Advanced Praise for *Leading Adult Learning: Supporting Adult Development in Our Schools*

By Eleanor Drago-Severson

"This book's major strength is its astonishing breadth and depth combined with an elegant dual framework concept which unifies large ideas into a whole. It draws from a great number of disciplines in evoking a model of leading learning and does so with remarkable anchors in the literature and in practice. The astounding range of material in this book begins to integrate elements of leadership and adult learning I have not yet seen adequately included and developed in any one book. This is a feat! I believe Leading Adult Learning will succeed as a master work and a major contribution to the field of education."

—Richard Ackerman, Associate Professor
The University of Maine, Orono, ME

"This is what practitioners need, and in fact, so do the college and university professors who prepare teachers and school administrators. This is a book to be cherished and reread until it is dog-eared, and you have to go out and buy another copy. It requires you to think, to attend, and to reflect."

—Deanna Burney, Director of Teaching and Learning
LEAP Academy University Charter School, Camden, NJ

"Building on the 'pillar practices' of her earlier work and animated with stories, exercises, and illustrations, this book offers both lucid explication of the powerful insights of constructive developmental theory and intensely practical partnership in how to put it all to work on Monday morning. In these hard times, this is a welcome and hopeful blueprint for the reanimation of our schools and the transformation of our communities."

—Laurent A. Parks Daloz, Senior Fellow
The Whidbey Institute

"There is no greater opportunity for improving public education than to make schools places where adults learn and lead together. In her rich and engaging book, Ellie Drago-Severson explores the challenge of this important work and shows us how success is both possible and deeply rewarding."

—Susan Moore Johnson, Pforzheimer Professor of Teaching and Learning
Harvard Graduate School of Education

"Brilliant, sensible and doable for any school that wants to become a Learning Center that seeks constant improvement!"

—Tim Kelly, Principal
Marysville Adult School, Marysville, CA

"This book is one of the best and most comprehensive works I have read in a long time. The author is clearly a brilliant scholar who understands how to take theory and make it instantly usable to the practitioner. The pillar practices, along with respecting and understanding the ways of knowing, offer solid, research-based professional development strategies for adults."

—Beth Madison, Principal
George Middle School, Portland, OR

*For the many teachers, principals, superintendents, and other educators
whose attentive and caring leadership transforms and brings joy to lives—and
especially for my greatest teachers and loves: Mama-San, Mrs. Betty L. Drago;
Papa-San, Dr. Rosario Drago; and David Severson, my Love.*

LEADING ADULT LEARNING

Supporting Adult Development
in Our Schools

ELEANOR DRAGO-SEVERSON

A Joint Publication

CORWIN
A SAGE Company

For information:

Corwin
A SAGE Company
2455 Teller Road
Thousand Oaks, California 91320
(800) 233-9936
Fax: (800) 417-2466
www.corwinpress.com

SAGE Ltd.
1 Oliver's Yard
55 City Road
London EC1Y 1SP
United Kingdom

SAGE India Pvt. Ltd.
B 1/I 1 Mohan Cooperative
   Industrial Area
Mathura Road, New Delhi 110 044
India

SAGE Asia-Pacific Pte. Ltd.
33 Pekin Street #02-01
Far East Square
Singapore 048763

Printed in the United States of America.

Library of Congress Cataloging-in-Publication Data

Drago-Severson, Eleanor.
Leading adult learning: Supporting adult development in our schools/Eleanor Drago-Severson; A Joint Publication with the National Staff Development Council.
      p. cm.
Includes bibliographical references and index.
ISBN 978-1-4129-5071-8 (cloth)
ISBN 978-1-4129-5072-5 (pbk.)

   1. Teachers—In-service training. 2. School administrators—In-service training. 3. Educational leadership. 4. Adult learning. I. Title.

LB1731.D7 2010
374—dc22   2009026777

This book is printed on acid-free paper.

09   10   11   12   13   10   9   8   7   6   5   4   3   2   1

Acquisitions Editor:	Dan Alpert
Associate Editor:	Megan Bedell
Production Editor:	Eric Garner
Copy Editor:	Paula L. Fleming
Typesetter:	C&M Digitals (P) Ltd.
Proofreader:	Susan Schon
Indexer:	Jean Casalegno
Cover Designer:	Dan Irwin

Contents

Preface

My work is inspired by the hope of making schools better places for both adults and children. I began as a teacher, program director, coach, and advisor to middle and high school students. My desire to make schools more effective learning environments for children and youth led me to attend graduate school to learn more about how to support adolescent development. While in graduate school, I learned that there was an entire field devoted to supporting adult development. I immediately became thirsty for more knowledge about the field and discovered that an important relationship exists between supporting adult development and child development.

I have dedicated myself to this work, to learning from courageous and generous school leaders and to sharing what I have learned (and continue to learn) with and from others, for nearly two decades. I am passionate about creating, and helping others shape, school contexts that better support the development of both children and adults. This is my resounding hope, inspiration, and commitment. The questions informing my research were drawn from this commitment, and my research has involved—and evolved from—paying careful and caring attention to the kinds of leadership that nurture adult development. There is perhaps no better time to pay this kind of attention to adult development among educators.

The work of educators has become dramatically more complex in the 21st century, especially since the passage of the No Child Left Behind Act in 2002. Building school capacity, managing reform, meeting accountability demands, caring for students' diverse needs, closing the achievement gap, and working effectively in an era of standards-based reform are some of the pressing issues facing all educators today. School systems around the country are changing in response to demands for increased accountability, greater diversity in the student population, and standards-based reform. Given these demands and the added complexity they create, as well as the extraordinary pressure to improve student achievement, researchers, reformers, school systems, and policymakers are searching for promising new approaches (Firestone & Shipps, 2005; Hargreaves & Fink, 2006; Kegan & Lahey, 2009; Wagner, 2007). Without the tools or support to meet such sizeable challenges, many principals, superintendents, and teachers feel ill equipped, and some leave the profession for more supportive environments (Donaldson, 2008; Murphy, 2006; Teitel, 2006).

Educational challenges such as those named above place new, complex demands on educators. Therefore, we must change the ways in which we work and learn together. As school leaders committed to supporting student learning, achievement, organizational change, and adult learning, we must first understand that authentic change starts with us. It must be a given that if schools are to adapt to current conditions, they need to be places where the adults as well as the children can grow.

Development of effective models of support for leadership, human capacity building, and leader development can make the difference. While principals, teachers, and superintendents certainly continue to need support to meet the technical requirements of their work (e.g., managing budgets, schedules, and personnel), they also need the kind of support that will help them adapt to the daunting demands of the new environment. As educators, we must build our developmental capacities (i.e., our cognitive, affective, interpersonal, and intrapersonal capacities) so that we can meet these adaptive challenges while we are *in the process* of working on them. Such a process requires ongoing support for adult growth and new ways of working, learning, and leading together, as opposed to training on specific topics and acquiring discrete skills. Much of this ongoing support must stem from the practice of leadership and the work we do together as we support each other's growth.

One way to facilitate the support and development of principals, teachers, and super-intendents is to shape schools and school systems more effectively as genuine *mentoring communities* or *learning centers*—contexts for collaborative learning—where educators support and challenge each other to grow. While supporting adult development is important for its own sake, such support will also strengthen teaching practice and, in turn, student performance (Donaldson, 2008; Elmore, 2004; Fullan, 2003; Guskey, 2000; Murphy, 2006). The research on which this book is based offers a promising path toward building these kinds of schools and school systems so that we can work through adaptive challenges while simultaneously building leadership and developmental (human) capacity. Doing so will enable us to serve better the development of both children and adults in schools.

Supporting adult learning is positively linked to improved student achievement (DuFour, 2007; Guskey, 1999, 2000; Roy & Hord, 2003), and opportunities for improving student learning depend on principal leadership and the quality of teaching (Firestone & Riehl, 2005; Levin, 2006; Marzano, Waters, & McNulty, 2005). However, to meet the complex challenges of 21st-century schooling and globalization, we will need new ways of working together that will support adult development (Childs-Bowen, 2007; Donaldson, 2008; Kegan & Lahey, 2009; Wagner et al., 2006). How can we create high-quality learning and growth opportunities for adults with different needs, preferences, and developmental orientations? Just as we adapt our instruction to care for the differences among children, we must differentiate our leadership practices to attend to differences in how adults learn and what they need to grow. My intention in this book is to offer ideas and practices to do just that.

This book is, in many ways, a response to the expressed needs of principals, super-intendents, and other school leaders for better supports for their own and other adults' growth in the service of children's learning. The new learning-oriented model of school leadership I present is one promising path that can help build our schools and school systems as learning centers, or mentoring communities for growth. Learning-oriented school leadership attends to the development of our capacities to handle complexities. My model, informed by developmental theory, offers a range of supportive practices, which I call pillar practices for growth. As pillars support a roof, these practices are supportive of and challenging to individuals at different developmental levels.

The four practices—teaming, providing adults with leadership roles, engaging in collegial inquiry, and mentoring—are developmentally robust, meaning that they can support the growth and learning of adults with different preferences, needs, and developmental orientations. In describing these practices in detail, I illuminate the importance of the relationship between a person and the environment, as well as the different kinds of supports and challenges that different people need in order to grow.

It is essential that we find more effective ways to support the adults who teach our children, especially given the complexity of leadership, teaching, and learning in our world (Ackerman & Mackenzie, 2007; Donaldson, 2008; Kegan & Lahey, 2009). This book illuminates the ways in which principals, teachers, and superintendents can use specific, developmentally oriented practices to support adult growth and learning. Moreover, the collective and individual strategies outlined herein suggest a promising new way to work towards the important national goals at the forefront of our educational agenda. After all, effectively exercised leadership in support of adult growth is important for its own sake, as well as being directly tied to improved quality of teaching and the growth of children.

This book is intended, therefore, for several audiences. It offers practices for supporting adult learning and growth to adults who serve in schools and school systems—teachers, principals, assistant principals, superintendents, teacher educators, professional development providers, and other leaders. It is also for those who work to support and teach aspiring leaders in preservice and inservice graduate programs. In addition, I hope it helps adult learning theorists, organizational theorists, researchers, and policymakers. Since the ideas and practices in this book draw from multiple knowledge domains—adult learning, developmental theory, leadership practice, and organizational collaboration—I hope that a wide audience will find the ideas and practices helpful and informative. This book was written for anyone who wants to learn how to support adult development better in an educational, organizational, or even a personal context.

In writing *Leading Adult Learning,* my primary purpose and heartfelt intention was to offer this new perspective and to illuminate practices that can support adult development within schools and across school systems. I very much hope it offers a map that you can use to support adult development in *your* learning community. I invite and encourage you to let me know how, if at all, what follows helps in the noble and inspiring work you do. It would be an honor to learn from you about how the ideas and practices presented help you in your leadership, the support of others' growth, and your own growth. I am hoping, with all my heart, that they do.

Acknowledgments

I see the opening of your potential in you as you see it in me.

—From a Tibetan/Nepali greeting, *"Namaste"*

I have been holding this book in my heart, mind, and soul ever since finishing *Helping Teachers Learn* (2004b). This book is offered in gratitude to all who have taught me and have opened their hearts and minds so generously and courageously. The lessons shared represent the collective contribution of many people.

I have deep awareness of the importance, power, blessing, and gift of the many precious connections I have with cherished individuals and of all the different and important ways in which their bright lights and oh-so-big-and-generous hearts and minds inspire, encourage, and strengthen me. One thing that I know for certain is that no meaningful endeavor—whether it is raising a child, caring for an aging parent, or writing a book—is done alone. When any important work is brought to fruition, there is always a team or tribe of generous people behind it who have come together over many years to offer their gracious and thoughtful help and support. The encouragement and inspiration I have benefited from are impossible to measure, and the individuals as well as institutions who contributed are impossible to count. I am deeply grateful to all of them and ask forgiveness from anyone whom I fail to mention here who also made a difference to this project.

I am deeply indebted to so many wonderful human beings—friends, colleagues, partners in thought, and family—who have contributed to this book in meaningful and different ways. Each of you is a bright light and shines with so many gifts. In these next few pages, I hope to acknowledge you in some way—though what I can say represents only a fraction of the deep gratitude I feel in my heart and soul.

First, I want to express deep appreciation for a few friends, colleagues, and partners in thought who have contributed to this book in meaningful and different ways. I trust you know why I mention you here: Janet Aravena, Ira Bogotch, Maria Broderick, Tom Buffett, Larry Daloz, Linda DeLauri, Betty Drago, Howard Gardner, Hillary Johnson,

Robert Kegan, Peggy Kemp, Lee Knefelkamp, Neville Marks, Yesenia Mareno, Victoria Marsick, Patricia Maslin-Ostrowski, David McCallum, Kathleen McCartney, Robert Monson, Peter Neaman, Aliki Nicolaides, and David Severson.

Part of the early research on which this book is based was made possible by a grant from the Spencer Foundation. I gratefully acknowledge and express my appreciation to the Spencer Foundation for its support. The data presented, the statements made, and the views expressed are solely my responsibility as author.

Deep gratitude and greatest thanks go to the 25 principals who participated in one of the studies reported on in this book and to *all* of the teachers, principals, assistant principals, superintendents, and other school leaders who participated in my research since 2004. Your remarkable, courageous, and inspired sharing have made this book what it is. The way you listened to and shared your insights on many of the ideas presented in this book helped inform and improve what appears in the pages that follow. You trusted me and generously shared your experiences by opening your hearts and minds so that all of us could learn from your good work, dedication, leadership, and passion. Thank you for giving freely of your time and for teaching me. Thank you for welcoming me into your schools, your thinking, your hearts, and your lives. Thank you for inspiring me. I am grateful to each of you for the privilege of learning from the gifts of your insights into the triumphs, struggles, and joys of leadership, all shared in the mutual hope that our work will improve schools, better support adult development, and provide a better education for our children and youth, who deserve our very best. I thank all of you for your genuine interest in this work and for your meaningful contributions to making it all it has become. I shall not forget you, your generosity of heart and mind, or your leadership. While I'm not able to name all of you here, I want you to know that the lessons shared in this book came from all you have taught me. I hope you feel my soulfelt gratitude.

I would also like to express warm gratitude for the organizations and the people behind them that have enabled my learning, including the Executive Leadership Institute of New York City and, especially, the leaders affiliated with the Advanced Leadership Program for Assistant Principals: the mentor-principals, the assistant principals, Janet Aravena, Peter McNally, and Ada Dolch. My heartfelt gratitude also goes to the Cahn Fellows Program at Teachers College, Columbia University, and in particular to Benefactor Chuck Cahn, Director Krista Dunbar, and all of the principals and assistant principals with whom I have been privileged to work and learn. My deep appreciation also goes to the National Academy for Excellence in Teaching at Teachers College and Director Dr. Douglas Wood, Key Administrator Claire Evelyn, as well as to all of the leaders of small schools in the Bronx who have generously shared their experiences with me.

During earlier ethnographic research that informed and inspired my current work, I had the honor of learning from Dr. Sarah Levine. Sarah contributed her best thinking and energies to my study over numerous hours and many years. She welcomed me into her school, her practices, and her heart and mind as she shared her thinking with courage and tenacity. I thank Sarah for believing in my work and in me and for the gift of our enduring friendship.

Gratitude goes to my colleagues and friends who generously agreed and, in most cases, offered to read and share their insights on early drafts or chapters of this book. Each of them and their thoughtful contributions strengthened the book: Jessica Blum, Anne Jones, Robert Monson, Julie Porter, and Craig Richards. I would also like to express my appreciation for Alexander Hoffman, who assisted in many ways, including offering his wise thinking about images for Chapter 2 and investigating how to secure permissions for potential images for the cover of this book. Thank you Alex, from my heart.

I offer heartfelt gratitude to Dr. David McCallum and Dr. Aliki Nicolaides, cherished friends, dear colleagues, and partners in thought. Thank you for your belief in this work and for the many important contributions you have made to it and my life. In particular, for now, I would like to voice my deep appreciation for thinking with me about the ideas related to inclusion of the self-transforming way of knowing. Thank you, also and enormously, for your willingness to share your experiences in this book. I am deeply grateful for your help in making this part of the work rest on a solid foundation. I cherish each of you and thank you with all my heart.

I have been blessed with the precious gift of learning from and with Dr. Robert Kegan of Harvard's Graduate School of Education for more than 20 years. First, Bob was my teacher, advisor, and wise mentor. Now, he is a cherished friend, trusted mentor, and treasured colleague. Bob, your friendship, your modeling, and your brilliant teachings have been and always will be an inspiration and gift to me. Not only are you a master teacher and wise mentor, but you are also a true humanitarian, wonderful person, and generous soul. Both as colleague and friend, I have been moved and inspired by your goodness, generosity, kindness, and commitments, as well as by your gifted ways of nurturing, encouraging, holding, and caring. This work and my own learning and development would not be as strong without your wisdom, support, and kindness. Thank you for developing your constructive-developmental theory, which enlivens the learning-oriented model presented in this book. You have changed the directions and contributions of my life in ways I could never adequately acknowledge. My deepest gratitude to you, Bob, for your company, your friendship, and your support and for helping me grow and for standing with me—each and every step along the way.

My thanks also go to Dr. Kristina C. Pinto for reviewing early drafts of several chapters and for sharing her insightful suggestions. Much appreciation to you, Kristina.

Deepest gratitude goes to India Koopman, who generously shared her wise thinking and vast expertise throughout this project, including during extended conversations about how best to present the ideas in this book. I thank you, India, with all my heart, for sharing your brilliant thinking with me; for your careful attention to words and ideas; and for your careful reading, thoughtful suggestions, and editorial suggestions. Thank you for your company throughout this long journey. I deeply appreciate your attention to my work and me. The greater gift is the lifelong friendship we now share. I thank you for that and so much more than I can adequately express. Thank you for the peaceful calm and wisdom that you offered so freely during this writing, especially when it was most needed. Thank you for the present of your company, for your presence, and for *running* alongside me. For me, you embody the ideals of big heart, big soul, and big mind. I thank you for the precious gifts you gave, including your thoughtful questions offered in the spirit of making this work more accessible. You are a treasure. I am deeply grateful for you.

Editors Robb Clouse and Rachel Livsey, both formerly of Corwin, started this journey with me. I thank each of you for your support, faith in this work, and gracious help and care during initial phases of this project. Special gratitude goes to you, Robb. Thank you so very much and most sincerely for noticing my work, for supporting it steadfastly over time, and for believing in its value.

Editor Dan Alpert of Corwin/Sage has continued to inspire me with his patience and firm belief in what he calls "the lessons" and potential of this book. Dan, thank you for your patience, availability, and enduring belief in this work and in me. Your continuing support and encouragement for this work continues to mean a lot to me. Thank you for keeping communications open throughout this journey and for always making time to think through ideas together. Thank you for your caring attention and willingness to respond so thoughtfully to my questions and for your openness to ideas. Heartfelt thanks to you and to Megan Bedell for the valuable suggestions offered so generously that helped improve the transformation of this work from research into accessible ideas for educators everywhere. I thank you both for staying with the promise of my work during development. I feel very fortunate to know and learn from both of you.

Corwin Production Editor Eric Garner has been generous as well. Thank you, Eric, for your thoughtful communication, leadership, and support during final stages of this work. I am very grateful to you. Anthony Paular of Corwin has also been tremendously helpful. Thank you, Anthony, for your willingness to consider my ideas for the cover of this book and for offering your creative and wise thinking. I appreciate all of your sage ideas.

Corwin Copy Editor Paula Fleming has also been wonderful and a gift to this work and me. Paula, I thank you deeply for your patience, careful reading, excellent editorial suggestions, and help in bringing this work to completion. I also need to thank you, with all of my heart, for your thoughtful and careful help and attention during the last phase of this journey and for offering your best thinking with me. Your sage suggestions and care have made this work much stronger. I appreciate your enduring attention and, more than that, your care.

In addition, I would like now to express sincere gratitude to the leaders who reviewed an earlier draft of this book. Thank you for sharing your insights and for carving out time to do so. Your thoughtful suggestions made this work so much better. Heartfelt thanks go to Principal Beth Madison, George Middle School, Portland, Oregon; Dr. Gail Coffin, Howard County Public Schools, Ellicott City, Maryland; Peggy Morrison, Pinecreek Farm, Acton, Ontario, Canada; Deanna Burney, Haddonfield, New Jersey; Principal Tim Kelly, Marysville Adult School, Marysville, California; Professor Richard Ackerman, Brooksville, Maine; and Professor Gayle Moller, Franklin, North Carolina. My deepest heartfelt thanks to each of you.

Many others have helped improve and support this work in important and sometimes subtle ways. Gratitude goes to Dr. Howard Gardner, Dr. Robert Kegan, Dr. Victoria Marsick and Peter Neuman, Dr. Patricia Maslin-Ostrowski, Dr. Ira Bogotch, Dr. Craig Richards, Dr. Robert Peterkin, Dr. Susan Moore Johnson, and Dr. Eleanor Duckworth for your thoughtful support, wise counsel, and encouragement. Among the many excellent students who have helped advance this work, I would especially like to thank the students, including new and seasoned Turtles, the SPA leaders, and other leaders, in my classes at Teachers College and Harvard's Graduate School of Education. I also want to express gratitude for Anila Asghar, Jen DeForest, and Jenni Roloff Welch. To all, your teachings, insights, questions, and curiosity have made this work stronger. Thank you all for all you teach me.

My acknowledgments conclude with deepest gratitude for the love and support from those people most associated with shaping my life—my family. My late father, Dr. Rosario Drago, and mother, Betty Drago, have been my finest teachers. With wisdom, joy, hard work, and care, they modeled loving, learning, and leadership that continues to inspire me. Holding me all along the way, they helped me learn to love and stand for something. I thank them for the impossible-to-measure gifts, encouragement, and great love they have given to my life. By example, my father and my mother taught me to love learning and hard work and instilled in me the value of making a contribution to the lives of others. Their belief in me and their support for all I have chosen to do are but two of the precious life gifts they have given me. There are oh-so-many more. It is on their shoulders that I continue to stand to see farther. I thank my parents for showing me how to build a happy, fulfilling, and productive life. I thank you, Mom, for all that you have modeled for me and for your loving and lovely goodness. After years of your asking me with your loving care, "Are you finished with that book yet?" I can now finally say, "Yes, I am." Thank you, dearest Mom—more than words could ever express—for being so beautiful—inside and out—and for all the joy and inspiration you give others and me. You and your courage and love strengthen my life and me. You are LOVE.

I thank my siblings and their families for their love. My five brothers and sister, all but one older than I, traveled some paths before I did. They taught me and continue to teach me very important lessons about leadership, love, life, as well as the importance of what can be found and what can be lost. I thank you and your children for teaching me.

Anyone who has engaged in a labor of love and heart such as this knows that it requires sacrifice of so many kinds: patience, love, and support from many, especially one's lifelong soulmate. I now will do my best to voice my heart and soulfelt appreciation to my loving husband and sweetest Love, David Severson. How can I adequately thank the Sunlight in my life? While no words can adequately express the depths of my love and gratitude for you, Greatest, I will try to offer a fraction of it here. Thank you for believing in me and for the impossible-to-detail sacrifices and compromises you have made with joy and love. Thank you for the treasure of your companionship and friendship every step along the way. Thank you, David, for the insights you make and give so freely. Thank you for your enduring support, for all you teach me, for the many ways in which you help me to grow, for the gift of you and your light in my life, and for sharing your own learning journeys with me. Thank you for being my cherished love, angel, touchstone—and for being in my life. I happily and with deepest joy and appreciation dedicate this book to my greatest loves—you, Mom, and Dad—with enormous love, admiration, and appreciation for the generous ways in which you hold me and have held me and for the precious, wonderful love each of you gives to me and all each and every day—by being.

Corwin and Eleanor Drago-Severson gratefully acknowledge the thoughtful contributions of the following reviewers:

Richard Ackerman, Associate Professor
The University of Maine, Orono, ME

Deanna Burney, Director of Teaching & Learning
LEAP Academy University Charter School, Camden, NJ

Gail Coffin, Leadership Development Facilitator and Certified Coach
Howard County Public Schools, Ellicott City, MD

Tim Kelly, Principal
Marysville Adult School, Marysville, CA

Beth Madison, Principal
George Middle School, Portland, OR

Gayle Moller, Professor Emeritus
Franklin, NC

Peggy Morrison, Educational Consultant
Halton Hills, Ontario, Canada

About the Author

Eleanor (Ellie) Drago-Severson is an Associate Professor of Education Leadership at Columbia University's Teachers College. She earned her master's and doctoral degrees from Harvard, where she taught from 1997–2005. Her research and teaching passions include leadership for supporting adult development in K–12 schools, ABE/ESOL, and university contexts. Her work is inspired by the idea that schools must be places where adults as well as children can grow. Ellie is the author of two additional recent books: *Becoming Adult Learners: Principles and Practices for Effective Development* (2004) and *Helping Teachers Learn: Principal Leadership for Adult Growth and Development* (Corwin, 2004). *Helping Teachers Learn* was awarded recognition as the National Staff Development Council's 2004 "Book of the Year."

Ellie has served as teacher, program designer, director, consultant, and professional developer in a variety of educational contexts, including K–12 schools, adult education community centers, and universities. She served as lead researcher on the Adult Development Team of the National Center for the Study of Adult Learning and Literacy (NCSALL) at Harvard University with Robert Kegan. She consults to leaders and educational organizations on matters of superintendents', principals', and teachers' personal and professional learning and development, as well as leadership that supports adult development domestically and internationally. Ellie has been awarded three distinguished teaching awards from Teachers College (2007), the Harvard Graduate School of Education's Morningstar Award (2005) for excellence in teaching, and Harvard Extension School's Dean's Award for Excellence in Teaching (1998).

She grew up in the Bronx and lives in New York City with her husband, David.

Never doubt that a small group of thoughtful,
committed citizens can change the world. Indeed, it's the only thing that ever has.

—Margaret Mead (attributed)

PART I

Foundations

1

A New Model of Leadership for Adult Growth and Learning

I was recently working with and learning from a group of about a hundred superintendents, principals, and teachers who had gathered to learn about some of the ideas I'm about to present in this book. Several of them, at different points during our time together, said, "Thank you for making me feel so special and for recognizing the challenges and complexity of my work." As one seasoned leader explained, "In my work, it is so rare that I ever feel special . . . appreciated." My response to each of them was, "You *are* special. The work you do is so important. Thank you for all you do." With all my heart, I meant every word.

Teachers, principals, and superintendents face increasingly complex educational challenges in working to serve students and support their achievement and well-being. All adults who serve in our schools and school systems are being called upon to lead and assist in building collaborative learning centers that nurture children and adults' growth and learning. How can we build schools as learning centers that can nurture the growth of adults with different needs, preferences, and developmental orientations? How can we build schools so that they are mentoring communities—true learning centers?

I have been studying teacher development, professional development, and leadership development—as well as how such adult development can make schools better learning centers—for more than two decades. I have worked on the ground as teacher, program director, coach, school counselor, staff developer, and consultant in several middle and high schools, and this experience informs my research and the learning I hope to share in this book. I dedicate my teaching, research, and writing to supporting diverse constituencies (teachers, principals, assistant principals, superintendents, graduate students, and adult literacy teachers) who serve in a variety of educational contexts (K–12 schools, school districts, workplace learning centers, and universities). My work bridges theory and practice, and I seek to use each to inform, build, and strengthen the other. In other words, not only do I share with practitioners practices for supporting adult development that are informed by theory, but also I feed back what I learn from practitioners to build theory and enhance practice. This dynamic dialogue between theory and practice is a centerpiece of my work.

I have observed what growth-enhancing—even magical—places of learning schools and school systems can be for all who participate in them. I have also experienced the challenges and problems that can exist in schools and school systems. More specifically, as a teacher, I first noticed that children's well-being and academic achievement seemed to be positively influenced by teachers and principals who felt supported in their own development. I also observed the reverse. I set out—years ago—to understand why it was so difficult to support adult development in schools. How might school leaders do this better? What practices might support adult development?

My overarching goal for this book is to answer these questions, by offering a helpful map that shows *how* we can better support our own and each others' growth within schools and school systems. I hope this book offers a response to the urgent calls from the field for better supporting the personal and professional growth and learning of all adults who serve in schools and school systems. In today's complex and ever-changing world, we must all be learners who are invested in supporting each other's growth. In particular, school leaders across the system—principals, teachers, superintendents, and others—need to lead adult learning in the service of the complex adaptive challenges that schools face. I hope this book is of help as we journey forward—together.

IN THIS CHAPTER

In this chapter, I introduce the need for a new learning-oriented model of school leadership and explore the connections among the fields of professional development, adult developmental theory, adult learning, organizational development, and leadership practices. I discuss the complex, adaptive challenges educators face and emphasize the need to find more effective ways to support adult development within schools and across school systems. I introduce an important distinction between informational and transformational learning—or growth. In so doing, I point to themes in the professional development literature that emphasize common and urgent calls for schools and school systems to support better the growth of teachers, principals, superintendents, and other school leaders. Supporting adult learning across the system will enable all to meet more effectively the implicit and explicit demands of leadership, teaching, learning, and life.

I also briefly introduce the developmental principles that inform my model and present a short overview of the four pillar practices of my learning-oriented model: teaming, providing adults with leadership roles, engaging in collegial inquiry, and mentoring. As pillars support a roof, these mutually reinforcing, broad forms of adult collaboration are supportive of and challenging to adults at different developmental levels. An overview of all of the chapters in the book, a summary of this chapter, and reflective questions conclude the chapter.

MEETING ADAPTIVE CHALLENGES

I recently facilitated a workshop for experienced principals on robust ways to support adult development within schools and across districts. In their leadership work with the National School Leaders Network, these participants were responsible for the learning and development of newer principals. In the beginning of this workshop, Jane, a seasoned principal in a high-performing, overcrowded New York City high school (4,200 students and 200 teachers), shared that the changes in the city's educational system (that is, new membership in the empowerment schools where principals have more autonomy) are "putting so much on us." The demands on her had become "so great" that she was not sure how much longer she could manage. I looked around the room and noticed other experienced principals, from around the country, nodding in agreement.

Toward the end of the workshop, one participant, John, who had served as a New York City principal for more than 20 years, said,

> I have a master's degree in educational administration and have taken many courses and workshops on different aspects of leadership and administration since earning my degree. None of my coursework has focused on understanding how adults learn. Without this workshop, I wouldn't have even realized how much I needed to learn—as a principal, I *need* more knowledge about how I can support adult learning and growth.

John's desire to learn how to support adult learning for his staff and for the newer principals he mentors is emblematic of the great desire many principals have to support adult learning and development more effectively.

At the start of my workshops, I ask participants to share their hopes for learning. Over the years, school leaders have consistently expressed similar ideas. Dan, an experienced teacher of 22 years in urban Philadelphia, captured the essence of what others have voiced. He explained,

> My hope is that this workshop provides a space where I am intellectually fed, nurtured in my own learning and development, and to have a space to engage in reflection. It's so rare that I ever have any time to reflect, to be in conversation with colleagues about my work, and to learn. I invest almost all of my time into caring for my students' learning and development. I almost feel guilty taking out this time for my own learning and reflection, even though I know it's important.

Another experienced teacher, May, followed Dan's comment by saying,

> And the other thing I've been thinking about is that while we say that at our school we value adult learning and learning from our mistakes . . . what really happens when adults make mistakes? Are they really opportunities for us to learn?

It is important for us to consider how we can shape schools as mentoring communities—or learning centers—in which mistakes are valued for the learning that can be gleaned from them. *Learning centers,* as defined in this book, are schools and school systems that nurture and support the growth and learning of children, youth, *and adults.*

In my work with principals, teachers, and superintendents, domestically and internationally, I have found that they yearn for opportunities to learn. They need time and space for dialogue and learning in the company of colleagues, and they feel that such dialogue will support their growth, their ability to lead, and their personal development.

As noted in the Preface, educators today work in a context of increasing complexity and increasing accountability, and they do not always have the tools or support to thrive in this environment. As Richard Elmore (2004b) rightly notes, successful school reform must grow "from the inside out." In addition, he emphasizes that developing a deeper understanding of how to support adult growth and learning is an area in which further research and attention are essential. Only recently, however, have we started to examine these complex issues (Firestone & Shipps, 2005; Gardner, 2007; Hargreaves & Fink, 2006).

School systems around the country are changing in response to the call for increased accountability, greater diversity in the student population, and standards-based reform. Given these leadership demands and the extraordinary pressure to improve student achievement, school systems, researchers, policymakers, and reformers are searching for promising new approaches (Blankstein, Houston, & Cole, 2007; Wagner, 2007). We must develop fresh strategies because the challenges we face require more than the approach we have in hand—what leadership scholar Ronald Heifetz (1994) calls a "technical fix." Technical problems are those for which we have both the problem and solutions clearly defined. With regard to the challenges we encounter in education today, we have not been here before. Rather, we are facing profound *adaptive challenges.*

By *adaptive challenges,* Heifetz (1994) means situations and problems for which neither a problem nor a solution is known or has been identified. This kind of problem requires new approaches and is solved as we are "*in the act of working on it*" (Wagner et al., 2006, p. 10). Without the appropriate tools and supports needed to meet such challenges, many principals, superintendents, and teachers leave their professions for more supportive environments (Donaldson, 2008; Moller & Pankake, 2006; Murphy, 2006; Teitel, 2006). The use of effective support models for leadership development in schools helps us build our cognitive, affective, interpersonal, and intrapersonal capacities. Increasing these capacities can make the difference in adaptively addressing complex challenges. We will have to learn our way into understanding what these problems are and toward developing a more adequate response. And we will have to do it together.

While principals, teachers, and superintendents certainly need support to meet the traditional technical requirements of their work, the new demands of the 21st century are adaptive challenges, and these will require new approaches. Educators will have to address these challenges while *in the process* of working on them. Thus, ongoing support for adult growth and new ways of working, learning, growing, and leading together—not just specific training or discrete skill acquisition—is critical to fulfilling our visions for our school communities. While some supports can be provided externally, many must come from within the school through the practice of leadership and the work we do together as we support each other's growth. In light of the many adaptive challenges school leaders face, supporting adult growth in schools is important both for its own sake as well as for the contributions it can make toward improving student achievement (Guskey, 1999).

One way to facilitate the development of principals, teachers, and superintendents is to shape schools and school systems more effectively into what I call genuine *mentoring communities;* that is, contexts for collaborative learning where educators support and challenge each other to grow. Such communities will strengthen teaching and, in turn, student performance (Desforges, 2006; Donaldson, 2008; Elmore, 2004b; Fullan, 2003; Murphy, 2006; Parks, 2005; Wagner, 2007). The research on which this book is based offers a promising path toward building mentoring communities, helping educators work through adaptive challenges while simultaneously building developmental leadership capacity. It must be a given that if schools are to adapt to current conditions, they need to be places where adults as well as children can grow, and we must change *the ways in which we work, grow, and learn together.*

We know that a direct link exists between supporting adult learning and enhanced student achievement (DuFour, 2007; Guskey, 1999; Wagner, 2007), and opportunities for improving student learning depend on principal leadership and the quality of teaching (Firestone & Riehl, 2005; Levin, 2006; Marzano, Waters, & McNulty, 2005). However, we need a deeper understanding of the practices that can support adult development and learning. As Hayes Mizell (2007) writes, "The more often educators are engaged with their peers in effective professional learning, the more they will learn and the more likely it is their practice will improve" (p. 2). Like others, Mizell emphasizes that to meet the complex challenges of 21st-century schooling and globalization, we need new ways of working together that will support adult development (see Childs-Bowen, 2007; Donaldson, 2008; Kegan & Lahey, 2009; Wagner et al., 2006).

Improving school-based professional learning for all adults—teachers, principals, and superintendents—must stay at the forefront of our educational agenda. In fact, the National Staff Development Council (NSDC) (2008) states that its purpose is to build schools in which "every educator engages in effective professional learning every day so every student achieves." In stepping forward to meet the multiple, complex demands of 21st-century schooling with courage and hope, we must support our own and each other's growth. This special kind of developmental capacity building will enable educators to increase student achievement and improve schools so that they can be true learning centers where all—adults and children—can grow.

Building Developmental Capacity

Traditionally in education, two kinds of capacity have been necessary for improving student achievement: *school or organizational capacity*—the school's collective ability as a functioning, working whole to increase achievement (Newmann, King, & Youngs, 2000; Spillane & Louis, 2002)—and *instructional capacity*—teachers' ability to provide effective instruction (Cohen & Ball, 1999; Hoerr, 2008). But a third kind of capacity is also needed, and this book addresses it: *developmental capacity.* Educators must be supported in pursuing adult learning and development. Developmental capacity concerns the cognitive, affective, interpersonal, and intrapersonal capacities that enable us to manage better the demands of leadership, teaching, learning, and life. The new mental demands placed on educators often exceed our developmental capacities (Kegan & Lahey, 2009).

For example, principals need to help teachers prepare K–12 students to prosper in a global knowledge economy. Yet many principals are not trained in these tasks, and many are not supported to meet such new challenges (Elmore, 2004b; Kegan & Lahey, 2009). Moreover, some principals may not yet have the developmental capacities or educational training to do so.

Similarly, as mentioned, teachers are called upon to assume more responsibility and demonstrate even greater authority in schools. Recently, there has been a great deal of discussion about helping teachers to increase their capacities to build schools as learning centers where both children and adults grow (Ackerman & Mackenzie, 2007; Moller & Pankake, 2006). For example, research shows that teachers who are change leaders engage in several productive behaviors: they navigate the complex structures of schools, cultivate relationships with each other, help each other manage change, and challenge conditions in schools by illuminating children's needs and voices (Barth, 2006; Silva, Gimbert, & Nolan, 2000).

The complexity of teaching and leading in the 21st-century places increasingly complex demands on all educators—teachers, principals, superintendents, and others—and school communities (Donaldson, 2008; Gardner, Csikszentmihalyi, & Damon, 2001; Kegan, 2000, Kegan & Lahey, 2009). Such complex demands cannot be addressed in isolation. As noted above, what is needed are new ways of working together in support of each other's growth and development so that together we can meet the implicit and explicit demands of 21st-century schooling.

Acknowledging Developmental Diversity

In addition to the various forms of diversity that school leaders typically consider when supporting the growth and learning of adults in their schools (e.g., race, ethnicity, years of experience, religion, and sexuality), they also need to attend to what I call *developmental diversity.* Caring for and attending to developmental diversity means being mindful of the qualitatively different ways in which we, as adults, make sense of our life experiences. In other words, because we take in and experience our realities in very different ways, we need different types of supports and challenges to grow. This book is about how we can do just that.

Since research suggests that in any school, team, or group, it is likely that adults will make sense of their experiences in developmentally different ways, we need to attend to this type of diversity. It is therefore necessary to incorporate learning-oriented leadership practices that will support and challenge adults in different ways. As one leader recently remarked,

> By acknowledging developmental diversity, I will be better able to understand people's attitudes, behaviors, and expectations and be better equipped to support teacher learning in the service of student learning. I hold very near to my heart the possibility of helping adults grow into this profession of servicing kids and providing students with opportunities to achieve and attain success. (Teacher-leader and aspiring principal, July 2007)

Although adult learning theories can be a powerful tool for understanding how to support adult development in K–12 schools, they are underutilized (Cranton, 1996; Drago-Severson, 2004a, 2004b; Hammerman, 1999; Kegan & Lahey, 2009; Levine, 1989; Mezirow, 2000). Table 1.1 provides a brief example of how adults with different developmental orientations communicate with others, as well as how they orient toward working together.

The adults listed in Table 1.1 make sense of communicating and working collaboratively in qualitatively different ways, which means they need different supports and challenges in order to grow. The qualitatively different ways in which they are making sense—or making meaning—of their experiences represent their *ways of knowing*.

As I wrote in my first book, *Helping Teachers Learn: Principal Leadership for Adult Growth and Development* (2004b), a way of knowing is actually a person's meaning-making system through which all experience is filtered and understood; it is often referred to as a developmental level or stage. A person's way of knowing dictates how he or she will make sense of reality. It is the filter through which people interpret their experiences, largely determining their capacities for perspective taking on self, other, and the relationship between the two. As such, it determines how learning experiences (and all life experience) will be taken in, managed, understood, and used. A person's way of knowing is not connected to gender, age, or life phase, but there is a progression of increasing complexity from one way of knowing to the next. A person's way of knowing shapes how she understands her roles and responsibilities as a teacher, leader, and learner. It also informs how she thinks about what makes a good leader, what constitutes effective leadership practice, and the supports and challenges she needs to grow from various forms of adult collaboration.

Of the six primary ways of knowing (Kegan, 1982, 1994, 2000), the first two (stage 0 and stage 1) are prevalent in infancy and childhood. Three more ways of knowing—the *instrumental, socializing,* and *self-authoring* ways of knowing—are most common in adulthood. While less common, a sixth, which I call the *self-transforming* way of knowing, is becoming slightly more prevalent in today's society, given the complex challenges of living, learning, teaching, and leading. Awareness of these ways of knowing, which I discuss in depth in Chapter 2, helps us to understand adults' developmental diversity so that we can support their growth accordingly, bringing us closer to the goal of establishing schools as true learning centers for all.

Table 1.1   Adults' Different Perceptions of Communication and Collaboration

Leader	Orientation Toward Communicating	Orientation Toward Collaborating
Mel	• Emphasizes rules for communication; orients toward facts, right way to do things, and concrete goals.	• Everyone in the school or team needs to do their work the "right" way (there is one right way). • Achieving concrete goals is most important.
Fran	• Emphasizes his or her own and other people's feelings. • Communicates feelings and personal experiences (internal sense of self). • Orients toward making sure all are in agreement.	• Needs the school, group, or team to agree on a shared goal that they work toward.
Daye	• Emphasizes ideology, philosophy, and feelings when presenting her perspective to others. • Seeks to understand diversity across similarities and differences in perspectives.	• Understands and appreciates that adults will bring different perspectives, values, and experiences that enrich collaboration. • Values coming together for a common purpose.
Pat	• Seeks to negotiate multiple boundaries of diverse stakeholders who bring different needs, gifts, and experiences to a school. • Orients toward stretching his own capacity to support interpersonal and organizational processes.	• Values a collaborative spirit of accountability in the group so that each person can work to capacity and share responsibility for leading, teaching, and learning, while being flexible so each person can rely on the group. • Values structure and process when they are based on collaboration and what each person brings to and needs from the group. • Appreciates when space is created where each person's gifts and abilities can come forth. Considers it important for groups to be able to balance the personal circumstances of their members with achieving the tasks and/or goals for the group.

The Power of Transformational Learning: Its Promise Across the System

Whereas teachers struggle to improve student achievement and support each other's growth and learning, principals, in their role as instructional leaders, struggle to create conditions that support teacher learning. Principals today are being asked to add leadership of instructional improvement to their managerial responsibilities. To do this, they must become primary adult developers and architects of collaborative learning communities. As they assume these diverse roles under challenging conditions, they must find ways to support themselves and teachers with differing needs, developmental orientations, and levels of experience.

Just as the demands placed on teachers and principals have become increasingly complex, so too have the demands placed on superintendents (Elmore, 2004a). Superintendents have the tremendous responsibility of shaping the culture in which all members of the school system operate. Recently, their work has changed: no longer only primarily responsible for *running* the school system, they are now responsible for *transforming* the school system in response to new demands. Yet in their training, many superintendents have not been prepared for this role (Kegan & Lahey, 2009). It is clear that the demands of leading and teaching in the 21st century require important changes across all levels of the school and the district (Donaldson, 2008; Kegan & Lahey, 2009; Wagner et al., 2006).

In today's global society, both the implicit and explicit expectations of what leaders are supposed to accomplish, within and across education, have changed. Many acknowledge how complex the work of teaching and leadership in the school has become and how expectations are changing constantly. Educators are expected to lead in ways in which they were never taught to lead and they themselves have never experienced. How can we help each other to develop the capacities needed to lead through the complex demands of leading and teaching?

Here I need to make an important distinction between two kinds of learning: informational learning and transformational learning. *Informational learning*, often the goal of traditional forms of professional development, focuses on increasing the amount of knowledge and skills a person possesses. *Transformational learning*, on the other hand, relates to the development of the cognitive, emotional, interpersonal, and intrapersonal capacities that enable a person to manage the complexities of work (e.g., leadership, teaching, learning, adaptive challenges) and life. With transformational learning, or growth (I use these terms interchangeably), a qualitative shift occurs in *how a person actively interprets, organizes, understands, and makes sense of his or her experience.* This kind of learning is associated with an increase in individual developmental capacities, which enables a person to have a broader perspective on him- or herself, on others, and on the relationships between self and others (Cranton, 1996; Kegan, 1982, 1994, 2000; Kegan & Lahey, 2009; Mezirow, 1991, 2000). While both types of learning are important and necessary, we need opportunities to develop our internal capacities if we are to meet the implicit and explicit new and complex demands of the 21st century. And we need help in doing this. No one can do it alone. As human beings, we need different kinds of supports and challenges in order to grow.

In fact, Kegan and Lahey (2009) contend that many leaders—and adults in general—have not been prepared to meet adaptive challenges, which require both new knowledge and new ways of thinking, and do not yet have the developmental capacities to manage these challenges effectively. In other words, the adaptive challenges we face today often outpace our capacities (Kegan, 1994, 2000; Kegan & Lahey, 2009). However, adults can develop these capacities by engaging in practices that support transformational learning, since this kind of learning changes the ways in which we understand and make sense of our reality and often causes changes in our fundamental beliefs and assumptions. As Kegan notes in an interview (Sparks, 2002):

> Major change requires alteration in some of our basic, underlying beliefs. That is transformational learning. . . . Technical challenges require harnessing already existing kinds of thinking and knowledge. Adaptive challenges, on the other hand, require creating new knowledge and new ways of thinking. Heifetz says that one of the biggest errors leaders make is addressing adaptive challenges through technical means. We're saying something similar—that the challenges school leaders face are adaptive and require transformational learning (p. 70).

THE NEED FOR A NEW MODEL OF LEADERSHIP

The school leaders I've worked with and learned from for over two decades have taught me many important lessons, and in this book I share some of them. One thing I've learned is how palpable and widespread the need is for more opportunities to collaborate. During workshops, I ask educators, "What kinds of practices do you feel support your own and other people's learning?" Regardless of their position—teacher, principal, superintendent, staff developer, coach, or curriculum coordinator—they name practices that center on collaboration. Most often they also remark, as one district leader put it, "It is both difficult and important to privilege time for collaboration and reflection. I know we need more flexibility in the agenda to accommodate this." The new learning-oriented model I present in this book takes into account the need to build healthy, strong school systems where collaboration is part of the fabric of day-to-day life.

In my work with practicing school leaders and those who attend my university classes, I continue to be inspired by how much these adults teach each other (and me). Michael Nakkula and Sharon Ravitch (1997) developed the concept of *reciprocal transformation* from developmental research that focuses on mentorship between children and adults. I employ this concept to highlight the importance of reciprocity when adults are collaborating with each other.

Just as the boundaries between teacher and student in graduate classrooms differ from those in the classrooms of decades ago, so too do the boundaries between adults in different kinds of leadership capacities in schools differ from what they were. To build capacity and support adult development in schools, mutuality, reciprocal learning, and shared leadership are needed.

Building capacity and practicing shared leadership also require a good *holding environment*—a concept discussed in some detail in Chapter 2. Briefly, and for our purposes here, a good holding environment both supports a person where he or she is in terms of making meaning of life experiences and challenges the person to grow beyond that, but without conveying any urgent need for change. In other words, it joins a person in his or her meaning making, or way of knowing. It also seeks to bring the individual's voice into the conversation, whether that person is a teacher, a student, a principal, or a superintendent. It is the kind of environment created by teachers in effective classrooms, by thoughtful leaders in effective schools, and by developmentally mindful superintendents in outstanding school systems. In these contexts, all leaders meet learners where they are, provide challenges for growth and learning, and stay around while the learner is demonstrating a new way of thinking and acting. This may sometimes mean that the leader needs to empower the quieter or less empowered learners. Children feel the difference when the adults in their school are thriving and well supported in their work.

Roland Barth (2006) underscores the importance of building trusting, generous, helpful, and generative relationships among the adults in a school and emphasizes that the quality of these relationships has "a greater influence on the character and quality of that school and on student accomplishment than anything else" (p. 8). He continues by pointing out the need for a collegial culture and how important it is to have conditions where colleagues can help each other learn. As he puts it,

> A precondition for doing *anything* to strengthen our practice and improve a school is the existence of a collegial culture in which professionals talk about practice, share their craft knowledge, and observe and root for the success of one another. Without these in place, no meaningful improvement—no staff or curriculum development, no teacher leadership, no student appraisal, no team teaching, no parent involvement, and no sustained change—is possible. (p. 13)

In essence, Barth is referring to trust and trusting relationships, and as you know, these are fundamental to supporting growth in *all* human beings. Trusting relationships lead to growth-enhancing cultures of learning and development for all, regardless of age. As Alan Blankstein et al. (2007) remind us, developing trust among teachers, administrators, parents, and all persons within schools and school systems is a vital foundation for adult learning and development. Research consistently shows that supporting adult learning is directly and positively linked to enhancing children's achievement (Donaldson, 2008; Guskey, 2000; Leithwood, Louis, Anderson, & Wahlstrom, 2004; Roy & Hord, 2003; Wagner, 2007).

We need new ways of shaping schools to be true learning centers, places where adults and children are well supported in their learning and development. I hope that the pillar practices (described at the end of this chapter and in more detail throughout this book) that compose my learning-oriented model of school leadership will help educators to support adult growth and build capacity across the school system: principal to principal, principal to teachers, teacher to teacher, superintendent to principal, and superintendent to superintendent. The four pillar practices—establishing teams, providing adults with leadership roles, engaging in collegial inquiry, and mentoring—can support effective, differentiated approaches to adult development in schools. Informed by principles of adult learning and developmental theories, these pillar practices are developmentally robust, meaning any one of them can support adults with different needs, preferences, and developmental orientations. And they can help us to attend to the different needs for growth that we bring to our learning and leadership.

According to adult learning and developmental theory, we must understand the underlying assumptions we hold about how the world works because we accept them as truths until we become aware of them. Our assumptions guide our thinking and our behaviors. Developing greater awareness of our assumptions can help us to grow. The pillar practices create structures, or holding environments (as described above), that allow us to engage in shared reflection and examine our assumptions about leadership, teaching, and learning and then to test these assumptions, revise them, and grow.

In other words, just as teachers must accommodate all types of learners to support their learning and development, so too must adults work to support other adults' development. The best teachers create lessons and structure class activities in ways that both support and challenge ("stretch," in a developmental sense) all learners. The new learning-oriented model, the pillar practices, and the examples of these practices that I present in this book can support the development of adults with different preferences, needs, and developmental orientations (or ways of knowing). They offer a new and promising pathway to establishing true learning communities through a developmental approach. In effect, they help us to understand that we need to differentiate our leadership in support of each other's learning and growth. And they provide a map that shows us how to do so.

SUPPORTING LEARNING ACROSS THE SYSTEM

> *Improvement requires fundamental changes in the way public schools and school systems are designed and in the ways they are led. It will require change in the values and norms that shape how teachers and principals think about the purposes of their work, changes in how we think about who leaders are, where they are, and what they do, and changes in the knowledge and skill requirements of work in schools. In short, we must fundamentally redesign schools as places where both adults and young people learn.*
>
> —Elmore, 2000, p. 35

As Richard Elmore (2000) emphasizes in the above quote, we need to find more effective ways to support the continual learning of adults across levels of the system and to make fundamental changes in the system itself. Similarly, as Michelle LaPointe and Stephen Davis (2006) point out, relatively "little is known about how to design programs that can develop and sustain effective leadership practices" (p. 16). In this section, I highlight a few common themes from the literature about professional development for central office district leaders and staff, principals, and teachers; I then focus on each group individually.

First, the primary way in which teachers, principals, and superintendents are supported in their personal and professional growth is through professional development programs, often referred to now as professional learning programs. Second, the literature emphasizes a critical need for more time to be devoted to these programs (Blaydes, 2002; Cochran-Smith & Lytle, 2001; Donaldson, 2008; Kegan & Lahey, 2009; Peterson, 2002). Third, research shows that supporting learning and development for each group decreases the individual's sense of isolation, making it possible for all three groups to influence student achievement positively (Donaldson; Guskey, 2000; Leithwood, Seashore-Louis, Anderson, & Wahlstrom, 2004; Peterson, 2002). Traditionally—and unfortunately—professionals in schools and school systems carry out their work and practices on their own, without the benefit of a supportive yet critically thoughtful observer. Thus, many times their good work is not replicated, built upon, examined, or celebrated. In addition, many issues with which adults need help are left undiscovered. Last, these three groups have a common need for meaningful professional development, which entails job-embedded, ongoing, safe opportunities (rather than single-shot or "drive-by" experiences) and engagement in meaningful dialogue about their work and its inherent challenges (Guskey, 1995; Hoffmann & Johnston, 2005; Johnson et al., 2004; Kegan & Lahey, 2009; Teitel, 2006).

Superintendents

Superintendents have the important leadership responsibility of sustaining school- and district-level improvement (Elmore, 2004a; Levine, 2005; Teitel, 2006). Central office professionals are also responsible for supporting and monitoring the effectiveness of school-based professional development (Blankstein et al., 2007; Roy & Hord, 2003). Yet how are central office staff supported in their efforts to accomplish this? For more than a decade, scholars have argued that it is essential for districts to offer support to principals, teachers, and professional development committees (Blankstein et al.; Johnson, 1996; Roy & Hord). In addition to their other responsibilities, say Pat Roy and Shirley Hord, districts need to

> prepare administrators and teachers to use a variety of data to determine the focus of professional learning, to build collaboration skills and structures, to use job-embedded professional development designs, and continue to focus on long-term support for the development of new classroom-based skills. (p. 3)

Their examination of district support for school-based improvement reveals that while building district capacity to support schools is possible, it requires "redefining everyone's role—not only the principal's role but also that of central office staff, superintendent and school board members" (Roy, 2007, p. 3). Roy further notes, "District staff also found that their current structural features did not easily support new approaches to collaboration and professional development" (p. 3).

How do we support the learning and growth of superintendents? Recently, a superintendent remarked before one of my workshops, "I have served as a senior superintendent of [a large urban district] for many years. I have felt overwhelmed and undersupported [in my own development and learning] most of the time." Fortunately, more attention is being paid to developing effective initiatives and programs for supporting the learning and development of superintendents, given the complexity and importance of their work (Blankstein et al., 2007; Kegan & Lahey, 2009; Teitel, 2006; Wagner, 2007; Wagner et al., 2006).

In his examination of effective professional development programs for school superintendents, Lee Teitel (2006) finds that superintendents valued the following about their executive learning experiences:

- Being able to talk about the real issues they face in a "safe space," where they can talk openly without compromising their authority
- Being with peers to whom they can relate and whom they respect
- Learning about their own leadership
- Sharing practical ideas that they can apply to their work at the district level

It is necessary to emphasize the importance of creating a "safe" context in which superintendents can share concerns and issues. Being able to share honestly about the complexity of their work and their own leadership challenges is central to learning and growth and a necessary feature in bringing about change (Garmston & Wellman, 2009; Rallis, Tedder, Lachman, & Elmore, 2006).

Teitel (2006) also finds that the effective programs he surveyed could be characterized as *professional learning communities* in which superintendents shared their practice with each other, engaged in problem solving together, and developed shared norms and values. As a result, they hungered for more opportunities to engage with these types of communities.

Teitel (2006) argues, "If the current 'boom' in programs for sitting superintendents is to have any lasting effect (sustainable beyond any future reductions of interest and funding), capacity must be built" (p. 9). He further questions where this capacity is being built: "Is it in the superintendents? In the districts? In the sponsoring organization? In the approaches programs are using?" (p. 9). I suggest that the learning-oriented model I present in this book offers one promising path for building capacity within superintendents individually and as a group. Furthermore, my research indicates that adopting my learning-oriented model can help superintendents better support the growth of the adults who serve in their schools.

Principals

While outside stakeholders highly value accountability, scholars and practitioners maintain that principals are expected to fix schools and communities without having the necessary resources, a situation that has led to a critical shortage of principals (Donaldson, 2008; Fullan, 2005; Murphy, 2006). The global shortage of principals is attributed to a cascade of events in which they are blamed for the problems in their schools, lack the time and energy to sustain a balanced life, and suffer from the resulting stress (Boyatzis & McKee, 2005; Byrne-Jiménez & Orr, 2007; Coleman & Perkins, 2004; Donaldson, 2008; Houston,

1998). Principals are increasingly resigning due to this stress, which is also fed by inadequate training (Moller & Pankake, 2006), insufficient compensation, professional isolation, bureaucratic micromanagement, uncertainty related to role expectations, inadequate support (Arnold, 2005; Donaldson), and the burden of inculcating youth with a knowledge base on which leaders cannot agree (Langer & Boris-Schacter, 2003; Oplatka, 2003; Wagner, 2007). For instance, a 2002 survey conducted by the National Association of Elementary School Principals (NAESP, 2002) found that 66 percent of its membership would be retiring in the next six to ten years. Kent Peterson (2002) notes that districts expect to replace more than 60 percent of all principals over the next five years.

Principals, like superintendents and teachers, face new challenges of standards-based reform and increased accountability (Donaldson, 2008; Elmore, 2004a, 2004b; Sparks, 2004), challenges that are even more difficult when attempted in the context of a troubled school attended by many low-income and/or nonnative English speakers. Support for principal leadership is particularly important in the climate of high-stakes accountability systems.

The shift from being managers to instructional leaders has also placed new and increasingly complex demands on principals. More specifically, districts are asking them to adapt from a chiefly managerial role (scheduling, budgeting, and imposing discipline) to being a school's primary adult developer and architect of the collaborative learning community (Samuels, 2008).

The friction between complex work demands and an adult's developmental capacities also factors into principals' job stress and their ability to meet their leadership challenges (Drago-Severson, 2007). Principals must take on a diverse set of roles, supporting both themselves and teachers who have differing needs, developmental orientations, and preferences. Many principals are not equipped or given the support needed to meet these challenges (Donaldson, 2008; Elmore, 2004b; Kegan & Lahey, 2009; Kelley & Peterson, 2002; Wagner et al., 2006). As a result, many teachers and principals leave the profession in search of more supportive places of employment. Principals need to be adult educators and advocates to retain teachers and to sustain themselves under adverse conditions.

Research shows that supporting new and experienced principals' learning by creating opportunities for reflection on practice is crucial to everyone in a school (Byrne-Jiménez & Orr, 2007; Donaldson, 2008; Leithwood & Jantzi, 1998; Wagner et al., 2006). While principals benefit from practices such as skill development and training provided by their district, they also need time and resources for reflective practice with fellow principals (Byrne-Jiménez & Orr; Coleman & Perkins, 2004; Kegan & Lahey, 2009). Peterson (2002) references the National Staff Development Council (NSDC) description of the kinds of structural and cultural qualities that professional development for school leaders needs to incorporate. The NSDC states that effective programs of professional development take place over the long term, are carefully planned, are embedded in the job, and focus on student achievement and how it can be reached. Such programs, the NSDC emphasizes, should include opportunities to develop positive norms, examine assumptions, and engage in reflective practice with peers about issues related to work. Karen Osterman and Robert Kottkamp (2004) define *reflective practice* as a method for developing a greater self-awareness about the nature and influence of leadership.

Thus, one way to support principal development is to provide school leaders with ongoing opportunities to reflect on their own and others' leadership in a group setting, thereby focusing on how they make sense of their experiences. The research points to the importance of creating regular opportunities for principals to engage in dialogue with peers. The purpose of such opportunities is to step back from the immediacy of one's own experiences and gain new insight into practice (Boyatzis & McKee, 2005; Donaldson, 2008; Drago-Severson, 2004b; Kegan & Lahey, 2009; Wagner et al., 2006). When we as educators re-examine our assumptions and belief systems, we can transform our practice, in turn improving our ability to facilitate change and support adult growth in schools and in ourselves. The pillar practices offer a promising path for achieving this.

Gordon Donaldson (2008) and Mónica Byrne-Jiménez and Margaret Terry Orr (2007) have developed effective professional development models that center on inviting principals to engage in reflective practice with colleagues over time around leadership dilemmas. Byrne-Jiménez and Orr's framework extends Victoria Marsick's (2002) model for supporting adult learning in for-profit organizations through *action learning conversations*. Byrne-Jiménez and Orr's model, like Marsick's, draws on adult learning theories (Knowles, 1978; Mezirow, 2000) and emphasizes the importance of dialogue and reflection to support learning and development (see Osterman & Kottkamp, 2004). Their powerful and low-cost model, like Donaldson's (2008), coincides with what Silverberg and Kottkamp (2006) recommend in terms of the importance of examining assumptions and learning collaboratively.

My learning-oriented model is similar to those discussed above in that it, too, centers on dialogue and shared reflection. However, my model differs in that it is informed by adult developmental theory. It focuses on the person as an active meaning maker, the ways in which adults make meaning of their experiences, and the different kinds of supports and challenges adults need in order to grow. The pillar practices themselves are effective holding environments for supporting growth and are robust enough to support adults with diverse ways of knowing.

Teachers

Principals are responsible for creating conditions that nurture teachers' growth in schools. Often, though, the demands of being the central designer and developer of adult learning communities outpace leaders' preparation and capacities (Johnson, 1990; Kegan & Lahey, 2001, 2009; Lugg & Shoho, 2006). To be effective leaders, principals need to understand what makes for effective professional learning that supports teacher development.

In a meta-analysis of 35 years of research on school leadership, Robert Marzano, Timothy Waters, and Brian McNulty (2005) find that a highly effective school leader can have a dramatic and positive influence on students' overall academic achievement. Furthermore, as Roland Barth (1990) maintains, "Probably nothing within a school has more impact on students in terms of skills development, self-confidence, or classroom behavior than the personal and professional growth of teachers" (p. 49).

The primary way in which teachers are supported in their personal and professional growth is through professional development programs. In their 1990 study, Dennis Sparks and Susan Loucks-Horsley identify five distinct models of staff development. My developmentally oriented review of the literature furthers theirs by illuminating the assumptions that undergird the models, the developmental demands of these models, and the different supports and challenges that adults need in order to grow from engaging in professional development initiatives. I have identified six types of professional development models that are currently practiced (Drago-Severson, 1994, 1996, 2004b):

- Training
- Observation/Evaluation and Feedback assessment
- Involvement in an improvement process
- Inquiry/collaborative action research
- Individually guided or self-directed
- Mentoring (sometimes referred to as "developmental coaching")

The sequence of models presented in Table 1.2 reflects an increasingly internal or self-developmental focus. As shown in Table 1.2, there is a lack of clarity and consensus as to *what* constitutes teacher development, *how* to support it, and *how* models are translated into practice (Cochran-Smith & Lytle, 2006; DuFour, 2007; Lieberman & Miller, 2001; Peterson & Deal, 1998).

Currently practiced models of teacher growth operate on different assumptions and expectations about how teacher growth can be supported (Drago-Severson, 1994, 1996, 2004b, 2007). Scholars have emphasized that new visions for professional development are sometimes implemented in different ways (Cochran-Smith & Lytle, 2006; DuFour, 2007; Hord & Sommers, 2008). Similarly, other educational researchers and practitioners emphasize the need to reassess what constitutes professional development (Darling-Hammond, 2003; DuFour; Lieberman & Miller, 2001), and they acknowledge that the ideas and assumptions informing the models are sometimes misunderstood, interpreted differently, and implemented incorrectly (Cochran-Smith & Lytle; DuFour; Hord & Sommers).

Scholars maintain that principals must allocate resources to support school-based and job-embedded professional development for teachers (Blankstein, Houston, & Cole, 2007; Hord & Sommers, 2008; Roy & Hord, 2003). Roy (2007) also notes that job-embedded (on-site and school-based) professional development for teachers "includes both informal and formal interactions among teachers who develop lessons, share instructional strategies, examine student work, analyze achievement data, and observe each other and give feedback" (p. 3). She emphasizes that this kind of professional development centers on the classroom and focuses on increasing teachers' knowledge and skills so that students will profit.

Table 1.2 Characteristics of Professional Development Models

Defining Characteristics	Training	Observation/ Evaluation & Feedback Assessment	Involvement in School Improvement Process	Inquiry/ Collaborative Action Research	Self-directed	Mentoring/Coaching
Focus: Target of development	Information, increasing knowledge, and skills development	New or improved teaching methods through skill development	Increased knowledge and skills needed to participate effectively in decision making	Improved decision-making skills, collegiality, collaboration, communities of practice	Increased self-direction, pursuit of self-defined interests	Psychological development of self through the context of the interpersonal relationship
Methods: Types of initiatives	Most inservice, some coursework, Hunter model	Peer coaching, clinical supervision, teacher evaluation	Curriculum development, research into better teaching, assessment of student data, improvement processes	Collaborative action research, collaborative research, study groups, roundtables	Self-directed learning, journal writing, evaluation with teacher setting goals	Supportive, longer-term interpersonal relationship
Goals	Improved student achievement, enhanced teacher knowledge and skills	Improved student achievement through improved teacher performance	Improved classroom instruction and curriculum	Improved teaching practices and greater student learning	Improved collegiality and opportunities for reflection	Psychological development of self
Mode of delivery	Are mostly single-shot or "drive-by" experiences.	Several conferences and/or meetings occur over a period of time.	Longer term—may span several years.	Variable—depends on context and current problems, issues, and dilemmas.	Variable—depends on context and current problems, issues, and dilemmas.	Usually longer term—may extend over several years.
Underlying assumptions	Techniques and skills are worthy of replication.	Colleagues' observations and feedback will enhance reflection and performance.	Adults learn most effectively when faced with a problem to solve; that is, issues of practice that are meaningful to them.	Process is self-managed and nonhierarchical; teachers have knowledge and expertise that can be brought to the inquiry process.	Adults are capable of judging their own learning needs; adults learn best when they are agents of their own development.	Development occurs in the context of a relationship, a constellation of relationships, or a team; mentoring skills can be taught to adults.

SOURCE: Adapted from Drago-Severson, 2004b.

Recently, scholars have argued that effective professional development approaches have several common features. They (1) work to link improved instructional practice and student learning, (2) address the needs of student and adult learners, (3) are collaborative and ongoing experiences, (4) create a culture of excellence, and (5) allocate time for reflective practice that nurtures learning and application (Blankstein, Houston, & Cole, 2007; Easton as cited in Roy, 2007).

Research highlights the sensitivity of professional development to teachers' needs for active learning (Corcoran, 2007), as well as informal, diverse, and continuous development practices that are spontaneous rather than planned (Blankstein et al., 2007). Joellen Killion (2000) discusses informal learning as "teacher planning, grade-level or department meetings, conversations about students, reflection on students' or teachers' work, problem solving, assisting each other, classroom-based action, research, coaching and supporting one another, making school-based decisions, developing assessments, curriculum, and instructional resources" (p. 3). Creating these types of learning opportunities, Killion emphasizes, ignites and sustains teachers' excitement for learning, growing, and altering their instructional practices. Furthermore, she contends that these types of experiences could be created in schools regardless of financial resources, provided that nonfinancial resources, such as human resources and time, are available. She, like others, finds that teachers say the "alignment of school goals with student learning needs" (p. 3) is key to their development preferences (see Corcoran; Roy, 2007). Adequate resources in terms of time and funding, as well as a strong principal, are also paramount.

Peter Youngs and M. Bruce King (2002) conducted a multiyear, qualitative study to explore principal leadership of teachers' professional development in four urban elementary schools. They found that effective principals fostered trust, created structures for teacher learning, and directed faculty to outside expertise or helped teachers to learn on-site. These practices complement what others have emphasized as key to supporting teacher learning. A collaborative approach to leadership for teacher learning is essential because collaboration provides greater access to pertinent information and alternative perspectives, nurtures reflective practice, helps develop a culture that supports learning and growth, and facilitates change (Ackerman & Mackenzie, 2007; Blase & Blase, 2001; Donaldson, 2008; Fullan, 2005; Hargreaves, 1994; Rallis & Goldring, 2000). According to Gayle Moller and Anita Pankake (2006), the principal's role is to be a facilitator or "matchmaker." As these authors explain, principals need to match their information about professional learning opportunities with their teachers' interests to foster professional growth.

RE-ENVISIONING STAFF DEVELOPMENT

In pointing out the need for new ways of leading and providing better support for the individuals who care for our children, Andy Hargreaves (2007a, 2007b), like Richard Elmore (2000, 2004b), advocates new ways of supporting adult development within schools. In so doing, he challenges educators to consider how we can alter old ways of delivering staff development to serve learners better in the future. He uses the words *integrity, equity, innovation*, and *interdependence* to describe staff development at its best. To create the interdependence Hargreaves advocates, we need more effective practices for supporting adult learning throughout the system. In fact, Hargreaves maintains that students will not be able to learn and develop unless teachers are learning and developing. And for teachers to be supported in their learning and development, we must help all educators in their learning and development: principals and superintendents, as well as teachers.

Similarly, Michael Fullan (2005, 2007) advocates dramatic shifts in how we conceptualize professional development, envisioning very different contexts for the work of both teachers and students. According to Fullan, we must ensure that we foster the highest standard of learning among the adults in our schools.

Likewise, Shirley Hord (2007) furthers the discussion for building schools with collective learning at their center. To accomplish this, schools and their staffs need to support the learning of communities of professionals. She argues that such support has two requirements: (1) creating a rich learning community for adults requires human and material resources, and (2) "relational conditions" are essential to establishing a community of learners. Future schools, she explains, must be places of learning for all students and adults. Creating true learning communities that attend to adults' differing learning and developmental needs is a promising path to achieving this new vision and emerging call from the field.

Today's teachers, not just principals and superintendents, must assist in building these collaborative learning communities. How can we build schools as learning centers that can support adults with different needs, preferences, and developmental orientations? How can we build schools so that they are mentoring communities—true learning centers?

As educators committed to supporting student learning and achievement, organizational change, and adult learning and development, we must understand that change begins with us. As Kegan (as cited in Sparks, 2002) puts it,

> The most powerful driver for behavioral change is a change in how one understands the world. If you want powerful ongoing changes in teaching or leadership, you have to get at the underlying beliefs and conceptions that give rise to behaviors. (p. 70)

The pillar practices, informed by adult developmental theory, are robust and can help us to examine our assumptions and underlying beliefs that give rise to our behaviors. Employing these practices can help us grow.

THE RESEARCH INFORMING THIS BOOK

The research on which this book is based includes and extends my prior research, which I presented in *Helping Teachers Learn: Principal Leadership for Adult Growth and Development* (2004b). In that study, 25 principals from across the United States discussed how they worked to support teachers' learning and development *within their schools*. What I learned from these leaders, a few of whom are no longer practicing principals, extended what I had learned from an earlier four-and-a-half-year ethnography (Drago-Severson, 1996) in which I examined how one principal, Dr. Sarah Levine, exercised leadership on behalf of teacher development in her school. This was one of the first studies that examined this type of leadership process in schools.

In this book, I reference the 1996 study, the later sample of 25 principals, and the research I have conducted since then with principals, teachers, superintendents, and other school leaders in the workshops, institutes, and classes in which I teach the pillar practices. It was from listening to the stories these school leaders told about how they support adult learning and development in their schools that I developed what I now refer to as the *learning-oriented model of school leadership.* In the research appendix, I describe the research methods on which my development of this model is based.

A NEW LEARNING-ORIENTED MODEL OF SCHOOL LEADERSHIP

During a retreat for experienced teachers in the last year of an evaluation cycle, I introduced the pillar practices and the developmental theory that informs them. I invited the teachers to consider how these might inform their teaching and leadership work, their current and future goals, and the supports and challenges (logistical and developmental) they felt they needed in order to grow and achieve their goals.

One 15-year veteran, Kara, asked, "How are the administrators in our school supposed to support us if they do not understand the pillar practices for growth and the developmental theory informing them?" Another teacher, Dave, elaborated,

> We need administrators and supervisors to understand the ideas—the pillar practices and the theory behind them—if they are to support us in our development. They need to understand what we're talking about when we share with them our needs for support and challenge and why we want to use certain pillar practices.

After the workshop, the teachers voiced this concern to their administrators. The administrators wanted to learn more about the pillar practices and the theoretical principles informing them to support their teachers' learning and growth. This example illuminates how adult learning can be supported when the school is viewed as a learning center in which adults share a common language for development, understand how to support and challenge each other, and employ the pillar practices to enable growth.

This book is, in many ways, a response to the concerns of teachers like Kara and Dave. It is an opportunity to introduce—to educators and administrators—the kind of leadership that fosters adult growth, or transformational learning. It is also a response to the principals, superintendents, and other school leaders who expressed the need for better supports for their own and other adults' growth. The ideas informing my learning-oriented model are aligned with a growing realization in the field that we need more effective ways to care for the growth and development of leaders across school systems. Furthermore, to build schools as learning centers, or mentoring communities for growth, we all need to be more active in supporting each other's development. As we know, learning-oriented school leadership needs to attend to more than practice and improvement; it also needs to support the development of our capacities to handle complexities. My model, informed by developmental theory, offers a range of practices that are supportive of and challenging to individuals at different developmental levels.

Developmental Underpinnings of the Model

Robert Kegan's constructive-developmental theory informs my learning-oriented model. In particular, this theory helps us to understand how differences in our behaviors, feelings, and thinking are often related to differences in how we *construct,* or make meaning of, our experience. It also helps to explain why even as adults we have different developmental capacities and different needs for growth. Understanding the key principles of this theory provides us with a *language* we can use to discuss adult development. Importantly, it also helps us to understand that growth is possible in adulthood. In fact, adulthood can be a period of significant development if a person is provided with developmentally appropriate supports and challenges.

The pillar practices and the developmental theory informing them help us to understand that we need to differentiate the kinds of leadership we provide according to the different needs of the adults with whom we are working, just as we do for young learners. My work shows that professionals will experience the same curriculum or developmental initiative differently and that it is necessary to modify our approach accordingly. In this book, I draw on a variety of developmental theories to illuminate how the pillar practices can help adults develop their cognitive, emotional, and interpersonal capacities to support others and themselves. Providing this kind of differentiated support will enable us to build true professional learning communities through a developmental approach.

Adult learning and constructive-developmental theory help us to understand the developmental underpinnings of the pillar practices and ways in which adults learn and grow when engaging in them. In this book, I illuminate the interplay between a person's developmental capacity (or way of knowing) and his or her readiness to engage in these practices. Since Kegan's theory illuminates how people construct experience and considers how contexts can provide both supports and challenges, it offers a way to help adults grow.

The pillar practices can serve as robust holding environments for supporting adult growth. Any one of the pillar practices can be used to support adults with different needs, preferences, and developmental orientations.

The Four Pillar Practices for Growth

In *Helping Teachers Learn* (2004b), I presented principals' perspectives on and experiences with supporting adult learning in their schools. From my original research with 25 principals, I developed a new model of learning-oriented leadership, which is composed of four pillar practices. This book extends and enriches the content of my first book on this topic in several ways:

- I offer more in-depth, concrete examples of the pillar practices.
- I share insights gleaned from new research conducted with a variety of educators serving in different types of leadership positions.
- I discuss the self-transforming way of knowing and how to offer developmental supports and challenges to help these adults grow.
- I include application exercises to help you, the reader, translate your knowledge into the action of supporting adult growth in your school or school system.

While I wrote *Helping Teachers Learn* primarily for school principals, I have written this book to help all adults in school systems learn and grow. The example practices can be implemented across districts and by different kinds of district leaders.

Perhaps the most important thing to say in introducing the pillar practices is to emphasize that they are *distinct yet mutually reinforcing* initiatives that were designed and should be applied with the intent of supporting adult development in a collaborative environment. They can support transformational learning by creating contexts—dynamic spaces—in which adults can engage in different modes of reflection and shared dialogue within the school and school system. I introduce the pillar practices briefly below.

Teaming

Engaging in teams provides adults with opportunities to question their own and other people's philosophies and assumptions about leadership, teaching, and learning. It provides a context in which adults can examine and question their assumptions and beliefs about the ways they implement a school's core values—in the curriculum and elsewhere, reflect on their teaching and leadership practices and challenges, examine their school's mission in light of new accountability demands, and make decisions collaboratively. Teaming creates an opportunity for adults to share their diverse perspectives and learn about one another's ideas, perspectives, and assumptions, as well as to challenge each other to consider alternative perspectives and to revise assumptions toward growth. Learning to appreciate others' perspectives can enable individuals to manage better situations with multiple perspectives and to develop broader perspectives.

Providing Adults With Leadership Roles

In assuming leadership roles, adults are invited to share power and decision-making authority. As adults, we grow from being responsible for an idea's development or implementation, as well as from different opportunities to assume leadership. In these contexts, we learn about other people's perspectives and ourselves. A leadership role is an opportunity to raise not only one's own consciousness but also a group's consciousness with respect to the ideas, perspectives, and assumptions we bring to our practice. These roles are a way for the members of a school community to benefit from other adults' expertise. I use the phrase "providing leadership roles" rather than the commonly used "distributive leadership" because of the intention behind these roles. In contrast with assigning tasks, providing leadership roles offers supports and challenges to the person taking on the role so that he or she can develop. Working with others in a leadership role helps people to uncover their assumptions and to test out new ways of thinking and acting. It's important to note that many adults assume informal leadership roles and that these experiences can also provide opportunities for growth.

Engaging in Collegial Inquiry

Collegial inquiry is an example of a larger developmental concept known as reflective practice, which can occur individually or in groups. I define *collegial inquiry* as a shared dialogue that involves reflecting on one's assumptions, values, commitments, and convictions with others as part of the learning process. In other words, while we can engage in reflective practice alone, we need at least one partner to engage in collegial inquiry. Collegial inquiry also creates a context in which adults can reflect on proposals for change, new initiatives, and schoolwide issues (e.g., developing a school mission), as well as build individual and systemwide capacity. Setting up situations in which adults talk regularly about their practice in the context of supportive relationships encourages self-analysis and can improve the individual's and the school's practice.

Mentoring

Mentoring creates an opportunity for adults to broaden perspectives, examine assumptions and beliefs, and share expertise toward supporting growth. Mentoring as a practice takes many forms, including pairing experienced teachers with new teachers or university interns, pairing teachers who have deep knowledge of the school mission with other teachers, pairing new and experienced principals, and group mentoring.

Bringing the Practices to Work

In this book, I offer examples of how adults with different ways of knowing will experience the pillar practices and of the kinds of support and challenge they will need in order to grow from engaging in these practices. I also share specific examples of how the pillar practices can be used to facilitate adults' transformational learning.

At the end of a workshop for district leaders who served in different positions, the participants and I discussed how they might use some of the pillar practices to strengthen each other's development. Immediately, they expressed a desire for more time to collaborate. Betty voiced the following, which resonated with others:

> We've [always] known that our primary concern and agenda have been to support children's growth, learning, and development. It occurs to me, now, how rarely I've thought about the need to support adult learning. This is really important and needs to be part of our shared agenda in our district.

ORGANIZATION OF THE BOOK

In the chapters that follow, I hope to serve as your guide as you explore the pillar practices and the developmental theory informing them. I hope that as you read, you will consider how these practices and ideas might help you to support other people and your own personal and professional growth. The two chapters in Part 1 provide a foundation for understanding the chapters in Part 2, which consist of an in-depth exploration of the pillar practices for growth.

Throughout, I have provided case studies and numerous examples of how the theories and practices here have been applied in different real-world educational settings. Also included throughout are application exercises and reflective questions that invite you to consider deeply how the ideas and practices presented might be helpful as you work to support your own and others' growth and development.

Part 1: Foundations

The first two chapters are offered to provide a solid foundation for understanding the ideas and concepts that follow. My intention in Chapter 1 is to introduce the need for a learning-oriented model of school leadership, especially in light of the adaptive challenges leaders face across every level of our school systems.

Chapter 2 reviews the foundational ideas of Harvard psychologist Robert Kegan's constructive-developmental theory of adult growth: (1) theoretical principles, (2) the most common "ways of knowing" in adulthood (which account for adults' differing developmental orientations), and (3) the central aspects of a "holding environment"—an environment that encourages growth and learning in all of its diverse members.

Part 2: Pillar Practices for Growth

Each of Chapters 3 through 6 is devoted to exploring one of the four pillar practices. In each chapter, I present main themes from both the professional learning literature and the adult developmental literature and then discuss the pillar practice from a developmental perspective to illuminate how it supports adult growth. In addition, I share case examples of how leaders employ the practice under consideration in a variety of school contexts. Chapter 7 provides case examples showing how school leaders have actually employed the pillar practices, and Chapter 8 shows how the four pillar practices can be adapted for different settings. More detailed reviews of Chapters 3 through 8 follow.

Chapter 3 focuses on how the practice of teaming can be used to promote personal and organizational learning through various forms of collaboration. I review the literature on teaming and discuss important features for structuring teams from a developmental perspective. I also relate the ways in which adults with different developmental orientations will experience the practice and the types of supports and challenges they will need in order to grow through teaming. This chapter includes a discussion of how variations of teaming can support adults with different developmental orientations and specific examples of ways to structure teams and use developmental protocols to support adult development optimally. Through case examples, I show how leaders organize their schools for teamwork and describe how teaming opens communication, decreases isolation, supports growth, and builds interdependent relationships. Toward the end of the chapter, I present a case from a principal who serves in a large, urban high school, which illustrates how this leader implemented teaming from a developmental perspective.

Chapter 4 presents the practice of providing adults with leadership roles. I review the theoretical literature on leadership roles and then explore (1) why these roles are essential in today's complex educational world, (2) the principal's role in inviting other adults to assume leadership, (3) how providing these roles cultivates schools as learning centers, and (4) how inviting teachers to assume these roles in schools can create a pathway to individual and organizational growth. I also discuss how to support adults in these roles from a developmental perspective, how adults with different developmental orientations will experience the roles, and what types of supports and challenges they will need in order to grow from assuming these roles. Using real-life examples, I describe how leaders employ the practice of providing leadership roles and how it supports learning, builds capacity and positive school climates, decreases isolation, nurtures relationships, and supports adult development.

Chapter 5 explores the practice of collegial inquiry—investing time in meaningful dialogue about practice. After a review of the literature on adult and professional development, I discuss how to structure collegial inquiry from a developmental perspective, how adults with different developmental orientations will experience the practice, and what types of supports and challenges they will need to grow from it. After illuminating why school leaders believe collegial inquiry supports adult learning and what conditions are necessary to facilitate it, I provide examples of how it has functioned and the forms it has taken in different schools. I discuss how principals and assistant principals employ this practice with teachers and other adults in their schools, how principals engage in this practice with fellow principals, and how teachers use it with fellow teachers. In addition, I present a case example of how one school leader used collegial inquiry as an opportunity to reflect on her practices and assumptions and ultimately grow.

Chapter 6 describes the practice of mentoring as an initiative that school leaders can employ to promote personal, professional, and organizational growth through a more private relationship or series of relationships. I briefly introduce the origins of mentoring as a growth-enhancing practice that supports human development and review the mentoring literature. I then discuss how adults with different ways of knowing will experience this practice and what types of supports and challenges they will need to grow from it. Next, I explain why school leaders value mentoring and how they think it supports adult learning, and I clarify the adult learning and developmental principles behind it. I illuminate how mentoring program purposes vary from "spreading a mission" to exchanging information to providing both new and experienced educators with emotional support. Through these examples, I show how leaders employ this practice and describe what effective mentoring *means to them;* why they value it; and how it opens communication, decreases isolation, builds interdependent relationships, helps adults to manage change, and supports adult growth.

Chapter 7 includes several in-depth cases written by leaders who employ the pillar practices in service to adult development. This chapter illustrates how teaming, providing leadership roles, engaging in collegial inquiry, and mentoring can together create a true center for adult learning and growth. The cases illustrate how the pillar practices help adults broaden their perspectives, build community, manage change, and grow. As you will see, while these leaders employ the pillar practices, they adjust them to meet the needs of the adults with whom they are working—that is, they adapt the pillar practices to the context of their work. In presenting developmentally oriented examples from these leaders' experiences with the pillar practices in diverse contexts, I hope to make the pillar practices more immediately practical and accessible.

Chapter 8 discusses ways in which school leaders can adapt and use the four pillar practices in different settings. I emphasize the importance of each school's particular characteristics in supporting the learning of all its members. In addition, I discuss some of the implications of the learning-oriented model of leadership. While no universal remedy can be applied to every school context and system, this model is especially promising for the very reason that it can be adapted to different school cultures and systems that nonetheless share the same purpose: supporting the growth and learning of the community.

In illuminating this learning-oriented model, the pillar practices, and practical examples, as well as by sharing the experiences of leaders like yourself, this book provides a new entry point for joining the conversation about building schools as learning centers. It also helps us to increase our capacities to meet the adaptive challenges of schooling and leadership today by implementing practices that will help adults grow *within* schools and school systems. My greatest hope is that this work will take us one step further toward realizing our collective desire to support adult learning in schools by building cultures responsive to adults' developmental needs.

SUMMARY AND CONCLUSION

> *"What is honored in a country is cultivated there."*
>
> —Plato's *Republic*

In this chapter, I introduced the need for a learning-oriented model of school leadership, exploring connections among the fields of professional development, adult developmental theory, adult learning, organizational development, and leadership practices. I introduced how adult learning and adult developmental theories, and in particular how adults' different ways of knowing, inform my learning-oriented model of school leadership. Then I briefly described the four pillar practices supporting my model: teaming, providing adults with leadership roles, engaging in collegial inquiry, and mentoring.

To galvanize a movement that will build capacity in schools—especially in light of the adaptive challenges schools face—leaders at all district levels need to be aware of practices that support adult learning. To be true mentoring communities and learning centers, schools and school systems must be places where the adults as well as the children can grow.

REFLECTIVE QUESTIONS

Please take a moment to reflect on these questions. They are intended to help you consider the ideas in this chapter through internal reflection and group discussion.

1. What are two challenges you currently face in your practice? Do you consider them to be technical or adaptive? How so? What kinds of supports would help you better manage these?

2. What do you feel are the ingredients needed to help yourself and other adults grow?

3. Before reading Chapter 2, consider your current ideas about what growth in adulthood means. How do you think growth is supported?

4. What do you consider to be the most important features of a professional learning community? Why? If you have been working to build such a community, what challenges have you experienced? Why? If you have not yet done this work, what do you anticipate in terms of challenges? Why?

5. In what ways does this chapter help you think about the challenges you face as a school leader? What, if anything, resonates with your own experience?

6. What are two practices you engage in regularly by yourself or with colleagues to support your own growth? How are they working?

7. What are two practices you employ to support other people's growth? How well do you think these practices are working?

2

How Constructive-Developmental Theory Informs the Pillar Practices

Learning about constructive-developmental theory has enabled me to put a name to why we have to connect with each adult in a different manner.

—John Quattrochi, principal, public middle school, March 2008

Constructive-developmental theory is powerful to me because it not only offers insight [into] why different individuals respond differently in similar situations but also helps explain how my own leadership has changed and developed over time.

—Charter school principal, May 2006

My aim in this chapter is to provide a detailed discussion of Robert Kegan's constructive-developmental theory, with particular emphasis on how understanding and attending to adults' different ways of knowing can enable us to build schools that serve as rich and dynamic contexts that support adult growth. Because constructive-developmental theory informs both my learning-oriented model of leadership and the pillar practices introduced in Chapter 1, I think it is important to invest some time in discussing it. I hope you find this discussion enriching and meaningful.

I've organized this chapter into six major sections. First, I explain why Kegan's constructive-developmental theory is a helpful lens through which to view the qualitatively different ways we make meaning of our experiences. In the second major section, I provide an overview of the key ideas from Kegan's theory (1982, 1994, 2000), including the ways of knowing and the transitions between them. Third, I present examples to illuminate why and how ways of knowing matter when considering how to best support adult growth in schools. Fourth, I discuss how we can better shape school cultures to support adult growth and why it is important to consider the fit between a person's developmental capacities and the explicit as well as the hidden demands of the environment.

In the fifth section, I describe the key features of robust holding environments and why these matter in schools and school systems. Last, I discuss my learning-oriented model of leadership and the ways in which it provides a new foundation for leadership that can support adult growth. More specifically, I illuminate the ways in which this model—and the pillar practices that are at its heart—can serve as robust holding environments that support the growth of adults with diverse ways of knowing.

I then offer an application exercise aimed at applying and expanding your understanding of the theory. Also included are my responses to some frequently asked questions (derived from my work with leaders across the country). The chapter concludes with reflective questions for discussion.

WHY CONSTRUCTIVE-DEVELOPMENTAL THEORY?

In my work with principals, assistant principals, teachers, and superintendents, I often discuss going to the eye doctor to make a point about the value of any given theory. An optometrist typically will invite you to cover one eye while a lens is placed over the other to determine if it improves your vision. The doctor might say, "Tell me what you can read on the chart." After you try the first lens, she might offer another and say, "Tell me what you can see now." The idea is that each of the lenses makes certain images appear clearer, while others appear blurred. Like lenses, certain psychological theories enhance our perspectives on different aspects of our experiences.

Throughout this book, I employ one lens in particular because it informs my learning-oriented model of leadership and the pillar practices that support it. I draw from Kegan's (1982, 1994, 2000) principles of constructive-developmental theory because they illuminate the ways in which we make sense of our experiences. His theory also provides us with a language to use in conversing about the ways we make sense of our experiences and about adult growth and development in general. My learning-oriented model of leadership, informed by this theory, can help leaders across school systems differentiate the kinds of leadership needed to encourage the growth of adults at different levels of development. In other words, it can help us vary the kinds of support and challenge we provide to foster adult growth. In addition, as noted in Chapter 1, constructive-developmental theory and adult learning theories offer a fresh perspective from which to understand leadership practices and current models of teacher development.

Of course, like any theory, constructive-developmental theory has both strengths and limitations, and frameworks other than constructive-developmental theory could illuminate different aspects of leadership practice. In fact, I do draw from other sources in my analysis and examples of the pillar practices (e.g., Ackerman & Mackenzie, 2007; Ackerman & Maslin-Ostrowski, 2002; Boyatzis & McKee, 2005; Brookfield, 1987, 1995; Daloz, 1986, 1999; Donaldson, 2006; Moller & Pankake, 2006; Osterman & Kottkamp, 1993, 2004; Sergiovanni, 1995, 2000; Taylor, Marienau, & Fiddler, 2000; Wagner et al., 2006; York-Barr, Sommers, Ghere, & Montie, 2001, 2006). For example, I could interpret the stories of research participants (i.e., principals, teachers, superintendents, and assistant principals) through the lenses of women's development (e.g., Belenky, Clinchy, Goldberger, Tarule, 1986; Beukema, 1990; Surrey, 1991), men's development (e.g., Kindlon & Thompson, 1999; Newberger, 1999; Pollack, 2000), empathic intelligence (e.g., Arnold, 2005), emotional intelligence (e.g., Goleman, 1997, 2007), gender and leadership development (e.g., Shakeshaft, Nowell, & Perry, 2000), intellectual and ethical development (e.g., Gardner, 1983; Gardner, Csikszentmihalyi, & Damon, 2001; Perry, 1970), or moral development and exemplary leadership (e.g., Gardner, 1997, 2007; Parks-Daloz, 2005; Sobol, 2002). While these frameworks do enhance our understanding of how to foster adult development, I chose Kegan's theory because of the very direct and multifaceted ways in which it informs my learning-oriented model of leadership.

First, constructive-developmental theory focuses on a person as an active meaning maker of experience, considering cognitive, affective, interpersonal, and intrapersonal experiences. In particular, the theory focuses on how these aspects of experience intersect. In so doing, this theory helps us to understand ourselves and others. Other theories concentrate on just one of these aspects. Second, many developmentally oriented theories focus on children's development and articulate adult development in less depth than Kegan's theory does. Third, his theory offers hopeful principles about how to support adult growth so that we can better manage the complexities of 21st-century life, especially in terms of leadership in the educational workplace. In particular, this theory helps us to understand how adults—including ourselves—will make sense of issues related to their relationship to authority, responsibility, ambiguity, and complexity. Last, it asserts that development is *not* intelligence.

It was important in my own earlier research, published in *Helping Teachers Learn* (2004b), to highlight the developmental principles that inform the pillar practices and the supports and challenges embedded in them. My primary interest was to learn how the principals in my research supported adults' transformational learning, meaning changes in *how* a person knows rather than in *what* a person knows. In my research since then, I have wanted to examine how these theoretical ideas that inform my model and the pillar practices are helpful to school leaders who serve in different positions across the school system. What do they find helpful? How would these ideas and pillar practices transfer to and help them with their practice? In fact, nearly all of the principals in my original research wanted to learn more about how this learning-oriented model could inform their practices. The same has been true for the school leaders taking part in my research and workshops and those I have mentored and coached since my 2004 work. When I explain the key characteristics of how adults make sense of their experiences and how the pillar practices can support growth, many principals, superintendents, and other school leaders nod in agreement. The following exemplifies the ways that constructive-developmental theory resonates with school leaders:

> Learning about constructive-developmental theory has enabled me to put a name to why we have to connect with each adult in a different manner. In my position during the day, I instinctively connect with each staff member differently. Now I am able to use the centrality of language to describe why. (John Quattrochi, principal of PS/MS 43Q, Far Rockaway, NY, mentor to assistant principals, March 2006)

> Constructive-developmental theory is powerful to me because it not only offers insight [into] why different individuals respond differently in similar situations but also it helps explain how my own leadership changed and developed over time. (Charter school principal, May 2006)

For many years, scholars such as Daniel Levinson (1978, 1996) and Gail Sheehy (1974/2006) have conducted research to learn how age might organize adult development. This approach is commonly known as the *age-phasic* (or *phasic*) approach to adult development. In years past, this family of theories guided the way many people viewed their lives as they unfolded with each passing decade. The strength of this approach is that it enables us to expect some common themes in each phase and/or decade of life. For example, when adult children leave home, American parents often experience "the empty nest syndrome," creating a common theme for this phase of parenthood.

While offering some common themes, which can be very helpful, a phasic approach does not necessarily predict how a person will *make sense* of the experience of a grown child moving away. One partner in the relationship might experience the child's departure as a time of freedom to pursue other life passions after years of sacrifice happily offered to raising the child. In contrast, the other partner might experience the event as a period of loss. This experience might be a time of redefining the self and reconstructing identity. While an age-phasic approach has many strengths, including helping us to anticipate our responses to life events, it does not help us to interpret how we will make sense of these events or explain *how* we experience them.

Of course, as I said above, no one theory can explain everything. William Perry, a beloved developmental psychologist, instructs us that as human beings we require different theories for different situations since every theory has both strengths and limitations. He says that to understand anything well—including ourselves and others—we need at least three good theories (as cited in Daloz, 1986, p. 43; see also Gilligan, Kegan, Sizer, 1999).

INFORMATIONAL LEARNING VERSUS TRANSFORMATIONAL LEARNING

Before explaining the central ideas of constructive-developmental theory, I want to make a very important distinction. As mentioned in Chapter 1, both Kegan (2000) and I distinguish between transformational learning, which helps adults to better manage the complexities of work and life, and informational learning, which is simply an increase in knowledge and skills. Informational learning, increases in what we know, is thought to bring about changes in adults' attitudes, skills, and even their competencies (e.g., navigating different forms of technology, knowing how to use data to assess students' academic achievement, or acquiring skills to allocate resources in budgets). While informational learning is needed and has a crucial purpose in the 21st century, limiting ourselves to this kind of learning will not equip us to handle all of the challenges in our schools, nor will it enable us to build leadership capacity within school systems.

As noted in Chapter 1, we currently face what Ronald Heifetz (1994) refers to as "adaptive challenges," situations in which both the problem and the solution are unclear. Given that there are no known solutions to these kinds of problems and situations, they require new tools and greater cognitive capacities so that we can "solve the problem *in the act of working on it*" (Wagner et al., 2006, p. 10). While school leaders might need support in fulfilling technical aspects of their work (e.g., budgets, schedules), new demands (e.g., standards-based reform) mean that some challenges are adaptive as well. As a result, we will need to develop new capacities and learn new approaches that allow us to develop and grow *in the process* of meeting the adaptive demands of our work.

Without the tools or support to meet their sizeable challenges, many school leaders leave their professions for more supportive environments (Donaldson, 2008; Moller & Pankake, 2006; Murphy, 2006). To build our capacities to manage the complexity of these situations, we require a different kind of learning—transformational learning. While some supports can be externally provided, many must come through a practice of leadership and learning that transforms one's perspective.

As this book will help you discover, the pillar practices can assist with supporting this kind of genuine growth. While interested in informational learning, my research focuses on how the pillar practices can be implemented in schools to support adults' transformational learning.

Transformational learning changes *how* a person knows. To support the process of transformational learning, we must first understand an adult's current way of knowing, since it shapes how a person interprets all experiences. This means meeting a person where he or she is. Kegan (2000) calls this a process of "meaning-forming" (p. 52). Next, we need to attend to "reforming our meaning-forming" (Kegan, p. 52); when transformational learning occurs, there is a change in the *structure* of a person's meaning-making system.

As you might imagine, self-examination and transformational learning are closely related (Brookfield, 1987, 1995; Cranton, 1994, 1996; Mezirow, 1991, 1994, 1996, 2000). An adult who has undergone transformational learning is able to take a broader perspective on herself, others, and the relationship between the two (Kegan, 1982, 1994). For such changes to occur, we must pay careful attention to the ways in which she interprets or makes meaning of her experience so that the context can provide developmentally appropriate supports and challenges. This kind of change is at the heart of Kegan's constructive-developmental theory (1982, 1994), which informs my learning-oriented model of leadership.

CONSTRUCTIVE-DEVELOPMENTAL THEORY: AN INTRODUCTION

The constructive-developmental view of adult growth and development derives from 40 years of research (Basseches, 1984; Baxter-Magolda, 1992, 2009; Belenky et al., 1986; Gilligan, 1982; Kegan, 1982, 1994, 2000; King & Kitchener, 1994; Knefelkamp & David-Lang, 2000; Kohlberg, 1969, 1984; Perry, 1970; Piaget, 1952). Although constructive-developmental theory can be powerful for understanding how adults grow in K–12 professional development programs (Cranton, 1996; Drago-Severson, 2004a, 2004b, 2007; Drago-Severson et al., 2001a, 2001b; Hammerman, 1999; Kegan, 2000; Levine, 1989; Mezirow, 2000), it is only beginning to be considered. This theory helps us to understand and attend to developmental diversity in addition to the other forms of diversity (e.g., race, ethnicity, class, gender, religion, sexuality) that educators strive to address. I invite you to "rent" the theory for a while since it informs my learning-oriented model of leadership. And I hope that you will find it helpful in your leadership practice in support of adult growth.

History of the Theory

Swiss psychologist Jean Piaget (1952, 1963, 1932/1965) dedicated his life to understanding the development of children's cognition, as well as their moral and social reasoning. Since many of the same ideas that form the foundation of Piagetian theory also serve as foundation for constructive-developmental theory, the latter is often referred to as a neo-Piagetian theory.

More specifically, Kegan's theory applies many of Piaget's ideas to the development of adults; however, his theory includes additional lines of development—emotional, interpersonal, and intrapersonal. Like Piaget, Kegan imagines discrete stages of development and focuses on the processes involved in moving from one way of knowing to the next. In addition, Kegan's theory attends to the interplay between a person's way of knowing and his or her psychosocial context to illuminate the robust interaction between the two. Moreover, Kegan sees development as a dynamic, lifelong, interactive process between the person and the environment. The process of development does not end in late adolescence but is a critical part of adulthood as well.

Meaning-Making Systems

Kegan's theory attends to the structure and the process of an individual's meaning-making system. It is based on three primary ideas:

1. *Constructivism:* We actively construct and make meaning of our experiences and create our realities with respect to cognitive, emotional, intrapersonal (the self's relationship to itself), and interpersonal pathways of development.

2. *Developmentalism:* The ways in which we make meaning and construct reality can develop over time and throughout the life span, provided that we benefit from developmentally appropriate supports and challenges.

3. *Subject-object balance:* This balance centers on the relationship between what we can take a perspective on (hold as "object") and what we are embedded in and cannot see or be responsible for (are "subject to").

Understanding these three big ideas sheds light on the developmental principles of my learning-oriented model and on the ways in which the pillar practices can support transformational learning.

What I call a person's way of knowing, or meaning-making system, as introduced in Chapter 1, Kegan refers to as an order of consciousness (1994) or a developmental level or stage (1982). Kegan (2000) explains that what Jack Mezirow calls a "frame of reference," which consists of a habit of mind and a point of view, is essentially a meaning-making system. It is the lens through which all experience is filtered; it enables an individual to interpret life actively. In Kegan's (1982) words, "There is no feeling, no experience, no thought, no perception independent of a meaning-making context" (p. 11).

Self and Other, Subject and Object

Kegan (1982, 1994) defines growth as a process of increasing differentiation and internalization, a process of constant compromise or renegotiation between what constitutes *self* and *other*. He called this a renegotiation of the subject-object balance, asserting that a way of knowing hinges on the subject-object balance. According to this theory, the self "is" what it is subject to, and the self "has" what it can take as object. Put simply, we cannot take a perspective on what we are *subject to* because we are embedded in it; it is not separate from our selves. In contrast, that which is taken as *object* can be organized and reflected upon by the self. As we grow, we develop greater developmental capacities for perspective taking. Growing from one way of knowing to the next requires that the self emerge from being subject to a familiar and particular environment (e.g., its needs, its interpersonal mutuality, or its own authorship and ideology). As the self emerges, it is able to reflect on that frame of reference as an object.

A person's way of knowing dictates how learning experiences will be taken in, managed, used, and understood as objects. The components of our way of knowing that we hold as objects can be considered and compared; we can be responsible for and manage them. An example might help to ground these ideas in familiar circumstances. Let's consider an infant's development during the first 18 months of life. Kegan (1982) refers to this as the *incorporative* stage of development. During this time, an infant is subject to her own reflexes, sensing, and moving and does not hold anything or anyone as object. In other words, the infant *is* its moving and sensing, and its reflexes are the basic structure of her individual organization. As Figure 2.1 shows, in stage 0, or the *incorporative* stage (the infant at birth), an oval represents the self, and the bar inside it represents what the infant is subject to.

Figure 2.1   The Incorporative and Impulsive Stages of Development

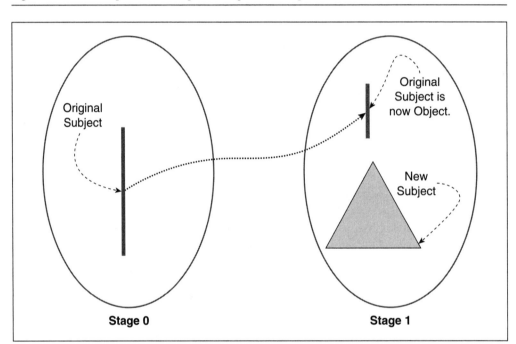

Notice that the infant is subject to everything; there is no distinction between it and the world. Over time, an infant develops the capacity to coordinate and mediate its reflexes; this is the point at which movements can become objects. As indicated in Figure 2.1, a new system, stage 1, or the *impulsive* stage, takes over (Kegan, 1982). This change is represented in the figure by a dotted arrow. In growing from one stage to another, the infant becomes subject to something else, as indicated by the triangle. The triangle represents something a little more complex than the bar (sensing, moving, reflexes). This developmental achievement marks the first time that the infant recognizes the existence of a world separate from himself. This is a process of transformation in the infant's way of knowing about himself as a subject and the world as an object. Transformational learning can continue throughout our lives, provided that we benefit from developmentally appropriate supports and challenges.

Ways of Knowing

Kegan's constructive-developmental theory is composed of six qualitatively different systems of thought, or ways of knowing, as I call them. Research (Broderick, 1996; Goodman, 1983; Kegan, 1982, 1994; Kegan, Broderick, Drago-Severson, Helsing, Popp, & Portnow, 2001a, 2001b; Lahey, 1986) shows that one's way of knowing is not associated with gender, age, or life phase. The *instrumental, socializing, and self-authoring* ways of knowing are most common in adulthood. In addition, a sixth way of knowing, *interindividual* (Kegan, 1982), which I call *self-transforming*, is becoming increasingly prevalent in postmodern society given the complex implicit and explicit demands of work, leadership, and life (McCallum, 2008; Nicolaides, 2008; Torbert, 2004). According to Kegan (1994), research in the 1980s and 1990s shows that the self-transforming way of knowing was less prevalent then than now and not ordinarily found in any population before midlife. I focus the discussion below and throughout this book on all four of these ways of knowing to illuminate how we can help ourselves and other adults, through engagement in the pillar practices, travel diverse paths toward growth. Table 2.1 summarizes the essential characteristics of these four ways of knowing and incorporates the earlier stages mentioned above, the incorporative stage and the impulsive stage.

Although there are discrete, broad stages in a person's development of way of knowing, it is important to note that there are also distinct and identifiable transitional stages (see Drago-Severson, 2004a; Lahey, Souvaine, Kegan, Goodman, & Felix, 1988). I will briefly explain how these transitions occur after describing the ways of knowing.

As I mentioned, a *way of knowing* is my term for developmental levels that profoundly affect how we as human beings make meaning of experiences and dictates how we make sense of reality. In the context of education, our way of knowing shapes the way we understand our role and responsibilities as a teacher, principal, superintendent, or learner and the way we think about what makes a good teacher or a good superintendent. A person's way of knowing is not random; it is stable and consistent for a period of time and reflects a coherent system of logic. A way of knowing might feel more like the way we *are* rather than something we *have* (Drago-Severson, 2004a; Kegan, 1982, 1994; Kegan et al., 2001a).

Each way of knowing incorporates the former into its new, more expansive meaning-making system. Although this theory is hierarchical, one way of knowing is not necessarily better than another, unless the demands of the environment call for higher-level capacities. I think the best way to look at this question is in terms of the goodness of fit, or the match between our way of knowing and the challenges we face and others' expectations of us. If the complexity of our way of knowing is sufficient to meet the implicit and explicit challenges we face in work and life, it would not necessarily be better for us to construct experiences through a more complex way of knowing. However, if the inherent developmental demands of work and/or life outpace our developmental capacities, a change in our way of knowing would help us to manage the complexities better. This is not to say that anyone is a better person for having a more complex way of knowing.

Table 2.1   Ways of Knowing According to Kegan's Constructive-Developmental Theory

Stage→ Kegan's (1982) Terms→ Way of Knowing→	Stage 0 Incorporative	Stage 1 Impulsive	Stage 2 Imperial Instrumental	Stage 3 Interpersonal Socializing	Stage 4 Institutional Self-Authoring	Stage 5 Interindividual Self-Transforming
Orientation of self			*Rule-based self*	*Other-focused self*	*Reflective self*	*Interconnecting self*
Underlying thought structure *Subject* (S): What a person is identified with *Object* (O): What a person can reflect on and take perspective on	S: Reflexes (sensing, moving) O: None	S: Impulses, perceptions O: Reflexes (sensing, moving)	S: Needs, interests, wishes O: Impulses, perceptions	S: The interpersonal, mutuality O: Needs, interests, wishes	S: Authorship, identity, psychic administration, ideology O: The interpersonal, mutuality	S: Interindividuality, interpenetrability of self-systems O: Authorship, identity, psychic administration, ideology
Definition of self			Orients to self-interests, purposes, and concrete needs.	Orients to valued others' (external authorities') expectations, values, and opinions.	Orients to self's values (internal authority).	Orients to multiple self-systems; open to learning from other people.
Orienting concerns			Depends on rules and the "right" way to do things. Is concerned with concrete consequences. Decisions are based on what the self will acquire. Others are	Depends on external authority, acceptance, and affiliation. Self is defined by important others' judgments.	Self generates and replies to internal values and standards. Criticism is evaluated according to internal standards.	Is committed to self-exploration. Engaging with conflict is an opportunity to let others inform and shape thinking.

| Stage → | Stage 0 | Stage 1 | Stage 2 | Stage 3 | Stage 4 | Stage 5 |
| Kegan's (1982) Terms → | Incorporative | Impulsive | Imperial | Interpersonal | Institutional | Interindividual |
Way of Knowing →			Instrumental	Socializing	Self-Authoring	Self-Transforming
			experienced as help or obstacles to meeting concrete needs. Person does not yet have the capacity for abstract thinking or generalizing.	Is oriented to inner states. Self feels responsible for others' feelings and holds others responsible for own feelings. Criticism and conflict threaten the self.	Ultimate concern is with one's own competence and performance. Self can balance contradictory feelings. Conflict is viewed as natural and enhances one's own and others' perspectives to achieve larger organizational goals.	Conflict is viewed as natural to life and enhances thinking. Is able to understand and manage tremendous complexity. Is substantively less invested in own identity and more open to others' perspectives. Constantly judges and questions how self-system works.
Guiding questions for self			"Will I get punished?" "What's in it for me?"	"Will you (valued other/authority) still like/value me?" "Will you (valued other/authority) approve of me?" "Will you (valued other/authority) still think I am a good person?"	"Am I maintaining my own personal integrity, standards, and values?" "Am I competent?" "Am I living, working, and loving to the best of my ability?" "Am I achieving my goals and being guided by my ideals?"	"How can other people's thinking help me to enhance my own?" "How can I seek out information and opinions from others to help me modify my own ways of understanding?"

SOURCE: Adapted from Drago-Severson (2004b, 2007). "Underlying Thought Structure" (row 3) is from Kegan (1982), *The Evolving Self*, pp. 86–87.

All that said, it is important to note that certain kinds of positions—including leadership positions—do call for the ability to demonstrate more complex developmental capacities. For example, leaders must be able to understand other adults' perspectives while simultaneously having the capacity to hold onto their own perspectives (Kegan & Lahey, 2009). In 1994 Kegan argued that many of the demands of modern life outpaced most adults' developmental capacities, a challenge that will become more important as the world becomes increasingly complex. Stephen Covey (2005), a scholar who has dedicated his life to understanding how to help adults become more effective at work, notes in *The 8th Habit: From Effectiveness to Greatness* that eight habits are important to functioning effectively in the modern workplace. Many of these habits, such as beginning with the end in mind, owning one's work, and being able to engage in conflict and take a stand for one's beliefs, call for self-authoring developmental capacities, which many adults cannot yet demonstrate, according to Kegan's (1994) analysis.

Take, for example, Kegan's (1994)[1] analysis of the rates at which people demonstrate the different ways of knowing, based on a socioeconomic composite from three studies (see also Dixon, 1986; Goodman, 1983; Greenwald, 1991). As shown in Figure 2.2,[2] only approximately 18 percent of adults in 1994 demonstrated a self-authoring (stage 4) way of knowing. Forty-three percent of adults made meaning with a socializing way of knowing (stage 3, 12 percent and 31 percent between stages 3 and 4), an instrumental and socializing way of knowing (between 2 and 3, 23 percent), or a socializing and a self-authoring way of knowing (between 3 and 4, 31 percent). Note that the darker gray areas in the pie chart

Figure 2.2   Distribution of Ways of Knowing (1994)

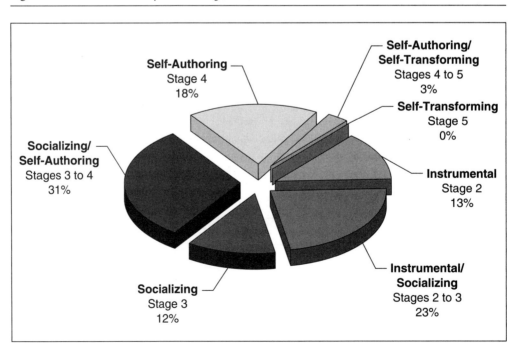

represent adults who made meaning between two full stages (i.e., with two ways of knowing) and the lighter gray areas represent adults who made meaning with exclusively one way of knowing. The majority of adults made meaning with two ways of knowing (57 percent versus 43 percent of the adults in the research studies mentioned above).

In general, according to constructive-developmental theory, people tend to engage the same way of knowing within different roles and across different contexts. (For a more detailed discussion of very rare exceptions to this, see Kegan, 1994, p. 371.) David McCallum (2008), using a developmental lens to explore how a group of adults experienced a group-relations conference, finds that under periods of extreme stress, some adults tend to "fall back"—that is, they temporarily demonstrate less complex ways of knowing. This kind of temporary falling back is also noted in Lee Knefelkamp and Timothy David-Lang's (2000) work.

The Instrumental Way of Knowing: "Rule-Bound Self"

An adult with an instrumental way of knowing has what I refer to as a "rule-bound self." In other words, this person has a very concrete orientation to the world, asking, "What do you have that can help me? What do I have that can help you?" A person with this way of knowing is defined by his own concrete needs, desires, and purposes, and in general, an instrumental knower cannot take another's perspective fully. However, the person understands that situations have a reality separate from his own point of view (e.g., when seeing the ground from an airplane, the person knows that buildings and trees are not shrinking).

Instrumental knowers are able to take perspective on and control their impulses. They do not, however, have this same sense of perspective on their needs, wishes, and interests; they are subject to their desires. Other people are perceived as either helpers or obstacles to getting one's own concrete needs met, and another person's needs and interests are important only if they interfere with the interests of the instrumental knower. For example, a person making meaning in this way might think, *I'll have a better chance of getting your help to get the things I want and need if you like me. If you don't like me, you will not help me do what I need to do or get what I want* (Popp & Portnow, 2001). While they understand that other people have feelings, preferences, and beliefs, they do not yet have the developmental capacity to accommodate their perspectives to the perspectives of another person.

Instrumental knowers are aware that their preferences and feelings remain consistent over time, but they lack the capacity for abstract thinking or making generalizations from one context to another. Experiences are organized by the following concrete qualities:

- Attributes, events, and sequences (I am good at my job; I like baseball.)
- Noticeable actions and behaviors (Good teachers follow rules, work hard, do things the "right" way, and get the "right" answers.)
- One's own point of view, needs, interests, and preferences (If I do this at work, I will have a better chance of getting a raise or a promotion.)

People with this way of knowing have dualistic thinking; they believe there are "right" and "wrong" answers, "right" ways to think and "right" ways to act. They generally want to learn "the rules," whether the rules dictate performing a task as a teacher, solving a problem with team members, or helping students with homework.

A real-life example might help to illuminate how instrumental knowers cannot generalize from one context to another. A principal approached me during a break at one of my recent workshops. She said,

> I finally understand. One of my teachers came to me last fall and said that things were not going well with colleagues on her team. She said she needed help working with her cross-grade-level colleagues. I asked her to explain what was happening, and after she did, I offered some strategies for building more effective communication within the team.

The principal continued,

> We met once a week for a few weeks to check in. She seemed to be doing much better and thought that things were working well in terms of improved communication with all team members. I felt good about it too.
>
> Then, this spring after our break, this same teacher came to me and asked for my help. She said that as her fourth-grade class was shifting focus to prepare more for the state exams, a few parents were voicing a lot of discontent to other parents about the class.
>
> As she described her role in all of this, I kept thinking to myself, "This sounds very similar to the situation with your team that we worked on last fall. Why are you not making the connection? Those same skills and strategies will help you here too."

The principal didn't share her thinking with the teacher, though. Instead, she offered strategies to help her with the parents. The principal wondered, "Why can the teacher not see that these two situations were calling for the very same set of skills and strategies? Was she listening the first time?"

And then the principal shared her epiphany from the workshop:

> Today I realized that while the situations were very similar *to me*—I could see the connections between them—for this teacher they were not related at all. She couldn't abstract her experience from one situation and generalize to the other.

The principal then said, "Now I understand this and I know how to support her."

While instrumental knowers orient toward their own concrete goals and interests, they are not self-absorbed and can be as kind-hearted as anyone else. In other words, instrumental knowers will feel comforted by concrete, more tangible expressions of support, such as the direct suggestions offered by this principal to her teacher.

Table 2.2 describes some developmental supports and challenges that will help instrumental knowers grow.

Table 2.2   Instrumental Knowers: Supports and Challenges for Growth

Supports	Challenges (Growing Edge)
• Set clear goals and expectations. • Provide step-by-step procedures for dialogue and working with other colleagues. • Share examples of rules, purposes, and goals—and how to share them with others. • Engage in dialogue that provides specific advice, skills, and information about practice.	• Provide opportunities to learn about multiple perspectives through dialogue. • Create tasks that demand abstract thinking and scaffolding knower through the process. • Encourage movement beyond "correct" solutions and toward other perspectives. • Discuss how multiple perspectives could build abstract thinking and increase perspective broadening.

As illustrated in Table 2.2, encouraging these adults to open up to multiple perspectives will help them to broaden their perspectives over time.

The Socializing Way of Knowing: "Other-Focused Self"

A person who makes meaning primarily with a socializing way of knowing has an enhanced capacity for reflection. Unlike instrumental knowers, socializing knowers have developed the capacity to think abstractly—to think about thinking—to make generalizations, and to reflect on their actions and the actions of others. They are able to be conversational and participate in a shared reality. When people have grown into a socializing way of knowing, they can identify with and internalize other people's feelings. A teacher might ask herself, "What does my principal think I should do? Will my teammates still like me if I disagree with them?" The self is identified by its relationship to valued others (e.g., a spouse or a boss) or ideas (e.g., religious or political ideologies, societal expectations), and the person constantly seeks approval and acceptance (Kegan, 1982). Because of this, I refer to adults with this way of knowing as having an "other-focused self." One school leader, after learning about this way of knowing, explained her understanding. She said, "I understand this. It can be summed up as 'you are my mirror.'"

An individual with this way of knowing has the capacity for empathy and can subordinate her own needs and desires to those of others. However, she is not yet able to have a perspective on her relationships. Socializing knowers feel responsible for other people's feelings and hold other people responsible for their feelings. Interpersonal conflict is experienced as a threat to the self; thus socializing knowers avoid conflict because it is a risk to the relationship and is experienced as a threat to the coherence of a person's very self.

As Table 2.1 shows, socializing knowers are concerned with abstract psychological consequences, asking, "Am I meeting your expectations of me? Will you still like/love and/or value me?" Likewise, socializing knowers do not yet have the capacity to look inside for their own expectations for themselves. Kegan (1982) discusses a socializing knower's identification with relationships: "You are the other by whom I complete myself, the other whom I need to create the context out of which I define and know myself and the world" (p. 100). In other words, socializing knowers do not have the capacity to consider that point of view from a distance and evaluate it.

An example might demonstrate how we can best support and challenge adults with this way of knowing. For several years, I worked with a young teacher, whom I'll call Yee, as she worked to complete an important project. When we would meet, she often asked me, "What do *you* think I *should* do about this?" After several meetings in which I worked to help her feel accepted, I began to say, "I will share what I think, but before that, I'd love to learn what you think is the best path for *you?*" She would offer some ideas, and I would say something like, "That sounds good to me. Please try it and we can talk more afterwards."

Over time, she began to voice her own thinking before asking me what I thought she should do. After Yee had completed her project, she called me and said, "Do you remember when you used to always ask me what I thought when I would come to you for advice?" She continued,

> Well, in the beginning when you did that, it was frustrating for me, since I wanted to know what you thought. But soon I realized that I did have ideas about what to do, and I appreciated your listening to them and validating that they were ideas I could pursue! Now when I work with my teacher interns in a college, I find myself doing the very same thing. I constantly ask some of them, "What do you think you should do?" I do this because it helped me to grow and I hope it will help them.

I assessed that Yee was using a socializing way of knowing, and I tried to support her by creating a space where she felt safe and could risk sharing her perspective and develop her beliefs. Initially, she looked to me (a teacher in a position of authority) for direction in her decision making. She needed, from my perspective, to be supportively challenged, over time, to look first to herself in her decision making.

Table 2.3 describes several supports and challenges that will help socializing knowers to grow.

Table 2.3 Socializing Knowers: Supports and Challenges for Growth

Supports	*Challenges (Growing Edge)*
• Ensure that learner feels known and accepted. • Beliefs are confirmed by authorities. • Supervisors and valued colleagues and/or loved ones show acceptance. • Provide opportunities to share perspectives in pairs or smaller groups before sharing with larger groups. • Ensure that interpersonal relationships are not jeopardized when differences of opinion arise.	• Provide opportunities to develop *own* beliefs, becoming less dependent on others' approval. • Encourage this knower to construct own values and standards, not coconstruct them. • Support the acceptance of conflicting points of view without feeling threatened. • Support this knower in separating own feelings and responsibilities from another person's. • Support this knower in distinguishing own perspective from need to be accepted.

As Table 2.3 shows, encouraging these adults to look inwardly and to express their own perspectives, rather than adopting authorities' solutions and perspectives, will support growth.

The Self-Authoring Way of Knowing: "Reflective Self"

Adults with a predominantly self-authoring way of knowing have grown to take perspective on the interpersonal context and society's expectations of them. In other words, they can hold, prioritize, and reflect on different perspectives and relationships. I refer to these knowers as having a "reflective self" because they have grown from being made up by their relationships to being able to regulate them. Kegan (1982) discusses this as a developmental shift from "'I am my relationships' to 'I have relationships'" (p. 100).

Self-authoring knowers can control their feelings and emotions and are able to discuss their internal states. They also have the capacity to hold opposing feelings simultaneously and not be torn apart by them. As Table 2.1 shows, socializing knowers are preoccupied by asking, "Do you still value me? Will you still think I am a good person?" while self-authoring knowers ask themselves, "Am I maintaining my own personal integrity, standards, and values? Am I competent? Am I living, working, and loving to the best of my ability? Am I achieving my goals and being guided by my ideals?"

Self-authoring knowers have self-regulating capacities, including the capacity to reflect on their multiple roles as leaders, parents, partners, and citizens. They can construct a theory about their relationships and have an understanding of how the past, present, and future relate. They generate their own systems of values and standards and can identify *with* abstract values, principles, and longer-term purposes. Competence, achievement, and responsibility are the uppermost concerns of people who make meaning in this way.

A limitation, or area for growth, for adults who are self-authoring knowers is that the self identifies with or is made up by its ideology; it is identified with its own assertions and theories. In other words, a self-authoring knower cannot take perspective on her own self-system because it is embedded in her own ideals and principles. As Kegan (1982) puts it, "The self is identified with the organization it is trying to run smoothly; it *is* this organization" (p. 101).

In my advising and coaching work with adults who demonstrate the self-authoring way of knowing, I try to offer both supports and challenges to help them grow. For instance, I have been working with a school leader (I'll call him John) who is trying to choose from among several career alternatives for himself. Recently, we met to discuss his ideas. As he sat down, he said, "I'd like to tell you about the options I'm considering for the next phase of my career." I said, "Okay, good. I've been thinking about possibilities for you and have come up with some ideas since the last time we met."

Immediately, he replied, "Ellie, I'll listen to what you have to say, but I may not follow your advice. I'm going to do what I think is best. What would help me most is if you could engage with me—think with me—around these ideas and critique them so that I can improve them. In the end, though, I'm going to decide for myself what I should do." John's idea of support was for me to listen to him and offer additional perspectives for his consideration.

I also offered developmental challenges to support his growth. For example, I asked him questions and offered ideas for consideration that did not coincide with his own, encouraging him not to dismiss them without consideration. As a self-authoring knower, John has the developmental capacity to integrate another person's perspective, including criticism, as one perspective among many possibilities. He sees himself and others as knowledge generators. He made it clear that he would evaluate my suggestions according to his own standards and values. In sharing his ideas with me and seeking my counsel, he *consulted* with me to enhance his goals, his perspective, and his authority.

Table 2.4 describes several supports and challenges that will help these knowers grow.

Table 2.4   Self-Authoring Knowers: Supports and Challenges for Growth

Supports	*Challenges (Growing Edge)*
• Provide opportunities to learn about diverse points of view. • Provide opportunities to analyze and critique ideas and explore own goals. • Ensure that learning from the process takes place. • Support learning about and demonstrating own competencies. • Emphasize competency. • Invite demonstration of competencies and dialogue.	• Challenge knower to let go of own perspective and embrace diametrically opposing alternatives. • Support this knower's acceptance of diverse problem-solving approaches that differ from own. • Challenge knower to set aside own standards for practice and open up to other values. • Support critique of own practices and vision. • Encourage the acceptance of diverse ways to explore problems.

As shown, helping these adults to become less invested in their own perspectives and more open to opposing views will support their growth over time.

The Self-Transforming Way of Knowing: The Interconnecting Self

In this section, I provide a sense of life beyond the self-authoring way of knowing. Theorists (e.g., Cook-Grueter 2004; Torbert, 2003, 2004) have explored even higher stages of development beyond the self-transforming way of knowing, using different assessment tools based on their theories. They have specifically examined how developmental capacities influence the ways in which people lead. William Torbert (1976), for example, conducted a study of how workplaces might cultivate greater capacities for supporting development beyond the self-authoring way of knowing. Kegan (1982) refers to the perspective beyond self-authoring as *interindividual,* and while he illuminates its central characteristics, his discussion emphasizes the ways of knowing that are more common. He did describe, however, the gradual movement from self-authoring to a fully and solely operating interindividual—or what I call *self-transforming*—way of knowing.

While this way of knowing is less common, I explain it for a couple reasons. First, in my work with school leaders, many have voiced a desire to understand better how to offer supports and challenges to self-authoring knowers. Second, with leadership and life—and the world—becoming more complex, it can be helpful for us to learn how to support each other to grow further in our development. Third, given the complexity of life in the 21st century, more adults are growing into the capacity to make meaning in this way (McCallum, 2008; Nicolaides, 2008). I hope what follows provides a sense of this way of knowing and what supports and challenges self-transforming people might appreciate.

Before describing the central characteristics of the self-transforming way of knowing, I want to explain the difficulty of articulating *specific* behaviors or personality characteristics of such an abstract way of knowing, which makes it challenging to describe (McCallum, 2008; Nicolaides, 2008; Torbert, 2004). For this reason, I will describe the central characteristics of this way of knowing and, in the chapters that follow, share vignettes of how adults who make meaning in this way describe their experience of engagement in the four pillar practices.

During the transition from a self-authoring to a self-transforming way of knowing, a person can experience a sense of loneliness and dissatisfaction with his or her self-system (Kegan 1982, 1994). All developmental movements involve some form of philosophical crisis, pain, emergence, and rethinking of what was taken previously to be of ultimate importance. For instance, self-authoring knowers are identified with the smooth running of their own self-systems because their systems are, as Kegan (1982) puts it, "a way of seeing" (p. 225). Self-transforming knowers, on the other hand, have developed the capacity to see through their system. This is an important and challenging developmental shift. Writing of the difficult transition from self-authoring to self-transforming, Kegan (1982) explains,

> The positive [side of this transition] might include relaxation of one's vigilance, a sense of flow and immediacy, a freeing up of one's internal life, an openness to and playfulness about oneself. But viewed from the old perspective [the self-authoring way of knowing], in which [a person has] long been invested, the same loosening up may be experienced as boundary loss, impulse flooding, and, as always, the experience of *not knowing*. This last can speak itself in terms of felt meaninglessness. (p. 231)

In Figure 2.3, I present images to depict the transition from a self-authoring to a self-transforming way of knowing. The large head on the left indicates the self-authoring knower, and the large head on the right represents the self-transforming knower. The smaller heads on both the left and right represent other people who have opposing perspectives. The different shapes (e.g., stars, squares) represent different aspects of a person's identity, perspective, and values. Notice that self-authoring knowers tend to focus on the differences in opposing perspectives when faced with these extremes, indicated by the smaller heads on the left that show only squares, rather than the interrelationship of self-systems shown on the right. A self-transforming knower has the capacity to be less invested in identity, point of view, and standards and is more open to others' perspectives. As indicated in the diagram, this knower has the capacity to experience forms of interconnectedness in perspectives (the self can recognize and appreciate elements of circles and squares in self and others).

Figure 2.3   Transitioning From the Self-Authoring to the Self-Transforming Way of Knowing

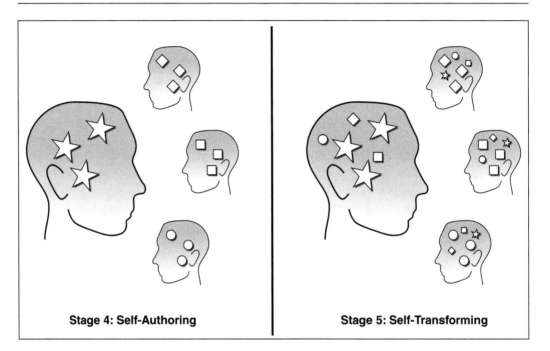

Stage 4: Self-Authoring   Stage 5: Self-Transforming

As Table 2.1 shows, adults with a self-transforming way of knowing have grown into the developmental capacity to take perspective on their own authorship, identity, and ideology, forming a meta-awareness. In other words, a person's self-system is available to him or her for attention and constant judgment; there is an appreciation for and frequent questioning of how one's self-system works. Self-transforming knowers have the capacity to examine issues from multiple points of view and, most important, to see the way seemingly opposing perspectives overlap. They are also able to understand and manage tremendous amounts of complexity. Self-transforming knowers are substantively less invested in their own identity and more open to others' perspectives.

Another central characteristic of self-transforming knowers is their orientation to contradiction, inconsistency, and paradox, which no longer threaten their self-system. These things become recognizable to the self-transforming knower, who becomes conversant with the relationship between the extremes in perspectives and self-systems instead of feeling the need to choose between them. Rather than prioritizing the protection of their self-system, self-transforming knowers are open to the relationships between self-systems. Along with this, self-transforming knowers experience a new sense of freedom to express the self and let others be themselves.

Adults with this way of knowing understand that one's own perspective is incomplete and that one's self is also incomplete without intimate relationships with others. Thus, intimacy with others is essential. Kegan (1982) notes that this form of intimacy is different from what feels like intimacy for a socializing knower; for the self-transforming knower, intimacy is "the self's aim rather than its source" (p. 238). A person experiences a new balance between feelings of agency and intimate relationships.

As an adult more fully demonstrates a self-transforming way of knowing, his or her inner life intensifies and grows deeper, as do his or her yearnings for mutuality. Self-authoring knowers might work to hold tightly to their perspectives and the running of their own self-systems; they may be more oriented toward changing others rather than themselves. Self-transforming knowers, however, want to be changed by others; they hunger for this kind of growth. Adults with this way of knowing have highly developed strategic capacities; decisions are based on the common good for families (a generational perspective), society, and organizations within society.

As Table 2.5 shows, self-transforming knowers make sense of the self as emerging and changing constantly. They are committed to self-exploration. They experience other points of view as opportunities to shape their own thinking. Conflict is natural to life and can lead to enhanced thinking. Self-transforming knowers thrive on involvement with multiple, diverse communities in which they can learn from varied perspectives.

Table 2.5   Self-Transforming Knowers: Supports and Challenges for Growth

Supports	Challenges (Growing Edge)
• Provide opportunites to grow from supporting others and having deepening relationships with self and others, especially in diverse contexts. • This knower learns, contributes, and grows from self, others, and the larger social system. • Learning from complex projects emphasizes cocreation and intimacy, with a focus on learning about self, others, and processes. • Another person is present as this learner explores deepening relationships and sense of intimacy with self and others. • A coach, mentor, guide, and/or system is in place such that deeper meaning can be made in the midst of the complexity to which this learner is capable of responding.	• Someone is present as the person makes sense of the paradoxes of life and the tensions generated by inner contradictions. • Situations and work involve others with diverse perspectives such that there is an openness to exploring tensions, incongruity, and synergy. • Offer recognition of the challenge this adult experiences (i.e., that there are limits to what the self can learn and how the self can know, that inspiring a system to transform itself is really tough). • Offer a way to make sense of the frustrations that this knower confronts when (a) the limitations of others' and one's selves slow the process of transformation and (b) one's good intentions for effective expansive, systemic change in both work and personal contexts encounter barriers.

Transitions: Growing From One Way of Knowing to Another

Growing from one way of knowing to the next is a gradual and progressive process; it occurs step by step. Kegan (1982) uses a helix to illustrate the movement of growth, as in Figure 2.4.

Figure 2.4 Trajectory of Growth Through the Ways of Knowing

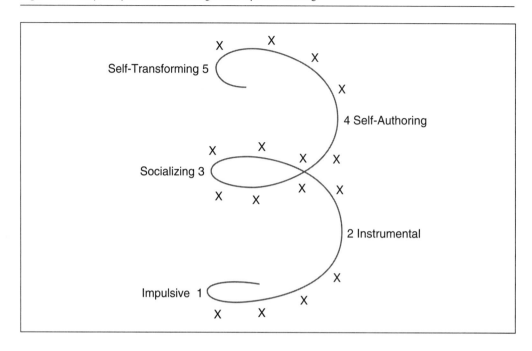

As Figure 2.4 shows, there are four identifiable, distinct, and qualitatively different transitional places (Lahey et al., 1988) between each of the named ways of knowing, noted by an *X* (e.g., between instrumental and socializing). Each of these represents a new meaning-making system for how adults make sense of their experiences, themselves, and their various roles. A person can only make meaning with ways of knowing that are adjacent to each other in the growth process. We grow from a simpler way of knowing to a more complex—bigger—way of knowing at our own pace, depending on the supports and challenges provided by the environment. While the rate of growth varies from individual to individual, and development from one full way of knowing to another can take years, the trajectory is predictable (Kegan, 1982, 1994, 2000).

More specifically, Lisa Lahey and colleagues (1988), in *A Guide to the Subject-Object Interview: Its Administration and Interpretation,* present a system for identifying the transitional phases in which two ways of knowing operate. In this system, *X* indicates a person's current way of knowing, and *Y* is the way of knowing the person is growing toward. The notations $X(Y), X/Y, Y/X,$ and $Y(X)$ are used to show these transitional ways of knowing and the movement from one to the next. This movement is typically represented in the following manner: $X \rightarrow X(Y) \rightarrow X/Y \rightarrow Y/X \rightarrow Y(X) \rightarrow Y$. This notation shows that as a person grows from one way of knowing to the next, two ways of knowing coexist. At first, the former way of knowing dominates, and the emerging way of knowing appears only a little. Gradually, the former way releases its dominance and the new way takes over, until the former is no longer operating and the new way of knowing operates exclusively. The former becomes part of the new way of knowing; it is subsumed in it.

We make meaning in these transitional phases for most of our lives. And regardless of how an individual is making sense of experience, the self strives to make itself cohere (Drago-Severson, 2004a). This coherence is preserved until a person is no longer able to incorporate new experiences into the existing way of knowing. Then the subject-object balance is slowly renegotiated, and a new, more complex subject-object balance evolves.

David McCallum (2007, personnel communication) shares a helpful image to represent what movement from each place on the development continuum might feel like. Envision a bucket of water sitting on the ground; this represents a person in a developmental position, whether in a full way of knowing or a transitional space (an *X*). If the bucket of water is swung from side to side, the water moves vigorously; this represents what it might feel like as a person grows from one way of knowing to the next. Eventually, if the bucket is placed on the ground, the water will settle; this represents the person settling into a new way of knowing.

Figure 2.5 depicts the three most common ways of knowing in adulthood and how growth from one stage to the next gradually occurs. The arrows in Figure 2.5 show the direction of growth. The image above each way of knowing represents the self—a coherent, whole system. The images toward the bottom of the oval represent the things a person is subject to. What the self can take a perspective on, be responsible for, control, and manage— what is object—is toward the top of the oval. Figure 2.5 shows that as we grow, what we were once subject to becomes something we can hold as object.

Figure 2.5   The Incorporative Nature of Growth in Ways of Knowing

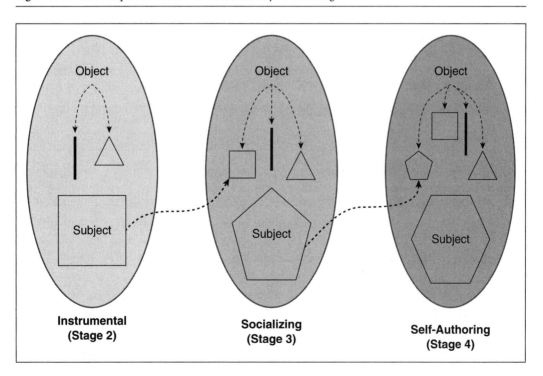

What we are subject to differs in each system; Figure 2.5 illustrates that the shape of what is subject changes, as does the shading in each way of knowing. In other words, the new subject within each way of knowing has more sides to it, indicating that it is more complex. We do not lose things as we grow; rather, a layering occurs, and the old system is incorporated into the new, more complex system.

As noted, moving from one transitional space to the next is gradual and incremental. In fact, in all of the longitudinal data, movement from one transitional phase to the next has not occurred in less than one year (Drago-Severson, 2004a; Kegan, 1982, 1994, 2000; Kegan et al., 2001a, 2001b). However, there is no maximum amount of time for these kinds of changes to occur; again, growth depends on the presence of appropriate supports and challenges.

WHY WAYS OF KNOWING MATTER
WHEN SUPPORTING ADULT GROWTH

Understanding Kegan's constructive-developmental theory and the ways of knowing will help readers understand the developmental basis of the learning-oriented leadership model and the pillar practices. In addition to facilitating growth, these practices also help us to move away from labeling people on the basis of behaviors alone (Levine, 1989). A developmental perspective offers a lens through which we can better view people's attitudes, behaviors, and expectations and understand how to support growth in individuals with different ways of knowing. For example, some adults might appear resistant to new initiatives when there might be a developmental reason for their resistance. In effect, this theory enables us to understand how adults might experience participation in programs designed to support their learning. Providing developmentally oriented support means recognizing, acknowledging, and affirming a person and how she is actively—in the moment—making sense of her experience. Providing developmentally oriented challenges means posing helpful questions and/or offering an alternative perspective to push gently at the edges of a person's thinking and feeling to foster new ways of thinking and feeling. I refer to this as *standing at the edges of someone's thinking (and feeling).*

Mindfulness of developmental diversity helps us understand how teachers, principals, and superintendents will experience the pillar practices and other efforts intended to support their learning in different ways. It also helps us to understand that sometimes our expectations of colleagues may exceed their developmental capacities. (And the reverse is also true in terms of their expectations of us.) I suggest that developmental diversity, like other different types of diversity, is essential for us to attend to as educators (Drago-Severson, 2004a, 2004b; Drago-Severson et al., 2001b; Kegan et al., 2001a, 2001b). I hope this discussion of developmental diversity will help to shed some light on the unrecognized demands that schools, leadership opportunities, and professional learning models can make on self-knowledge.

In Table 1.2, I showed how assumptions about adult growth not only drive the professional development models in common use today but also, importantly, can inhibit efforts to provide adults with growth-enhancing experiences. In some cases, these situations demand that teachers, principals, and superintendents have self-authoring capacities to participate effectively in implementation. This means that they must be able to take a stand for their beliefs, exercise authority, act upon their values, and take responsibility for themselves and their work. Socializing knowers do not yet have the developmental capacity to take such steps because they rely on external authority for answers and solutions. However with appropriate supports and challenges and engagement in the pillar practices, they can grow to develop these capacities.

SHAPING SCHOOL CULTURES: NOBLE EXPECTATIONS AND HIDDEN DEVELOPMENTAL DEMANDS

With what you now know about how constructive-developmental theory informs the learning-oriented model of leadership and the pillar practices, I invite you to consider the inherent and unintentional developmental demands in the following principals' noble efforts to shape school cultures in which teachers can learn and grow (Drago-Severson, 2004b). These school leaders work fearlessly to empower adults in their schools. Consider the following two questions as you read about their efforts:

1. What developmental capacities might teachers need to meet the expectations inherent to these efforts?

2. What types of supports and challenges would teachers with different ways of knowing need to thrive in these school cultures?

The names supplied below are pseudonyms. The quotations are from my research with school principals.

Mark: That's part of what I'm saying to the faculty all the time, that you're not just a teacher here, you are an educational leader. And part of leadership is taking risks and trying on things and reflecting upon them. You know . . . if you've been doing the same thing for 25 years, that it's for a reason. And that you've reflected on that reasoning, other than it's just easy or efficient. I think there should be ownership about the entire enterprise, the entire school [and teachers' participation in committees enables them to make decisions that shape the direction and climate of the school]. Professional growth and faculty learning must be driven by the faculty. We are a community of learners. The kids aren't the only ones in the school learning. And part of learning as an adult is continuously questioning the status quo. Even if you land on the status quo after [considering] that question.

Martha: I tell my teachers that the people who like it here [at the school] and stay are people who are self-starters. . . . So that if you have an idea, you see [the assistant principal] and you say, "I've thought about doing thus and such," and she says, "Great.

Go ahead." And that really means go ahead. It doesn't mean she's gonna sit down with you and do it for you. You're the one who wants to do it, [so go and do it]. . . . The assumption is that if you have an idea, you will make it happen. And if you need resources, come and say so.

Mae: I think schools can treat faculty members as children. And I think I really learned . . . and continue to learn that faculty members are adults and institutions need to treat them as such. And that's where I say, "You'll be successful here if you have an idea, you don't wait around for me to come back and say, 'So, how can I help you do it?'" . . . That's part of treating people as professionals. And as I say, I think sometimes schools don't.

James: We value professional development here at school, and I want teachers to value learning and growing as well. I tell teachers that all the time, if you try something even for a week or two and it's not working, for God's sake, stop it. Don't do it all year because you made a commitment to do it. . . . What's important is whether it's working for you personally. Whether it's working for your class. How do you know that it's making you a better teacher and a better person? That is really where [teachers] want to try to go.

Graham: In a good strong faculty, I think something that you will find is the ability to take on different perspectives. . . . That's important, because when you put a team together, or when you're looking for input, you try to get all the perspectives. . . . All the perspectives [need to be] acknowledged and people [need to] feel free to express them because they're all important to the decision making.

Pat: [I don't want teachers to be] looking to me for answers all the time. They need to provide their own answers and do their own thinking.

As you may have observed, all six of the school leaders above are calling for self-authoring capacities. The descriptions of their expectations and their sincere, noble hopes for the adults working within their school cultures likely place demands on teachers' ways of knowing, albeit unintentionally. In some cases, the demands might be beyond the capacities of the teachers. Principals, assistant principals, teachers, superintendents—any adults, for that matter—who are mindful of developmental diversity will be better equipped to support adult learning.

THE HOLDING ENVIRONMENT AND WHY IT MATTERS IN SCHOOLS

At this point, you might be thinking about the implications of your own way of knowing and what sorts of supports you may need in order to grow. Knowledge of constructive-developmental theory and the ways of knowing naturally leads us to this consideration—no matter what our way of knowing. An essential component of constructive-developmental theory is that growth—in particular the growth involved in transitioning from one way of knowing to the next—always takes place in some context, which is referred to as the holding environment (Kegan, 1982). A holding environment is the nurturing context in and out of which a person grows.

Similar to the conditions provided to facilitate a child's growth, holding environments offer developmentally appropriate supports and challenges to adults who make sense of their experiences in different ways. A developmental challenge presents a person with helpful, stretching sorts of questions and alternative perspectives—over time and when he or she is ready—to gently push or stand at the edges of his or her thinking, feeling, and knowing. This growth-promoting engagement raises the bar just a little bit—enough to give the person something to strive for while standing beside the person to spot his or her reach.

D. W. Winnicott (1965) originally developed the term *holding environment* in reference to the types of special kinds of care and challenges needed to support an infant's development in early life. Such environments, according to Winnicott, need to be responsive to the child's development and changing needs as he or she grows out of infancy. Kegan (1982) extends the application of the holding environment concept to a human being's entire life span, defining *holding environment* as the "form of the world in which the person is, at this moment in his or her evolution, embedded" (pp. 115–116). Holding environments must change as we develop if they are to offer appropriate forms of support and challenge.

As teachers, principals, assistant principals, and superintendents, we need to shape schools as holding environments for children's growth and our own. As was written in the Talmud, "Every blade of grass has its Angel that bends over it and whispers, 'Grow, grow.'" Leadership practices supportive of adult growth can enhance the ways in which we learn and work together and improve the design and implementation of professional learning initiatives. Holding environments can consist of a relationship with one other person, a series of relationships, situations that engage the pillar practices, or a complex organization like a school. In the classes I teach and the workshops I deliver to school leaders about how leadership practice can support transformational learning, participants often ask, "Can a holding environment be a person, a group, a team, or a school context?" The answer is yes to all—and it can also be a mix of these.

In shaping a holding environment that will best support adults with different ways of knowing, there are two fundamental principles to consider. The first concerns the way in which a strong learning environment is created: holding environments need to offer a healthy balance of both high support and high challenge. For example, challenging instrumental knowers toward growth could take the form of encouraging them to be more flexible and to follow alternative pathways to a goal or problem. They might also be encouraged to understand the meaning of goals and the steps toward achieving them in abstract terms. At the same time, supports for an instrumental knower would provide a stepwise process for achieving goals.

The second principle of shaping a holding environment concerns the goodness of fit, or match, between the holding environment and an adult's way of knowing. For example, if educators participating in teams are expected to take a stand for their beliefs or to exercise authority, the socializing knowers among them will need to be gently supported and challenged to develop these capacities. Since socializing knowers look externally (e.g., to a supervisor) for solutions, their growth can be fostered by supportively challenging them to begin to examine what they think and by encouraging them to share their thinking about a potential solution before hearing what a supervisor or another authority figure thinks.

In addition to maintaining these principles, a good holding environment serves three functions (Kegan, 1982). Like the teaching and learning process, it needs to "hold well" by meeting a person where he or she is in terms of meaning making. In other words, it must recognize, honor, and confirm who the person is, without pushing urgently for change. Second, when the person is ready, good holding environments "let go" by offering challenges that permit the person to grow toward a new way of knowing. Last, a strong holding environment needs to stay in place, or "stick around," to provide continuity, availability, and stability during the growth process. In other words, it remains in place as a person is reforming what constitutes his or her self (i.e., the subject-object balance) in the more complex way of knowing so that the person can be re-known in a new way supporting who he or she has grown to be (Drago-Severson, 2004a, 2004b, 2007; Drago-Severson et al., 2001a; Kegan, 1982, 1994). Sticking around is sometimes challenging for a variety of reasons, one of them being the prevalence of shorter-term professional development programs. However, the pillar practices that support transformation can be adapted to school contexts, which can then serve as holding environments that fulfill all three functions. A robust holding environment that serves these functions can enable a person to move from one place to the next on the developmental continuum. By way of gentle reminder, the process of growth is not often comfortable or easy; it is frequently painful as we let go of what we held tightly to—our old self—and strive to rebalance who we are growing to become.

THE LEARNING-ORIENTED LEADERSHIP MODEL

As education and leadership have become more complex in the 21st century, improving professional learning for principals, assistant principals, teachers, and superintendents must be at the forefront of our agenda. As our work becomes increasingly challenging, the need for sharing leadership among all educators becomes even more palpable, as does the need for understanding how to help each other grow. My model of learning-oriented school leadership, informed by the principles of constructive-developmental theory and built on my research (see the Research Appendix for details), can help educators grow and develop their capacity to lead. Constructive-developmental theory helps us understand why the pillar practices support transformational learning among adults with diverse ways of knowing. As you will see in the chapters that follow, the pillar practices and the developmental lens through which they are presented can help all school leaders—teachers, principals, assistant principals, and superintendents—support each other's growth. The pillar practices and constructive-developmental theory can also help us to understand the nature of the expectations we hold for ourselves, our colleagues, and our supervisors. Expectations that exceed adults' developmental capacities risk overwhelming and intimidating them. On the other hand, unintentionally low expectations can lead some adults to disconnect from the experience.

Thinking about adult growth as a movement through periods of stability and change can help us understand how each individual experiences leadership practices, the pillar practices, and other initiatives aimed at supporting learning. Helping adults in schools to grow, regardless of their positions in the hierarchy, is important for its own sake, for building learning centers, for building capacity, and for improving student achievement. Leadership that supports adult learning is directly tied to improving teaching and fostering children's development and achievement (Guskey, 2000).

I have learned that school leaders across the system and around the world hunger for a better understanding of how to support the growth of adults as well as children and enhance leadership capacity. At the end of one professional learning institute I facilitated, I asked the school leaders how they might use some of the ideas we discussed to strengthen their leadership in support of adult development. In addition to wanting more time to learn together, they agreed with one participant who said, "Having an understanding of adults' ways of knowing and the pillar practices enabled me to gain perspective as to how to work with others and where I want to position myself professionally." My work with scores of adults who serve in schools has taught me that implementing these pillar practices can move us forward in building better schools—schools that are learning centers where we help each other learn and grow.

CHAPTER SUMMARY

What the eye sees better the heart feels more deeply. We not only increase the likelihood of our being moved; we also run the risk that being moved entails. For we are moved somewhere, and that somewhere is further into life, closer to those we live with. They come to matter to us more. Seeing better increases our vulnerability to being recruited to the welfare of another. It is our recruitability, as much as our knowledge of what to do once drawn, that makes us of value in our caring for another's development.

—Robert Kegan, 1982, pp. 16–17.

I opened this chapter by discussing Kegan's constructive-developmental theory, which is key to understanding my learning-oriented model of leadership. I briefly introduced an age-phasic approach to adult learning (Levinson, 1978, 1996; Sheehy, 1996, 1974/2006) as a counterpoint to Kegan's framework. I introduced the concept of transformational learning and discussed several key principles of constructive-developmental theory: constructivism, developmentalism, and the subject-object balance and how this balance changes with growth. I also described the four qualitatively different ways of knowing of adults (three of which are more common than the fourth) and presented examples to illuminate why ways of knowing matter when considering how best to support adult growth in schools. In addition, I discussed how the nature of an adult's way of knowing shapes the types of supports and developmental challenges he or she will need in order to grow.

I pointed to the importance of considering a person's developmental capacities and goodness of fit with the demands of the environment, and I described the key features of a holding environment and explained how the pillar practices serve as robust holding environments for growth. Since Kegan's theory considers how context can be shaped as a holding environment that contains both supports and challenges, it offers a way to understand the explicit and hidden developmental demands that are placed on us—often unintentionally. Such demands call not just for a change in the skills to be deployed (i.e., informational learning) but may also call for a change in a person's way of knowing (i.e., transformational learning).

In later chapters, I engage constructive-developmental theory, as well as other adult learning and developmental theories (Brookfield, 1987, 1995; Daloz, 1983, 1986, 1999; Kegan, 1982, 1994, 2000; Kegan & Lahey, 1984, 2001, 2009; Mezirow, 1991, 2000; Osterman & Kottkamp, 1993, 2004; Taylor, 2000), to illuminate the developmental underpinnings of the pillar practices and how they can serve as robust holding environments. I also highlight the interplay between an individual's developmental capacity and his or her engagement in these practices and offer ideas about how to maximize the use of the pillar practices with different forms of support and challenge.

These supportive learning opportunities potentially can lead to greater retention of teachers, superintendents, principals, and assistant principals; higher job satisfaction; better teaching and leadership at the instructional, organizational, and interpersonal levels; and greater student achievement. And all of these will lead to stronger and more caring schools that will be true learning centers for children and adults.

FREQUENTLY ASKED QUESTIONS

In this section, you will find some of the more common questions that adults ask after learning about this theory and considering how to best apply the pillar practices in their leadership.

1. *Is there a quick assessment tool—perhaps a questionnaire or a checklist—that would help me to understand how the adults in my school or principals in my school district are making meaning?*

A quick questionnaire of this type does not exist. It can be valuable though to apply the broader principles of constructive-developmental theory—ways of knowing, holding environments, and the pillar practices—to support adults in your own context. Employing a developmental perspective does not mean that you need to assess each adult's exact way of knowing, as depicted in Figure 2.4 on the helix, however. The descriptions of the different ways of knowing and the examples of the pillar practices that appear later in the book will enable you to understand and support adult growth better in general. Asking questions and probing for how a person is making sense of an experience is a good way to understand an adult's way of knowing.

That said, even if there were an assessment tool that could be administered in five minutes, it would still take time to interpret the results. In other words, it's important to understand the broader principles of development and know how to listen for them in order to use any tool and consider the implications of what the tool indicates. Think about the ways in which a master and novice teacher assess a room of students. A master teacher is able to sense where the students are in terms of their learning, to understand their learning needs, and perhaps to recognize and anticipate trouble spots for learners much more quickly than a novice teacher. Just as it takes time to help a novice teacher grow to perform as a master teacher would, it takes time to interpret a person's way of knowing. Please be patient.

2. *Superintendents often ask, how can I understand my principals' ways of knowing so that I can support them? Likewise, principals usually ask, how can I understand my teachers' ways of knowing so that I can support them? And teachers sometimes ask, how can I understand my colleagues' ways of knowing so that I can support them?*

I believe it is very important to invite adults to determine where they themselves fall along the developmental map. Doing so can be very powerful. In many cases, all the members of a school community are asked to assess themselves. With the knowledge gained from self-assessment, these adults can then seek out particular types of developmental support and challenge as they engage in pillar practices. Below I provide an application exercise that can be helpful in providing an opportunity for this type of self-assessment.

3. *Is it desirable for me, as a principal, to hire all self-authoring knowers to be teachers in my school? Are self-authoring knowers better teachers?*

Absolutely not! We need to recognize and appreciate that developmental diversity, like other forms of diversity, is important in any organization. If supports and challenges are in place to help adults grow, we can build stronger schools. The hopefulness of this learning-oriented model that is informed by developmental theory is that it, along with the pillar practices, can help us to offer supports and challenges for growth. Two of the biggest ideas to take away are as follows: (1) as leaders, we need to recognize and celebrate developmental diversity because it is present in any group of adults, and (2) the pillar practices can be employed to support the growth of adults with diverse of ways of knowing.

4. *How can I use my understanding of adult development to help with hiring? Supervision?*

I will discuss these kinds of questions in the remainder of this book. For now, though, I will say that asking developmentally oriented questions can help with this. For example, educators involved in the hiring process might find it helpful to ask of applicants, "Can you tell me about the kinds of supports you think you will need from us as you join our school so that we can best support you?" Questions such as this can help us to understand the goodness of fit, as well as how best to support adults with different ways of knowing as they engage in the pillar practices. It is important to recognize, however, that assessing someone's way of knowing requires time and probing questions to determine how he or she constructs experience. One of the great promises of the pillar practices and the theory informing them is that they move us away from labeling people based on their behaviors and help us instead to support growth.

APPLICATION EXERCISE: ATTENDING TO WAYS OF KNOWING

This section is an opportunity to apply your understanding of constructive-developmental theory. It can also be used as a tool for beginning to assess your own way of knowing as well as others' ways of knowing, whether of teachers, principals, or teaching colleagues. Figure 2.6 contains passages from four adults with diverse ways of knowing. They respond to these questions: In what ways is your principal helpful to you in your work? How is your principal unhelpful? (If you are a superintendent and would like to invite principals in your district to assess their ways of knowing, you can replace the word *principal* in the questions and in Figure 2.6 with the word *superintendent*. Likewise, if you are a team leader or teacher and would like to invite your colleagues to assess their ways of knowing, you can replace the word *principal* with the term *team leader* or *colleague*.)

Questions to Consider in Relation to Figure 2.6

1. Please first read the passages privately and underline/circle phrases or sentences that help you to understand each person's way of knowing. Some questions to consider as you read are these:

    a) What is each adult's expectation for the principal?

    b) What is important to each adult about his or her relationship with the principal?

    c) With which way(s) of knowing is each person constructing experience?

2. After marking the passages and assessing each person's way(s) of knowing, work with a colleague or two and discuss the ways of knowing demonstrated in the excerpts. In addition, consider the following questions:

    a) What is each person's way(s) of knowing?

    b) Could the principal be the same person each teacher is describing?

    c) If you were the principal, what kinds of supports and challenges would you offer to help each person grow?

Figure 2.6   Vignettes

Mel

How is your principal helpful to you in your work? How is she unhelpful?

Her feedback is what helps me most. Whether it's on goals that we discuss or my teaching, it is really helpful. Her comments make me feel like I'm doing a good job. And when she offers suggestions for improving, I know that she is offering them because she really cares about me—not just as a teacher, but as a person. That makes a huge difference. It makes me want to do more for her and to be an even better teacher. Sometimes, when I answer a question during a faculty meeting, she tells me that I didn't get the whole thing correct, but she always has something good to say about what I said. She makes me feel like I got part of it, like I am contributing—even if I didn't get it all. She makes me feel like at least I'm learning something about the new curriculum. And she is very patient with me. When she encourages me during an observation or after a faculty meeting, it makes me feel like I really belong here. If she didn't do that, I think I'd feel like, "What am I doing here? Maybe I should just quit." She works really hard at helping us to have a sense of our school as a real community—a place where we are making a difference. It's hard being a teacher. Sometimes, when she tells me that I didn't do something quite right in my teaching, I feel so badly. I don't like to disappoint her. When she says something like this, she also lets me know that she knows that I'm really trying and that makes me feel better. A lot of times at school, she'll say, "Mel, what do you think about this or that?" It's really not helpful to me when she does this after I've asked her a question about something that I don't understand. I'm not sure how I'm suppose to learn new practices if she doesn't tell me what I should know. I ask her a question because I don't know what I think.

Fran

How is your principal helpful in your work? How is she unhelpful to you?

My principal is very helpful to me. She always tells me exactly what I need to do. In our school there are rules so that none of us can say that we don't understand what to do. I like that. She gives us clear directions and explains everything. Every policy is written down for us. That's good. When we meet after an observation, she tells me what I did right and what I need to do to improve my teaching. It's not just that. When I ask her how I should implement the improvement, she helps me by showing me other models for doing it and explains the steps. It's very helpful. The one thing that I'm confused about is that she makes us do these freewrites at the start of some faculty meetings. She tells us, "Just write what you're thinking." And sometimes she asks us how we're *feeling* about school or our work. She asks us to write what we think about a question that she puts on the overhead or on the board. I don't think this is helpful. I already know what I'm thinking, so why do I need to write it down? Plus, she doesn't even collect it. She says, "It's just for you!" I just need to know what to do because if I do what I need to then I'm going to do well here. I wish that she would just focus on what I need to do for my annual evaluation. That's what would really help me.

(Continued)

Figure 2.6 (Continued)

Daye

How is your principal helpful in your work? How is she unhelpful to you?

My principal is most helpful because she encourages me, and everyone at school, to think for ourselves. We learn *a lot* from each other. I've had other principals who don't do this; they just wanted me to follow *their* rules and do what they want. That works okay when you have to follow a new policy, where there are clearly right and wrong ways. But not in all situations. I really appreciate that my principal makes room for us to discuss things—she allows us to do our own thinking. That's what really helps me feel satisfied at work. I know that she trusts me as a professional. She respects my decisions—she doesn't need or want me to check in with her about every instructional choice I make in my classroom or with my team. I also appreciate that she looks out for my own growth as a teacher-leader. She suggested I be appointed to our school's parent-school council—and that's been a terrific experience in many ways. It's been a help to me as a person and a help to me professionally. Not only that, but she even took the time to introduce me to parents on the school's board who she thinks would be good for me to know. The part that is hardest for me is that sometimes she gets frustrated and annoyed when I critique her practices or ideas for improvement or give her feedback on things. Like the time when so many teachers in a recent faculty meeting had no clue about what she was talking about or why she wanted to implement the initiative when the old one was working so well. We just didn't understand her reasoning. And I told her about that and how I thought she could help us. At school, and in my life, I question things. Just because she's the principal, I'm not going to stop that. I'm not going to take something as truth just because she says so. I guess that's something that I find unhelpful.

Pat

How is your principal helpful in your work? How is she unhelpful to you?

Most helpful? What I think is most helpful about my principal is that she strives to create a school culture that aims to empower all of us [teachers and students] to make our own choices. That's how she exercises her leadership. When I say choices, I mean that she really wants us to create our own goals and to experiment by trying on different roles in the school and in our leadership and different ways of teaching. I like that I'm able to experiment in my own classroom while encouraging a learning process I believe in. She's supportive of that, and I'm grateful to serve in a school like this. She's also incredibly loyal to folks here and tremendously dedicated to our school's survival, even in the complex situation with AYP [annual yearly progress]. Even though our scores for the past two years have been very low, I truly believe that we will be okay and not need to close, despite the predicament we're currently in. While she feels a deep responsibility to continue running our school in the way she sees fit—and I understand that—she seems unwilling to consider other possible paths to achieving more success in terms of students' improved achievement. From my view, this limits our school and our students' possibilities and potential. I think that if she could become more open to the questions about practice and the possibilities for improvement that are embedded in the evaluators' criticisms, it would better serve our school and students. Sometimes when I offer an alternative for future direction, she interprets it as a criticism and defends *against it*—rather than seeing it as a perspective I'm offering to look beyond our school's current needs and the situation we're in and toward the best interests of the school's future. And, while I know that it's difficult to move from the way things are now and to shift our direction, I think that if we kind of joined together in exploring more thoughtfully—and critically—what we are doing now and alternatives as potential possibilities for change—especially the criticism we've received from our evaluators—we could learn from them and further develop our school's potential and programs. "What kind of long-term impact might shifting our direction now have on the school in the future?" I asked her. "How might viewing the last evaluators' suggestions for improvement as a way to examine our mission, practices, and culture and open new possibilities to help us build for the future?" Rather than protect our school from criticism in order to preserve what we have here, I want to engage with the criticism and the questions and the possibilities and to learn from them because exploring these together could make us and our school more open to growing, improving, and possibly reorganizing ourselves. It's this kind of joint inquiry into evaluators' criticism and the possibilities for change that would make our school an even richer learning context in the future.

Sample Responses

During a recent workshop, I invited participants (principals, assistant principals, and other district leaders) whose schools did not meet Annual Yearly Progress (AYP) to work with vignettes similar to those above (i.e., Mel, Fran, Daye). They worked in groups of four or five to develop the differentiated supports and challenges they would offer to adults with instrumental, socializing, and self-authoring ways of knowing. They were not asked about supports and challenges for self-transforming knowers; thus, I have not included that way of knowing here. A summary of their thoughtful work is shown in Table 2.6.

Table 2.6 School Leaders' Views of Supports and Challenges for Adults With Different Ways of Knowing

Way of Knowing	Supports	Challenges
Instrumental Knowers	• Invite this detail-oriented person to read policy/procedure and then to report on it. • Collect reflections and give positive feedback/praise. • Give clear, concise written and oral feedback. • Offer concrete advice and feedback. • Clarify the purpose of reflective writing.	• Encourage this learner to expand beyond information given. • Provide the opportunity to take on a leadership role in planning a grade-level assembly. • Use teamwork such that this person encounters situations where one must consider another perspective. • Give permission and encourage "thinking outside of the box" and being "constructively critical." • Encourage reflective writing.

(Continued)

Table 2.6 (Continued)

Way of Knowing	Supports	Challenges
Socializing Knowers	• Affirm performance. • Work with collaborative learning teams.	• Provide this knower the opportunity to become a facilitator. • Ask open-ended questions that call for person to voice own views.
Self-Authoring Knowers	• Encourage dialogue. • Make time for sharing feedback on performance and goals. • Encourage self-evaluation. • Value the person's ideas. • Validate this person's critical thinking and willingness to challenge the status quo. • Provide leadership opportunities with plenty of time for dialogue with the principal.	• Encourage person to critique own ideas. • "Know when to hold them and when to fold them." Encourage person to practice "wait time" and to self-regulate. • Invite learner to assume a leadership role among staff (e.g., to clarify confusions, facilitate discussions, and dialogue at a staff meeting). • Expose person to people with opposing points of views and encourage learner to withhold decisions until all points of view, especially opposing ones, are considered. • Discuss differences in opposing perspectives.

REFLECTIVE QUESTIONS

Please take a moment to consider these questions, which can be used for independent reflection or in group conversation. They are intended to help you and your colleagues consider the ideas discussed in this chapter.

1. *What are your conceptions of change in adulthood? What are your conceptions of growth—and how it happens—in adulthood? For growth to take place, what supports do you think need to be available? Why?*

After reflecting on these questions on your own, please share your reflections with colleagues. After you talk through your responses, look below to read some of the responses from teachers, principals, assistant principals, and superintendents who responded to similar questions in my research and workshops. First, I share some of their responses related to their conception of *change*.

a. Being flexible, open to new ideas, willing to take risks
b. Attending to changes: deaths in the family can spur growth, if one rises to the occasion.

   c. Knowing it can be hard to make a decision to change; sometimes you need to sacrifice the present in order to move and look to the future.

   d. Understanding that intentional change is different than things that pop up

   e. Dealing with how others view you

   f. Resisting the change after it was made—you hope that you made the right decision and that the change will be positive.

   g. Seeing the difference between making changes right after college versus later in life; you have more responsibilities, and opportunities are fewer.

   h. Seeing change as long-term, not a temporary alteration (e.g., a diet, as opposed to a lifestyle change)

   i. Perceiving change optimistically

After reading how some educators perceive change, now you can read how other school leaders perceive *growth*.

   a. Sometimes you have to unlearn something before you learn new things.

   b. Growth means shifting paradigms.

   c. "If you don't stay fresh you lose what you know."

   d. Growth means being able to accept feedback.

   e. Growth is when you are capable of responding differently to things that used to cause you to act irrationally.

   f. Growth happens when you "have to change." Change is losing ten pounds. Growth is keeping the pounds off.

   g. Growth requires input; something new is added to the mix.

   h. Growth comes from self-learning. First one needs to learn from oneself and then from others.

   i. For growth to happen, it needs time.

2. *In what ways do any of the practices you named in Chapter 1 serve as a holding environment for your own or other people's growth and/or learning? What common elements do you notice in the practices you and your colleagues named? In other words, why do you and others feel those practices are effective in terms of supporting growth?*

After you have had a chance to talk through your ideas, please look below at some of the responses from school leaders who were asked similar questions:

   a. Allow space for reflection and dialogue.

   b. Involve writing, in most instances.

   c. Center on sharing and learning from others and ourselves.

   d. Create spaces where we can talk.

   e. Emphasize collaboration.

3. *What kind of things, if they were to happen more in your school, would better support your own and other adults' growth? What small steps could you take to build these into your practice?*

4. *How will you secure the needed time to take the first small steps you listed in response to question 3? How could you work together with colleagues to do this?*

PART II

Pillar Practices for Growth

3

Teaming

Growth Opportunities for Individuals, Organizations, and Systems

In this chapter, I discuss the pillar practice of teaming as one that school leaders can employ to promote personal and organizational learning through collaboration. I begin by exploring discussing major themes from the theoretical literature on teaming as an effective approach to professional learning in schools and school systems. While teaming in and of itself is fairly common in the field, my intention is to illuminate how teaming can be employed as a developmental practice that supports the growth and learning of adults with diverse ways of knowing. Next, I highlight how adults with different developmental orientations tend to experience teaming and the kinds of supports and challenges they will need so as to grow from engaging in this practice.

Third, I introduce themes that have emerged from my research with school leaders about why they find teaming to be an effective way to support adult learning and provide examples of how these leaders implement teaming in their unique contexts. These case examples show how leaders organize their schools for teamwork and describe how teaming opens communication, decreases isolation, builds interdependent relationships, and supports adult development.

Fourth, I introduce specific examples of ways to structure teams and use developmental protocols to support adult development. Toward the end of the chapter, I present a case example from a principal who serves in a large, urban high school that illustrates how this leader implemented teaming from a developmental perspective. An application exercise and reflective questions are included at the end of the chapter.

Almost all of the school leaders in my research—principals, assistant principals, superintendents, and teacher-leaders—use teaming to promote individual and organizational learning through various forms of partnering and adult collaboration. Many organize their schools for teamwork because they think that teaming enables teachers to "take a broader perspective on themselves and their work." Teaming, most of these school leaders explain, is a practice that is "vital to success" and "makes a big difference in supporting adult learning."

ABOUT EFFECTIVE TEAMING AND ITS VALUE

In this section, I discuss prevalent themes in the theoretical literature. Scholars and practitioners agree that the practice of teaming is crucial to securing opportunities for critical reflection and to building schools and districts as learning centers. This holds true for district-level leaders (Childress, Johnson, Grossman, & Elmore, 2007; Richardson, 2008; Wagner, 2007), principals and assistant principals (Byrne-Jiménez & Orr, 2007; Donaldson, 2008; Sparks, 2002), teachers (Ackerman & Mackenzie, 2007; Moller & Pankake, 2006), and others who devote themselves to caring for our children in schools. My research echoes what the literature illuminates: teaming can take diverse forms. Teaming may focus on team teaching, pairing veteran and new teachers, forming school leadership teams, examining student work and/or teacher practice, or working collaboratively on reform or improvement issues. Researchers argue that teaming builds individual, school, and systemwide capacity for learning and improvement since it builds human capacity (DuFour, 2007; Hannay, Wideman, & Seller, 2006; McAdamis, 2007). In fact, today, teaming, especially teaming designed to improve student achievement, is at the center of professional learning (DuFour, 2007; McAdamis, 2007).

School change and improvement are shared responsibilities. Jeff Johnston, Mary Knight, and Laura Miller (2007) remind us, "Finding time for teams to work in school is both a necessity and a responsibility" (p. 15). In fact, they, like others (Leithwood, Seashore, Anderson, & Wahlstrom, 2004), maintain that student achievement increases as districts increase adult collaboration in teams.

Likewise, Robert Garmston and Bruce Wellman (2000, 2009) advocate for the use of teaming to build collaborative cultures in which adults exchange ideas and share ownership and decision-making responsibilities. Garmston (2007) reminds us that it is important to provide adults with training and tools and emphasizes the importance of "balanced conversations" (p. 57) for exchanging ideas and making decisions in teams. Doing so, he explains, will accomplish the following:

- Produce change and other positive results.
- Give rise to a sense of shared ownership among team members, which will increase understanding, commitment, and follow-through.

- Create a collaborative culture that identifies and reaches measurable goals.
- Increase metacognitive skills as well as individual and team effectiveness.

However, he also alerts us to three challenges that teams must resolve: airtime imbalance, talkative leaders, and insufficient protocols for securing input from all team members. To overcome such challenges, he recommends providing tools for conversation (processes, strategies, and protocols) and creating structured opportunities for reflection (allocating time for speaking and writing).

Teaming creates opportunities for group and individual reflection, reduces isolation, engenders innovation, builds capacity, and establishes knowledge-based management systems (Barth, 1996, 2006; Wagner et al., 2006; York-Barr, Sommers, Ghere, & Montie, 2006). It creates a context in which adults can engage in dialogue (that is, the art of thinking *together* and looking at an issue *together* versus discussion—pressing forward with one's own views). One can think of dialogue as being like percussion with a drum kit, in the sense that various timbers and rhythms combine to drive the music forward. Teaming enables us to share expertise and support each other's learning.

As Roland Barth (2006) writes, adults engage in these interpersonal interactions in four common ways:

1. *Parallel play* is characterized by teachers (whose territories are the classrooms) and principals (whose territories are the schools) who keep to their own territories.

2. *Adversarial relationships* are characterized by competition among teachers (e.g., over differences in how they teach) and a lack of idea exchange between teachers and principals. This means that when professionals leave the school, they take their knowledge and good practices with them, burdening new teachers with the need to figure out things anew.

3. *Congenial relationships* consist of positive and friendly social interactions that are not necessarily learning oriented or growth enhancing.

4. *Collegial relationships* are harder to develop than congenial relationships but can occur when teachers
   a. *talk about practice* (e.g., curriculum, team teaching, assessments);
   b. *share craft knowledge* (what works, what doesn't);
   c. *observe one another* (class visits that include follow-up conversations and feedback); and
   d. *help one another* (teachers helping struggling teachers).

Barth (2006) emphasizes that principals can promote collegial relationships by stating expectations clearly from the start, modeling collegiality, and rewarding those who engage in collegial relationships (e.g., with recognition, materials, or funding). I believe that teaming provides a rich context for building such collegial relationships, not just among teachers but also among other adults across and within a school system.

KEY ELEMENTS OF SUCCESSFUL TEAMING

According to Richard DuFour (1999, 2002, 2007) and others (Johnston et al., 2007; York-Barr et al., 2006), the success of teaming as a practice depends on the following:

1. Allocating time (during the school day and year), support, and parameters to focus on a specific task (e.g., for teachers, the focus would be student learning)

2. Clarifying the purpose and product of collaboration (e.g., creating a clear objective, being explicit about expectations and questions)

3. Inviting team members to discuss how they will work together:
   a. Developing procedures for how the team will operate (starting and ending on time, attending all meetings)
   b. Defining consensus (all team members participate, equal distribution of workload)
   c. Developing an assessment for team effectiveness (articulating and exploring reasoning)
   d. Discussing how team members will resolve conflicts

4. Establishing "SMART goals: Strategic and specific, Measurable, Attainable, Results-oriented, and Time bound" (DuFour, 2002, p. 77), which enable teams to identify and pursue specific, measurable performance goals

5. Giving and learning from feedback that is relevant to practice

6. Securing time for celebrating improvements by conveying that a difference is being made

Similarly, Johnston et al. (2007), who discuss teams composed of board of education members, district officers, building principals, and teachers, recommend securing needed time by releasing students early one day per week, starting school late one day per week, or changing the annual calendar so that it allows for one full day for staff development per month. Second, they suggest that monthly professional learning teams assume responsibility for addressing specific goals. Third, they emphasize the importance of districts providing support and explicit expectations about the work of teams. Last, like others (Eaker, DuFour, & DuFour, 2002), they strongly advocate for using questions to guide inquiry and conversation.

What do educators value about teaming? Joan Richardson (2008), for example, describes what a "network" of superintendents in Connecticut appreciated about working as a team. She highlights how much they valued the trust that existed in the team and how it enabled them to be more vulnerable and more open to learning than before. This basis of trust, mutuality, and respect among team members provided "a safe space" (p. 7) for them to wrestle with challenging issues. In addition, the expectation of confidentiality encouraged team members to explore issues more deeply and to learn and grow from their participation on this team.

As noted above, effective teaming that supports adult development is not without challenges. Among the more common challenges are securing time for teachers and administrators to work together and procuring additional funding for teaming that occurs outside of school hours. In addition, human resistance to change while working in teams is a natural phenomenon (Evans, 1996, 2001; Fullan, 2005; Severson, 2006). However, Weiss and Cambone (2000) find that while teachers sometimes resist teaming initially, giving them the opportunity to participate in shared decision making with principals can change their assumptions and eliminate ineffective ways of working. It is also important to acknowledge the challenge of translating essential elements of teaming into different kinds of environments—each of which has unique strengths and presents unique challenges.

THE TEAM AS A SOURCE OF INDIVIDUAL GROWTH AND DEVELOPMENT

Teaming has great value for the school as a whole, supporting the goal of making it a richer learning and growth-enhancing context. Of course, this overall atmosphere is made up of numerous developmental support strategies for the individuals who make up the school environment. Engaging in reflective practice and attending to developmental diversity are two important sources of individual developmental support.

Engaging in Reflective Practice

Karen Osterman and Robert Kottkamp (2004) refer to reflective practice as "a way of thinking" (p. 1). According to them, reflective practice is a process of identifying, assessing, challenging, and altering the fundamental beliefs and assumptions that influence our behaviors. Teaming provides a fresh pathway for this as it centers on adult collaboration and dialogue.

Osterman and Kottkamp's work on reflective practice builds on the work of Chris Argyris and Donald Schön (1974, 1978), who put forth the importance of examining thought and action to improve practice. Osterman and Kottkamp extend this notion by emphasizing how context and culture influence thought and action. In addition, they maintain that the central components of reflective practice focus on systematically observing, collecting, and analyzing data drawn from practice and then attending to thinking, actions, feelings, and consequences, as well as opportunities for experimenting with new ideas, ways of thinking, behaviors, and strategies (please see Osterman & Kottkamp for techniques for surfacing assumptions).

Assumptions, sometimes referred to as "action theories" (Osterman & Kottkamp, 2004, p. 9), are the ideas and beliefs we hold about how the world should and does work

(Argyris & Schön, 1974). These *big truths,* as I call them, guide our thinking and actions. We do not question them unless we develop awareness that we are holding these assumptions. As human beings, we all hold assumptions. For example, superintendents hold assumptions about what makes a school system work well, principals hold assumptions about leadership that guide their thoughts and actions, and teachers have assumptions about pedagogy. Developing an understanding of our assumptions by examining them critically through reflective practice cultivates meaningful personal and professional learning, behavioral change, and improved performance. This process allows us to test our assumptions and gives us opportunities to revise them (Brookfield, 1995; Kegan & Lahey, 2009).

As Osterman and Kottkamp (2004) and others (Cambron-McCabe, 2003; Donaldson, 2008; Kegan, 1994, 2000; Kegan & Lahey, 2001, 2009; Schön, 1987) argue, individual change is a precursor to organizational change, and reflective practice supports both. Like Osterman & Kottkamp, I argue that for reflective practice to support the growth of individuals and organizations, it must be anchored in a community where open and honest communication is the norm, where critical dialogue is a priority, and where a supportive, trusting environment encourages and embraces risk taking. Dialogue about change must be part of the fabric of the entire community for organizational change to occur.

Attending to Developmental Diversity

In addition to all of the ways in which teaming helps to build strong, nurturing learning communities in schools and districts, it also serves a number of developmental purposes, including creating a safe context, or what I refer to in Part I of this book as a dynamic holding environment (Kegan, 1982), for learning and growth. How does this happen?

Teaming provides a context for perspective broadening, taking risks, engaging in reflective practice, examining assumptions (our own and other people's) and behaviors, and over time, possibly reframing them. Several principles of constructive-developmental theory inform how teaming supports the process of transformational learning: teaming enables adults to learn from diverse perspectives by affording greater opportunity for individuals to reflect on their own and other people's ways of knowing in a safe place. This process can help us to release ourselves from identifying so strongly with our own perspective and create an opening for better understanding other people's points of view.

A developmental mindfulness helps us to understand that adults with different ways of knowing will experience teaming in different ways. Importantly, the extent to which individuals are able to benefit from this practice depends on their developmental orientations and the availability of appropriate supports and challenges for growth. Table 3.1 shows how adults with different ways of knowing tend to experience teaming and the supports and challenges needed to support them in this pillar practice. Next, I discuss how adults with different ways of knowing experience working together in teams.

Table 3.1 Potential Ways Adults Experience Teaming Based on Their Way of Knowing

Way of Knowing	Experience of Teaming	Supports for Growth	Challenges (Growing Edge)
Instrumental Knowers	Working with a team may supportively challenge these knowers to think differently about not only their own but also other team members' perspectives on teaching practice, reform initiatives, the school, and other issues discussed in team meetings.	• Set clear expectations and guidelines for teamwork. • Explicitly state a timetable and concrete goals to be achieved by certain dates. • Provide clear, step-by-step descriptions of ways to proceed and rules for proceeding the right way with teamwork. (There is one correct way.) • Emphasize the following of concrete and agreed-upon procedures for achieving goals and working together in a prescribed manner. (Deviation from the agreed-upon, correct way to proceed is experienced as doing "something wrong.") • Focus on this knower's concrete need to achieve desired results.	• Create tasks (e.g., writing in response to questions related to team issues under discussion/debate and discussing responses in pairs) that require abstract thinking and scaffolding this knower through the process. • Encourage learner to move beyond what is seen as the "correct" way to proceed or "right" solution and toward consideration of other viewpoints to stretch thinking. • Provide opportunities to follow alternative paths to reach team goals, supporting recognition, acceptance, flexibility. • Support this knower in growing to understand team goals and steps toward them in more abstract terms, with an understanding of a multiplicity of meanings and pathways toward achievement.
Socializing Knowers	Working with a team, for these knowers, may serve as a safe context for learning about other colleagues' experience, practices, ideas, and perspectives, as well as their expertise. A team context would likely be a safe place in which they have the opportunity to broaden their own perspectives by learning	• Authorities and valued others on the team validate, acknowledge, and accept this knower's self and voiced perspectives and, in so doing, create a team context in which this adult feels safe asking questions and seeking help when unsure about what to do. (Such affirmation enables this knower to feel safe asking questions and seeking help when unsure about what to do.)	• Provide gentle encouragement to look to self and own views when asked for input on team-related issues under discussion and when making team decisions. • Support the construction of own values and standards rather than coconstructing them.

(Continued)

Table 3.1 (Continued)

Way of Knowing	Experience of Teaming	Supports for Growth	Challenges (Growing Edge)
	from valued colleagues, to whom they would look for approval and acceptance of their own ideas. Acceptance from important others and authorities is ultimate; adhering to unquestioned doctrines and societal or authorities' expectations is most important. Conflict and disagreement are threatening. As long as all of the team members share a similar outlook, which would, in these knowers' views, protect relationships with other team members, difference of opinion is acceptable. These knowers will rely on absence of conflict to feel safe in this context.	• Colleagues on the team provide acceptance, which helps this knower feel recognized and safe in taking risks and sharing own perspectives. • Provide opportunities for this learner to share own perspectives in pairs or smaller groups of colleagues before sharing with the whole team. • Focus on realizing an abstract goal and on the best ways to achieve it. • Include goals that are derived from a sense of obligation or loyalty to a team member, another person, team, or cause. • Provide guidance from experts on the team or authority figures about the best way to accomplish team goals.	• Challenge this knower to tolerate and accept conflict, such as conflicting points of view on an issue under discussion or solutions, without feeling that interpersonal relationships with team members are threatened. • Support this knower to see conflict as part of relationships and effective teamwork. • Challenge this knower to create autonomously own procedures for team-related tasks and own standards for evaluating teamwork. These need to be separate from and perhaps in contradiction to the views of team experts and authorities.
Self-Authoring	Teaming for these knowers would likely serve as a context in which they learn from other people's perspectives and opinions about teaching, practice, reform initiatives, and school improvement. Adults with this way of knowing would use the learning, ideas, and information that they learn from other team members to help themselves in their own	• Create opportunities within teams where this knower is exposed to diverse points of view so as to consider and benefit from different perspectives. • Provide opportunities to identify own goals for teamwork and to share them and learn from other's ideas. (For these knowers, it is important to discuss all possible ways to accomplish goals before deciding how to proceed.)	• Support this knower in dealing with the socioemotional (interpersonal) dimensions of teamwork. • Challenge the learner to recognize the relative and constructed nature of own goals and plans and be willing to pursue and attend to goals that previously felt diametrically opposed to own.

Way of Knowing	Experience of Teaming	Supports for Growth	Challenges (Growing Edge)
	self-understanding and improvement. These knowers will evaluate (internally) suggestions, ideas, and perspectives provided by fellow teammates, and if these new ideas are deemed desirable, these knowers will integrate them with their own. Unlike adults who are socializing knowers, these knowers will experience conflict as a natural occurrence in teamwork and learning, which can lead to more effective decision making.	• Carve out time during teamwork to analyze and critique presented proposals and/or ideas for achieving goals or accomplish some smaller team task. • Decide through dialogue what path to take given all complexities of each goal and this learner's and the team's talents, capacities, and resources. • Create opportunities for these knowers to design initiatives and to lead the team. Allow time for this adult to explore self-determined goals in relation to the work of the team.	• Challenge this knower to let go of investment and identification with own standards and values—or to set them aside—and embrace/acknowledge values of other team members that may be in opposition to own. • Support the embrace/acceptance of different approaches to the process of exploring a problem or solving it that are not aligned with this knower's way or approach. • Challenge this adult to experience *self* as being process driven.
Self-Transforming (Early)	The strength of knowers in the early phase of this stage is that they have a deep respect for other people's perspectives as well as their own. Adults with this way of knowing prefer collegial exchange, cooperation, and consensus building. They have a developing capacity for—and willingness to—focus not only on the task, goal, or purpose at hand but also on the socioemotional (interpersonal) dimensions of team building. These knowers are more capable of helping to harmonize multiple conflicting points of view when entertaining possible goals, pathways toward achieving them, and issues under discussion.	• Value this knower's felt sense of independence and provide opportunities that do not restrict deep inquiry and self-expression. • Ensure support by a broad diversity of team members and perspectives (age, gender, race, social location, experience, orientation to task/process) and forms of participation. (This knower prefers such diversity to working with more homogeneous groups or teams.) • Provide team structures that are open to change and adaptation.	• Support this knower in sorting through multiple points of view. • Challenge learner to cope with and manage hierarchy. • Encourage this adult to identify beyond the team with authorities.

(Continued)

Table 3.1 (Continued)

Way of Knowing	Experience of Teaming	Supports for Growth	Challenges (Growing Edge)
Self-Transforming (Later)	The strength of fully autonomous self-transforming knowers is their capacity to situate the work of teams in a larger systemic framework due to their ability to manage complexity and to hold multiple points of view while, simultaneously, discerning and acting on the basis of superordinate principles and values. These knowers have a tendency to exercise leadership roles on teams.	• Ensure that the structure and form of group process can emerge organically and, along the way, expand or contract as necessary from meeting to meeting and from team task to task. • Allow the freedom to assume different kinds of roles in teams. • Provide goals and purposes that are complex, challenging, and oriented toward long-term and broadly encompassing values (e.g. sustainability, the common good, communal self-actualization). • Provide opportunities to work with teams wherein this knower experiences learning and growing—and contributing to team members' learning and growth and to the growth and enhancement of larger system. • Ensure that hierarchies have enough perspective to support the development of people wherever they are in their ways of knowing.	• Challenge this knower to be patient with others so as to let them work at their own pace and not to take over in teams or collaborative settings.

The Instrumental Knower as Team Member

An adult with an instrumental way of knowing is identified with his or her own concrete needs, desires, and self-interests and does not yet have the capacity to think abstractly or make generalizations. Instrumental knowers will be most concerned with following guidelines and established rules for how to work in a team. Adhering to rules enables them to know what the *right* goals are and how to accomplish goals in the *right* way. In other words, these adults will feel supported if the team names the concrete goals it will pursue and agrees upon the steps it will take to achieve its goals.

For these adults, a causal relationship exists between their behaviors and consequences (e.g., if I work hard and follow the rules, I will get the "right" results and be rewarded in a tangible, concrete way). Adults with this way of knowing will orient toward team tasks by adhering to the rules they need to follow to complete any task they are assigned.

Decisions are based on what the self will acquire. In other words, how will doing or not doing something directly and tangibly benefit me? What will I get if I go along with you and the team? While instrumental knowers have a concrete, give-and-take orientation to the world and to their own goals and interests, they should not be understood as self-centered and manipulative. They can be as loving, kind, and giving as adults with any way of knowing; however, instrumental knowers express these traits in a concrete manner (e.g., giving and receiving love and affection in concrete, tangible, palpable ways). Over time, teaming can help these knowers to think differently about their own and other people's perspectives on teaching practices, proposals, reform initiatives, student work, and other issues discussed in teams. Establishing clear expectations and guidelines for their own work and for teamwork will help them feel supported. Explicitly agreeing on a timetable, tasks to be accomplished and by whom, and setting deadlines will also support them.

Teaming can also challenge these knowers to grow since it creates a space to learn about multiple perspectives through dialogue. With encouragement, these adults can grow beyond what they see as the only right answer toward open-ended discussion of other viewpoints that could stretch their thinking. Engaging in teaming can help these adults to develop flexibility and follow alternative paths to reach team goals. In other words, over time, teaming can provide the support and challenge needed to help them to see team goals in more abstract terms with a multiplicity of meanings and pathways toward achieving them.

The Socializing Knower as Team Member

An adult with a socializing way of knowing has the capacity to think abstractly, to make generalizations, and to reflect on his or her own actions and the actions of others. At the same time, a socializing knower is identified with his or her relationships with valued others (e.g., authority figures, important friends, cherished family, and supervisors) and society's expectations of him or her; these cannot be reflected on. In other words, other people are a socializing knower's source of internal validation. Acceptance and approval from important others and/or meeting societal expectations is of ultimate importance.

As long as all team members share a similar outlook, a socializing knower's relationships with other team members feel safe. However, conflict and team disagreement are experienced as threats to the self. Socializing knowers do not yet have the capacity to take a stand for or fully own their work or perspectives; they look to authorities and valued colleagues for decisions and answers to situations that the team encounters. Although these knowers can feel internal satisfaction when they have succeeded with a task assigned by their team, they need the acknowledgment of valued others to confirm their actions and perspective.

When learning in a team context, these knowers will focus on realizing abstract goals and want to focus on best ways to achieve them. These adults construct goals based on a sense of obligation or loyalty to a team member, authority, team, or cause. Socializing knowers will feel supported if the team sets goals, a plan for achieving them, and the steps needed to be taken based on what the expert members of the team or authority figures recommend.

To support these adults, team members could encourage socializing knowers to think through the challenges of implementing new curricula, serve as mentors, help them to see themselves as experts in a specific area and encourage them to see themselves as capable of voicing and acting on their own points of view. Working with colleagues can offer these knowers a safe context for learning about diverse perspectives and for understanding that conflict in discussions can help team members grow and lead to improved decision making. In time, these adults can grow to accept conflict as an important part of effective teamwork, without feeling that it threatens their relationships with team members.

Teaming can help these adults to develop the capacity to share their own perspectives on issues by looking internally for what they think. This can occur by gently encouraging individuals to look to themselves when asked for input on an issue and when making team decisions. Eventually, teaming can help socializing knowers to grow the capacity to create independently their own procedures for team tasks and their own standards for evaluating teamwork.

The Self-Authoring Knower as Team Member

In contrast, a self-authoring knower has developed the capacity to take responsibility for his or her work and to look internally to his or her own set of guiding values when making decisions that are part of teamwork. These knowers value the opportunity to learn from fellow team members' diverse perspectives and feel supported when there are opportunities for them to identify their own goals for the team and to consider all of the possible ways to accomplish them. Similarly, when considering goals the team might want to accomplish, self-authoring knowers prefer that time be allocated for discussing all possible ways to accomplish goals before deciding how to proceed. In other words, they prefer to make decisions by engaging in dialogue about what path to take, given the complexities of each goal, everyone's talents, capacities, and resources.

A self-authoring team member might feel best supported if colleagues encouraged him or her to assume more responsibility and leadership within the team, school, and/or district. Likewise, these knowers are more likely to embrace opportunities that invite them to take a stand for their beliefs and to exercise authority, while considering classroom, organizational, or interpersonal issues. For example, creating spaces for these adults to design initiatives and critique existing proposals will be experienced as supportive. Teaming provides a context for sharing their own internally generated perspectives and for learning from other perspectives and from the process of collaboration. Allocating time during team meetings to analyze, critique, and refine proposals and/or tasks will feel supportive to these adults.

Conversations that gently challenge them to let go of their investment in their standards and values—or to set them aside—and question their own beliefs or acknowledge other team members' values will help them grow over time. Their growing edge is to recognize the relative and constructed nature of their own goals and plans and to be willing to pursue team members' goals that initially feel diametrically opposed to their own. Similarly, helping them to explore openly interpersonal dynamics and dimensions (i.e., relationships between members) in the team will help them grow.

The Self-Transforming Knower as Team Member

Describing the central characteristics of how self-transforming adults will experience teaming is a bit different from illuminating how adults with other ways of knowing will experience the practice. As mentioned in Chapter 2, this post-self-authoring way of knowing is challenging to describe because it is such an inclusive, deep, and complex way of knowing. In other words, these knowers show less propensity to conform to normative patterns. That said, I describe how adults with a self-transforming way of knowing will generally experience teaming. In Table 3.1, I illuminate how adults in the early and late phases of this way of knowing experience teaming, because these phases are quite distinct.

Adults in the early phase of the self-transforming way of knowing have the capacity to respect deeply other people's perspectives as well as their own. When working in a team, they yearn for collegial exchange, cooperation, and consensus building. They have a developing capacity to focus not only on the team's task or purpose but also on the interpersonal dimensions of team building. In addition, they are able to help with balancing conflicting points of view among fellow team members when entertaining issues, goals, and pathways toward achieving them.

Since an adult with this way of knowing is conversant with contradiction, which does not threaten the self's system, working in a team will feel supportive if opportunities arise to explore paradoxes in the team's work, for example in relation to the larger system. Since a self-transforming knower is dedicated to self-exploration, teaming creates an opportunity for fellow team members to shape this knower's own thinking. Adults with this way of knowing want to be changed by others. Since they are not directed by needing to maintain the smooth running of their own ideologies, working with team members enables these knowers to explore and learn from multiple perspectives while questioning their own self-systems.

Figure 3.1 contains one vignette drawn from the life experience of Dr. David McCallum, SJ, a Jesuit priest who has been a high school and university teacher. A variety of assessment tools have identified David as a self-transforming knower. Figure 3.1 shares his experience of engaging in teaming. His words illuminate how adults with this way of knowing tend to experience the practice of teaming.

Figure 3.1   In His Own Words: A Team Member With the Self-Transforming Way of Knowing

---

David on Teaming: "I valued the diversity of our group."

Context and Process

I joined a group (team) to give and receive support for a statistics class I took last semester. The group consisted of a 23-year-old white female, a 26-year-old African-American female, a 29-year-old Filipino female, a 38-year-old white male, and a 44-year-old white male. While I initiated the group and made arrangements for our meeting space each week, the structure of the group process emerged along the way, flexing or contracting as necessary from week to week and task to task. The youngest member of the group, the 23-year-old white female, became the group tutor with the mutual consent of the members based on her expertise and skillfulness in explaining the material. At the same time, each member of the group took responsibility for completing as much of the homework as possible for each assignment and for leading the group through problems from time to time. We met between three and six hours a week over the course of the semester (12 weeks).

We began each meeting by checking in to see how each person was doing in the general sense, giving people space to share what was important to them at that moment. For example, one woman was anticipating the first anniversary of her mother's death with some sadness, the older male was supporting a friend in the last stages of cancer, and the youngest female was preparing for her wedding and a move. Then we spent the rest of the time working through statistics problems together, sharing insights or shortcuts using formulas, coaching/cheering/cajoling one another, reviewing for exams, or working independently and checking in with each other as needed. When the semester ended, we shared a meal together. Each person described how this had been the most effective, supportive, and fulfilling small-group experience that we'd ever had related to our school experience. We concluded the meal by each person sharing what was meaningful to them and what each person aspires to do in the future.

What David Learned

- It is so fascinating to me as well that issues of race, gender, social location, and religion all were or became explicit during the course of the semester in such a way that they did not become obstacles or impediments. In fact, *we explored and processed our differences rather openly and the result was that we functioned better . . .* enjoying our diversity. I realize that I anticipate conflict in diverse groups, that I trust in its value for the sake of creativity, and that I prefer to make space for it to emerge (where once I tried to stifle it).
- I valued the way that we managed to create a *collaborative spirit of accountability* in the group so that *each person worked to capacity and shared responsibility* for teaching/coaching where this was possible, while at the same time, there was enough *flexibility* for each person to rely on the group when necessary.
- I valued the way that the *structure and process emerged* based on who we were and what we brought to the group/needed from the group.
- I valued the way that *each person's gifts and abilities had space to shine* and that we seemed to strike the *balance between personal considerations and the tasks at hand.*
- I loved the way that *roles in the group seemed to rotate as necessary* and that no one of us seemed to have the need to overidentify with their authority, age, or expertise.
- I have a sense that while this group was temporary, there is a way in which we each came into one another's life at a key moment and *enhanced each other's lives in a way that transcended the task of the class.*
- The experience of this particular work group/team was valuable to my growth because it provided an *opportunity to help create a holding environment for myself and the other members of the group,* we developed a highly reflective style that was *conscientious about processing issues in the moment . . .* acknowledging and working through challenges and also giving expression to our feelings of gratitude or praise, and *I felt like a valued and interdependent contributor* to our individual/collective goals.

The Value of the Developmental Perspective in Teaming

Ultimately, teaming represents not only an important resource for supporting adult development but also for enacting positive change. A developmental perspective helps us to understand that the context of a team and its structure can provide a safe space in which adults can give voice to their thinking and learn from other adults' perspectives. Over time, teaming can help us develop greater capacities to manage the complexities inherent in our professional and personal responsibilities and can support transformational learning— changes in ways of knowing.

WHY AND HOW SCHOOL LEADERS EMPLOY TEAMING

Helping my team [of teacher-leaders] to reflect upon how we support and challenge each other can better solidify in their minds the importance of supporting and challenging the adults on the grade-level teams that we lead. I thought that leading my team to develop a meta-awareness of how and why we are so cohesive was a stroke of brilliance because it will not only serve our team well but also help us to identify concrete actions and behaviors we would like to see demonstrated on the teacher-led teams.

—Lead teacher and aspiring principal, 2007

A central theme that has emerged in my research with school leaders regardless of the position they held (superintendents, principals, assistant principals, teachers) is that teaming is a context for learning and for supporting adult growth. Below I discuss common themes that have emerged from my research with principals, assistant principals, and teachers. Put simply, what I learned from them is that teaming helps adults in the school to build relationships, decrease feelings of isolation, open communication, become aware of each other's thinking, learn from diverse perspectives, and share information and expertise. Another important theme that emerged was the challenge of securing substantial blocks of time. Most leaders emphasized that prioritizing blocks of time for teaming meant "fighting off other initiatives" and, often, finding other avenues to communicate/discuss issues that could be handled outside of team meetings (e.g., by e-mail). They highlighted that teaming is a context for the growth and development of both individual team members and the school.

Why School Leaders Use Teaming

Teaming was employed by nearly *all* of the principals in my 2004 study and by the principals in my research since then. In fact, across school type and resource level, teaming was *the* most frequently employed practice for supporting adult learning; this was also true for teachers and the assistant principals. The principals discussed three main reasons for using teams: sharing their leadership, building school community, and helping adults manage change and maximize diversity. For them, teaming provides a context for teachers—and themselves—to think, plan, and work together to support their learning and, in so doing, to support student success more effectively. In addition, most of the principals discussed the importance of establishing an effective school leadership team that models and promotes a healthy learning community.

Principals reported that teaming provides opportunities for individuals to articulate their thinking and develop a greater awareness of their own and other people's thinking. Several principals, for instance, explained how teams sometimes challenged well-established school norms, which, in many cases, catalyzed these principals and their schools to reassess and collaborate to create alternative strategies for change (e.g., literacy programs and technology plans).

While assistant principals and teachers in my research echoed many of the principals' reasons for why teaming is a robust practice for supporting adult learning, they also emphasized some additional reasons. Working in teams helps assistant principals to facilitate meaningful professional development with their teachers, allowing them to "gain richer insights" from one another and "share the burden" of the complex challenges and responsibilities of supporting teacher learning. This, as one assistant principal remarked, "lowers the anxiety" she encounters when working alone. The assistant principals agreed that the context of a team helps them to do their work "more efficiently," though they pointed out that sometimes the "downfall" is that "two or three people could end up doing most of the work."

Teachers who participated in my research shared many of the sentiments expressed by principals and assistant principals as to why they valued teaming. In addition, they emphasized the following reasons. Teaming creates an opportunity for them to (1) "question" their practices and have "time" to receive input and give feedback, (2) "think out loud about [their individual] practices and share them with others," and (3) think together about shared goals and responsibilities. As a group, teachers valued how team meetings create an opportunity for them to engage in collaborative planning during the school day. They appreciated the opportunity to engage in critical reflection on teaching practices with colleagues and remarked that it supports their learning.

The assistant principals and teachers voiced the following common themes about why they believed teaming supports adult learning and growth. Teaming creates a context for enhancing "camaraderie" and trust, securing spaces for reflection and learning, allowing all team members to see the "intrinsic value" in what is shared, and broadening knowledge through in-person and text-based discussion. One assistant principal summed up what others expressed: "learning is social," and teaming creates a context for "genuine learning."

How School Leaders Use Teaming

In this section, I present a few examples that show how teaming works from the perspectives of some of the principals, assistant principals, and teachers in my research. I selected these examples because they represent common themes. Table 3.2 lists the more common examples from my research of how teams are used.

Table 3.2   Most Common Examples and Practical Applications of Teaming

Type/Purpose of Team	How Team Supports Adult Learning
Cross-functional (e.g., cabinets, instructional leadership teams, quality review teams)	• Adults give and receive feedback on ideas, proposals, and practices. • Adults learn from multiple perspectives.
Teaching	• Adults give and receive feedback on ideas, proposals, and practices. • Adults learn from multiple perspectives. • Adults develop awareness of assumptions guiding practice.
Strategy development and shared decision making	• Adults are invited into conversations regarding schoolwide issues and plans. • Adults give and receive feedback on ideas, proposals, and initiatives. • Adults learn from multiple perspectives. • Adults share and include others in leadership and decision making.
Discussion of curriculum and student work (e.g., subject area teams, grade-level teams, and vertical teams)	• Adults meet regularly to discuss curricula and to share lesson and unit plans and what they have learned from implementing plans and curricula (success and challenges). • Adults alter practice based on feedback from peers, coaches, and supervisors and shared discussion of curricula. • Adults review curricula/student work to assess the effectiveness of curricula and/or their pedagogical practices, teaching strategies, and assignments to students. • Adults use protocols to analyze curricula and/or student work and examine data to understand students' needs.
Inquiry	• Adults meet regularly to discuss students and student work (success and challenges). • Adults review student work to assess the effectiveness of curricula and/or pedagogical practices and strategies. • Adults make recommendations and suggestions for altering practice based on shared discussion. • Adults use protocols to analyze student work and examine data to understand students' needs.
Critical friends	• Adults give and receive feedback on ideas and practices. • Adults learn from multiple perspectives. • Adults develop awareness of assumptions guiding thinking and practice.
Professional learning and development	• Adults meet regularly to create plan/vision, establish professional learning goals, and assess progress toward them.

(Continued)

Table 3.2 (Continued)

Type/Purpose of Team	How Team Supports Adult Learning
Instructional leadership	• Adults meet regularly to create plan/vision and assess progress toward it and to establish goals and plans for achieving it.
Study and discussion (e.g., a book group)	• Adults meet regularly to discuss pedagogy and share lesson and unit plans and what they have learned from implementing plans and curricula (success and challenges); they discuss and critique observed practice. • Adults alter practices based on peers' feedback and shared discussion of practice. • Adults review, assess, and offer ideas to enhance pedagogical practices and teaching strategies. • Adults use protocols to analyze pedagogy.
Engagement with outside experts and partnerships with other organizations	• Adults are invited into shared dialogue regarding schoolwide or curricular issues and plans. • Adults seek counsel and feedback on ideas, proposals, and initiatives. • Adults learn from multiple perspectives and mutually beneficial partnerships. • Adults share with and include others in leadership, benefiting from multiple thought-partners.
Action research	• Adults decide collaboratively or independently to investigate a problem/challenge/question related to practice. • Adults investigate issue/question through research (individually or in teams). • Adults meet regularly to discuss data, learn, seek alternative interpretations of data, share insights, and formulate questions for further exploration based on learnings. • Adults alter practices based on learning from research. • Adults review and assess learning and offer ideas and next questions to explore.

Across school type, I've found that one of the most common uses of teams is in team teaching. Most reported, as shown in Table 3.2, that teachers in their schools have also taken the initiative to form study groups, research groups, and book clubs. Teaming teachers also allows for in-school visits to one another's classrooms and, in some cases, to other schools to improve practice. The majority of these school leaders value teaming for sharing leadership, sharing decision making, discussing curricular issues, and examining student work. Nearly all of them expressed high value for schoolwide teams as important supports to adult development. In addition, while most of the high school principals and assistant principals focused on departmental teaming, the elementary and middle school principals and assistant principals generally discussed grade-level and cross-grade-level teaming for teachers.

Dr. Myatt, Fenway Pilot High School

While serving as principal of Fenway High School, a pilot school in Boston, which he also founded, Dr. Larry Myatt expressed a sentiment that was shared by many other school leaders. Like others, he told me that creating spaces for teachers to engage in meaningful reflection on their practice is vital to supporting to teachers' transformational learning. He shared that this happens in the context of teaming. However, two ingredients are essential for teams to be effective contexts for supporting adult learning: "giving teachers the time to talk [and work together in teams]—and this is a very important one—helping them to learn *how* to talk and engage in reflective practice" when working in teams. Many of the other school leaders also expressed the importance of teaching adults how to reflect by modeling and providing some structure for reflecting in teams (e.g., protocols).

When I asked Myatt how he does this, he explained by sharing an example of how, initially, it was easier for his humanities teachers to get together and "build curriculum or discuss pedagogy" than his math teachers, due to content and "personality" characteristics. Having an "example or model," of reflecting on practice while collaborating in a team, in his view, "really helped" the adults in his school to learn how to do this. The example he shared to illustrate his point was the Facing History and Ourselves Curriculum for which the teachers at his school learned to examine and critically "reflect on the set of questions that help to guide and shape their conversation" while engaging in teamwork.

Dr. Jim Cavanaugh, Watertown High School

Dr. Jim Cavanaugh, principal of a medium-size public high school in Watertown, Massachusetts, explained that his leadership in support of adult learning is informed by his prior positive experiences as educator (i.e., teacher, union president, and assistant principal). He shared that he has a very optimistic and trusting view of students and teachers, seeing both groups as interested in doing their best. In discussing the value of teaming as a practice supportive of teachers' (and his own) transformational learning, Cavanaugh discussed an example of his high school's leadership team of 16 members (teachers from various disciplines, curriculum coordinators, specialists, a few administrators, and Cavanaugh). The goal of this team, Cavanaugh explained, was to "build a collaborative learning community for the school," and the primary focus was on evaluating student work to inform lesson design and improve student learning. The team used a protocol of questions to assess student work. One of Cavanaugh's most important reasons for collaborating was that

> we want to have a process, which allows [team members] to achieve to the maximum of their ability and doesn't turn them off. And to do that, it needs more than one person walking into a room, shutting the door and doing what he or she wants. . . . It's [collaboration as a team] that's going to be the most productive in terms of creating an environment in which kids can achieve, feel valuable, and feel supported, feel like they can give their opinions.

Cavanaugh believed that having teams of teachers looking at student work is an effective way to nurture reflective practice, support adult learning, strengthen student learning, and build the school as a "collaborative learning community." He explained why he values teaming and why it is effective:

> [Working with others in a team] . . . exposes so much when you have five or six pairs of eyes looking at a piece of [student] work and asking questions. . . . They ask clarifying questions and then they ask . . . questions which make you think about what you did and how you set the lesson or you set the task as well as what the student has done.

Mr. Beshir Abdell, Assistant Principal, Bayside High School, New York City

In reflecting on his work with school-based teams, whether cross-functional leadership teams composed of teachers and administrators or teams of teachers, Beshir Abdell, an experienced assistant principal of a large high school in Queens, New York, shared his insights about building and sustaining effective teams that support adult learning. His thinking echoed that of other assistant principals. His goal for teaming, he explained, was "to build collegiality and support adult learning." When building a team and as team members work together, he believed it is critical that the team "choose a leader" and that team members openly discuss "issues of equity" in terms of making contributions to the work. In addition, Abdell explained that it is essential to "recognize that adults have different needs"; to attend to these needs and the health of the team, Abdell created spaces for team members to engage in periodic "post-teamwork reflection" by writing privately in response to process-oriented questions (e.g., "Do you feel your input was represented? What were you expecting to come out of our work?") and conversing about their responses. He added that when working in a team, it is essential to express "gratitude" for each member's contributions and make others "feel special."

Ms. Christina Vittiglio, Teacher–Leader, Francis Lewis High School, New York City

Several teacher-leaders in my workshops discussed the value they placed on teams where they could focus on what they referred to as "text-based discussions." For example, Christina Vittiglio, an experienced math teacher at a large urban high school in New York City, explained that while she appreciated all she was learning from her involvement in the school's Data Team, she also valued participating in a text-based discussion team because it supported her own and other adults' learning. Specifically, she remarked that discussing ideas from the text with colleagues "enhances and cements my under-standing." Making a commitment to this team and to the work of the team, she explained, gave her "deadlines" so that she was sure to allocate time for reading and reflecting on the text. Vittiglio emphasized that discussing ideas in relation to questions that link the text to real-life teaching practice and guide discussion was one aspect of the team that supported adult learning.

TEAM STRUCTURES THAT NURTURE ADULT DEVELOPMENT

We know that many conditions need to be considered when building teams that support learning. Some essential features that enable teams to harness energy and capitalize on learning include the following:

- Focusing on question posing instead of question answering, thereby inviting adults into the process of co-inquiring
- Providing resources (e.g., time, data, expertise—if needed) for teams to collaborate effectively
- Providing adults with relevant data to analyze (Boudett, City, & Murnane, 2005)
- Providing teachers with tools for accessing useable data and protocols for analyzing and discussing it (McTighe, 2008; Wiggins & McTighe, 2007)
- Considering membership (composition of the team) and the roles members might assume (York-Barr et al., 2006)

Jay McTighe (2008) discusses the three recommended roles for members of professional learning communities when they meet in learning teams: critical friend, analyst of student work, and continuous learner.

If the above are the essential features of effective teams and the most promising roles for team members, what we need to know is how to build these features into teams, how to structure team meetings in ways that support these roles, and how to support growth of adults as they engage in teaming. In the sections below, I discuss how to start the team off on the right foot by establishing ground rules that help to create a safe and productive space for learning, how to continue that process by framing questions in a way that attends to members' various ways of knowing, and how to conduct constructive assessments of team progress that ensure that the team continues to act as a medium of growth for all of its members. In my work with all types of school leaders, from K–12 through university, I have found that these approaches to teaming support authentic adult learning and development.

A useful tool that can be employed in facilitating these approaches to team progress is the protocol. Protocols are guiding questions used to structure team conversations. It is well documented that protocols can be helpful in structuring team conversations about important issues. Lois Easton (2009) emphasizes that protocols "are a code of behavior for groups to use when exploring ideas" and can be used to help adults "change the culture of school" (p. 1). The structure helps to guide reflection and oftentimes helps us to become more aware of the assumptions we hold about practice and leadership, for example, so that we can purposefully examine and question them rather than be run by them. Numerous examples of protocols are given below.

Establishing Ground Rules

How might we create a team-learning environment that provides a safe and productive learning context for adults with different ways of knowing? Since we know that what constitutes a safe and productive context might differ according to a person's way of knowing, it can be helpful to invite adults to engage in dialogue aimed at sharing their thinking about what constitutes a safe learning space before beginning their work together in a team. Securing time for this kind of opening conversation can increase adults' willingness to take risks in sharing their perspectives about issues under discussion and enhance collaboration.

If team members establish norms at the outset and record them in a document (artifact), they can revisit the ground rules periodically to assess their progress. This is especially important when conflict arises or when individuals feel that the team is not functioning as well as it needs to or is not completely fulfilling its purpose. Revisiting the written document of agreed-upon norms periodically can serve as an important entry point into this discussion.

To build a team in which each member feels that he or she has an equal say, feels respected as a contributor, and supported as a learner, it is important to establish norms for engagement and to agree upon how to attend to confidentiality. These steps are important regardless of the type of team or its purpose. Attending to norms about how to structure meetings, how to approach problems, how to work through conflict (e.g., related to different perspectives, workload), and how to hold team members accountable will help to establish a context in which adults feel comfortable sharing expertise and perspectives.

Safety in team contexts means different things to adults with different ways of knowing. Let's take, for example, how differently we might experience being interrupted. Some adults prefer that team members feel free to interrupt them when they are discussing a proposal. They feel most engaged in team learning when team members are comfortable interrupting, and they experience such interruptions as opportunities for team members, including themselves, to build on each other's ideas. On the other hand, others have shared that interruptions cause them to lose their train of thought, perhaps feel disrespected, and to shut down in the conversation. While these two experiences do not necessarily correlate to a person's way of knowing, understanding these kinds of differences before diving into content-related team discussions can be very helpful.

Let's also consider the importance of establishing a safe environment from a developmental perspective. Recently, while I was working with a team to establish a safe and productive learning space, one team member said that she felt best supported in her learning when she could just "explode" if she needs to. If she were angry about her school's quality review, she might need to vent her anger before she could proceed with teamwork. As I listened, I found myself appreciating her honesty and how important it was for her to say this and for others to hear this. I also thought about how important it was for the socializing knowers on the team to hear this, given how they would tend to experience conflict. Figure 3.2 presents a protocol I developed for inviting team members to engage in a conversation about establishing ground rules and a shared agreement about confidentiality to establish trust.

Other important issues to discuss before beginning work together as a team include the distribution of work, role rotation, and equity.

Figure 3.2   Protocol for Establishing Team Ground Rules

While the amount of time is not included below, it is wise to allocate specific amounts of time for each part of the process—for example, for a team of eight, 15 minutes for initial introductions and 25 to 30 minutes for discussion of safe learning environment and confidentiality. Of course, times will vary depending on the number of team members. A general guideline for how to go about establishing team ground rules follows.

1. Invite members to freewrite (i.e., write what comes to mind without censoring one's thinking) for two to three minutes in response to the following questions: What constitutes a safe, productive, and supportive team learning context for you? What makes a team learning space unsafe for you and your learning?

2. Before each team member has a chance to share—whatever he or she feels comfortable sharing with the group—one team member will want to volunteer to take notes on what is discussed, type the notes, and provide hard copies for all team members. The idea here is not to capture every word verbatim but rather to capture the essence of what is said, with direct quotations when possible.

3. Invite team members to share their thinking with each other. Doing so helps to develop ground rules or norms for engaging in team discussion and for creating a safe learning environment. This is especially important because team members will be sharing their personal experiences of work with teams.

4. At the next team meeting, distribute the notes from the previous meeting so that all team members can add to them, if needed. Periodically revisiting this ground rule document and checking in with team members around these important issues can strengthen collaboration and support learning and development.

5. After the safe and productive team learning environment discussion, if the topic hasn't come up already, the team will want to come to a shared understanding of what kind of confidentiality agreement they'd like. After the team has agreed how to handle confidentiality, the person who is taking notes will want to restate the agreement for the team and add it to the document, along with the team's thinking about what makes a safe and productive team learning environment. Team members may want to discuss how they want to handle confidentiality around issues discussed in the team with others within the school, for example.

During the fall of each year, I have the privilege of conducting a one-and-a-half-day retreat with groups of experienced teachers who serve in an urban school. These teachers are in the third and final year of their teacher-evaluation cycle. In addition to the teachers, their supervisors (i.e., department chairs, division directors, or deans) attend the workshop. At the start of our time together, school leaders (everyone at the retreat) consider the questions I've described above (a modified version of the protocol appears in Figure 3.2). What follows are the ground rules and confidentiality agreement that one group developed to support learning as they worked together as a team. Their sentiments echo themes that emerged in my research with school leaders. I wrote their words on flip chart-size sticky notes, which we kept on the walls of the room where we met. We revisited these ground rules (agreed-upon norms) and confidentiality agreements at the end of the first and the beginning of the second day and assessed how we were doing in relation to them.

- Keeping a "sense of humor."
- "What's said in the room stays in the room."
- "Double C" (i.e., double confidentiality): "It's the speaker's work and decision to pass along any information to others outside of the group here. It is totally up to the speaker. The listener will not share this."
- "It's okay to be inarticulate."
- We need to begin with the assumption that we are working together. "We are a working team."
- "All of us are here because we love the children."
- Shared agreement that we are going to "lean into discomfort."
- We will work to acknowledge "where we are as people."
- "Be crisp—say what is core."
- "Be okay with contradictory statements."
- Let's agree to have a "take-back chip. It's okay to take something that you said back. It's okay to change your mind."
- "It's important to listen actively."
- "Let's agree to allow for time to process as we transition to each new phase of the retreat and also as we transition back to work. [The person who organized this retreat] wants to be able to build more of this kind of thing, what we do in the retreat, into life at school. To integrate it more."
- "Don't make assumptions about what is said."
- "It's important that we bring an open mind."
- "Step up and step back. All voices need to be heard. Importance of making room for all voices around the table."

Framing Questions to Attend to Ways of Knowing

Working in teams enables adults to

- question their own and other people's philosophies of teaching, leadership, and learning;
- implement the school's core values in the curriculum and school context;
- reflect on the meaning of their school's mission; and
- engage in shared decision making.

Whether in a school district, school, university, or other educational setting, when I deliver a workshop or a class, I normally open sessions with a series of questions. I invite participating school leaders to consider them first by writing privately and then by sharing whatever they feel comfortable sharing with a partner or two. After the pairs or triads have had a chance to confer, I invite volunteers to share aspects of their conversation with the larger group. I do this not only to create a space for private reflection and focusing on the session but also so that I can get a sense of what feels important to participants in relationship to the topics we will be discussing. In many cases, we are discussing the pillar practices and how adult developmental theory informs them.

My questions are developmentally oriented. In other words, I structure the questions so that adults with different ways of knowing might lean toward responding to one of them in writing. For example, I usually design one question so that it asks a person to recall some fact, procedure, or learning from either a reading or a past gathering. In my experience, these kinds of questions help instrumental knowers to connect with the material or the context of the session.

I also create a question that invites participants to reflect on how they are feeling about the content to be discussed or the material that was assigned in the presession reading. Sometimes, I ask about how they feel about a best practice that was described in the reading. These questions invite participants to look internally and create an opportunity to share feelings. As such, they often appeal to socializing knowers.

The third question I ask usually creates an opportunity for adults to comment on the design of a practice, initiative, or policy or the philosophical underpinnings of a reading. Sometimes this question invites participants to critique a model or to offer ideas for redesigning an initiative or a theory. In general, self-authoring and, often, self-transforming knowers might feel more comfortable responding to these sorts of questions, which invite the respondent to synthesize and assess tensions among models or theories.

Why do I bring this up? I share this process of arriving at developmentally oriented questions—and a few examples of questions—because they are a way to engage adults in meaningful discussion in team meetings. Over time, these conversations may help to support growth in adults with different ways of knowing—help them take the risk to respond to questions at their growing edge; that is, slightly beyond their comfort level or at the edge of their ways of knowing.

After learning about the pillar practice of teaming and the developmental principles informing it, one group of school leaders created the developmental questions presented in Table 3.3. These are tools that can be employed to guide a team's discussion about instructional practice—and questions that attend to adults' different ways of knowing. (Note that the table does not reference the self-transforming way of knowing because participants had not yet learned about it.)

Assessing Team Performance

In my work with New York City principals who are part of the Cahn Fellows Program at Columbia University, Professor Victoria Marsick and I serve as faculty coaches. We work to support these principals over a 15-month period as they investigate leadership challenges by conducting research in their schools. In each meeting, we group the principals into smaller teams of four to six people. These teams share a common leadership challenge that focuses on supporting adult learning and development within their schools. Using a version of the ground rules document I described above helps with creating a safe and trusting context for sharing, as well as a way to assess performance. Usually, at about the midpoint in the program, we also invite these principals to complete a protocol that helps them to assess the effectiveness of their team to date.

Table 3.3   Sample Questions to Facilitate Dialogue About Instructional Practice in Teams

Way of Knowing	Questions to Guide Dialogue and/or Assess Instructional Practice			
Instrumental	What does high-quality instruction look like?	What are the components of good instruction?	How do you know you have a good lesson plan format?	What are three things good teachers do?
Socializing	What's an example of quality instruction in *your* practice?	Who are people *you* can rely on for good instructional feedback?	What instructional practices have *you* observed from school visits that seem to work?	What or who informs *your* ideas about what good instruction looks like?
Self-Authoring	What high-quality practices would you like to adopt from others and develop in your practice? Why?	How would you incorporate what you've learned into your own instructional practice?	What is one thing you would like to improve about your instruction?	What strategies would you design to implement your new ideas effectively?

We do this for four reasons. First, we want to learn how these leaders experience their team's performance. Second, we want the principals to have a chance to reflect on their team experience. Third, we want the teams to review their results and to consider how they might improve their performance. And last, we hope that the principals might consider using the instrument shown in Figure 3.3 in their schools to help teams assess their performance.

Additional Protocols for Furthering Team Progress

Figure 3.4 on page 99 presents an example of two protocols I developed and employed with school leadership teams—teachers, principals, and assistant principals—from small schools in the Bronx, New York. These leaders were collaborating with the National Academy for Excellence in Teaching (NAfET), directed by Dr. Douglas Wood, at Columbia University's Teachers College. They were working on their professional development goals for the year in light of their Quality Review Reports, and the protocol questions helped to structure their team dialogue.

The first protocol is the set of questions that guided school team members' conversations during the fall meeting. Teams worked in small groups for two hours to discuss these questions, which aimed to help the teams develop greater awareness of how individuals and the team as a whole were feeling and thinking about their professional plans and goals. The second protocol guided team conversations and assessed team progress during the spring of the following year. As you will see, this protocol invited team members to reflect on what they had accomplished and what supports would help with achieving goals and to envision what next steps they would take.

Figure 3.3   The High-Performance Team Instrument

One way to monitor the effectiveness of your team is for members to assess their work in the team periodically.

Directions: Circle the number that best reflects how true each of the below descriptions is for your team.

	Strongly Disagree					*Strongly Agree*
1. We engage in open and honest communication.	1	2	3	4	5	6
2. Everyone has a chance to participate in decision making.	1	2	3	4	5	6
3. We all feel comfortable expressing our thoughts and ideas during team meetings.	1	2	3	4	5	6
4. We listen actively to one another and try not to interrupt.	1	2	3	4	5	6
5. We cooperate to get the work done.	1	2	3	4	5	6
6. We all follow through on commitments made at previous meetings.	1	2	3	4	5	6
7. We clarify everyone's team responsibilities (e.g., leader, timekeeper, etc.).	1	2	3	4	5	6
8. We fully discuss the advantages and pitfalls of all ideas and options.	1	2	3	4	5	6
9. We try to generate all possible ideas and options before coming to any conclusions.	1	2	3	4	5	6
10. Conflicts associated with different points of view are dealt with constructively.	1	2	3	4	5	6
11. We don't come to conclusions unless we have consensus.	1	2	3	4	5	6

(Continued)

Figure 3.3 (Continued)

	Strongly Disagree					Strongly Agree
12. Everyone on the team does his or her fair share of work.	1	2	3	4	5	6
13. We accommodate and respect cultural differences.	1	2	3	4	5	6
14. We capitalize on cross-functional strengths.	1	2	3	4	5	6
15. We recognize the strengths and weaknesses of team members.	1	2	3	4	5	6
16. We seek feedback and give feedback to each other.	1	2	3	4	5	6
17. We celebrate our successes.	1	2	3	4	5	6
18. We regularly reflect on and evaluate our *task* progress.	1	2	3	4	5	6
19. We regularly reflect on and evaluate our *team* processes.	1	2	3	4	5	6
20. We learn from both our failures and our successes.	1	2	3	4	5	6
21. We clarify group tasks before ending a meeting.	1	2	3	4	5	6
22. We set objectives and stay focused.	1	2	3	4	5	6
23. We structure meetings using an agenda, objectives, and timetable.	1	2	3	4	5	6
24. We are aligned around the purpose and mission of our team.	1	2	3	4	5	6
25. There is a high level of trust among team members.	1	2	3	4	5	6

SOURCE: Adapted from Rimanoczy, I., Turner, E., & Pearson, T. (2000). *The learning coach handbook* (pp. 61–62). Aventura, FL: Leadership in International Management (LIM).

Figure 3.4   Sample Protocols for First and Follow-Up Team Meetings

---

Guiding Questions for Work Plan Professional Development Goals at the NAfET Leadership Forum

Team Session 1 (November):

1. How are you feeling about the work plan you and your team developed? What do you feel good about? What, if anything, do you need help fleshing out?

2. What are the two or three most important professional development (PD) goals you have set for the year?

3. How do your PD goals connect with one or more of the NAfET priorities?

4. At this point, how are you planning to attend to achieving your PD goals? What benchmarks has your team set for attaining your goals?

5. What, if anything, do you need help with at this time?

Team Session 2 (March):

1. What progress have you made toward achieving the two or three PD goals you have set for your school?

2. What data are you collecting to track progress? How is that going?

3. In what ways are you analyzing or assessing the data to help with understanding your goals?

4. What is going well?

5. What, if anything, are you struggling with at this time? How can NAfET and other colleagues help you?

Another useful protocol is one I developed in my work with school leaders individually and in classes. I use it to learn how the adults are experiencing the learning environment and to figure out how I might improve conditions to support their learning. I've adapted this protocol so that it can be employed to check in periodically with team members to learn more about their experiences on particular teams. In addition to offering individuals an opportunity to assess their experience of being part of a team, it offers a chance to consider how the team itself might better support adult learning.

The protocol (see Figure 3.5) can be used in two ways. First, it can be offered to individuals to complete privately. The participants would then share their responses with a team leader, who would assess all completed forms, summarize general impressions, and give these as feedback to the team. These learnings could then be a starting place for checking on how the team as a whole would like to address any of the issues raised and what, if anything, they would like to change.

Alternatively, the individual team members could complete the protocol and then discuss what they felt comfortable sharing in dyads or triads. In these smaller groups,

Figure 3.5   Midterm Reflections About Your Experience on Our Team

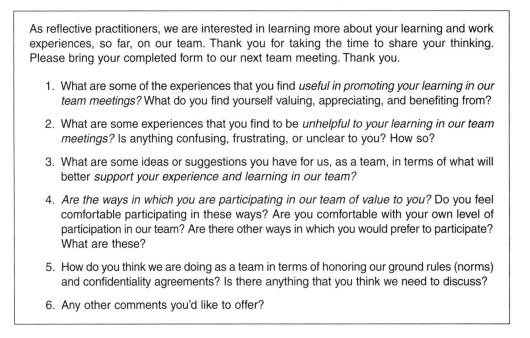

As reflective practitioners, we are interested in learning more about your learning and work experiences, so far, on our team. Thank you for taking the time to share your thinking. Please bring your completed form to our next team meeting. Thank you.

1. What are some of the experiences that you find *useful in promoting your learning in our team meetings?* What do you find yourself valuing, appreciating, and benefiting from?

2. What are some experiences that you find to be *unhelpful to your learning in our team meetings?* Is anything confusing, frustrating, or unclear to you? How so?

3. What are some ideas or suggestions you have for us, as a team, in terms of what will better *support your experience and learning in our team?*

4. *Are the ways in which you are participating in our team of value to you?* Do you feel comfortable participating in these ways? Are you comfortable with your own level of participation in our team? Are there other ways in which you would prefer to participate? What are these?

5. How do you think we are doing as a team in terms of honoring our ground rules (norms) and confidentiality agreements? Is there anything that you think we need to discuss?

6. Any other comments you'd like to offer?

one person could take notes of the themes under discussion (without any names attached). The note takers could share general themes that emerged with the full team, which could discuss them and share decision making about how they would like to move forward as a team. Team members might also discuss how they could work to support adult learning better.

IMPLEMENTING TEAMING: LESSONS FROM THE FIELD

Shirley H. Matthews, principal of a large urban high school in New York City, was a member of the 2006–2007 Cahn Fellows Program at Columbia University's Teachers College. I was her faculty advisor. After learning about the pillar practices and the adult developmental theory informing them, Matthews decided to invite teachers in her school to work in teams throughout the year. She wanted to "differentiate staff development, based on the demonstrated and expressed strengths and needs of the teachers, with a focus on improving students' learning for the demands of the 21st-century globalization."

Matthews's first step was to collaborate with her "Cabinet" (a cross-functional team of assistant principals, teachers, and Matthews) to design a needs assessment to develop a better understanding of how the 77 teachers in her school experienced professional development opportunities. She wanted professional learning opportunities to be relevant to teachers' needs. The Cabinet wanted all teachers to be heard and attended to, according to Principal Matthews. The results of this needs assessment indicated that teachers, in general, felt that

- they were disconnected from the professional development input process.
- their needs were not being met.
- they were not brought into the process of designing professional development.
- group sessions were boring.
- the topics offered in their professional development menu were limited.
- professional development did not connect with data.
- there was no sense of interdisciplinary community.

After learning from the survey, the Cabinet decided on a course of action. As Matthews explained, "We for a long time have known about the importance of differentiated instruction; now we also know that we need to differentiate professional development for teachers in order to attend to their developmental needs."

Teachers and staff at Matthews's high school were invited to join one of several teams. These teams focused on areas that were identified as "need" areas in the survey. Teams consisted of teachers, assistant principals, and other staff. Matthews was a member of several teams as well. The professional development teams' topics included the following:

- Continuing to Increase the Achievement of African-American and Latin Young Men
- Motivational Math
- Curriculum Mapping
- Infusing the Environment Into the Curriculum
- Integrating Technology Into the Curriculum
- Teaching 101
- PASCO Training for Classroom Demos and Lab Exercises

At midyear, Principal Matthews and the Cabinet learned from observations, summary notes from team meetings, and feedback that while nearly all teachers "were doing a great job with" and benefiting tremendously from the new professional learning opportunities, "a handful of teachers" needed a different group and closer monitoring. The school also received feedback from its Quality Review Report. At that point, professional development teams discussed the feedback and adjusted the focus of some of their groups. School members moved into the following groups for the second term:

- Homework That Helps
- African-American and Latino Boys II
- Success for All

- Integrating Technology Into the Curriculum
- Case Studies: A Closer Look
- Individual Education Plans (IEP)
- Curriculum Mapping: English (9–12)
- Curriculum Mapping: U.S. History (11–12)
- Curriculum Mapping: Global Studies (9–10)
- Curriculum Mapping: Science
- Curriculum Mapping: Math
- Curriculum Mapping: Environmental Seminar

At the end of the year, the Cabinet designed a follow-up survey to learn from teacher and staff feedback about their experiences working in these teams. What follows are the main results of this survey. Teachers and staff felt that the "new professional development (PD) approach" of working in teams

- created personalized PD.
- changed teachers' perspective of PD.
- encouraged teachers to take a more active role in PD, including some action research.
- increased learning/partnering with colleagues.
- engaged teachers in collegial inquiry.

Matthews also invited individual teams to complete the "High Performance Team Instrument" (Figure 3.3). She reported that this assessment helped to "expose those teachers who were not serious about professional development, [which allowed] administration to provide individual assistance as needed." She believed that using the practice of teaming that is informed by a developmental perspective helped both individuals and her school community to grow.

CHAPTER SUMMARY

In this chapter, I presented a theoretical perspective on teaming as an effective approach to professional development in schools and school systems to situate the practice as a developmental initiative within the field. Next, I discussed how adults with different ways of knowing will experience teaming and the kinds of supports and challenges they need to support their development. Third, I shared themes that have emerged from my research with school leaders about why they employ teaming and why they find it an effective way to support adult learning and development. I offered specific examples of how these leaders implement teaming. I also offered suggestions for different ways to structure teams to support adult development. Toward the end of this chapter, I included a case example from a school principal who described her experience of teaming in a large, urban high school.

Throughout this chapter, I have illuminated why school leaders use teaming to support adult development. To summarize, they think teaming does the following:

- Supports adult learning and perspective broadening
- Builds collegial relationships
- Improves instruction and schoolwide decision making
- Decreases isolation
- Helps adults adjust to change
- Helps adults to manage adaptive challenges
- Encourages pedagogical and curricular innovation
- Builds professional learning communities
- Empowers adults
- Develops and enhances skills for reflection and dialogue
- Builds leadership capacity on the individual, school, and system levels

In addition, teaming supports adult learning and development by affording teachers, assistant principals, principals, superintendents, and other school leaders with opportunities to exchange perspectives, thereby challenging themselves and each other to question assumptions and beliefs. The sharing of perspectives enables adults to develop practical ideas for curriculum and student assessment and assists them in uncovering the underlying beliefs that shape their actions. Developmentally speaking, this kind of perspective broadening allows adults to move to more complex ways of knowing.

In addition to perspective building, teaming creates a safe environment for adults to take risks. In teams, adults can brainstorm about new ways to approach old issues. Similarly, adults can benefit from thinking together about problems and proposals as they share decision making. In this way, teaming can be a holding environment.

FREQUENTLY ASKED QUESTIONS

1. *Should teams be composed of people with the same way of knowing?*

No. Just as in schools, classrooms, and any other community, developmental diversity on a team is needed and important.

2. *How can I create a team structure so that all adults can learn—even those with different ways of knowing?*

I hope that the protocols and ideas shared in this chapter are useful. It's important to imbue team meetings with enough freedom for creativity and enough structure for safety; doing so will offer both developmental supports and challenges to adults with different ways of knowing. It is helpful to create opportunities for adults to engage in dialogue in pairs, triads, and smaller teams. Inviting team members to engage in some writing, freewriting for example, can serve as a platform for deeper and more focused dialogue. Periodically revisiting ground rules and confidentiality agreements can build healthier teams that are safe, fertile places for adult growth.

APPLICATION EXERCISE

The following application exercise is offered to assist you in applying the ideas discussed in this chapter to your own context.

1. Knowing what you know about adults' ways of knowing and teaming as a developmental practice, what is one way you might use teaming or enhance the teams that exist in your school to support learning and growth in your work context?

2. What logistical or substantive concerns, if any, do you have at this time?

3. How might you secure needed resources to implement your idea from question 1? What kinds of supports would help?

4. Table 3.4 is a graphic that might help you frame your ideas for implementation in your unique context.

Table 3.4   Teaming: Supports and Challenges

Way of Knowing	Supports	Challenges
Instrumental		
Socializing		
Self-Authoring		
Self-Transforming		

REFLECTIVE QUESTIONS

Few needs are as pressing and as often go unmet in our world as the need for a place to converse. We all require somewhere, some circle of companions, where and with whom we can enter into the demanding task of trying to say what we experience and to understand what others say in response.

—Michael Himes (1995)

The following questions are offered to assist you in applying the strategies outlined in this chapter to your unique work context. They can be used for internal reflection first and then to open up a team-, school-, or systemwide dialogue.

1. What is one thing you've learned from this chapter that feels important to you? In stepping forward, how will you work to implement your learning?

2. What kinds of teams are in place in your work context? How do you think they work to support adult learning? What's working well, from your perspective? What would you like to see improved? Why?

3. What have you experienced as the benefits of working in teams? What have you noticed about other adults' engagement in teams? How, if at all, do the ideas presented in this chapter help you? In what ways, if any, might you apply them to your work context?

4. What kinds of successes have you noticed when adults in your school work in teams? What sorts of obstacles or constraints, if any, do you see as barriers to working in teams?

5. How do you think adults in your school would describe their experience of learning in teams? How do you experience their learning experience?

6. How, if at all, might any of the ideas in this chapter help you to enhance one of the teams of which you are a member?

7. Knowing what you know about adults who make meaning in developmentally different ways, how might you incorporate different structures discussed in this chapter to support adults with diverse ways of knowing?

8. What are two practical ideas for teaming that you have learned about in this chapter that you would like to implement or encourage in your school? What small steps will you take to implement these?

4

Providing Leadership Roles

Learning and Growing From Leading Together

We are each of us angels with only one wing and we can only fly by embracing each other.

—Luciano De Crescenzo, Italian writer and filmmaker (attributed)

In this chapter, I discuss how school leaders employ the practice of inviting adults to assume leadership roles to support transformational learning, to build organizational and human capacity, and to promote change. My central purpose is to illuminate how providing leadership roles can be a developmental practice that supports the growth of adults with diverse of ways of knowing. Viewing leadership roles from a developmental perspective helps us understand how to shape them, making sure to include careful and caring attention to the developmental supports and challenges that can be used to support authentic growth. Mindfulness of developmental diversity can help in creating roles that serve as contexts for developing adults' capacities to manage the complexities inherent in our professional and personal responsibilities.

Before presenting an overview of this chapter, it might be helpful to make a few important distinctions. First, I use the term *providing leadership roles* rather than the commonly used *distributed leadership* because providing adults with leadership roles is not simply allocating leadership tasks or responsibilities. Instead of only being assigned duties, the person is provided with supports and challenges by another professional (e.g., principal or colleague) so that he or she can grow from the leadership role experience. Second, sometimes leadership roles are offered because the person assuming the role requires little guidance to enact it. However, at other times, adults assume these roles because they have the potential to grow in them. While both reasons are valid, in this chapter, I focus on the ways in which people can grow from assuming leadership roles that provide developmental supports and challenges. Third, the practice of providing other adults with leadership roles can be intimately connected to the practice of teaming (Chapter 3) because adults assume leadership roles while working with teammates. Fourth, in some school districts, organizational charts illuminate roles, and often functions are connected to specific roles. If you find it helpful to think about functions instead of roles, please do.

In my research, I learned that superintendents, principals, and teachers offer different types of leadership roles to other adults. Nearly all of them emphasized that leadership roles support individual growth and learning, build the capacity of the system, promote change across the school, and strengthen learning communities. In addition, some leaders emphasized that one of the more important aspects of providing others with leadership roles is the influence doing so has on reducing the chattering that occurs underground. Inviting adults to assume leadership roles, they concurred, can support adults with different needs, preferences, and developmental orientations. It can create a holding environment (Kegan, 1982, 1994) that supports teachers, assistant principals, principals, and superintendents in their efforts to learn and grow.

In this chapter, I highlight theoretical perspectives on providing leadership roles: (a) why these roles are essential in today's complex educational world, (b) the principal's role in inviting other adults to assume leadership, (c) how providing these roles cultivates schools as learning centers, and (d) how inviting teachers to assume these roles in schools can create a pathway to individual and organizational growth. Next, I discuss how adults with different developmental orientations experience leadership roles and the types of supports and challenges they need in order to grow. I then present a few examples of how school leaders in my research used leadership roles to support their own and other adults' learning. Through examples, I describe how leaders employ the practice of providing leadership roles and how it supports learning, builds capacity and positive school climates, decreases isolation, nurtures relationships, and supports adult development.

This chapter also includes two cases to be used as opportunities for private reflection and case discussion to help you apply this pillar practice and these developmental ideas to your own context. The first case describes a principal who invited a teacher to assume a leadership role as an administrator. The second case illuminates a first-year teacher's experience of assuming a leadership role and the importance of providing appropriate supports and challenges to nurture growth. Reflective questions for discussing the cases, your own leadership, and your own contexts are included.

ABOUT PROVIDING LEADERSHIP ROLES

How can we respond to the complex demands of our time? How do we assist adults in developing the capacity to lead through the complexities of education, especially the adaptive challenges? Leaders cannot lead alone. The development of leaders and learners in school systems is critical in today's educational world. In calling for a new structure of leadership, Richard Elmore (2000, 2004) maintains that it is the work of school leaders to ensure that teachers continue to develop. His first two principles for his new structure of leadership are as follows: "the purpose of leadership is the improvement of instructional practice and performance, regardless of role," and "instructional improvement requires continuous learning" (2000, p. 20).

Like Elmore, other scholars and practitioners assert that leadership must be shared to build and sustain schools and districts as learning centers. In fact, the Paris-based Organization for Economic Cooperation and Development recently released the results of its study of 22 nations (excluding the United States), in which it found that the responsibilities of educational leaders have increased significantly in the last few decades (Olson, 2008). The researchers identified the global need to improve school leadership, adding that learning is enhanced "when teachers and others take on formal and informal leadership responsibilities" (Olson, p. 8).

Reflecting on the report, Michael Fullan (2008) comments on what its results mean for principals. He urges principals to exercise leadership that will foster "developing a collaborative culture among teachers that focuses on 'ongoing, relentless improvement of instruction'" (Olson, 2008, p. 8). Importantly, Fullan advocates developing school systems as professional learning communities where leadership is shared because these contexts are more effective than those where individuals work in isolation. At the same time, he and others have found that in some cases, "professional learning communities are being implemented superficially" (Fullan, p. 28), ideas and assumptions informing the models are misunderstood, and professional learning communities are implemented incorrectly (Cochran-Smith & Lytle, 2006; DuFour, 2007). As Fullan points out, sometimes concepts and terms become buzzwords, and the genuine intent of the concept is not applied. Building learning communities includes paying attention to how activities and progress will be assessed and monitored as well as developing accountability systems. He urges school leaders to build cultures of shared leadership by focusing on integrating "individual and organizational development" (Fullan, p. 28).

To build such school cultures, leaders must focus on supporting educators as they assume new leadership roles (Farrington, 2007; Lambert, 2002). Some leaders across the system may need to move away from a vision of leadership based on command and control, which emphasizes individual responsibility. Instead, they may need to develop and implement a shared leadership ethos (Farrington; Lambert). As Linda Lambert points out, "Instructional leadership must be a shared, community undertaking. Leadership is the professional work of everyone in the school" (p. 37). She further emphasizes that leaders are responsible for the learning of colleagues because learning and leading are firmly linked.

This type of school community where leadership is shared and adults are collectively responsible for student learning will build individual and organizational capacity, Lambert says. She stresses that shared instructional leadership occurs when adults assume different types of leadership roles and develop a shared vision, engage in inquiry to guide decisions and practice, and reflect (e.g., through journaling, coaching, dialogue, and networking) on what works and what does not.

In a qualitative study, Lorraine Slater (2008) examines the different forms of communication used by principals, parents, and teachers to encourage shared leadership and build human and organizational capacity. She finds that developing collaborative relationships among adults improves teachers' professionalism. It also builds collective leadership capacity in schools and enhances the school community's ability to respond to today's complex educational changes and leadership challenges. Furthermore, authentic collaboration improves student learning and contributes to teacher growth, morale, and retention. For this to occur, though, a culture of trust and respect is needed so as to decrease organizational fear and encourage the kind of risk taking essential for adults to be leaders.

In a similar vein, according to Slater (2008), building capacity leads to the following five outcomes:

1. School improvement, when leaders nurture leadership capacity in other adults

2. Teacher growth

3. Increased retention

4. Higher morale, when adults pursue their personal passions and concerns

5. Redistribution of responsibility by empowering others to assume leadership

In addition, building capacity and sharing leadership lead to redefinition of roles and relationships (Blase & Blase, 2000; Slater, 2008). So what is the principal's role in creating pathways for sharing leadership and conditions for building capacity?

Pathways for Sharing Leadership

Gordon Donaldson (2007) writes that "great schools grow when educators understand that the power of their leadership lies in the strength of their relationships" (p. 29). "Leadership," according to Donaldson, "is a particular type of relationship—one that mobilizes other people to improve practice" (p. 27). Working together, it is possible to improve the quality of our relationships, fulfill a school's mission, and carefully examine and improve instruction (Donaldson, 2006, 2008).

In this section, I discuss themes in the literature about the principal's role in building capacity and strengthening interpersonal relationships by inviting others to assume leadership roles. While my focus here is on the principal, I believe that these ideas hold true for other adults—superintendents, assistant principals, and teachers—who are in a position to build capacity and support adults as they grow through and in their leadership roles.

We know that principals' modeling and behaviors influence the school culture and that leading a school is complex work (Leithwood & Riehl, 2003; Simons & Friedman, 2008). Terry Dozier (2007), like Donaldson (2007) and others, stresses the important role the principal plays in promoting and supporting teachers as they take on new leadership roles because they need specific knowledge, skills, and dispositions to be successful change agents. In addition, Bradley Portin (2004) reminds us that whether and how a principal shares the different functions of leadership—instructional, cultural, managerial, human resources, strategic, external development, and micropolitical (Sergiovanni, 2001)—is related to a school's unique context.

Slater (2008) maintains that principals need to know the adults in their schools well to share leadership toward building capacity. The purpose is to build on their strengths when providing leadership roles while simultaneously creating the opportunity for growth. Donaldson (2007) emphasizes that principals need to secure resources to support teachers who assume leadership roles. One such resource is the time to support shared practice, planning, and professional learning. In addition, he notes the importance of the principal's explicit acknowledgment of teacher-leaders as essential and powerful partners in leadership.

Similarly, in discussing how to overcome the obstacles to sharing leadership and building capacity, Susan Moore Johnson and Morgaen Donaldson (2007) assert that principals should have well-defined qualifications, responsibilities, and a clear selection process for different leadership roles. Principals would be wise, they explain, to publish the qualifications and responsibilities of each leadership role and encourage all staff members to apply. Principals also need to help teachers who assume leadership roles by responding to other teachers' resistance. Johnson and Donaldson encourage principals to provide professional development to help teacher-leaders to respond respectfully to resistance while improving practice.

Echoing Johnson and Donaldson (2007), Charlotte Danielson (2007) offers additional ways for principals to support teachers as they assume leadership roles. Principals, Danielson explains, need to create a safe environment for teachers to engage in risk taking, delegate important tasks to teachers (e.g., leading meetings, analyzing data), and provide opportunities for teachers to learn leadership skills (e.g., curriculum planning, assessments, and facilitation). These skills can be acquired through participation in workshops, courses, readings, and consultation, she contends.

Current Thinking About Teacher Leadership

[Teachers] are leaders because their own capacity to teach and improve is infectious and helps others learn more effective ways of working with their own students.

—Donaldson, 2007, p. 29

As Donaldson reminds us in this passage, teachers are well positioned to take on leadership in schools and contribute special "assets" (p. 28) to strengthening school leadership. Some of the special characteristics teachers bring to their leadership roles include their

1. abilities to *build relationships* with other teachers through collaboration, which can enhance teacher culture;

2. capacity to *maintain a sense of purpose* by mobilizing others to action and improving the learning of all students; and

3. ability to *improve instructional practice* by encouraging the sharing of ideas.

"Whereas principals *can* shape teachers' beliefs, attitudes, and behaviors, other teachers *do* shape them" (p. 29), Donaldson eloquently notes.

In light of complex challenges, principals need help to lead in today's multifaceted educational world (Donaldson, 2007; Dozier, 2007; Phelps, 2008). Teacher-leaders are excellent candidates for additional leadership roles for many reasons, including their desire for additional leadership responsibilities while wanting to stay close to their students (Donaldson). Dozier reminds us that teachers know firsthand what is needed to improve student learning and that they are crucial for the success of any education reform effort. Similarly, Patricia Phelps (2008) emphasizes that collegiality increases when teachers assume additional leadership roles and this nurtures "open communication, support among colleagues, celebration of successes, and talk about teaching" (p. 122).

Many scholars and practitioners have illuminated the different types of leadership roles teachers are assuming in schools. For example, Danielson (2007) points out that sometimes teachers prefer formal roles (e.g., department chair, master teacher, or instructional coach), while others may opt for informal roles, such as spontaneously initiating inquiry into a dilemma or starting a new program. Both types of roles are invaluable.

Teachers can assume leadership roles in different contexts as well. For instance, Danielson (2007) notes that they can lead *within the department or team* by coordinating groups for teachers to explore student underperformance. They can also lead *across a school,* such as by scheduling and coordinating schoolwide activities or reconceptualizing practices such as report cards. And teachers can lead *beyond a school,* such as by leading districtwide committees on teacher evaluation or curriculum, representing teachers' views on the school board, and serving on a state's educational board. Further, Dozier (2007) comments that teachers can also lead as mentors to new teachers, as leaders in school improvement efforts and curriculum development, and as providers of professional development for colleagues.

Cindy Harrison and Joellen Killion (2007) offer a helpful framework of different leadership roles that teachers assume in their schools. (The terms in italics are theirs.) I summarize these ten roles based on their descriptions.

1. *Resource provider:* Shares learning and teaching materials with colleagues.

2. *Instructional specialist:* Stays up-to-date with research-based practices and helps colleagues differentiate instruction and plan lessons.

3. *Curriculum specialist:* Helps develop common assessments and pacing charts based on agreed-upon learning expectations.

4. *Data coach:* Leads data analysis discussions with colleagues to develop action plans that are based on student work.

5. *Classroom supporter:* Works in colleagues' classrooms to improve instructional practices (e.g., by doing demo lessons or observing and giving feedback).

6. *Learning facilitator:* Leads workshops and checks on the implementation after workshops (e.g., What's working, and what can be modified?).

7. *Mentor:* Serves as guide, role model, and coach, especially for beginning teachers as they enter the field for the first time.

8. *Instructional leader:* Participates in committees that provide opportunities for change and improvement (e.g., school improvement committee, grade-level or department chair, or district representative).

9. *Catalyst for change:* Encourages needed change when others are not pushing for change.

10. *Ongoing learner:* Continues to improve, learn, and apply learning to help others reach their full potential.

In addition, as I discussed in Chapter 3 on teaming, teachers assume leadership roles as team leaders.

Johnson and Donaldson (2007) caution us, though, about three aspects of school culture that have negative effects, potentially leading to isolation, limiting the exchange of ideas when teachers assume leadership roles, and suppressing the recognition of good young teacher-leaders. They refer to these as "the traditional norms of teaching" and name them in the following manner: *autonomy* (not open to being observed), *egalitarianism* (questioning of others peers' "power"), and *seniority* (resentment toward younger leaders' roles in the school). Further, they emphasize that these can adversely influence the work of teachers in leadership roles. As I noted earlier in this section, however, Johnson and Donaldson also offer important insights as to how principals can support teachers in leadership roles.

It is important to take workload and balance into account when considering additional leadership roles for teachers. For example, what might be taken away from a teacher's responsibilities if he or she is assuming a leadership role that might require a great deal of time? Attending to this issue can help avoid burnout (Lewis, 2008).

Despite these challenges, providing other adults with leadership roles can provide a context for transformational learning and, in turn, build individual as well as organizational capacity. As discussed above, scholars and practitioners highlight the need for expanded leadership roles, their many benefits, and some of the inherent challenges in inviting staff—especially younger teachers—to assume these roles. My research with school leaders who serve in different positions across school systems points to the importance of considering a school's context and an individual's strengths and areas for growth when issuing invitations to assume leadership roles.

Danielson (2007) and others (e.g., Phelps, 2008) help us to understand some of the important characteristics or qualities of adults who take on leadership roles. For example, Danielson emphasizes the following characteristics: expertise in their field, confidence, persuasiveness, open-mindedness, respect for others' views, the ability to listen, optimism, enthusiasm, decisiveness, perseverance, and flexibility. But how will adults with different ways of knowing demonstrate these qualities (decisiveness, for example) and experience leadership roles? What kinds of supports and challenges might enable them to enact and grow from assuming these roles?

I next address these questions and discuss how providing leadership roles can serve as holding environments that support adult development.

DEVELOPMENTAL BENEFITS OF PROVIDING LEADERSHIP ROLES

How might a developmental perspective help us to support adults in leadership roles? How might these roles serve as robust opportunities not just for managing continuous work demands but also for attending to development?

Before responding to these questions, I want to share what one principal conveyed after learning about the ideas and practices presented in this book as part of her 15-month fellowship program. On the last day of our time together, Mary, who had been a principal for more than 20 years, told me,

> I've had a powerful realization that I want to share with you. I now, after having learned about how adults develop and how to support their growth, realize that *all* of my teachers are stars! They are just stars in their *own way* and need different kinds of supports and challenges in order to shine brightly.

As mentioned, providing adults with leadership roles helps to build capacity in schools and districts. In addition, though, leadership roles serve a number of developmental purposes, such as creating a safe context or a healthy holding environment for growth. How does this happen?

When serving in a leadership role, we have the opportunity to develop a deeper awareness of our own beliefs, values, and assumptions about leadership; share our thinking with others; and learn about other's perspectives. Engaging in dialogue offers an opportunity for other people to challenge our thinking in ways that support the reshaping of assumptions. And as noted, broadening our perspectives is essential to development.

Heightening awareness of our assumptions enables us to examine their influence on performance. Through systematic reflection with colleagues, we become better able to view our thinking multiple times through the lenses of others, which can lead to opportunities for transformational learning. Feeling safe in this context can encourage risk taking and self-authorship, especially in an independent task or project.

Relating Leadership Roles to Ways of Knowing

As we know, practices that are aimed at supporting growth and learning have inherent developmental demands. Put simply, how we experience leadership roles and the supports, challenges, and risks depends on our ways of knowing. What kinds of supports and challenges might help adults with different ways of knowing to grow in leadership roles?

Table 4.1 highlights how adults with different ways of knowing tend to make sense of their experiences of exercising leadership and what would constitute appropriate supports and challenges to help them grow from and fulfill their roles. As Table 4.1 shows, adults with different ways of knowing have different capacities for self-reflection and perspective taking, which will influence their experiences of a leadership role and how they exercise leadership.

The Instrumental Knower as Leader

For instance, instrumental knowers focus on enacting their leadership role in the "right" way and lead and contribute by being very task oriented. They also expect others to follow rules and directions for completing tasks. They will feel best supported if authorities share concrete ideas for how to execute the role and offer feedback as to whether or not they are exercising leadership in the right way. Opportunities in which these knowers are forced—in the developmental sense—to consider other people's perspectives and alternative models for achieving goals will challenge their growth in a positive way.

The Socializing Knower as Leader

Socializing knowers *need* to feel safe asking questions of those in authority or support positions when they assume leadership roles. While they focus on developing more abstract goals, they still look to a valued other to learn the *best* way to exercise leadership and to be acknowledged in their way of exercising leadership. They tend to avoid voicing ideas that might conflict with a supervisor's or valued colleague's thinking, because such conflict tends to be experienced as putting the very self at risk. These educators will need more explicit affirmation from the person who is supporting them in their role to believe that things are going well.

A helpful support and developmental challenge would be to encourage the person to look to herself or himself for the best action to take (authorship). Another person may serve as a gentle guide, explicitly acknowledging the challenges and/or difficulties in making such a shift and recognizing the person's perspectives when they are voiced. For example, if a socializing knower is encouraged by a support person to voice out loud to a group a view that she or he feels might not be well received, the support person could help

(Text continued on page 121)

Table 4.1 Potential Ways Adults Experience Leadership Roles Based on Their Ways of Knowing

Way of Knowing	Orientation to Lead Role	Supports for Growth	Challenges (Growing Edge)
Instrumental Knowers	• These knowers tend to think about and enact leadership in terms of what they need to accomplish to get the job done the "right way". • Will engage in leadership roles and contribute by being very task oriented. • Will focus on enacting the role in the "right way" so as to be rewarded concretely for a job well done. • Will want others to follow the rules and their directions for completing tasks.	• Ensure that authorities or those in a support position to the person with the lead role set clear expectations about the role. • Ensure that authorities or experts provide guidance in terms of due dates, rules, deliverables, and process (step-by-step guidelines). • Ensure that authorities or person who assigned the role share concrete feedback as to how this knower is doing and whether he or she is performing in the *right or wrong* manner. • Ensure that authorities provide information and skills to help knower execute the lead role correctly. • Provide acknowledgment and affirmation when this learner is doing things the right way.	• Challenge this knower to move beyond a self-protective stance by building confidence and trust in self-worth. • Encourage knower to offer affirmation and encouragement to others. • Provide opportunities where this adult is forced to consider other people's perspectives. • Provide opportunities to write in response to questions that require abstract thinking about leadership challenges and then to discuss responses with authority (or person assigned to support the person in the lead role), who scaffolds learner through the process. • Encourage this knower to move beyond what he or she sees as the "correct" way to proceed or "right" way to exercise leadership and toward consideration of other viewpoints, perspectives, and or paths. • Challenge learner to recognize and develop a sense of flexibility so as to follow alternative paths in exercising leadership. • Support growth to understand organizational goals and steps toward them in more abstract terms and to understand that a variety of pathways exist for achieving them. • Support the development of greater sensitivity to other people's perspectives and values. • Provide opportunities to practice dealing with uncertainty and with less concrete goals. • Challenge learner to appreciate process as well as end product.

Way of Knowing	Orientation to Lead Role	Supports for Growth	Challenges (Growing Edge)
Socializing Knowers	• These knowers need to feel safe and comfortable asking questions and requesting help and guidance of authorities and valued others when they are unsure about what to do. • Approval of others is of extreme importance. • Conflict and disagreement with valued others may be experienced as a threat to the self. As long as all share a similar outlook, which in these knowers' view protects relationships, difference of opinion is acceptable and nonthreatening. These adults rely on absence of conflict to feel safe when enacting a leadership role. • These knowers want authorities and valued others to be available as sources of knowledge and for informed opinions about proposals under consideration, leadership decisions, and best ways to enact a leadership role. • Need authority to confirm and accept leadership actions, self, and own beliefs. • Emphasize loyalty and all group members coming to a shared understanding or solution.	• Ensure that authority and valued others confirm, validate, acknowledge, and accept this knower's self and own beliefs and, in so doing, create a context in which this adult feels accepted and safe asking questions and requesting help when unsure about what to do. • Provide acceptance from authorities and those being led (colleagues) to help these adults feel safe voicing their own perspectives. • Provide opportunities to share own perspectives with authorities before sharing them with those being led. • Provide guidance from authorities and/or experts about the best way to exercise leadership.	• Gently encourage this knower to consult with and look to self and own views when leading and making decisions. • Over time, provide opportunities to construct own values and standards rather than coconstruct them with valued authorities. • Challenge this knower to tolerate and accept conflict, such as conflicting points of view on an issue or solutions under debate, without feeling that it threatens interpersonal relationships. • Support this learner in growing to see conflict as part of interpersonal relationships rather than something to avoid. • Challenge this knower to create autonomously own procedures and standards for evaluating own leadership. These standards and procedures need to be independent from those of authorities and experts.

(Continued)

Table 4.1 (Continued)

Way of Knowing	Orientation to Lead Role	Supports for Growth	Challenges (Growing Edge)
Self-Authoring Knowers	• Understand that varying perspectives inform decision making and the self. • Experience a lead role as a context in which to learn from other people's perspectives. These adults will consider how other people's ideas can help them in their own self-understanding and improvement, as well as in exercising leadership. • Evaluate (internally) other people's suggestions, ideas, and perspectives, and, if they are deemed desirable, integrate these new ideas with their own. • Conflict is experienced as a natural part of dialogue that can inform decision-making or other leadership processes. • Use an internal focus on own value-generating system when making decisions. • Have capacity to listen and attend to new ideas, diverse points of view, and multiple perspectives on a situation and to challenge new perspectives without feeling self to be at risk. • Focus on solutions that include a diversity of points of view and that will move the team's interests and goals forward.	• Provide opportunities to learn about diverse points of view. • Provide opportunities to identify own leadership goals and to share them and learn from other's ideas. For these adults, it is important to discuss all possible ways to accomplish goals before making a decision about how to proceed. • Allocate time to analyze and critique proposals and/or ideas for achieving goals or tasks. • Ensure decision making through dialogue about how to move forward given all complexities, using interests, talents, and resources of this adult and those being led. • Provide opportunities to design initiatives when exercising leadership. • Allow time for exploration of and dialogue about self-determined goals in relation to leadership. • Create contexts for analyzing and critiquing proposals under consideration.	• Challenge this knower to recognize and develop deeper awareness of the relative and created nature of own leadership goals and ideas and be willing to pursue goals or pathways that previously felt entirely opposed to own goals, ideas, and perspective on leadership and self-identity. • Encourage learner to release self from total investment in and identification with own standards and values—or set them aside—and embrace/accept values of others that may be in opposition to own. • Support this knower in acknowledging/accepting different approaches to the process of exploring a problem or solving it that may not be aligned with own way or approach. • Support this adult in growing to experience *self* as being process driven.

118

Way of Knowing	Orientation to Lead Role	Supports for Growth	Challenges (Growing Edge)
Early Self-Transforming Knowers (4/5)	• Appreciate the value of leadership roles that enable them to bring people together in community. • These adults bring a spirit of collaboration, collegiality, and mutual respect to exercising leadership and enacting leadership roles. • As leaders, early self-transformers have the capacity to bring a greater depth of emotional intelligence to formal authority and leadership roles. • Their curiosity and willingness to challenge convention and socially accepted patterns of behavior or style can yield considerable creativity, though at times, they require other people's help in bringing that creativity into reality at the operational level.	• Ensure that the team, group, and/or organization has a culture of collegiality—with power equally shared among colleagues—and lots of room for creativity. • Provide room for using imagination—and embrace it—to develop new and original ideas.	• Challenge this knower to take up authority when appropriate, even if doing so feels difficult. • Support learner in dealing with complex responsibilities that require quick decisions. • Support this knower in delegating responsibility.

(Continued)

Table 4.1 (Continued)

Way of Knowing	Orientation to Lead Role	Supports for Growth	Challenges (Growing Edge)
Later Self-Transforming Knowers (5)	• These leaders bring a noticeable capacity to think and lead strategically; that is, they comprehend the way that systems work and interact, appreciate the political workings of organizations, and know how to manage these politics. • They have the capacity to project long-term planning that extends several years in duration. • They are agile and adaptable—moving quickly with skill and control—while in the midst of crises and conflict. • While able to work collaboratively, they also have a gift for decision making and delegation. • They experience a leadership role as an opportunity to support and challenge own growth. • They experience a leadership role as an opportunity to serve in supporting the leadership and development of others—and embrace this responsibility. • They appreciate shared and multiple dimensions of power.	• Acknowledge this knower's authority, autonomy, and sense of purpose. • Provide the room (spaciousness) and the resources to enact own visions. • Ensure this knower works with capable colleagues. • Provide appropriate rewards in recognition of skills.	• Support this knower in learning the limits of own capacity for complexity, of responsibility, and of own ambition and capacity for achievement. • Help this knower learn to restrain self from taking over when things are not moving to own satisfaction. • Challenge learner to commit to seeing things through when there is a lack of alignment with strategic purposes. • Challenge this adult to develop a tolerance of others' weaknesses (e.g., strength, determination).

this person think through what's at stake in sharing his or her view. In addition, it is important to note that an educator who has not voiced a readiness for leadership may not perceive another person's support as helpful. In other words, if an educator reluctantly takes on a lead role, another person's intended support might feel like something beyond that adult learner's reach.

The Self-Authoring Knower as Leader

Self-authoring knowers will likely experience a leadership role as a context for learning from other people's perspectives. These leaders consider how other people's ideas can help their own self-understanding, as well as how they exercise leadership. Recall that they have the capacity to generate their own standards, which guide their decision making and leadership. From their perspective, there is no one right pathway toward a goal, and every path has a set of pros and cons. Conflict is experienced as a natural part of dialogue that can inform decision making and other leadership processes. In fact, self-authoring knowers have the capacity to listen to new ideas and diverse points of view and to challenge new perspectives without feeling their selves at risk.

Supporting these people in leadership roles would involve providing them with the freedom to carry the project to completion, offering feedback as they evaluate their work, and discussing their work and goals. These adults would be challenged to grow when others ask that they set aside their own beliefs about how something should be accomplished and entertain opposing perspectives, thus gently pushing or stretching the edges of their thinking to expose new ways of knowing and acting.

The Self-Transforming Knower as Leader

In contrast to self-authoring knowers, self-transforming knowers have grown to understand that all goals are relative. They feel best supported when a supervisor joins with them in exploring the inner tensions, politics, and synergy of diverse goals and perspectives.

As mentioned in prior chapters, one of the distinct challenges in describing how self-transforming knowers make meaning is that there is greater differentiation among early, middle, and later experiences of this way of knowing than for the other ways of knowing. Further, it is quite likely that adults in the later stages of the self-transforming way of knowing may already be in positions of authority, usually with considerable influence on the organization in question. Here, I will discuss adults who make meaning with an early self-transforming way of knowing, though Table 4.1 describes both early and late phases.

Early self-transforming knowers appreciate the value of leadership roles that enable them to bring people together. When leading, these adults often create forums where they invite other adults to join them in challenging convention and socially accepted patterns of behavior in an organization or group, which can yield considerable creativity. At times, however, they need other people's help in bringing that creativity into practice.

For these adults, support in a leadership role would consist of leading

- a team, group, and/or organization with a culture of collegiality, where power is equally shared; and
- in a context with room for creativity and where the value of imagination is embraced to develop original ideas.

To support these adults' growth, they should be encouraged to assume their own authority because they often have difficulty taking up their authority even when it is appropriate. Since they have difficulty with complex responsibilities that involve *quick* decisions, another developmental challenge would help them manage this. They may also be challenged by the need to delegate responsibility and will need support to do so. Dialogue with others challenges their thinking in a way that can help them test and reshape their assumptions.

The Leadership Role as Holding Environment

Leadership roles can serve as a holding environment for an adult who makes meaning in the transitional space where more than one way of knowing operates. However, as noted above, it is also important to emphasize that people who are not yet ready for such a developmental move might experience the role as a disturbance to their way of making meaning.

That said, a leadership role can provide a growth-enhancing opportunity for adults who are ready and often yearning to assume more leadership. These roles enable us to experience the complexities of exercising leadership and to become more aware of our own and other people's assumptions, values, and perspectives. Table 4.1 illuminates the kinds of supports and challenges that we can offer each other in exercising leadership to nurture growth.

Why School Leaders Provide Leadership Roles

[Leadership is] role-taking as opposed to role-playing. . . . People never understand what it's like to be the leader unless they have an opportunity to be a leader.

—Dr. Sarah Levine, Belmont Day School, Belmont, Massachusetts

In this section, I discuss themes that emerged from my principal research study (2004) and in my research with principals, assistant principals, teachers, and superintendents since then. In many of their schools, teachers, staff, parents, and administrators were invited, at different times, to embrace leadership roles. Leading others can help uncover assumptions guiding actions and possibly test out new ways of acting. Nearly *all* of the school leaders explained that providing leadership roles created opportunities for

- supporting adult learning and growth;
- encouraging individuals to share their knowledge and expertise;
- making others' ideas and voices heard; and
- sharing responsibility and greater decision-making authority for the success of events, ideas, reform initiatives, or programs.

In addition, many of them commented on how these roles help educators acclimate to change, build leadership capacity, raise individual and organizational consciousness, and build healthier school cultures as learning centers.

Providing leadership roles, from most of the school leaders' perspectives, creates opportunities for adults to grow by gaining the responsibilities of a task, program, or initiative. The majority of school leaders explained that adults develop from leading both large and small initiatives. As Sr. Joan Magnetti, head of the Convent of the Sacred Heart School in Greenwich, Connecticut, put it, "Teacher initiative is a big thing," and it needs to be "nurtured." Teachers would feel stifled in their learning, Sr. Magnetti explained, if she were not able to support them when they want to assume leadership roles and implement *their* new ideas.

In fact, regardless of position (principal, assistant principal, teacher-leader, and superintendent), most emphasized that whenever possible, if a person approached them with a new idea, they encouraged that person to "run with it." Some invited adults to submit proposals if they voiced new ideas or inquired about opportunities for leadership. Even the work of developing the proposal, either independently or with colleagues, supported the development of certain skills or capacities. Jerry Zank, past principal of the Canterbury School in Fort Myers, Florida, captured what other school leaders expressed. These roles support "self-reflection and independent learning" as well as "self-discovery."

Table 4.2 summarizes why the school leaders in my research understood the practice of providing leadership roles as pivotal to supporting adult growth and building school capacity. This table also provides specific examples of how participants in my research employed this practice in their own contexts.

As Table 4.2 shows, these school leaders believed that undertaking the complexities of leadership helps adults in the school to grow by sharing leadership, knowledge, and authority for decision making. In addition to enhancing interpersonal relationships and school climate, leadership roles help adults to become aware of their own and others' thinking and to understand the influence of assumptions on thinking and behavior.

Leadership roles took different forms, as Table 4.2 indicates. A leadership role could be one in which a teacher acted as a meeting facilitator, a brainstorming session leader, a project manager, or a team leader. It could also be one where principals assumed different types of leadership roles with fellow principals. Depending upon the role, individuals assumed different degrees of responsibility and different levels of authority.

Table 4.2 Providing Leadership Roles: Reasons School Leaders Employed This Practice and Its Practical Applications

Reasons to Provide Leadership Roles	Examples
School leaders' philosophies and espoused beliefs about why providing leadership roles are important	• Share and include others in leadership. • Share knowledge, expertise, and authority for decision making. • Foster reflective practice and growth. • Build interpersonal relationships. • Develop a positive school climate.
Principals and assistant principals providing leadership roles to teachers	• Teachers and staff share knowledge and expertise. • Teachers serve as lead teachers and/or coaches. • Teachers become administrators or team leaders and/or department chairs. • Teachers lead grade-level meetings. • Teachers serve as leaders in curriculum development. • Teachers deliver workshops within and outside the school. • Teachers lead peer reviews (evaluation). • Teachers lead in technology. • Teachers serve as leaders in self-study. • Teachers lead program evaluation and various school improvement efforts. • Teachers serve as instructional coaches and/or data coaches. • Experienced teachers mentor associate teachers (graduate students, interns) and/or new teachers. • Teachers have authority for decision making (ownership) and for their own work. • Teachers are members of accreditation teams, and/or lead roles in self-study. • Teachers are members of schoolwide inquiry teams. • Teachers deliver workshops and/or presentations at conferences. • Teachers assume lead roles in peer evaluation. • Teachers develop expertise (through sabbaticals, research, or training) and teach others. • Teachers develop partnerships with universities and/or businesses. • Teachers develop courses to teach graduate students on-site.
Providing additional leadership roles to principals	• Experienced principals facilitate monthly meetings with newer principals. • Principals mentor assistant principals who aspire to the principalship. • Experienced principals coach newer principals.

The Challenges of Providing Leadership Roles

Many of the principals in my most recent research identified two common challenges when discussing how they provide adults with leadership roles. First, while these roles are important opportunities to share leadership, build capacity, and support adult learning, many felt strongly that they, the principals, were "ultimately responsible for" and "accountable" for their schools. Another prevalent challenge was that it was often difficult for some adults in leadership roles to provide critical feedback to colleagues. Despite these challenges, they emphasized that providing leadership roles is an important way to support adult growth and learning.

Learning From Leadership Roles

I think the most effective professional development in my experience has been when you can engage a significant and substantial group of faculty in the process.

—Mr. Jack Thompson, Palm Beach Day School, Florida

Leadership roles are critical for supporting adult learning since they create opportunities for adults to share leadership, decision-making authority, responsibility, and influence on the direction of the school. How does this work? In most cases, these school leaders reported that leadership roles were carried out in supportive contexts for risk taking and exercising authority. In some cases, leadership served as a context for an adult to assume and gradually take on more responsibility for an important piece of work that would benefit the school community.

The majority of these school leaders admitted that in today's complex educational world, providing leadership opportunities is important for getting work done well and building school capacity. For the most part, however, they thought about providing leadership roles as different from delegating "tasks." Dr. Sarah Levine, former head of Belmont Day School in Massachusetts, captured a key distinction that other principals shared. As she explained, sharing leadership

can have delegation, or better collaboration, as a component, but delegation by itself may not have anything to do with [sharing] leadership. In its most basic form delegation is simply assigning a task. [Sharing] leadership is anything but basic. It is a higher order of conception of common goals, mission, and purpose jointly owned and implemented. While colleagues who share leadership may delegate to each other certain roles or functions, [sharing leadership has] a collaborative feel.

For Levine and most of the school leaders in my current research, leadership provides a person with the opportunity to become more aware of personal ambiguities and his or her *own* lack of clarity about how to proceed, especially when working with others.

Learning and growing from leadership also gives individuals firsthand experience of the challenges of leadership. Levine spoke about a faculty meeting in which several teachers had assumed leadership roles in sharing a proposal for a new idea:

> What happened was they [the teachers in leadership roles] experienced viscerally how hard it is when you get in that *stuck place*. And when we got to "Well, what do we do next?" they [pause] really came up against the limitations of their differences.

Supports for Those Assuming Leadership Roles

Often, principals and assistant principals explained that when considering whom to invite to assume a leadership role, they thought carefully about a person's strengths and areas for growth. Is this role a good fit for a particular person? Who would best serve as a support to the adult assuming the role? Sometimes, principals themselves served in the support role, and at other times, other adults (e.g., administrators, teachers) in their schools with more experience or greater expertise provided necessary supports. The mutually supportive process of working with another, more experienced professional can serve as a holding environment for growth.

Having a relationship with someone who is both supporting and challenging allows the new leader to articulate the challenges in the role. The relationship also helps adults to differentiate their own perspectives and can become a context that supports the uncovering of the assumptions that guide their thoughts and actions. This relational space is often one where the adult in the lead role can test new ways of behaving and thinking so as to learn and grow from the experience of leadership. The supportive challenging of another's thinking, established by the provision of leadership roles, holds the potential to facilitate growth. Educators in these roles have the opportunity to broaden their perspectives by working closely with colleagues with whom they might not ordinarily work. The majority of these school leaders—principals, assistant principals, teachers and superintendents—believed that the provision of leadership roles facilitated adult growth, enhanced organizational capacity, and improved various competencies and capacities. For this growth to occur, though, the school leaders emphasized that a trusting relationship is crucial.

EXAMPLES OF SCHOOL LEADERS' USE OF PROVIDING LEADERSHIP ROLES

> *Indeed, it is clear that true teacher empowerment and the democratization of schools is unlikely to occur unless educational leaders support such actions by teachers and aggressively collaborate with teachers and others to pursue educational goals.*

> —Blase & Blase, 2001, p. 164

In this section, I offer several examples of the major ways that the school leaders in my research provided leadership roles. Table 4.2, presented earlier, displays the full range of examples of the practice of providing leadership roles that emerged in my research. Here, I first discuss the more prevalent types of leadership roles that principals and assistant principals offer teachers. Next, I briefly mention two types of leadership roles that principals have undertaken in addition to their roles as principals. Finally, I share a few of the leadership roles that teachers have assumed.

Principals Providing Leadership Roles for Teachers

Sometimes we [the administration] ask [faculty] to do things that they're delighted to do, and sometimes we ask [faculty] to try things that make them very nervous to do. And often the person who did not initially [want to assume a lead role] will say, "I never thought I would love this so much!" But our job is to imagine possibilities for people.

—Sr. Barbara Rogers, Newton Country Day
School of the Sacred Heart, Newton, Massachusetts

Across all school types, but to different degrees, principals in my research emphasized that regardless of the type of role, leadership creates a context for learning from diverse perspectives; for sharing leadership, decision making, and expertise; and for becoming more aware of assumptions. While these leaders invited teachers to assume leadership roles in many different ways, nearly all of the instances served as essential opportunities to support teachers' learning. As Principal Gary LeFave of Matignon High School in Cambridge, Massachusetts, explained, an important part of his role as principal is leaving "things open for people who have ideas that might want to do something." Listening to teachers' ideas about leadership by inviting them to assume such roles was a common theme.

As Table 4.2 shows, school leaders invite teachers to assume various leadership roles, including leadership in teams, peer observation, peer evaluation, program evaluation, program design, teachers teaching teachers, coaching, program coordinator, and conducting research within and outside of the school. Nearly all principals and assistant principals in my research remarked that encouraging teachers who have particular areas of expertise to share their knowledge inside and outside the school supports their own "self-discovery." It also builds the capacity of the school.

One additional theme that emerged in my discussions with principals and assistant principals is that they invited a variety of different teachers to assume leadership roles (if the teachers were interested) rather than always having the *same* teachers in these roles. For example, Ms. Kathleen Perry, principal of Lake Worth Community High School, Lake Worth, Florida, explained that she encourages many different teachers in her school to take on leadership roles so that "it's not the same people all the time who are taking advantage of" these opportunities. She, like other leaders, also discussed the importance of encouraging other teachers to look to and learn from the teacher with the leadership role. She urges fellow teachers to "sit down, one-on-one [and] talk to the person" with the leadership role. Doing so, in her view, creates an opportunity for reciprocal teacher learning—and both teachers benefit. It is important to give teachers with varying perspectives the opportunity to take on leadership roles, Kathleen explained, and to make sure the teachers assuming these roles are not afraid to disagree with the administration. They should be "brutally frank," Kathleen said, and be willing to critique and offer alternative ideas for change. Thus, those who agree with administrative perspectives are not the only ones given leadership roles at her school.

Most of the school leaders shared this point of view. As Kathleen put it, having "dissenters" assume these roles is important because of the "danger of . . . being blindsided" and the opportunity it creates for adult learning.[1] Since we all have blind spots—unconscious assumptions—it can be helpful, in Kathleen's view, to understand multiple and differing perspectives on any issue, idea, and/or proposal.

Below, I categorize the examples of leadership roles presented here into two types: those that are exercised inside the school and those exercised outside the school. Obviously, there is some overlap in terms of how these roles support teacher learning and organizational capacity building; however, I organized this section in this way because I thought it would be the most useful for readers who desire to apply leadership practices.

Teacher Leadership Roles Inside the School

In this section, I discuss a few of the more common ways that school leaders in my research invited and encouraged teachers to assume leadership roles inside the school.

Delivering Presentations. Many principals and assistant principals discussed inviting teachers to deliver presentations to other teachers at their own schools about an area of expertise or what they had learned while visiting other schools. The principals and assistant principals explained that such presentations provide important leadership roles for the presenting teachers and growth for those who learn from them.

Leading Faculty Meetings and/or Professional Development Workshops. Another common way in which teachers assume leadership roles is by leading department or schoolwide faculty meetings that focus on the area of expertise of an individual teacher. Many school leaders explained that inviting a faculty member to talk even for a short time during a school meeting provides a leadership role.

In addition, the assistant principals in my research highlighted that they often invite faculty with particular expertise to assume leadership in faculty and professional development workshops by leading a session from which others can learn. Common examples included teachers leading professional development on mentoring, using protocols, and analyzing data.

Sharing Ideas, Learning, and Expertise in Informal Ways. Many school leaders emphasized that teachers often take on important—though less visible—leadership roles by sharing ideas and expertise informally, in that way learning from each other. For example, they explained that teachers often assume leadership roles "more individually," such as "when they've read a book that they want to share" with others, as Jack Thompson of Palm Beach Day School, Palm Beach, Florida, put it. School leaders also made clear that teachers assume leadership roles by sharing what they've learned from conferences and workshops and demonstrating their learning for others—whether in a faculty, department, or grade-level meeting or informally.

Serving as Principal for the Day. Some of the school leaders discussed inviting teachers to assume leadership by taking on the role of "principal" for a day or other period of time. For instance, at Deborah O'Neil's school, St. Peter's in Cambridge, Massachusetts, each month a different teacher is invited to be "principal of the month." When serving in this leadership role, the teacher chairs the faculty meeting and invites colleagues to "engage in dialogue" about school issues. The teacher in this role also assumes responsibility for managing questions and situations that arise during the day.

Leading Peer Reviews: Examining Student Work and Teaching Practices. The majority of principals and assistant principals emphasized the importance of inviting teachers to assume leadership by conducting peer reviews of each other's teaching practices. Most see this as a critical opportunity for teacher learning.[2] I will share one principal's peer review process; this principal's perspective is emblematic of what many others explained.

"Teachers embrace and learn from having opportunities to observe and talk with each other about their practice," Principal Christina Tettonis of the Hellenic Classical Charter School in New York City explained. Christina wanted to enhance her school as a professional learning community during the 2007–2008 school year and sought professional development that would be "sustained, intensive, and ongoing." From her perspective, teachers needed leadership roles when building this kind of culture. While the teachers had multiple roles, Christina emphasized that the roles her teachers assumed in leading "peer reviews" were "the most powerful because teachers were sharing their work with each other." Assuming leadership of the peer review process created "opportunities to collaborate with peers [that included] co-observations of teaching." Christina explained that this created important learning opportunities for the teachers who were leading the process and those who were involved in other ways. In the peer review process at Christina's school, teachers observed each other's teaching and then discussed teaching practices and students' work. "Teachers began to talk about standards" in an ongoing and deep learning-oriented manner and "began to feel empowered."

These leadership roles became one of the more important supports for learning, from Christina's perspective. "Allowing adequate time" in the schedule for collaborative "reflection" and "dialogue . . . based on looking at the work [students' work and teaching practices]" was essential. From results of a year-end survey administered to teachers, Christina learned that the teachers—both those in lead roles and those not—"wanted more and more professional development" time for this kind of collaboration. As Christina summarized, "It's all about collaboration and sharing leadership."

Mentoring and Modeling for Student Interns. About a third of the schools in the 2004 study and many of the principals and assistant principals since then reported that their teachers have leadership roles in mentoring graduate student interns from local universities. In several schools, teachers also taught courses at their schools for graduate student interns. For example, Dr. Larry Myatt, like several other principals, had eight or nine teachers annually who mentored graduate student interns. Questions from the interns "push" mentor faculty "to think more deeply" about what they're doing and remind them how hard it is to do what they do. Larry believes that this experience supports their learning in a deep way and is "beneficial to both new faculty and veteran faculty."

Teacher-Leaders, New Programs, and Modeling Learning for Others. Across all school types, more than half of the leaders in my research explained that teachers assume leadership roles by developing and implementing new programs and models for practice. In addition to supporting their own and their colleagues' learning, these types of leadership roles serve as "models" for other teachers and "provide growth for everybody."

Researching, Adapting, and Implementing Models. Inviting teachers to research and implement new programs and models for practice is one very common way in which principals and assistant principals share leadership. For instance, when the Mary Lyons Alternative School in Brighton, Massachusetts, received the new standards for Boston public schools, Dr. Mary Nash suggested to the teachers "that they throw the Boston frameworks out in a barrel" and invited teachers to assume major leadership in developing a new framework for their school. Mary felt that the larger school system's frameworks were not helpful to the teachers in her unique context. The teachers tried putting the frameworks in their classrooms and invested time into reflecting on their "own work, looking for tools to help us in our work, [and] clarify our thinking."

A different example demonstrates how teacher leadership of a program influenced the entire school. Kim Marshall, while leading the Mather Elementary School in Dorchester, Massachusetts (a school with low financial resources), explained how the implementation of the literacy program at his school, ELLI, provided several teachers with important leadership roles. One teacher was even selected to leave for training to become the leader of this program, responsible for training other teachers within the school. This literacy program was implemented in similar ways at three other Boston public schools in the 2004 study, and literacy programs are a form of teacher leadership that leaders have noted in my research since 2004. At Marshall's school (as at most of the other schools), the teacher who received paid training returned to lead the training of other teachers on how to use this method of literacy education in their classrooms.

Similarly, as many principals and assistant principals explained, teachers lead efforts for researching, assessing, revising, and implementing peer evaluation systems for their schools. For example, at Sr. Joan Magnetti's school, Convent of the Sacred Heart in Greenwich, Connecticut, teachers research and determine the evaluation models that they feel will best support their growth and adapt these models to suit the school context. More specifically, Sr. Magnetti and members of her leadership cabinet invited teachers to be leaders in a task force to investigate the idea of peer evaluation and the corresponding models they could adapt to their school. The task force learned that many teachers preferred that their department heads continue evaluations because they believed some peers might not provide enough "critical feedback."

However, Sr. Magnetti felt strongly that having peers (faculty) involved in evaluations would provide important learning and growth opportunities. The leading teachers on the task force set out to reconsider the peer evaluation program models and were responsible for refining and implementing a model that would accommodate their school's unique context.

More commonly than they participated in peer evaluation systems, teachers assumed leadership roles by developing advisory systems for their schools. For instance, at Dr. Larry Myatt's school, Fenway High School in Boston, teachers assumed leadership roles by developing a system for the new student advisory program, which he explained was a key component of the school culture. The faculty in leadership roles learned from reflecting on questions related to the curricula, which, Larry shared, supported their growth and often challenged their assumptions. They also learned from the process of making decisions together.

Teachers as Leaders in Technology. More than half of the principals in my research discussed how they work to allocate space and time so that teachers can be "leaders in technology" for their divisions, departments, and/or schools. Below I present one detailed example of this, which illuminates many of the ideas other school leaders shared.

Technology is a key priority at the Canterbury School in Fort Myers, Florida. Principal Jerry Zank described how faculty set priorities in collaboration with him and implemented the technology program by facilitating and leading discussions in six areas related to technology. The technology coordinator introduced the "broad stroke sort of issues" to faculty and delivered a 45-minute demonstration on integrating technology into pedagogy. In Jerry's view, this was a "highly effective" learning opportunity for faculty leaders in the program and for the entire school. "People wanted to do it again," he explained.

Jerry believed that in addition to supporting individual teachers' learning, this initiative supported organizational learning. Jerry, like some other principals and assistant principals, felt that leaders in these improvement and learning programs should be teachers, not administrators. Such leadership roles, from his perspective, increase ownership of ideas and provide important learning and growth opportunities.

In his view, teachers in these types of leadership roles (e.g., the technology coordinator) need to meet certain criteria. The teacher needs to have "a little seniority," be "respected," and have "a little bit of experience" to "carry the credibility with senior teachers." Also, the person must have "credibility in the classroom" and represent more than just his or her own academic department. Given his smaller school context, Jerry did not think that the process of selecting the leader for these larger schoolwide initiatives needed to be formal, though he realized that this decision depends on the school context. He believed that the person needs to be appointed—that faculty expect administrators to appoint other faculty to these kinds of leadership roles. Faculty would be "puzzled" if he asked for a vote on a leader.

While Jerry, like a few other principals in my research, believed that teachers should be appointed to specific leadership roles, another, larger group of principals and assistant principals believed that teachers need to volunteer for these leadership roles. Also, nearly a third of the principals in my 2004 research and about half of the principals and assistant principals in my research conducted since then feel that teachers need to be paid for these leadership roles. In fact, some leaders explained that paying teacher-leaders is a legitimate use of Title I professional development funding set aside in budgets. (Districts under sanction by No Child Left Behind are required to set aside 10 percent of their Title I budgets, making this an excellent source of funding.)

Leaders in several schools with lower financial resources told me that teachers assume leadership by applying for grant funding for their school's technology initiatives. For instance, at Principal Gary LeFave's low-financial-resource high school in Cambridge, Massachusetts, the teachers who assumed leadership roles in implementing technology also had leadership roles in applying for grant funding from the archdiocese of Boston to secure training in software for their classrooms. After these teachers were trained, they assumed leadership in teaching their colleagues in the school. They eventually became the school's technology committee and assumed responsibility for making decisions about technology issues in conjunction with the technology coordinator.

Teacher Leadership Roles Outside the School

Principals and assistant principals invited and encouraged teachers to assume leadership beyond the school in several main ways. Delivering presentations and workshops at conferences and at neighboring schools was most common. I discuss some examples of these leadership opportunities below. It is important to note, however, that most leaders also emphasized that some teachers did not want to assume additional leadership roles outside the classroom or school and that it is critical to honor their feelings and preferences.

Delivering Workshops and Presentations at Conferences. More than half of the principals in my 2004 study and the majority of the principals and assistant principals in my research since then explained that they encourage teachers to deliver presentations at professional conferences. They believe that doing so is an important way to support teacher learning. While some schools have the financial resources to support teachers in delivering presentations at national or regional conferences, lower-resourced schools cannot fund teachers but still encourage them to deliver presentations. School leaders like to see teachers assume these roles because they believe that teachers who share their work support adult learning by modeling for other teachers. Teachers also are provided with opportunities to "develop their own ideas" and broaden their perspectives by learning from others in their field, as Scott Nelson, head of Rye Country Day School, put it. Many commented that "writing a proposal" for a conference workshop or presentation facilitates learning as well.

For example, Mr. Jerry Zank, of Canterbury School in Fort Myers, Florida, explained that he often encouraged teachers to deliver presentations at the Florida Council of Independent schools: "You ought to take this a little bit on the road." Jerry, like other leaders, felt that part of his role was to encourage teachers to assume leadership by trying new things, creating new goals, challenging their own and others' thinking and assumptions, and "reaching beyond" what they normally do. This, in his view, is a low-cost way to support "deeper learning" because it engenders "self-reflection and self-education," which he saw as key to growth.

Delivering Presentations/Workshops at Other Schools. Similarly, many of the school leaders reported that assuming leadership in delivering talks at other schools also supports adult learning. For example, Principal Deborah O'Neil encourages teachers from St. Peter's in Massachusetts to deliver workshops to other schools about portfolio assessment, alternative assessment, and the writing process. Deborah shared that principals value the power of faculty educating other faculty on a peer-to-peer basis. Other principals called Deborah to ask if one of her teachers could deliver a workshop at their schools "because [teachers will] listen to another faculty person." Like Deborah, other principals and assistant principals believed that these leadership roles stretch teachers and support their growth and development.

Principals Assuming Additional Leadership Roles

In this section, I briefly discuss two types of leadership roles that principals in my research assumed beyond their regular duties: mentoring assistant principals who aspire to the principalship and facilitating the learning of newer principals. These roles create contexts for learning for the experienced principals, the newer principals, and the assistant principals who aspire to the principalship. The leaders felt that these roles enabled them to learn from diverse perspectives, share leadership expertise, share in decision making, and become more aware of their own and other leaders' assumptions. In effect, these roles serve as holding environments for everyone involved.

Principals as Mentors to Aspiring Principals

For three years, I worked with a group of experienced principals from New York City who served as mentors to assistant principals who were aspiring to the principalship through the New York City Educational Leadership Institute (ELI). The mentors participated in three-hour workshops/seminars, which I delivered four times a year. Workshops focused on learning about the pillar practices, with particular emphasis on mentoring and adult developmental theory. In addition, workshops enabled the mentor-principals to engage in reflective conversations about how to apply the pillar practices and theory to their mentoring and the challenges and successes of mentoring. While I will discuss this in more depth in Chapter 6 on mentoring, I want to mention it here because mentoring provides a leadership role for the experienced principal. The mentor-principals experienced this leadership role as one that supported and challenged their *own* growth while supporting the growth of aspiring principals. As one mentor-principal shared, "I think the learning that I apply all the time . . . is providing leadership roles because this for me is an outgrowth of the distributive leadership theory as well as collaborative inquiry."

Principals as Facilitators of Conversations With Newer Principals

I regularly meet with a group of approximately 50 experienced principals from across the nation who assume leadership as facilitators of monthly discussions to support the development of newer principals. These principals are part of the National School Leaders Network (NSLN), which is lead by founder Dr. Elizabeth Neale. The facilitator-principals also meet with other facilitator-principals several times a year to learn from each other and to deepen their skills and understanding of NSLN's four key priority areas: supporting adult learning, building facilitation skills, learning about what Director Neale calls "change leadership," and deepening their understanding of racial and social inequities in education. These gatherings of the facilitator-principals, according to Dr. Neale, "offer a chance for the facilitators to learn together and to build their expertise so that they can, in turn, build their networks [groups of principals they facilitate]" and support growth.

These facilitator-principals expressed the same themes that emerged from my research with mentor-principals. They felt their work as facilitators enabled them to share expertise and to listen carefully as they learned from each other how to support and challenge the growth of newer principals. And they explained that engaging in "conversation" and "inquiry" with the group of facilitator-principals was a context supportive of their own growth, making it a holding environment as they served in these leadership roles.

Teachers Assuming Their Own Additional Leadership Roles

As I mentioned in Chapter 1, I have also conducted research with aspiring and practicing leaders who have taken my classes on the same ideas presented in this book. Specifically, I have studied how the ideas presented here (theory and practices for growth) informed their thinking and future practices about how they will support adult learning and development in their leadership practice. What follows are some of the ways that teachers in my classes described the types of additional leadership roles they hoped to assume after the course to support their colleagues' learning in their educational contexts.

After learning about the pillar practices for growth and the adult developmental theory informing them, common themes[3] emerged as to how teachers would assume leadership roles in their practice. Eleven out of the 12 students who were interviewed after one of several semesters and the majority of the 22 students who completed postcourse surveys planned to incorporate listening, dialogue, writing, and reflection as teacher-leaders who would take on the additional leadership role of supporting their colleagues' growth within their schools. They felt compelled to do so because these practices supported their own growth and development within the course. They were determined to do the following:

- Assume leadership by creating contexts for engaging with other teachers in reflective practice through the use of writing. They explained that these practices would help them and their colleagues to articulate their thoughts about their teaching practice and facilitate adult development over time.
- Assume leadership by helping their teacher-colleagues to "build relationships" by engaging in dialogue about their professional practice.
- Carve out "time" and "space" on a regular basis to engage with fellow teachers in "constructive" discussions about pedagogical and other challenges and dilemmas.
- Work to nurture "trust" and "shared decision making" among colleagues to create supportive environments for growth.
- Assume leadership by working with their principals and other leaders in their school systems to build interinstitutional "connections" that would support constructive change initiatives that could better support adult development.
- Provide appropriate supports and challenges to their colleagues in response to their specific developmental needs.

CASES AND LESSONS FROM THE FIELD

In this section, I present two cases that illuminate the potential of leadership roles as contexts for adult development. Peter's case is an example of a teacher who assumed a new leadership role as an administrator. This case focuses on how Peter experienced his new role and his principal's supports and challenges for his growth. The second case concerns a new teacher, Jenni, who became a lead teacher in her school.

Growing Into and From a Leadership Role—Peter's Story

Here I present the case of a teacher, Peter (a pseudonym, used to protect his privacy), who assumed a leadership role as an upper-school division director. I describe the efforts of the school principal, Dr. Sarah Levine, then principal of the Belmont Day School in Massachusetts, to support his learning and growth in this role.[4] This case brings together all of the pillar practices and, in so doing, highlights how leadership is shared and how the pillars support growth. The educational team consisted of Sarah; Betty (a pseudonym used to protect her privacy), who was the lower-school division director; and Peter. Together and in pairs, they examined their assumptions and values about leadership and the learning process. Sarah also engaged in mentoring and coaching Peter.

I have revised aspects of the case to include more on the school context and additional details that leaders in my workshops and research have inquired about when discussing the original case. In addition, I've included questions for discussion after the case. After the questions, I present the responses to many of these questions given by an experienced principal who has mentored aspiring principals.

You may wonder: Why did I select this case? I chose it because the case is a rich instance of both the joys and complexities of what often happens when a person assumes a leadership role. It also, from my view, illuminates a leader's gratification and struggle when balancing support for an individual's growth and an organization's development. And last, it sheds light on developmental leadership by bringing to life how leadership roles are contexts for growth and development.

Context

Sarah, the head-of-school, was about 50 years old and beginning her fourth year at the school when a position for upper-school director opened up. Peter, whom Sarah considered to be an excellent upper-school teacher, was in his early 40s and had recently experienced the joy of having his first child. Betty, the lower-school director, had served in this role for about five years and was in her mid-50s.

Sarah explicitly welcomed opportunities to invite community members into leadership. Providing leadership roles, from her perspective, was not just an essential way to share leadership, but also created a context for supporting growth. In general, when deciding whom to offer a leadership role, Sarah collaborated with division directors and shared the following criteria:

> I consider their *readiness* and their *desire* [for the role and to grow in and from it]. I consider their capability. I consider their ability to be disembedded from their own particular job description. I consider their *growth* and *potential.* And I consider their *perspective* on the issue. Although I have appointed people to leadership positions or asked them to take leadership positions when I know they don't have the same philosophy.

In Peter's case, Sarah considered all of these criteria. She believed that Peter would grow from this role.

The Case

Late in the spring before Peter assumed the new role, Sarah consulted with Betty before offering the position of interim upper-school division director to him. Peter, a talented, highly experienced, and well-respected upper-school teacher, had eagerly pursued the position. Peter's new duties included communicating with upper-school faculty about their concerns, keeping the Educational Team informed about those concerns, implementing policy, and advising the Educational Team on how his faculty might respond to changes under consideration. He also taught one upper-school class each day. It was important to Sarah that the division directors stay in touch with faculty needs and communicate them to her openly.

However, because Peter found his new responsibilities demanded more time than he had, Sarah allowed him to miss many of the weekly Educational Team meetings for the first few months.

Airing Concerns

Several months into Peter's new appointment, Sarah opened an Educational Team meeting in her office by sharing the meeting agenda. Looking uncomfortable and a little nervous, Sarah began the conversation with Peter and Betty by stating that she did not like the way the Team was working together this year. Sarah said that she appreciated that Peter felt overwhelmed by the amount of work he had. She told Peter that both she and Betty had been doing all they could to help him but she felt that Peter's "overload" was causing her to rely too much on Betty. Sarah concluded her opening statement by saying that it was not fair to Betty that Sarah needed to lean so heavily on her, since Betty had too much work of her own; she and Betty could no longer "cover" for Peter. Sarah and Betty told Peter that they were interested in "learning what was going on" with him.

Peter shared that he was still feeling "overwhelmed with the amount of work I have to do" and he was having trouble "staying above water." He felt that the position had too many responsibilities. After listening to Peter for some time, Betty and Sarah asked several questions to understand better what was going on. Sarah viewed this as an opportunity to engage together in collegial inquiry. Peter responded cooperatively while restating his feelings about how he was working "so hard."

At several points during the one-hour meeting, both Peter and Betty interrupted each other. When Sarah brought examples of unsatisfactory interactions among teachers to Peter's attention, he defended himself by saying that these situations were Betty's responsibility. Betty responded by saying that she felt "misunderstood" by Peter. Sarah said that certain things were responsibilities of both division directors; making clear that teachers worked together and "got along" was one of those things. Sarah wanted the division directors to do all they could to build interpersonal relationship among members of the school community. It was up to them to work effectively with all teachers so that this core value of community building could grow, she explained.

Sarah was puzzled that the two previous upper-school directors had been able to fulfill more responsibilities than she was asking Peter to handle. She reminded Peter that as a result of his new role, he had been relieved of some teaching duties. He interrupted Sarah, saying that although the previous division director had been able to do the work, she had been "stressed out" and that he did not want to be "like her." Peter soon reasserted his confidence in his ability to do the job, but he emphasized that since this was his first year in the position, he was "still learning." Sarah said gently, "I know you're working hard. I don't want you to work harder. I want you to work smarter." After taking a deep breath, she said firmly that she and Betty could no longer take on Peter's work in addition to their own.

"I hear what you are saying," Peter said to Sarah, "but it is not so easy for me to translate it into action." Sarah then offered several suggestions, based upon her own experiences, about how he might better handle his workload: "Do all of your written work at home. Use your downtime to talk with teachers and keep in touch with issues, and be in the loop. Get to know the kids more." Sarah also acknowledged during the meeting that Peter had to "learn how to say no." At the end of the meeting, Sarah reminded Peter of her support for him while also firmly telling him that he needed to "make changes" in his way of working. Sarah also suggested that the three of them meet with the school psychologist, either in pairs or all together, for help with communication.

As mentor and coach, Sarah invested time and effort into guiding Peter through a difficult time. She took several steps after the meeting to seek out Peter and provide support. She checked in first thing the next day, met with him several times to see how he was doing and to discuss further strategies, and continued to follow up in person and via notes. Knowing that community support was important for Peter's success, Sarah also told the Administrative Team (i.e., director of development, business manager, director of admissions) to encourage Peter, since he was having "a rough time."

Short-Term Outcomes

Peter's performance improved, Sarah noticed. While there were still areas where Peter needed to grow, he was better able to manage the responsibilities of his roles as division director and teacher. In addition to wanting to recognize these improvements and new developmental and leadership capacities, Sarah decided to offer Peter a contract because he responded to her mentoring and coaching and because his job performance had improved enough to make her want to keep him on as division director.

Several weeks later, Sarah conducted Peter's performance evaluation. In addition to discussing performance issues, including Peter's improvements, in the meeting, Sarah detailed how she saw his responsibilities changing during the next academic year. She emphasized that being an administrator would not be any easier than it had been this year. Peter would have more teaching duties (two classes of 20 students each instead of one class), and Sarah would have less time to mentor him because she would be involved in a capital campaign. Moreover, because some aspects of work done by the current Educational Team had fallen short of expectations, more changes in structure and responsibilities could be anticipated.

Sarah gave Peter some time to consider their conversation and to decide for himself whether to continue the administrative work along with his teaching responsibilities or to return to an exclusive teaching appointment. Peter "carefully weighed" the offer and wanted to continue as division director.

Leadership Dilemmas: Sarah's Perspective

In Sarah's view, adults at the school should be encouraged to take responsibility for themselves instead of relying on the division director to "clean up" messes. By encouraging teachers and administrators to take on more authority and responsibility, Sarah wanted to support and challenge them as they developed capacities to manage the complexities of their work. Sarah faced tensions as she tried to support Peter and help him grow and become more successful, while also supporting her other teachers and not abandoning her responsibilities to them.

Providing leadership roles involves more than just inviting people to assume those roles and then leaving them alone. Much more is needed to create roles that are a context for growth. Sarah was aware that even with a holding environment, development for those in transition is a complicated process because people grow at different rates, depending on available supports and challenges. Because of competing commitments, the implicit demands of the role, and the variation in individuals' ways of knowing, sharing leadership inevitably creates dilemmas for the leader as well as for the person assuming the role.

Getting the Work Done While Also Providing Support

Sarah's chief objectives as school leader were to get the school's work done and to provide the best education possible for the students. She saw herself as "ultimately responsible" for the organizational effectiveness of the school. If others in leadership roles were not performing up to standards, their deficiencies affected both her performance as school leader and the performance of the entire community. Sarah viewed the Educational Team meetings as a way to include others in her leadership. Thus, balancing a desire to support Peter in his new role by relieving him from some of the meetings with a desire to keep the Team's lines of communication open created a dilemma for her. Sarah concluded that she might have to forgo the product and ally with the process of development. Throughout Peter's transition, she knew she would continue to face the challenge of balancing her efforts to support adult development while supporting and nurturing the development of the school's children.

Stretching Competencies

In sharing her leadership, Sarah held high performance and growth expectations for herself and others. Sarah was able to handle a multitude of complex tasks in different domains in a way that made it all look easy. "Expectations are a great motivator," she once said. "When we know someone believes in us, we work hard to live up to those beliefs." Sometimes, however, she acknowledged that she worked "too hard."

Sarah also expected a great deal of others. She encouraged the stretching of competencies among adults in the school. She wanted Peter to broaden his leadership potential and to grow in his new role, and she expected him to succeed. Though always supportive of Peter, Sarah also appeared to have doubts. Were the demands of being a division director *and* a teacher too much to ask of him? How could all the work get done without compromising her own standards for supporting adult development in this community?

Caring for Future Success

Sarah saw Peter as a gifted teacher and told me that she would not have been disappointed if he "decided to return to full-time teaching." Although some might interpret such encouragement as a no-confidence vote in Peter's potential to be an effective upper-school director, Sarah wanted to support him in what he wanted to do. She understood that some teachers might not want to assume leadership roles outside the classroom. Before offering him a new contract, she and Peter discussed all aspects of his work and all options, airing their concerns together.

At this meeting, Sarah put her theory about conflict management into practice. She shared her concerns openly, listened attentively to Peter, and asked questions. Her questions aimed to come to a better understanding of the assumptions informing his thinking and behaviors, the situation, and where further development and improvement were needed. In follow-up interactions, Sarah seemed to act in ways that would support Peter. In her view, mistakes were "opportunities to learn," and she reminded Peter of this.

Sarah and Peter agreed that the following year, Peter would serve as both teacher and upper-school division director. In continuing to support Peter's development, Sarah saw herself doing what was best for the school *and* for Peter. Sarah inevitably continued to be concerned about how Peter would fare in the year to come with his increased teaching load and director responsibilities and about how well the school's mission and goals would be fulfilled. Nevertheless, she remained committed to supporting his and other adults' development, while acknowledging that the process would never be easy or readily quantifiable or its results immediately observable.

Peter's View of the Transition

About two months after the difficult Educational Team meeting described earlier, Peter talked with me about his new experience as an upper-school director. Three themes surfaced during our conversation: Peter's gratitude to Sarah for offering him a leadership role; his shared value for communicating openly with members of the school community (even though he occasionally found it hard to practice); and his pride in working with a community that demonstrated a commitment to adult growth, just as he did.

Peter believed that Sarah had offered him the leadership role because she saw him as capable of growing into the job. "If Sarah hadn't been a person who was open for people to learn, she would never have trusted me with the position." He also felt fortunate to work with Sarah and said he had learned a great deal from her, including how to mentor other faculty, how to give direct negative feedback in constructive ways, and how to stay focused on the mission and values of the school while handling many responsibilities. Peter's learning seemed to mirror Sarah's own mission and values.

Peter, like Sarah, believed that open communication was vital: "If you lose that, you lose everything, or you've really dug a hole for yourself." Although Peter still sometimes found it difficult to give direct feedback, especially when it meant giving a colleague "hard news," he knew that being direct would build respect. He acknowledged that he needed to "work on" his ability to do this. He told me that not long before, he'd had to deliver "hard news" to a colleague, but instead of taking responsibility for it, he "sort of blamed it on Sarah" by telling his colleague Sarah had told him to give the news. Reflecting on that situation, Peter explained how he would handle things now:

> Even if you're dealing with somebody who's your friend, when you need to tell him hard news, you have to sit him down and present the hard news and let the person know that you are open to discussing how the decision was made.

Peter appeared to be learning to take more responsibility in delivering clear but empathic feedback. This is developmentally significant, since Peter now was able to have a broader perspective on the relationship he had with teachers and to act on his thinking in new ways. He seemed to be demonstrating self-authoring developmental capacities.

Peter explained that the trust he had developed with upper-school teachers made an important difference in his relationships with them as their administrator. He seemed proud when he shared with me that he worked "really hard" to establish "good rapport" with his colleagues. He said that he, in turn, received a "great deal of support from them." He believed that "fair and direct communication" was the key to that rapport and mutual support. Community and colleague supports were important to Peter.

Being an administrator, Peter explained, included "dealing with differences of opinion." Both he and Sarah held "strong opinions" and respected each other's differences. Peter also discussed Sarah's belief in a shared mission among everyone at the school. He was aware of the need to be a "learner" to succeed in the school culture. He said that in his work as an administrator, he, like Sarah, worked to support and encourage adult growth.

When I asked about his leadership style, Peter said he would like to be able to give each of his many issues "equal billing" and "importance." He saw himself as favoring an approach different from that of Sarah, whom he saw as prioritizing and attending to issues in accord with their importance. When I asked if he thought he was learning in his leadership role, Peter answered, "Oh, most definitely. I hope, even if I become head someday, I hope I never get to the point that I think I know it all." One of the best parts of working in the community, he said, was that everyone was growing.

> One of the things I love about my position here, and about a lot of the people here, is that we're all in different stages of growth, but I don't think anybody feels that they want to just be stagnant here.

Though aspects of his new role remained "hard," Peter explained, "I do feel, personally, that I'm still growing. And that's what I want to be doing. That's the most important thing."

A Developmental View of Lessons From Leadership

Like many of the other leaders with whom I've worked, Sarah told me that one of the most difficult aspects of being school head was giving negative feedback; she saw it as uncomfortable and potentially very painful for the recipient. In the above case, Sarah wanted Peter to know that she recognized his hard work, but she also wanted him to know that he needed to become more effective in his role. For Peter to incorporate Sarah's advice to "work smarter," he had to grow toward a self-authoring way of knowing rather than looking for directions from external sources of authority. A self-authoring knower has the developmental capacities to assess a situation and look internally to decide what needs to be done better.

As a self-authoring knower, Peter would be able to look to himself, and his *own* values and standards, to decide what had to be done. Sarah gently challenged Peter's thinking by suggesting that he occasionally withhold his help from other adults at the school, especially when he was sacrificing his own efficiency. In this way, she was standing at the edges of his thinking by challenging his assumptions and offering an alternative way of thinking and acting for his consideration. By suggesting that Peter set boundaries and limits for his work with others, thus challenging his thinking in the context of their relationship, Sarah created a "holding environment" for Peter.

By encouraging Peter to develop more ownership of his own work and to establish boundaries with others, Sarah supported and gently challenged Peter's thinking to help him develop abilities for effectiveness in his leadership. First she created a safe context to meet him "where he was" by asking questions that invited him to reflect more deeply on his assumptions and current way of making sense. Next, she invited him to consider alternative ways of behaving and thinking about his role and how to enact it. In so doing, she introduced dissonance—or challenge—into his way of making meaning. Then, by offering concrete suggestions based on her experience, she guided and encouraged him to view his work in a broader context. In addition, she remained there to support him as he worked to demonstrate new competencies. In these ways, Sarah performed all three functions of effective holding environments.

After I have presented this case in workshops to leaders in K–12 schools, universities, and other adult education contexts, several participants have wondered what happened to Peter. The answer is that Peter flourished in his role as upper-school head. He continues to serve in this role and truly enjoys it.

This case models how difficult conversations can support growth. It teaches us why these conversations matter. While not easy and often painful, conversations like these—and the developmental intentions surrounding them—are essential given the complex demands of 21st-century leadership. This case illuminates in practical terms what the inherent complexities involved in developmental leadership, as well as the triumphs, *feel like*. To me, it offers hope of possibilities for individual and organizational growth.

Questions for Discussion of Peter's Case

The following questions are offered to assist you in considering Peter's case in light of your own context and leadership. They are also an opportunity to apply your understanding of developmental theory and the pillar practices. You might find it helpful to think through these first on your own and then to discuss your thinking with colleagues. As you will see,

I've included one principal's responses to most of these questions (1 through 4). I hope you find these responses useful and that they stimulate further discussion.

1. What kinds of supports and challenges (logistical and developmental) does Sarah offer Peter? How do you think Sarah uses principles from constructive-developmental theory and the pillar practices to support and challenge Peter?

2. How do you think Peter experiences Sarah's efforts to support his growth, especially in terms of *goodness of fit* between the supports and challenges used to support his growth and his way of knowing?

3. In what ways, if any, do Sarah's leadership dilemmas resonate with you?

4. How might constructive-developmental theory and the pillar practices help you in supporting adults' learning and growth as you invite them to assume leadership roles in your school or school system?

5. If you were Sarah, knowing what you now know about adult developmental theory and the pillar practices for growth, what would you do in this situation?

6. If you were Peter, knowing what you now know about adult developmental theory and the pillar practices for growth, what would you do in this situation?

One Principal's Reflections on Peter's Case

After a workshop I recently delivered to New York City principals who were mentoring assistant principals, the principal-mentors were invited to dialogue about the above questions to apply their learnings and to learn from each other. The workshop focused on many of the ideas discussed in this book. What follows is one principal's thinking about these questions; her responses show how she was considering the application of adult developmental theory and the pillar practices to her role as mentor to aspiring principals.

1. What kinds of supports and challenges does Sarah offer Peter? How do you think Sarah uses principles from constructive-developmental theory and the pillar practices in her approach to support and challenge Peter?
   - Challenge: Sarah could no longer cover for Peter.
   - Supports: Sarah invested time and effort in guiding Peter through his difficulties. After the meeting, Sarah sought him out to provide support, communicate about his progress, and further discuss strategies in person and via notes. She also asked other administrators to encourage and support him through a rough time.
   - Challenge: Sarah wondered, should Peter continue in an administrative role? How did Peter feel about working in this role next year? Sarah explained clearly to Peter that he would have more teaching duties. And Sarah made clear that she would have less time to mentor him since changes in structures and responsibilities were anticipated. Sarah also noted that the team had fallen short of some expectations.

- Supports: Sarah offered him the contract, listened attentively, and asked questions so she could understand his experience. Even though she had doubts, she was committed to support his development (best for Peter and the school).

2. How do you think Peter experiences Sarah's efforts to support his growth, especially in terms of *goodness of fit* between the supports and challenges offered to support Peter's growth?

- Peter was very appreciative and voiced his gratitude.

3a. In what ways, if any, do Sarah's leadership dilemmas resonate with you?

- Sarah was open for people to learn and committed to adult growth. She knew her organization had to achieve goals and needed to balance that. She understood that her organization might not achieve goals as quickly.

3b. In what ways do Sarah's leadership dilemmas resonate with you in terms of supporting your *mentees* (i.e., assistant principals who are aspiring principals)?

- It is difficult to give negative feedback. It's important to frame the feedback in a way to challenge the mentee. A mentor knows bigger picture and recognizes certain things have to be in place in the organization. It's vital to be patient and supporting—but one must bring mentee to the realization that is what he or she needs to do in the school.

4. How might constructive-developmental theory help in terms of offering supports and challenges to your *mentees*?

- You must understand the terrain.
- As a mentor, one must understand mentee's way of knowing.
- It's important to tailor your approach to each mentee and provide appropriate supports and challenges.
- A mentor needs to identify mentee's self-defined values, ideals, and goals. A mentor wants mentee to meet full potential.

Jenni's Story: Stuck in the Middle

Next, I share a case written by Jenni, a teacher-leader and student earning her doctorate. The case provides insight into how some new teachers might experience both the satisfactions and dilemmas associated with assuming leadership roles. I also share it as an opportunity to apply some of the ideas discussed in this chapter about supporting adult development. While this case is primarily about Jenni's experience of assuming a leadership role as a second-year teacher, it is also about her experience of being part of a team. Following this case, which was written by Jenni, are two sets of reflective questions. Jenni developed one set, and I created the other.

Case Context

This case encompasses the questions new teachers face when given leadership opportunities early in their careers. As I enacted my leadership role, I was torn between feeling appreciated and confident as a teacher-leader and feeling mistrusted and belittled by some veteran teachers I respected. This case raises the issue of how effectively to support and challenge new teachers in leadership positions while enlisting the involvement of veteran teachers.

My first teaching job after I completed my Master of Arts in teaching English was at a large, ethnically diverse suburban high school outside Chicago. The school, enticing in the eyes of new teachers because of its great diversity of students, was hiring six new teachers the year I was hired. After I joined the English department, I slowly began to understand the politics surrounding the process of hiring all of us. What I learned was that the department chair, Debbie, was actively recruiting graduates of the master's program from the university where I had just completed my degree. Debbie was in the process of rebuilding the English core curriculum and intended to include this university's model for teaching English and composition.

At the time I was hired, there was only one other teacher from this university's program; by the time I left three years later, there were six teachers with this master's degree at the school. All other teachers were from different schools, and I slowly learned that not all of them agreed with the approach taught at this university, although other veteran teachers were eager to learn from the new teachers. So there were mixed perceptions of this university's curriculum and the teachers who'd been schooled in it. However, the teachers from this university had the clear and obvious support of the Debbie, the chair.

My Case

At the end of my first year of teaching, my department chair assigned me to teach two accelerated classes and be the lead teacher for a group of new teachers who would teach sophomore English in the upcoming school year. Because I had taken a semester course on gifted education and had a master's, I was certified to teach accelerated classes.

During the first week of teaching a class of sophomores, I heard two veteran teachers, Kelly and Tom, talking in the hall. My students were in the midst of a test, so I went to close the door. Later, Kelly apologized to me for her conversation in the hall. Although I had not overheard the conversation, Kelly confessed that she and Tom, whom I'd trusted and asked for help during my first year, had been whispering about whether I should be given two accelerated classes at such an early point in my career. I was taken aback by their comments and lack of faith and felt deceived and distrusted by two teachers who had seemed to be my mentors. At that point, I began to notice that other teachers had become aloof since I'd been given the position of accelerated teacher and team leader.

Upset by the event earlier in the day, I confronted Tom in his classroom after school. He did not know Kelly had told me about their conversation, and he apologized, saying, "We think you'll do a fine job, but you're so young; there are other teachers with more experience to teach accelerated classes." Unfortunately, I also thought other people in the department would be great in the accelerated classroom, and I told my chair that maybe some other people should have the opportunity over me. Then she said that many of those people were not, in so many words, "accelerated teaching material."

Later in the fall, another veteran teacher, Karen, berated my part on the accelerated team, arguing loudly and publicly that students should be in all classes together. She was not angry I was part of the team but frustrated that there was a tracking system at all. I took it as a personal attack on both levels: that I was part of the team and that I believed in the accelerated curriculum. But at the start of the school year, I was not prepared to have this argument with this teacher, especially between classes in the open workroom among other teachers and students. I felt that veteran teachers were attacking me for being in positions of leadership that Debbie, my chair, had put me in.

At the end of the fall term, the sophomore English teaching team (of first-year teachers) that I'd been leading won an award for outstanding teamwork, which the principal presented to us at a faculty meeting in front of the whole school. The principal and chair showed great support of my efforts as a leader, but I was losing ground with some of the veteran teachers who seemed to see me as a "yes woman," "on the fast track," and having too much leadership as a novice (three years experience total) teacher.

I learned from my experiences that several of the veteran teachers did not agree with the system of working on teams, as they thought that we were creating cookie-cutter classrooms. They did not understand our process of planning and debriefing together but also did not take the time to learn more about our shared curriculum. For example, our team had created binders with volumes of materials for each novel and theme we would teach throughout the year. As two teachers on our team put the binders together in the workroom, some veteran teachers walked in and out, guffawing at the notion of all of us teaching the same materials, themes, and novels. Some veteran teachers laughed that new teachers needed the binders to be able to teach at all. A few of them said things like, "When I started, I was just given the text books, and that was it!" Not only did some of the veteran teachers disagree with the leadership positions given to new teachers, many of them also did not accept the concept of teaming or the new curriculum being developed. In essence, we sometimes clashed because teachers like me were willing and eager to be part of a team developing new curriculum.

On the other hand, new teachers seemed to thrive because of the teamwork and enjoyed the team as a means of sharing ideas, working out lesson plans, and considering revisions. We met every Friday morning before school without fail and met informally throughout every school day to ask each other questions, share ideas, and use each other as sounding boards for our experiences in the classroom. We worked hard, enjoyed each other's company, and really began to bond as a team. We greatly appreciated each other for the hours spent on lesson plans, classroom practices, and first-year teacher woes.

I felt proud of my accomplishments with the team but betrayed by trusted veteran teachers and uncertain of how my colleagues saw me. The chair put her faith in me, and the teaching team looked to me for support. But I was uneasy being in the middle of doubtful veteran teachers, earnest first-year teachers, a determined chairperson, and a proud principal. My awkward position in the department made me uneasy and distrustful of my coworkers, especially the veterans, from whom I had previously asked for support and would have appreciated real mentoring relationships. I felt I had a lot to learn from some of the veterans but felt too shunned by some to reach out to them. At the same time, I felt that I owed my best work, attention, and energy to my teaching and to my team. These issues made me feel even more pressure to succeed as a teacher and leader.

Update on Jenni's Case

My first reaction to what happened was to continue to do my work well and try not to worry about who approved of my achievements and who did not. Eventually, I also sought the mentorship of two other veteran teachers with whom I had reciprocal relationships. I wanted to learn from them, and they seemed to want to learn with me. I also maintained my friendship with the teacher who was the one whispering in the hallway. To this day, she is still a friend and colleague whom I can trust to be candid with me about what is on her mind. The department chair also continued to be a source of encouragement for me. In the end, I did gain the approval of most of the teachers, which is what I had hoped to do at that time. It was a learning and growing experience that I will not forget. It taught me about trusting others but most of all about trusting myself.

Jenni's Questions to Consider

1. How should I (Jenni) have dealt with the first event, the whispering in the hallway?

2. Who, if anyone, should I have consulted about my situation, besides the two I did speak with, Kelly and Tom?

3. How could I repair the relationship with Kelly and Tom, two teachers I admired and had trusted?

4. What could I have done to work on the relationships that I had hoped would succeed, such as the mentoring relationships with veteran teachers?

5. What caused the tension, and what could I have done to ease the tension of holding such leadership positions as a new teacher?

6. How, if at all, could the department chair and other leaders have been more effective in easing the tension for me in this leadership role?

Developmental Questions to Consider

As you reflect on Jenni's experience, I invite you to consider the following additional questions. I hope that they serve as starting places for engaging in inquiry with your colleagues, both veteran and newer teachers.

1. Knowing what you know now about adult developmental theory and leadership roles, how do you think Jenni was making meaning of her experience? What evidence of her way of knowing do you see?

2. What do you think might have happened if Jenni had openly shared with Debbie, her chair, how she was experiencing her leadership role? What do you think may have been at risk for Jenni in voicing how she was feeling (developmentally speaking)?

3. What do you think was hardest for Jenni as she was "losing ground with some of the veteran teachers who seemed to see me as a 'yes woman,' 'on the fast track,' and having too much leadership as a novice"?

4. What kinds of developmental supports and challenges do you think would have been helpful to Jenni? If you were the chair, how might you have created a holding environment for Jenni and/or for the veteran teachers who seemed upset by the teaming and Jenni's leadership role as a younger teacher?

5. If you were in Jenni's position, what do you think you would have done or said and to whom? Why?

CHAPTER SUMMARY

In this chapter, I first presented a theoretical perspective on leadership roles as an effective approach to supporting adults' development in school systems. I discussed the literature on (a) the importance of leadership roles in today's complex educational world, (b) the principal's role in inviting other adults to assume such roles, and (c) the importance of these roles as a support for individual and organizational growth.

I also discussed how adults with different developmental orientations experience leadership and the types of supports and challenges they need in order to grow from these roles. Next, I illuminated why and how the school leaders in my research understood and employed leadership roles to support transformational learning and to enhance organizational capacity building. Examples from my research included school leaders' conceptions of how this practice invites others to share ownership of leadership, expertise, and ideas as they work toward building learning communities and promoting change.

This chapter also included two cases showing how educators who had assumed leadership roles in their schools experienced them. I included these to highlight the powerful rewards and unforeseen struggles that arise both for the adults who assume these roles and for those who seek to support their development. In Peter's case, we see how Sarah worked to hold Peter in a developmental sense by offering supports *and* challenges. This case sheds light on how Peter, who was not fully ready for this role, could grow from developmental supports and challenges to meet the inherent demands of the role.

The second case illuminates the struggles and need for supports and growth-oriented challenges when a new teacher assumes a leadership role. While this role was offered, I think, to celebrate Jenni's strengths and capacities, it highlights how unforeseen challenges and needs for support can undermine well-intentioned practice. From this case, we come to understand the importance of developmentally appropriate supports and challenges to nurture growth.

Below, I have included two sets of reflective questions to invite you to consider what additional leadership roles you might like to assume and to consider what kinds of leadership roles you might like to invite other adults to assume in your school.

REFLECTIVE QUESTIONS

Questions for You

<u>Risk</u>
And then the day came,
when the risk
to remain tight
in a bud
was more painful
than the risk
it took
to Blossom.

—Anaïs Nin (n.d.)

1. Knowing what you know about adults' ways of knowing and providing leadership roles as a developmental practice, what is one way you will use this practice to support your own learning and growth in your work context?

2. What kinds of supports would you need to grow in a new role? What kinds of challenges do you think would be most helpful to you?

3. What logistical or substantive concerns or implementation challenges, if any, do have at this time about assuming a new role?

4. What are the biggest questions you have about assuming a new role?

5. When assuming a new role, what do you think will feel most satisfying and/or most difficult as you work to exercise leadership and achieve your goals?

Questions for You in Your Educational Context

I became a teacher in 1966. But I am not now the same teacher I was in 1966, or in 1975, or 1990. As we all do, I have changed a great deal over the years, and so have my practices and ideas about teaching. The changes did not occur without warning; they have been responses to experiences that I have had as a teacher, teacher educator, mentor, mother, grandmother, scholar, and researcher. I have lately become more introspective about where I began, where I am now, and why and how I have changed along the way.

—Sonia Nieto, 2003, p. 10

1. What kinds of leadership roles are offered to adults in your work context? How do you think they support adult learning? What's working well, from your perspective? What would you like to see improved?

2. What is one thing you've learned from reading this chapter that feels important to you?

(Continued)

(Continued)

3. What have you experienced as the benefits of supporting adults who assume leadership roles? What have you noticed about other adults' engagement in them? In what ways, if any, might you apply learnings from this chapter to your work context?

4. What logistical or substantive concerns, if any, do have at this time about inviting adults to assume leadership roles?

5. How might you secure help to implement your hopes for inviting other adults to assume leadership roles?

6. What kinds of successes have you noticed when adults in your school or school system assume leadership? What sorts of obstacles or constraints, if any, do you see in terms of supporting adults in these roles?

7. How do you think adults in your school would describe their experience of leadership roles? Why?

8. What criteria do you use when inviting adults to assume leadership roles? And why? How might you use what you know about our ways of knowing to support adults in leadership roles?

9. Knowing what you know now about adults who make meaning in developmentally different ways, how might you use the various structures discussed in this chapter to support adults with different ways of knowing as they assume leadership roles?

You might use Table 4.3 as a worksheet to help you implement your ideas in your specific context.

Table 4.3   Providing Leadership Roles: Supports and Challenges

Way of Knowing	Supports	Challenges
Instrumental		
Socializing		
Self-Authoring		
Self-Transforming		

5

Collegial Inquiry

Engaging in Shared Dialogue and Reflection on Practice

The process of telling about and reflecting on one's teaching life . . . can stimulate changes in teaching behavior and classroom procedures.

—Intrator & Kunzman, 2006, p. 41

In this chapter, I discuss collegial inquiry and the ways school leaders can shape contexts and secure time to invest into meaningful dialogue about practice. After reviewing the relevant literature on both adult and professional development, I discuss how adults with different developmental orientations will experience collegial inquiry and what types of supports and challenges they will need to grow from it. I then discuss why school leaders believe it supports adult learning and what conditions are necessary to facilitate it, and I provide examples of how it has functioned in different schools. In so doing, I also relate the different forms of collegial inquiry—reflection through writing, dialogue, conflict resolution, and decision making. I discuss how principals and assistant principals employ this practice with teachers and other adults in their schools, how principals engage in this practice with fellow principals, and how teachers use it with fellow teachers. In addition, I present a case example of how one school leader used collegial inquiry as an opportunity to reflect on her practices and assumptions and, ultimately, grow. Toward the end of the chapter, I introduce the practice of convening (case-based learning) and provide protocols for structuring convening and collegial inquiry from a developmental perspective. Application exercises and reflective questions appear at the end of the chapter.

COLLEGIAL INQUIRY:
A KIND OF REFLECTIVE PRACTICE

Reflective practice is thought to improve teaching, build leadership, and enhance student achievement. But we can more effectively shape positive school communities and systems if we engage in *collaborative* reflective practice, or what I call collegial inquiry. The difference between reflective practice and collegial inquiry is fairly simple: whereas a person can engage in reflective practice alone or in the company of colleagues, collegial inquiry, as I define it, is a dialogue that takes place between two or more people—it is not done alone. It is, however, a kind of reflective practice in that it involves purposefully examining and reflecting on one's assumptions, beliefs, values, commitments, and convictions as part of the learning, teaching, and leadership process. Recall that in Chapter 3, I made a distinction between *dialogue* and *discussion*. Dialogue refers to the art of thinking together and looking at some issue together, which is what we do when engaging in collegial inquiry. This is different from discussion, which is more about pressing forward with one's own views—sort of like percussion.

Collegial inquiry can help us to become more aware of the assumptions that inform and guide our thinking, behaviors, and approaches to problem solving and to alter those assumptions, freeing us to engage fully in learning and grow. It can support principals, assistant principals, teachers, and superintendents as they develop the capacities to manage the complexities and challenges of their work. One goal of collegial inquiry is to stop events so they can be re-viewed—the power is in the re-viewing and consideration of alternative and more effective ways of thinking and responding. Once issues and assumptions are raised to a conscious level, adults can then take steps to address, rethink, and revise them in safe contexts. In this section of the chapter, I discuss the adult and professional development literatures that address the theoretical underpinnings of reflective practice and collegial inquiry.

WHAT THE ADULT DEVELOPMENT LITERATURE
CAN TEACH US ABOUT REFLECTIVE PRACTICE

When I discussed teaming as a pillar practice supportive of growth in Chapter 3, I reviewed central learnings from the literature on reflective practice. In particular, I focused on the role of examining and questioning assumptions to test new ways of thinking and acting. In addition, I pointed out how teaming can be a support to both individual and organizational learning and development. Since I discussed these aspects of reflective practice in Chapter 3, in this section I will focus on how the literature describes the goals of reflective practice, why scholars and theorists advocate its use for all adults—including teachers *and* administrators—and how engaging in reflective practice nurtures a culture of learning and increases possibilities for school- and systemwide improvement. I will also briefly highlight the role that examining our assumptions plays in facilitating personal and professional learning. All of this is offered to illuminate how collaborative reflective practice connects to the *shared* dialogue that is at the heart of collegial inquiry.

Goals of Reflective Practice

Engaging in reflective practice is a learning tool for individuals and organizations. School leaders and theorists have identified reflective practice as a mechanism that supports personal and professional learning and growth in both teachers and administrators (Brookfield, 1995; Kegan & Lahey, 2009; York-Barr, Sommers, Ghere, & Montie, 2006). Improving one's teaching, which means paying attention to one's emotional and intellectual well-being and development, is one main goal of reflective practice (Brookfield; Osterman & Kottkamp, 2004). When teachers, or any adult for that matter, engage in reflective practice, they have the opportunity to become aware of their own and others' thinking and assumptions (which guide behavior). This awareness can, in turn, clarify thinking and help us better understand our behaviors, leading to growth. The ultimate goal of schoolwide (collective) reflective practice is, according to Jennifer York-Barr and her colleagues, increased student learning.

Who Should Engage in Reflective Practice

Just as it is important for teachers to engage in reflective practice to improve instruction and facilitate their own learning and growth, Brookfield (1995) and others emphasize the importance of administrators engaging in reflective practice (Kegan & Lahey, 2009; Wagner et al., 2006; York-Barr et al., 2006). For example, Brookfield highlights the importance of principals and superintendents publicly acknowledging private mistakes and "going public with their own learning" (p. 255). It is in fact essential that all of the adults in a school engage in reflective practice, since doing so stimulates individuals to think more carefully and deeply about their own beliefs and the issues under discussion, to consider and grow from exploring alternative possibilities and perspectives, and to understand the consequences of their actions (Brookfield; Kegan & Lahey). As reflection increases, the decisions and actions involved in leadership become more effective (York-Barr et al.).

How to Build Cultures of Reflective Practice

To build a school that is a true learning center—a place that nurtures adults and children's learning and development—reflective practice and collegial inquiry need to become a part of the fabric of that school's culture. Brookfield (1995) points out that to create such cultures, trust is essential; he writes that he himself "has to earn the right to ask colleagues to think critically about their practice" (p. 258). Similarly, Osterman and

Kottkamp (2004) emphasize that in shaping cultures of learning, it is especially important that school principals be able to acknowledge when they do not know how to proceed, admit that they do not have all of the solutions, and be able to request others' help. Research indicates that principals, superintendents, and other leaders who adopt this courageous mind-set establish a culture of reflective practice through their openness to learning with and from others and by engaging in the growth process themselves (Elmore, 2004; Kegan & Lahey, 2009; Osterman & Kottkamp).

Osterman and Kottkamp's (2004) perspective on reflective practice aligns with the earlier work of Chris Argyris and Donald Schön (1974, 1978) in that it also stresses thinking and actions (behaviors) as "integral processes" (Osterman & Kottkamp, p. xi). However, their work builds upon and extends that of Argyris and Schön in its consideration of "how context and culture shape thought and action" (p. xi). Reflective practice, from these authors' perspectives, centers on inviting individuals to work together to examine carefully and seriously their own practices and to resolve important challenges or problems. Certain organizational conditions are required. As Osterman and Kottkamp explain, "to engage in reflective practice requires an environment of support. It requires an organizational climate that encourages open communication, critical dialogue, risk taking and collaboration" (p. 21). Given the adaptive challenges leaders face today, I believe that it is essential to build school cultures in which collegial inquiry is a core element—something in which all of the adults in the school engage. Such a culture will decrease isolation, improve leadership, facilitate learning and growth, and enhance student learning.

From my perspective, it is also important to consider how adults with different ways of knowing will engage in collegial inquiry. What does collegial inquiry mean to adults with different ways of knowing? What developmental supports and challenges might be needed to help adults with different ways of knowing grow from engaging in this practice?

How Examining Assumptions Can Support Personal and Professional Learning

Stephen Brookfield (1995) defines assumptions as "the taken-for-granted beliefs about the world and our place within it that seem so obvious to us as not to need stating explicitly" (p. 2). The most distinctive feature of critical reflection, he maintains, is how it helps us to track down, or develop an awareness of, our assumptions. He continues, "In many ways we *are* our assumptions. Assumptions give meaning and purpose to who we are and what we do" (p. 2). Brookfield also refers to assumptions as "mostly unchecked acts of faith" (p. 266).

Robert Kegan and Lisa Laskow Lahey (2009) help us to understand even more deeply the power of what they call our "big assumptions"—the system of beliefs that forms "our mental models" (p. 58). As they explain, "We call them 'big assumptions' because they are not currently viewed as 'assumptions' at all. Rather, they are uncritically taken as true" (p. 58). They gently remind us that while our assumptions "*may* be true . . . they may not be, but as long as we simply assume they are true, we are blind even to question them" (p. 58).

How does reflective practice help us to identify our assumptions? Because our assumptions are embedded in us and guide our thinking and behaviors, and since we hold them as the *Big Truths* about how the world works, we do not question them or how they guide our behavior. Since we *assume* them to be true, we need other people's help to identify them and their influence on our thinking and actions.

Examining and modifying our assumptions promotes growth and learning. As Brookfield (1995) explains,

> Without this habit [of critical reflection], we run the continual risk of making poor decisions and bad judgments. We take action on the basis of assumptions that are unexamined and we believe unquestioningly that others are reading into our actions the meanings that we intend. (pp. 3–4)

When we engage in reflective practice, we are intentionally working to understand thinking, behaviors, and events from a variety of perspectives. We have opportunities to reformulate our thinking; clarify, explore, and evaluate our thoughts, governing values, and actions; and possibly reframe thoughts, feelings, and actions; as well as test and reconceptualize our assumptions (Kegan & Lahey, 2009; York-Barr et al., 2006).

Scholars recommend that after identifying a problem or an assumption, we peruse data about it from multiple sources. This strategy enables us to imagine and often experience alternative solutions because we are able to examine our actions critically and understand them more fully (Kegan & Lahey, 2009; Osterman & Kottkamp, 2004). This description of the problem or assumption should incorporate both cognitive and emotional aspects, and it should be drawn from as broad a range of data as possible. Processes of writing and shared reflection (dialogue) can help us identify the hidden assumptions underlying our ideas and actions (Brookfield, 1995; Drago-Severson, 2007; Kegan & Lahey, 2009). The act of listening to excerpts from others' journal entries, for example, may further illuminate our own and other people's ambiguities, fallacious reasoning, and points of confusion.

However, this kind of increased awareness can be challenging to attain, because theories-in-use (the assumptions that inform and direct our behavior) are not easy to name. In other words, our assumptions are not transparent to us since they are not easy to characterize or explain. Most often, we have a longing to view events from a positive perspective and see problems or challenges we encounter as a sign of incompetence or failure. In addition, we are often unaware of the assumptions we hold (Kegan & Lahey, 2009; Osterman & Kottkamp, 2004). When we are motivated by a personal desire to improve, examination of assumptions and the resulting self-awareness enable us to reconceptualize our assumptions, theories-in-use, and habits.

As Donald Schön (1983) wisely points out, "When a practitioner becomes a researcher into his own practice, he engages in a continuing process of self-education" (p. 299). Engaging in reflective practice can help us to develop deeper understanding of the influence of our assumptions on our thoughts and actions. Reflective practice can also help us achieve greater self-awareness about the nature of our performance. These increases in our awareness create opportunities for personal and professional learning, growth, and development.

WHAT THE PROFESSIONAL DEVELOPMENT LITERATURE CAN TEACH US ABOUT REFLECTIVE PRACTICE

For years . . . teachers have developed expertise in the art and science of teaching, but they've done it on their own. That's the hard way to do it.

—Robert Marzano, 2007, p. 3

In this section, I briefly discuss major themes in the professional development literature that highlight urgent calls for establishing collaborative cultures within schools by engaging adults in reflective practice. As I discuss below, establishing these cultures is one of the essential ways in which principals, assistant principals, teachers, and superintendents are building capacity and supporting adult learning in schools today. As Marzano points out in the above passage, it is "hard" to improve our practice alone; we need each other to grow best.

What do we know? Scholars and practitioners mostly agree that professional learning opportunities for teachers should center on reflective practice. These educators and researchers believe that teachers who engage in reflective practice will improve their instructional practice and, in turn, enhance student learning and achievement (Ball & Cohen, 1999; Cochran-Smith, 2006; Darling-Hammond, 2003; Elmore, 2000; Elmore & Burney, 1999; Fullan, 2005; Hawley & Valli, 1999; Johnson et al., 2004; Mizell, 2006). In fact, Killion (2000) advocates for "structuring staff development experiences to encourage teachers to analyze their practices and share what they have learned with colleagues" since she believes that doing so will "increase collaboration, commitment to implementing alternative strategies, and build teachers' knowledge about research-based teaching" (p. 3). Creating collaborative cultures wherein teachers engage in reflecting on their practice is a promising way to encourage risk taking, share leadership, learn together, and consequentially build individual and organizational capacity. It can also support transformational learning.

We also know that the principal has one of the key roles in building a collaborative school culture and in securing resources needed to support teachers' ongoing and school-based engagement in reflective practice (Ackerman & Mackenzie, 2007; Curry, 2008; Donaldson, 2006, 2008; Hirsch & Killion, 2008; Leithwood & Hallinger, 2003). The principal's role in such a culture, as Joseph Blase and Jo Blase (2001) note, "becomes one of communicating, coordinating, fostering mutual problem solving, and providing resources for effective work" (p. 77). Principals play a crucial role in systematically establishing structures that support the process of dialogue, critical reflection, and shared governance. Such structures enable entire schools to benefit from collaboration.

Developing structures for reflection and shared dialogue about instructional matters is a vital step, as noted by Blase and Blase (2001), among others (Curry, 2008; Moller & Pankake, 2006; Wideman, Owston, & Sinitskaya, 2007). Such structures include the physical act of allocating time in the master schedule for collaborative meetings; including faculty and staff in a collaborative, shared decision-making process; and engaging with faculty and staff as equal partners in this process. Developing such structures often requires school leaders to distribute leadership as they work to create a culture with a shared mission and a shared sense of purpose (Hackney & Henderson, 1999; Leithwood, Aitken, & Jantzi, 2006; Neuman & Simmons, 2000; Spillane, 2006). As these scholars have noted, flexibility in leadership, innovative approaches to problem solving, collaborative decision making, and constant experimentation are also necessary conditions for growing collaborative communities.

In discussing the urgent need for schools to invest in more effective professional learning opportunities, Stephanie Hirsch and Joellen Killion (2008) echo Robert Marzano's (2007) sentiments quoted earlier: it is ineffective to create isolated staff development experiences that focus only on the individual teacher. They have found that nearly two-thirds of schools and school districts engage in professional learning that hampers excellent teaching for each student each day. Effective professional learning opportunities, they maintain, meet teachers' learning needs and enhance student learning. Hirsch and Killion emphasize that given today's complex educational challenges, every educator must be a learning educator. For this to occur, teachers need to meet regularly to engage in collaborative adult learning experiences that center on dialogue and reflection on instructional practice (e.g., pedagogical lessons and assessments). This, in Hirsch and Killion's view, will create schools that promote great teaching for all students, instead of hindering it.

Similarly, Robert Garmston (2007) discusses this urgent need to establish and sustain collaborative cultures in schools; though admitting that developing such cultures is a complex endeavor, he affirms that it is worthwhile and needed. As I mentioned in Chapter 3 when discussing the practice of teaming, his work helps us to understand the importance of building collaborative cultures by inviting adults to engage in what he calls "balanced conversations"—conversations in which all participants are active contributors to the discussion underway and share ownership in the decisions. Engaging in these "balanced conversations" helps develop a collaborative culture; builds capacity, understanding, commitment, and follow-through; and thus promotes shared ownership (Garmston & Wellman, 2009).

As I mentioned in Chapter 3, Garmston (2007) highlights three challenges to achieving balanced conversations at school: airtime imbalance, which results in a decrease in ownership; talkative leaders, who ask and respond to their own questions; and the failure to use protocols, which can secure input from all engaged in the conversation, especially on topics that are difficult to discuss. To overcome such challenges, he recommends providing tools for structuring conversations (processes, strategies, and protocols) and creating structured opportunities for engaging in reflective practice (allocating time for speaking and writing). In particular, he, like others, emphasizes the ways in which asking adults to reflect in response to questions invites them to consider their instructional practices and to reflect on their participation in balanced conversations and the shared decision-making process.

Practitioners and researchers highlight additional ways in which collaborative cultures can be developed in schools: by creating learning opportunities for teachers to engage in reflective practice as critical friends, such as by providing peer-review feedback (see Curry, 2008; McTighe, 2008); by engaging in action research; by engaging in collaborative goal setting (see Marzano, 2007); and by analyzing student work. Several threads are woven through each of these opportunities to build collaborative cultures wherein teachers engage in reflective practice.

- These opportunities center on reflection and collegial conversations about the practice of teaching and learning that occur over time. Put simply, they are inquiry driven.
- These opportunities focus on building adults' capacities to share ownership in decision making and to influence instructional improvement.
- Most of these initiatives advocate for teachers to reflect on and contemplate questions as one way to support learning.
- Finally, all are oriented toward increasing teacher learning and student learning.

It is important to emphasize, I think, that more recently, researchers and practitioners stress the need for school principals and superintendents to engage in reflective practice as a support to their learning and development. In fact, many highlight the potential benefit of this model for school leaders (see Ackerman & Maslin-Ostrowski, 2002; Byrne-Jiménez & Orr, 2007; Donaldson, 2008; Kegan & Lahey, 2009; Normore, 2007).

Thus, we have learned that engaging in shared reflective practice is important for all adults, regardless of position, in our schools and school systems. Doing so will enable us to build and strengthen collaborative cultures to nurture learning.

HOW COLLEGIAL INQUIRY ATTENDS TO DEVELOPMENTAL DIVERSITY

How often do we invite each other to "please go and reflect on that"? And how often do we invite our teams to do the same? A developmental perspective helps us to understand that *how* we engage in reflective practice and collaborative work will vary depending on how we make sense of our experiences. Also, as we know, the kind of supports and developmental challenges that will stretch us and promote our growth will vary as well.

How might engaging in collegial inquiry over time provide a context—a holding environment—for a person's ongoing growth? What kinds of supports and challenges do adults with different ways of knowing need to engage effectively in this process and to grow from it? How might we best encourage and support each other to grow as we engage in this practice and articulate thinking, experiences, assumptions, and reflections about issues under discussion? How might we lead to shape cultures in which all adults—including superintendents and principals—feel safe to take the risks needed to grow? When we engage in collegial inquiry, we have the opportunity to share our own perspectives, to listen to and learn from other people's perspectives, to understand our own and other people's assumptions and how they guide our thinking and influence practice, and to offer support and challenges and benefit from those others offer to us in the spirit of helping us grow. As we know, it is important to establish trust and a safe context to have a fertile soil in and out of which adults feel secure in sharing their perspectives and willing to engage in risk taking.

Engaging in collegial inquiry is a developmental practice and a *process*. Over time, engaging in this practice and process creates a context for us to develop greater awareness of our beliefs, convictions, values, and assumptions; to reflect with others in ways that may allow us to envision and perhaps test the validity of our assumptions about practice; and to entertain and test alternative ways of thinking, acting, or behaving. When school leaders— principals, assistant principals, teachers, and superintendents—engage in collegial inquiry, a space is created for growth; the process and context of engaging in collegial inquiry becomes a holding environment.

As noted earlier in this chapter, collegial inquiry can include, for example, the process of collaboration focused on assessing instructional or leadership practice and examining student work. It can also be central to creating or evaluating a school's or a department's self-study report and/or designing alternative forms of assessment. Any of these forms of adult collaboration will likely require adults to engage in shared decision making to make informed decisions about practice. However, adults will experience collegial inquiry in any of these shared experiences differently, depending on their ways of knowing.

Relating Collegial Inquiry to Ways of Knowing

Table 5.1 illuminates how adults with different ways of knowing tend to make sense of their experiences of engaging in collegial inquiry. It shows what constitutes developmentally appropriate supports and challenges so that adults will be *both* well held (or supported) and appropriately challenged—in a developmental sense—to experience growth.

As the table shows, our way of knowing influences our capacities for perspective taking and *how* we will experience collegial inquiry.

The Instrumental Knower and Collegial Inquiry

Adults who are instrumental knowers will feel supported by establishing and adhering to ground rules for dialogue while engaging in collaboration and shared decision making. They will orient toward following step-by-step guidelines and rules about how to participate in collegial inquiry. In other words, clear agreements about and descriptions of ways to proceed with group dialogue and/or reflective writing (e.g., guidelines, step-by-step outlines of processes to be followed, specific questions to be addressed) will be experienced as supportive. When offering their perspectives, they will share the concrete details of their practice and whether it is "right" or "wrong." Engaging in dialogue with others will feel

Table 5.1   Potential Ways Adults Experience Collegial Inquiry Based on Their Way of Knowing

Way of Knowing	Supports for Growth	Challenges (Growing Edge)
Instrumental Knowers	• Establish ground rules and step-by-step guidelines as to how to engage in discussion and how to engage in shared decision making. • Share concrete examples and details of this knower's practice and explicitly state whether it is "right" or "wrong." • Provide opportunities to engage with others in conversation that provides concrete advice, examples or models to emulate, skills, and information about practice, for example. • Ensure that colleagues are experienced as resources who possess information and skills. • Provide clear descriptions of ways to proceed with conversations, reflective practice, and/or reflective writing. • Address concrete needs for improving practice (e.g., learning better skills or more effective rules to follow).	• Provide opportunities that require thinking differently—and more abstractly—through discussion and reflection about own practice and other people's practices. • Provide opportunities and conversations that require this adult to understand and evaluate self through another person's point of view.
Socializing Knowers	• Provide opportunities to meet the expectations of valued others (e.g., supervisors and respected colleagues) and evaluate self based upon what these important people think of own ideas. • Provide acceptance from colleagues and supervisors, which will help this knower feel recognized and safe in taking risks and sharing own perspectives. • Provide opportunities for this knower to evaluate practice through writing or engaging in dialogue with a colleague before engaging in dialogue with the larger group. • Provide opportunities to share perspectives and feelings in pairs or smaller groups of colleagues before sharing perspectives and feelings with larger groups. • Model that differences of opinion are experienced as tolerable by colleagues remaining connected and interpersonal relationships not being jeopardized.	• Challenge learner to develop own beliefs and values independent of what valued others think this adult should be thinking or doing. • Support this knower in becoming less dependent on the approval and judgment of others.
Self-Authoring Knowers	• Provide opportunities to demonstrate own competencies. • Provide opportunities to critique issues and proposals under consideration. • Provide opportunities to design initiatives. • Ensure this knower has the opportunity to learn from the process. • Ensure this knower has the opportunity to learn about own capabilities and competencies. • Provide opportunities for this knower to evaluate and critique instructional and/or leadership practices, decisions, and vision within the larger context of the school and/or school system.	• Challenge this knower to question own belief system. • Support learner in becoming less invested in own identities, ideology, standards, and points of view and becoming more open to and welcoming of standards, values, and points of view that are directly opposed to own.

Way of Knowing	Supports for Growth	Challenges (Growing Edge)
	• Emphasize becoming more competent and extending own options to achieve self-determined goals. • Invite this knower to create some of the structures for proceeding with the process of collegial inquiry (i.e., allow this adult to demonstrate some competencies and provide this adult some freedom within the structure of group conversations). • Include conflict in collegial inquiry context: this knower understands conflict to be a natural part of dialogue that can help the group arrive at better solutions, more effective practice, and/or ideas for implementation.	• Challenge this adult to experience *self* as process driven.
Self-Transforming Knowers (Early 4/5)	• Collegial inquiry in pairs, triads, or larger groups is an ideal context for this knower, since the practice provides a structure for inquiry that is open yet containing, with boundaries and deadlines. • Provide opportunities to voice, appreciate, and learn from a broad diversity of perspectives. • Ensure that a shared value exists within the partnership and/or groups for valuing and prioritizing conversation, process, and inquiry. • Prioritize resources (e.g., time and space) in favor of inquiry processes. • Include conflict in collegial inquiry context, but be aware that while this knower can endure, tolerate, and appreciate the value for and of conflict, this adult prefers the harmony of multiple perspectives working together.	• Challenge this knower to move from the process of inquiry to action. • Support learner in identifying or affiliating with authority or impersonal systems. • Help this knower to accept that some differences cannot be resolved. • Support this adult in not getting stuck by absolutizing "flat," nonhierarchal approaches and in own capacity for relativism.
Self-Transforming Knowers (Later 5)	• Ensure that a clear rationale for engaging in inquiry exists. • Ensure that stakeholders have a felt sense of commitment. • Ensure that a shared sense of a strategic vision exists. • Provide freedom within the structure of inquiry to experiment with a variety of forms of inquiry. • Allocate resources to support inquiry and ensure that follow-through will occur on actions determined by the group, team, or system. • Include conflict in collegial inquiry context: this knower takes conflict among a diversity of perspectives for granted and is capable of helping to harmonize conflicting perspectives and appreciates having opportunities to do so.	• Challenge this knower to remain committed when the sense of purpose is unclear. • Help this adult to appreciate the time it takes to reach a practical end when others may not move at the same pace. • Challenge learner not to take over and rush the process. • Coach this adult to be sensitive to the feelings of those who do not have the same capacity (e.g., for conflict).

supportive to them when it provides them with concrete advice, skills, and information about practice. Gradually encouraging these adults to move beyond what they see as the "right answers" toward open-ended dialogue wherein multiple perspectives are discussed and considered will broaden their perspectives and support their growth. Over time, engaging in dialogue and reflection on teaching practices or ideas for school improvement holds the potential to challenge these knowers to think differently—and more abstractly—about their own practices and other people's practices and to understand and evaluate themselves through other people's points of view.

The Socializing Knower and Collegial Inquiry

Adults who are socializing knowers will feel supported to engage in collegial inquiry with colleagues if a safe environment has been established, since such an environment will enable them to take risks in sharing their perspectives. Socializing knowers need the approval of valued colleagues and supervisors to feel secure and will likely look to them for direction in their decision making before voicing their own perspective as to how to move forward with a decision or proposal. Recall that socializing knowers experience conflict as a threat to the self and their interpersonal relationships. They will need to be supportively challenged over time to look to themselves first for direction in decision making. Over time, such support will help these adults grow to generate and look to their own set of internal values and standards when collaborating with colleagues and supervisors and to state explicitly their own viewpoints, independent of what valued others and supervisors think they should be thinking or doing.

The Self-Authoring Knower and Collegial Inquiry

Self-authoring knowers have grown to have the capacity to look internally—to their own set of values, beliefs, and standards—when engaging in collegial inquiry and making decisions. They have the capacity to hold, coordinate, and consider multiple perspectives when making decisions or voicing their perspectives on situations. Self-authoring knowers experience conflict as a natural part of dialogue. Engaging in collegial inquiry with colleagues is experienced as an opportunity to come together in the spirit of learning from the *process*. When engaged in dialogue and decision making, these adults will focus on evaluating and enhancing their own practices and decisions within the larger context of the team, group, school, or system. Collaborating with others is an opportunity for them to learn about and from multiple and diverse perspectives and to evaluate and integrate colleagues' perspectives and ideas with their own. When engaging in inquiry and decision making, these knowers will look internally to determine whether or not they are meeting their *own* standards for instructional and/or leadership practices. Collegial inquiry and its inherent sharing of ideas and perspectives are experienced as a way to expand their own options and ways of thinking about practice, leadership, proposed ideas for reform, initiatives under consideration, and feelings about impending changes.

A developmental challenge for adults who make meaning in this way is to consider alternative perspectives opposite their own. To support a self-authoring knower's growth, colleagues could engage in dialogue about the strengths and limitations of each presented perspective and highlight ways in which differing perspectives might be brought together and/or emphasize similarities between them. Asking questions about how each person arrived at a particular perspective and inviting all to elaborate on their perspectives about issues, proposals, or initiatives, while pointing to their interconnectedness or observable similarities, could facilitate growth. Self-authoring knowers might be challenged to grow while engaging in the process of collegial inquiry by opportunities in which they are called on to examine their own assumptions about issues under discussion and to consider their own self-evaluation by asking a person to share his or her reflections and thinking, by posing questions that require a person to examine and question his or her beliefs, and by offering alternative ways of viewing the issue under discussion or situation.

The Self-Transforming Knower and Collegial Inquiry

Adults who are self-transforming knowers will appreciate the process of collegial inquiry since it presents opportunities to articulate their own perspectives and to learn from a broad diversity of perspectives, including those that are diametrically opposed to their own. They will value an open structure for engaging in inquiry and the boundaries and deadlines inherent in the process. Engaging in this practice with colleagues and supervisors will feel most supportive to them if group members share a value for experiencing it as a partnership—one that prioritizes the process and dialogue inherent in that process. While they experience conflict in ideologies as a natural part of group processes, they usually have a preference for a harmony of multiple perspectives working together and will work to facilitate this. These knowers will feel supported if others engaging in the process (colleagues and supervisors) are interested in exploring the process of inquiry, the decisions they make together, the *paradoxes* of work and life, and the many tensions that are generated by inner contradictions. Collegial inquiry will be experienced as an opportunity to deepen the interpersonal relationships they share with team or group members. Encouraging and prioritizing some space and time for shared inquiry (dialogue and reflection) to develop a deeper understanding of their own and other team members' assumptions, mental models, intentions, and corresponding strengths and limitations will be experienced as both a support and a developmental challenge that will help them grow.

To bring these ideas to life, I'd like to present the views of Drs. David McCallum and Aliki Nicolaides, educational leaders, whom a variety of developmental assessments have identified as self-transforming knowers. They have shared their experiences of engaging in collegial inquiry over time in the same "action learning" group composed of seven developmentally diverse members. I hope their experiences shed light on how adults with this way of knowing tend to experience collegial inquiry.

Both Aliki and David commented on how important it was to them that a process of collegial inquiry with group members be one wherein they and all group members could "bring their lived personal and professional experiences into the holding environment provided by the group," as David explained. One of David's "nonnegotiables" was to have the group "establish a sufficient level of trust and safety [so that all group members] feel secure enough to risk being vulnerable, experiencing conflict, receiving feedback, and taking up leadership." And he believed this had to happen up front—before any of the work in collegial inquiry began. About his own experience of growing from the process of collegial inquiry with group members, David shared, "I find it valuable when the members of the group simultaneously respect and value my input and at the same time, exercise freedom in calling me on any hypocrisy, posturing, or other pretenses that they perceive."

Aliki appreciated opportunities within the process of collegial inquiry to "experiment with my intentions, action, and impact moment to moment and meeting to meeting." Like David, she valued and wanted to learn from "feedback in the moment from peers whom I trust and admire." Both appreciated the process of collegial inquiry and group members' commitment to learning across many levels. In Aliki's words, she valued the group's "mutual commitment to . . . learning as individuals, as a group and as part of a larger social context." Working closely with others while engaging in collegial inquiry can help us to identify the ideological or systematic assumptions we hold by surfacing these assumptions and learning from each other's points of view.

Collegial Inquiry as a Path to a Different Way of Knowing

As I've discussed, the process of collegial inquiry is robust in that it can support growth among adults with diverse ways of knowing. The way in which we engage in collegial inquiry (e.g., collaborative work and/or shared decision making) varies depending on our way of knowing. Collegial inquiry invites us to reflect internally on our own thinking and to share it in dialogue with others. To participate in this practice, we are invited to listen carefully; consider diverse points of view; and work to understand the similarities, differences, and overlapping points of multiple perspectives (which can include theoretical, emotional, and political perspectives) and the intersections among various diverse viewpoints. Participants are invited not only to listen to divergent points of view but also to listen to new ideas and challenge old ones. Conflict and contradiction may emerge naturally as part of these conversations as colleagues arrive at the best options or solutions, depending on context. When divergent perspectives or solutions are presented, it is best if a person can see the potentially helpful nature of conflict and the ways in which conflict often serves to clarify a solution.

I suggest that engaging in collegial inquiry can support a person's growth to a more complex way of knowing. Over time, adults will become more aware of gaps or inconsistencies in their own and other adults' perspectives. Engaging in collegial inquiry creates opportunities for adults to consider seriously and deeply new perspectives, especially those that are not aligned with their own, and to test the validity of their own assumptions. With appropriate supports and challenges, adults can grow from this process.

Goal Setting and Ways of Knowing

To illustrate a little more concretely the importance of attending to our ways of knowing, I discuss briefly how adults with different ways of knowing experience the goal-setting process, a common practice employed across school systems with leaders—superintendents, principals, assistant principals, teachers, and others. Robert Marzano (2007) comments, "The problem in low-performing schools . . . is not getting people to work hard; it's getting people to do the right work" (p. 3). His research indicates that "district leadership matters, and that getting district leadership aligned on the right work will translate into big student achievement gains" (p. 3). He and his team of researchers identify "collaborative goal setting" and "monitoring and tailoring instruction for goal achievement" as two essential aspects of "the right work" (p. 3).

Goal setting is a practice that can be employed by individuals, teams, schools, and school districts. For example, some school leaders in my research have employed schoolwide goal setting to develop goals related to how they want to integrate issues of diversity into the curriculum. Often, they began with a discussion that surfaced adults' differing conceptions of diversity. "What does diversity mean to you?" was frequently the opening question for reflection through writing before engaging in collegial inquiry. Other leaders worked with school communities to engage in the following school goals: How can we, as a community, help students from a range of socioeconomic backgrounds? How do we, as a community, teach diversity, infuse it into our curricula, and appreciate it in our daily lives?

Take, for example, this noble request, offered by a school principal to empower her teachers by engaging them in the process of collegial inquiry and goal setting to support their growth and development:

> The self-evaluation portion of your overall teacher evaluation is an opportunity for you to reflect on and share with [your supervisor] the "highs and lows" of your teaching, along with your professional and personal goals. Please make sure that you answer questions one and two; you may use the rest of the questions listed below as loose guidelines for the framing of your self-evaluation. It need not consist of specific answers to the questions below unless you prefer to write it that way. If you have any questions, please let me know. (1) Assess your progress on goals and explain what you have left to do. (2) In what ways to do think you carry out your goals? [How do they align with the mission of our school?] . . . How does your teaching reflect them? . . . In what areas do you consider yourself a successful teacher?

What kinds of developmental capacities would be needed to conduct a self-evaluation? How might adults with different ways of knowing respond to the questions above, which were offered with the best of intentions toward supporting growth, reflection, and eventually the process of collegial inquiry? How will adults with different ways of knowing experience the goal-setting and monitoring process to which Marzano (2007) refers in the above passage? What kinds of developmental supports and challenges might enable us to engage more effectively in this process and to grow from it? How might adults' very willingness to take risks in setting goals or sharing assumptions be influenced by their knowledge of an evaluative component to this process?

How might the supervisor's way of knowing influence how he or she approaches and engages in the goal-setting process? What types of feedback from supervisors during collaborative goal setting might best support adult learning? Since we bring developmental needs to the goal-setting process, we need to attend closely to adults' understanding of goal setting to support growth.

In Table 5.2, I describe how adults with different ways of knowing tend to experience the goal-setting process, the expectations they have for supervisors, and the kinds of

Table 5.2 Collaborative Goal Setting and Expectations of Supervisors: A Developmental View

Way of Knowing	Adults' Expectations of Supervisors in the Goal-Setting Process	Practical Supports	Challenges (Growing Edge)
Instrumental Knowers	Supervisor knows the right goals and should tell them what the right goals are.	• Give this knower goals and explain, step-by-step, the process for achieving them. • Share examples of goals. • Engage in dialogue that provides concrete advice, specific skills, and information about how to achieve goals that will improve instruction and practice.	• Suggest goals that require abstract thinking (in the psychological sense) and scaffold this knower through the process. • Encourage movement beyond "right" goals and toward goals that are inclusive of colleagues' collective needs.
Socializing Knowers	Supervisor knows the best goals for them out of many possibilities.	• This knower does generate some goals internally. If these are voiced, support the adult by acknowledging the goals as those he or she should pursue.	• Encourage this adult to generate own goals, becoming less dependent on supervisor's approval of goals. • Help learner to separate own goals and responsibilities from another person's. • Support this knower in distinguishing own perspective on goals from need to be accepted by important others.
Self-Authoring Knowers	Having generated their own self-determined goals, these adults expect their supervisor to engage in dialogue with them about their own goals and to offer additional goals for consideration.	• Offer feedback on and critique of goals and engage in joint inquiry around the process for selecting them. • Engage in joint inquiry oriented toward analyzing, critiquing, and exploring goals.	• Encourage this adult to consider letting go of own goals and moving toward divergent alternatives. • Challenge this learner to become less invested in own goals and more open to and welcoming of experiencing *self* and goals as being process driven.

Way of Knowing	Adults' Expectations of Supervisors in the Goal-Setting Process	Practical Supports	Challenges (Growing Edge)
Self-Transforming Knowers	These knowers hope that the supervisor will be a companion in exploring goals through the interpersonal relationship they share. Goals might center on how to deepen relationship and intimacy with self and others.	• Be present to this adult as he or she explores more profoundly the paradoxes of work and life and the many tensions that inner contradictions generate.	• Encourage and create opportunities for coinquiry (dialogue and reflection) into developing a deeper understanding of assumptions, mental models, and intentions and their strengths and limitations. • Conduct shared exploration of tensions, contradictions, ironies, and paradoxes of diversity of goals.

developmental supports and challenges that will best support their engagement in the process and their growth.

WHY AND HOW SCHOOL LEADERS EMPLOY COLLEGIAL INQUIRY

The majority of school leaders in my 2004 and more recent research believed that inviting adults to engage in collegial inquiry—"meaningful dialogue" or "real conversations," as most of the leaders referred to it—creates opportunities for authentic growth and learning in individuals and organizations over time. Recently, I asked a group of principals about the practices they felt best support adult learning and development in their schools. I present their ideas below. Please notice how many of these practices pivot on engaging in the practice and process of collegial inquiry.

- Taking Learning Walks across grade levels and across curriculum
- Having informal conversations
- Having collegial inquiry study groups
- Holding retreats where teachers have opportunities to engage in real conversations about students' work and their teaching
- Having real conversations with staff
- Hiring substitutes so that teachers can engage in professional development (grade-level)
- Having an open-door policy (for principals) after hours so that teachers can come in and talk
- Making time to listen to teachers' concerns
- Meeting with teachers on a regular basis to check in
- Reaching out to teachers and offering feedback
- Addressing concerns that have been voiced
- Listening to staff
- Conferencing with teachers
- Analyzing student performance
- Engaging in collegial inquiry as a school community
- Building relationships with teachers through dialogue
- Being reflective with staff; having conversations
- Engaging in goal setting (benchmarks, aspirational, partnerships)

It might be helpful to keep in mind that not all of the school leaders employed every strategy listed above; also, a few leaders let me know that they sometimes feel unprepared to support teachers when they are asked questions about discipline-specific teaching practices. This sentiment highlights the importance of having a safe place for principals themselves to ask questions, seek advice, and engage in collegial inquiry. I discuss an example of principal-to-principal support through collegial inquiry later in this chapter.

Many of the leaders explained that they employed collegial inquiry because it creates a context in which adults can reflect on proposals for change and schoolwide issues (e.g., developing a school mission), as well as build individual and systemwide capacity. A central theme that emerged among school leaders was their belief that setting up situations in which adults talk regularly about their practice in the context of supportive relationships encourages self-analysis and learning that can improve the individual's and the school's practice.

Key Reasons for Collegial Inquiry

As Table 5.3 shows, for the most part, the principals and assistant principals in my research reported that they employed collegial inquiry for four central reasons: (1) it helped them to share and include others in leadership, (2) it was an opportunity to learn from diverse perspectives and to build relationships, (3) it facilitated individual and organizational learning, (4) and it helped adults to manage change and complexity. In Table 5.3, I not only summarize why these school leaders felt collegial inquiry was a vital way to support adult growth, but I also provide examples that illustrate the diverse ways in which school leaders used collegial inquiry to support adult learning, how principals employed the practice to support their own and other principals' growth and learning, and how teachers employed this practice with fellow teachers in support of each other's learning and development.

Inviting adults to engage in collegial inquiry was also a way to share power and authority by asking others for their honest thinking on and feelings about ideas for change, school practices, curricula, instructional issues, proposals for change, reform initiatives, and policies. The majority of these leaders worked to create contexts in which they engaged in inquiry together. These contexts were spaces for adults to express their concerns, interests, feelings, and ideas. Many shared that much of this process involved encouraging and modeling open and honest communication. For them, this also meant modeling and encouraging others to learn from diverse perspectives. Doing so, many voiced, strengthened individual and organizational learning, deepened interpersonal relationships, and built capacity within the school.

Conditions Necessary to Collegial Inquiry

Providing Structures for Dialogue and Reflection

Just about two-thirds of the principals in my 2004 research and more than half of the principals and assistant principals in my research since then emphasized that to support teacher learning, it is essential to create "structures" for supporting teacher reflection. In addition, almost all of these leaders mentioned the importance of building "time into the master schedule" (job-embedded professional learning time) so that teachers can collaborate and reflect on instructional, curricular, and improvement issues.

For example, Muriel Leonard, principal of a low-resource middle school in Boston, was one of many principals who emphasized the importance of implementing school structures that support teacher reflection. Much like other school leaders, her idea was that the kinds of planning, collaboration, and learning she wanted to support among teachers would not happen unless the school and schedule were designed in ways that intentionally involved

Table 5.3 Collegial Inquiry: Reasons School Leaders Employed This Practice and Its Practical Applications

Reasons to Provide Opportunities for Collegial Inquiry	Examples
Principals' and assistant principals' philosophies and espoused beliefs about how collegial inquiry supports adult learning in their schools	• Share leadership. • Learn from diverse perspectives to build relationships. • Facilitate individual and organizational learning. • Help people to manage change and complexities, as well as foster diversity.
Principals and assistant principals employing collegial inquiry with other adults in the school	• Freewrite or journal privately in faculty, department, or grade-level meetings before hearing perspectives with a larger group. • Brainstorm before engaging in discussion of ideas and proposals under consideration. • Engage in dialogue when participating in roundtable discussions about problems in instructional practice as well as innovations. • Ask for feedback on practices and initiatives and proposals. • Engage in dialogue and "real conversations" about ideas. • Conduct Learning Walks (across grade level and curriculum). • Meet with teachers on a regular basis to address their concerns. • Offer feedback to teachers and staff and receive feedback from them. • Set goals with adults in the school (assistant principals and teachers). • Write in journals privately before sharing of thoughts about issues under discussion. • Engage in reflection and discussion after community events. • Engage in open and honest discussion for conflict resolution. • Engage with adults in the school community in reflection and dialogue related to classroom, teaching, and leadership practices. • Engage in writing and reflection for school's self-study, self-evaluation, and/or quality review. • Engage in dialogue and reflection about assessment options, altering curricula or practices, and/or refining systems. • Conceptualize and write proposals for grants, professional development, conference presentations or workshops, and/or articles. • Reflect on philosophical questions related to assessment, pedagogy, mission, testing procedures, and/or leadership. • Write proposals (for grants, new programs, sabbatical, and/or graduate study). • Engage in reflective practice and critical inquiry in faculty meetings. • Take sabbaticals, in and out of house. • Engage in inquiry teams that investigate how to improve student achievement. • Engage in reflection through writing and shared dialogue about teaching evaluation.

172

Reasons to Provide Opportunities for Collegial Inquiry	*Examples*
Principals employing collegial inquiry with fellow principals to support their own and others' learning and growth	• Experienced principals engage in reflection and dialogue with newer principals in monthly meetings, with experienced principals serving as facilitators in these groups. • Experienced principals serve as mentors to assistant principals, meeting throughout the year to engage in reflection and dialogue with other mentor-principals about the challenges and successes of mentoring.
Teachers employing collegial inquiry with fellow teachers to support their own and others' learning and growth	• Form book clubs with other teachers to engage in writing, reflecting, and dialoguing about books and their connection to practice. • Form study groups to read, reflect, and dialogue about instructional practice. • Engage in research groups wherein they investigate an aspect of instructional practice. • Engage in reflection, research, writing, and dialogue to write grant proposals and/or conference proposals.

173

and "prioritized" these forms of work. Even when the structures were put in place, there was still some resistance to working within them. In her view, "reshaping a school culture takes time." She explained the high priority she placed on creating structures in which adults could learn from each other in this way.

> Part of [supporting teacher learning] is really providing structures and forums for teachers to interact with each other, and to learn from each other. I think that there's a tremendous amount of skills and expertise that a lot of the teachers in our schools . . . have that they don't get credited with or recognized for. And that often as we pursue professional development by bringing in people from outside, . . . by attending professional conferences, . . . we don't spend enough time learning from each other. And learning from each other occurs through cluster meetings, when you're doing problem solving, by setting up classroom practices or having roundtable discussions where people are presenting how they solved some problem or mastered some content that they had been struggling with their students.

Muriel further expressed that recent school change and restructuring efforts in Boston had "pushed" her and other leaders to "to recognize and appreciate the importance of scheduling and prioritizing common planning time." Like many of the other school leaders in my research, Muriel worked to create forums and prioritize opportunities for adults within the school to benefit from "learning from each other."

Serving as a Model of Dialogue and Reflection

To learn from reflection and dialogue, many of the school leaders commented on the need to "model" these habits of inquiry and to make time to teach other adults in the school "how to reflect on practice." For example, like Muriel and the majority of school leaders in my research, Dr. Larry Myatt, while serving as principal of the Fenway Pilot High School in Boston, told me that creating spaces for teachers to engage in meaningful reflection on their practice was vital to supporting teachers' learning and growth. While allocating time in the schedule for teachers to engage in dialogue and reflection was "essential," he also emphasized what he saw as another indispensable ingredient for supporting this type of learning: "helping [teachers] to learn *how* to talk and engage in reflective practice."

When I asked him how he did this, he explained by sharing an example of an experience that helped him to learn this. He told me of an instance that occurred very soon after he and his school community had agreed to devote three and one-half hours each week to engaging in reflective practice with colleagues in their departments. During this block of time, Larry said that he would visit different departments to learn from them as they engaged in reflective practice and to see if he could do anything to support individual departments. During one of his visits, when he walked in the room where a department was meeting, he noticed that several of the teachers were working independently at their computers, one was correcting tests, and another was preparing a lesson plan. When he asked them what they were doing, one of the teachers replied, "We're working *together.*" Larry explored what this meant to them and realized that it was important to teach teachers *how* to engage in reflective practice and to share protocols that might assist them in the process.

As Larry reflected on that experience and what he learned from it, he shared that he understood that it might be easier for his teachers in a particular discipline to get together and "build curriculum or discuss pedagogy," as compared to teachers in another discipline, due to differences in content matter and "personality" characteristics. Sharing an "example or model" of different protocols and "modeling reflection" and how to engage in dialogue, in his view, "really helped the school to learn how to do this." The example of a protocol and curriculum he shared to illustrate his point was the "Facing History and Facing Ourselves Curriculum," whereby the teachers at his school learned to examine and critically "reflect on the set of questions that help to guide and shape their conversation."

Some of the teachers, Larry explained, were initially resistant to some of the conversations about curricula and various other school issues, but after engaging in the process, they looked forward to them. Collegial inquiry became part of the culture of the school.

Many of the principals and assistant principals in my research echoed Larry's sentiments about the essential need to model reflective practice themselves and to dedicate time to helping teachers and staff learn *how* to engage in shared reflection and dialogue. Using protocols and writing in meaningful ways were two common strategies used to facilitate reflective practice.

Increasing Awareness by Engaging in Meaningful Dialogue and Reflection

"Engaging in the process of reflection with colleagues is a powerful way to support adult learning" was a common theme that emerged from my 2004 and more recent research with principals and assistant principals. Nearly all school leaders mentioned how important it was for them and other adults in their schools to create spaces where teachers and other adults could purposefully engage in reflective practice, and they discussed how doing so "increases self-awareness." Many of them made a link between increasing self-awareness and its relationship to supporting increased student achievement.

For example, Mr. Jim Cavanaugh, while serving as principal of Watertown High School in Watertown, Massachusetts, placed great importance on "being reflective" himself and shared that he worked very hard to allocate time and space for teachers and other adults in his school to reflect purposefully on their practice and to grow in terms of self-awareness. This is the best way to raise student achievement, he explained. Jim believed that it is "crucial" that teachers and staff, including him, become aware of their assumptions and how they influence practice; they must examine their assumptions so that they can be tested. "Self-knowledge is just so important," he emphasized, and he explained that engaging in the process of reflection and dialogue enhances self-knowledge. This, in his view, is tied to making "student learning and performance the priority." In addition, modeling reflective practice among teachers can also help kids to become "lifelong learners."

Acclimating Teachers to a New Culture

Several school leaders mentioned that it is often difficult for some teachers to acclimate to the change from one kind of culture to a culture that prioritizes reflective practice. For example, Dr. Sarah Levine, while serving as head-of-school at Belmont Day School in Belmont,

Massachusetts, and suburban Polytechnic School in Pasadena, California, invited teachers and staff to reflect on their practice through writing and shared dialogue in faculty and team meetings. Often she invited all community members to reflect on how school values were "implemented" in their instructional practices and through their actions and interactions with others within the school context. Not all members of the faculty embraced these opportunities, Sarah explained. While some faculty appreciated the opportunity to reflect on larger issues, others did not. Sarah was sensitive to the frustrations experienced by some members of the school community when she asked such open-ended, philosophical questions:

> Some people get very frustrated with me, and they say that they want to get on with the day-to-day business. They don't necessarily see the connection between these abstract ideas [and their daily work]. But I'm convinced of the importance of it.

Sarah recognized that while many adults in schools appreciated the process of engaging in collegial inquiry, some did not, and some needed time to acclimate to this cultural change. Interestingly, engaging in reflective conversations provided a context for teachers and other adults within the school to articulate their perspectives about issues under discussion and to engage in dialogue about concerns. These reflective conversations created opportunities for all members of the school community to appreciate, learn from, and better understand each other's perspectives. One common theme these leaders expressed was that in general, but particularly in situations where conflict developed around proposed changes or instructional practices, it was important for them to "model" the importance of "listening" to varying perspectives, regardless of whether the group's hoped-for outcome aligned with their own expectations. Engaging in collegial inquiry, as many of these leaders explained, supports increased ownership and often supported successful and improved implementation of initiatives under consideration.

PRACTICES SCHOOL LEADERS USE TO INITIATE COLLEGIAL INQUIRY

In this section, I first discuss a few examples of the more common ways in which principals and assistant principals employ the practice of collegial inquiry with teachers and other adults in their schools. Next, I briefly mention one way a group of principals in my research engage with other principals in the practice of collegial inquiry on a regular basis. Last, I share a few of the ways in which the teachers I learned from in my research engage in collegial inquiry with other teachers to support each other's growth and learning.

Practices Used by Principals and Assistant Principals With Teachers and Other Adults

The practices below are grouped into four large categories that emerged in my recent research with principals and assistant principals. The practices illuminate how these leaders make use of collegial inquiry with teachers and other adults in their schools; each practice is a developmental tool that supports adult learning and development.

Before describing the practices in some detail, I think it would be useful to share what several principals and assistant principals have said about why they believe these practices are useful. Sometimes, they employed the phrase *reflective practice* to refer to their belief that teachers should know why they are doing what they are doing in their classrooms and with their instructional practices. This wording seemed to refer to their belief that teachers need to have a sense of *purposefulness* about their instructional practice (and the many components of it) and a faithful attention to what works in terms of supporting their students' learning and achievement. Put another way, most of these school leaders believed that their teachers needed to be able to articulate these purposes to others in order to learn from themselves and others.

At other times, these school leaders used the term to refer to their belief that teachers— and themselves—need to have a certain kind of *awareness* or *mindfulness* about themselves as teachers.[1] In this case, *reflective practice* was used in a way that pointed to its potential as a questioning, reflective, and learning tool that teachers need to be able to use to assess what is working well for them and their students and what's not.

Practice 1: Reflection Through the Process of Writing

I think you must put [your thoughts] down [in writing] to see where you are, how you got where you are, and then to pull together your ideas: what works, what problems you've encountered, what would be the best advice you give or what is one thing you wouldn't do over again? [Writing] requires a real examination and a weeding of the kinds of things you do and the important things. And I think it helps in development.

—Principal Kathleen Perry

As Kathleen Perry, principal of Lake Worth Community High School, Lake Worth, Florida, explained in the above passage, she employed writing as a mechanism to help herself and other adults in her school examine their thinking and feelings. Most of the school leaders in my research employed writing as a tool for reflection and clarification of ideas, feelings, and perspectives. These school leaders invited teachers and, often, other adults to engage in a variety of forms of writing: freewriting, journal entries, goal setting, self-evaluations, proposals for grant funding or for their own professional development, and/or conference presentations.

In general, writing helps us to formulate and articulate our thinking and feelings. It creates opportunities for teachers and other adults to identify their thoughts, feelings, beliefs, and assumptions about issues under discussion or proposals for change. While the majority of school leaders *invited* adults to use writing as a reflective tool, they also were sensitive to and respectful of adults' varying preferences. They emphasized three important aspects of employing writing as a tool for reflection: (1) inviting adults to freewrite must be an invitation and not a "requirement"; (2) not all adults find the practice of freewriting or journaling meaningful, and that must be respected; and (3) it is essential that an invitation to write be connected to writing about and carefully considering something meaningful.

These school leaders employed the practice of freewriting on paper or in a journal to invite teachers and other adults to respond to a question (e.g., What was the most powerful learning you had about your instructional practice this year?), a sentence stem (e.g., When I think about my upcoming self-evaluation, I feel . . .), or a quotation by writing their uncensored thoughts and impressions in response to the prompt. When freewriting, a person is invited to write down exactly what he or she is thinking and/or feeling, giving no attention to self-censuring for a particular audience or to grammar or syntax. The central idea is to think honestly and openly on paper about whatever comes to mind in reaction to the prompt. After freewriting, adults are invited, usually, to share whatever they feel comfortable sharing with a partner, small group, or large group. Freewriting was employed to help adults focus their thinking and/or feelings and to clarify them before engaging in dialogue.

Another form of writing these school leaders emphasized was journal keeping. Many of them encouraged teachers and administrators to engage in journal writing before engaging in discussion and to use their journals as places to reflect on their instructional practice, leadership challenges, annual goals, and issues and concerns as they arose. Many of these school leaders wrote in journals as well. A common theme that emerged was that these school leaders believed that writing in journals created a private space for clarifying thinking, feelings, and concerns for teachers and themselves. This space enabled them to identify and consider their own beliefs, assumptions, questions, and values about both personal and professional matters.

For example, Ms. Barbara Chase, head of Philips Academy in Andover, Massachusetts, emphasized the importance of creating spaces in which teachers can step back regularly for reflection through the process of writing, "to think about *who they are* and *what they care about* and how that relates to *what they're doing* on a day to day basis . . . in their jobs." Nearly half of the school leaders commented that in addition to the individual benefits of journal keeping for adults, it also offers a powerful and important model to children and youth.

In most of these schools, and especially in the independent and Catholic schools in my 2004 and more recent research, teachers were invited to write proposals to request that funding be allocated to support their professional development over the summer and/or during the year (e.g., graduate coursework, workshops). Writing proposals to apply for funds for professional development requires teachers "to reflect on what they want to learn," as Barbara Chase put it. In many schools, teachers were required to report back after they completed their project as a way to share their learning with others. Leaders explained that writing creates a space for teachers to consider what they want to do and learn and to plan ahead in terms of what would be helpful for their instructional practice in the next school year. Many of these leaders also invited teachers and administrators to write proposals to clarify their thinking about proposed ideas for change and about their responses to other people's ideas or initiatives.

Another very common way in which these school leaders used writing as a tool for reflection was to invite teachers and, often, staff to write up their self-evaluations and annual goals or assessments of them. These leaders emphasized how important this was, since doing so creates a space for private reflection and clarification of ideas. This kind of writing, like proposal writing, encourages teachers take responsibility for identifying and addressing their own professional and personal needs and goals. Sr. Joan Magnetti, head of Convent of the Sacred Heart School in Greenwich, Connecticut, echoed many other school leaders when explaining why writing about the goal-setting and self-evaluation process was vital to supporting teachers' growth. Her comments centered on how these processes help teachers to "try new things" and become "open to criticism, honest criticism, so they can grow." Often these processes, in her view, offer important opportunities for teachers to be supportively stretched or challenged "to rethink," "broaden," and/or test ideas and assumptions. And when teachers engage in this type of reflection, they model it for their students. "That's what learning should be about," she explained. The benefits of such modeling were noted by many of the school leaders.

Practice 2: Reflection Through Dialogue

Because of the deeply ingrained nature of our behavioral patterns, it is sometimes difficult to develop a critical perspective on our own behavior. For that reason alone, analysis occurring in a collaborative and cooperative environment is likely to lead to greater learning.

—Osterman & Kottkamp, 1993, p. 25

The school leaders in my research saw engaging in dialogue, as well as encouraging and creating opportunities for adults to give and receive feedback—and embrace it as a learning opportunity—as a very important way to support adult learning and growth. Many school leaders also commented that it was not "an easy thing" for teachers to provide critical feedback to each other. That said, most of the school leaders continued to encourage these practices, and they implemented a variety of structures to support such dialogue. Some of the structures were generated and implemented by teachers themselves (e.g., study groups and research groups). Others were implemented by the principals and assistant principals:

- Grade-level or cross-grade meetings that were dedicated to engaging in inquiry about instructional practice and to examining student work
- Providing books to groups of teachers who were interested in applying theory to their instructional practices
- Making Learning Walks part of the fabric of the school
- Changing the focus of faculty meetings so that they were occasions for "meaningful conversations" about important reform or instructional issues

Below I discuss a few of these examples.

The Quality Review Report. As mentioned in Chapter 3, I work as a faculty advisor for small schools in the Bronx, New York, that are part of the National Academy for Excellence in Teaching (NAFET). Dr. Douglas Wood directs NAFET. Together, faculty advisors, coaches who visit schools, and the school teams themselves, which are composed of the school principal, assistant principal, and a few teachers, meet during the year to focus on improving literacy development, leadership, differentiated instruction, and supports for new teachers. These teams meet about monthly with NAFET faculty to engage in dialogue about different aspects of the quality review report, including their schools' self-assessments, feedback from the review, and how to address both the strengths and weaknesses of programs in their schools. They engage in collegial inquiry about how to strengthen areas that need further work and development, and they develop action plans that they, as a team and in conjunction with other leaders, will implement to develop and address schoolwide goals that will support student learning and enhanced achievement.

What follows is an example of how six teams from different schools employed dialogue to engage in reflection about their schools' self-assessment process, called the *quality review process*. I present this example because it brings together a host of rich themes that emerged from talking with other school leaders in my research. Please keep in mind that these teams participated in several workshops that I had delivered in which they were exposed to the same kinds of ideas (ways of knowing, pillar practices) that I'm sharing with you in this book. This particular three-hour session's focus was to invite members of these six teams to work together in their school teams to engage in dialogue about the following question: How might employing collegial inquiry assist you and others in your school to engage meaningfully in and benefit from the Quality Review process? This example describes how they used dialogue as way to support individual and organizational learning. At the start of the session, team members were invited to reflect privately in writing on the following questions, which I created for them.

1. What process will you use or have you used to complete the Quality Review School Self-Evaluation Form?

2. What worked well? What would you like to change?

3. How might you use collegial inquiry to improve this process?

After reflecting privately in writing journals, members of each team were invited to share whatever they felt comfortable sharing with the rest of the team. After a short discussion, the teams engaged in dialogue to create practical strategies and examples of how they could, given their school resources and limitations, use collegial inquiry and, in particular, invite other adults in their school communities to engage in dialogue to discuss student work and engage in comprehensive assessment. The teams also engaged in dialogue in relation to this question: What are some effective ways you can use collegial inquiry, and dialogue in particular, while engaging in the Quality Review process and developing effective ways to gather and make sense of additional data that can help with developing a comprehensive review of strengths and areas for improvement?

Teams from each school engaged in dialogue to address the above questions, as well as to reflect on concerns that emerged and to develop action plans. In addition, they engaged in dialogue about the following questions: How can you, as a team, structurally support collegial inquiry in your school? What is not in your Quality Review that you feel would be helpful to understand? What other data might help you in making a comprehensive assessment? How might you employ different forms of collegial inquiry to understand additional data? School teams worked together as they engaged in dialogue about these questions, and toward the end of the three-hour session, each team reported creative ideas, challenges, and main next steps.

Each team used dialogue as a tool for giving and receiving feedback. Several team members commented on how valuable it was for them to be exposed to fellow teammates' perspectives and the importance of the "trust" that had been established in their teams. For example, while discussing the forms of student work to be examined in their schools, team members often would ask each other questions that challenged some underlying assumptions about why one type of student work was used and not another.

Several school leaders, teachers, principals, and assistant principals commented on how important it was to "listen to each other without interrupting or judging" when engaging in this type of dialogue. A few told me that these conversations and colleagues' questions helped them to "better understand how I learn, what I think, and to ask myself why." As teams were developing their action plans, I heard several principals and teachers ask each other, "How do you want me to support you in this?"

They were engaged in what several leaders referred to as "meaningful conversation" to address questions that helped them think through their strengths, areas for improvement, and future action plans. I invited teams to look at cases of other schools' Quality Review Reports and to consider how their school's report could be informed by the case examples. Toward the end of the session, they engaged in dialogue about this question: How can you use collegial inquiry in your school in team/grade/subject meetings to engage in shared decision making about collecting additional data to inform your decisions about next steps? This question was adapted from the *Quality Review Self-Assessment* (Bloomberg, Klien, & Liebman, 2007). At the close of the meeting, teams engaged in dialogue in response to the following questions: (1) After engaging in today's session, what structures and supports can you encourage the teams in your school to use when engaging in collegial inquiry (CI)? (2) What additional forms of data do you and others in your school want to collect to create a more comprehensive assessment of your school?

Walk-throughs. Another very common practice that I've seen school principals and assistant principals use, both with individual teachers and teams, is "walk-throughs" or "Learning Walks." Two of the main purposes in conducting walk-throughs, many leaders explained, are (1) to support teacher learning and development by inviting adults to learn from and with each other and (2) to improve instructional practice. "Gathering evidence and engaging in dialogue about observations" with teachers enables everyone—teachers, principals, superintendents, and assistant principals—to learn from each other and to become more informed about how to improve instructional practice. Engaging in Learning Walks fosters learning from collaboration and builds schools that are "professional learning communities," as many explained, where adults engage in collegial inquiry on a daily basis and learn together.

The walk-through is also a practice that all of the New York City mentor-principals in my research since 2004 used to support learning and development in assistant principals who were aspiring to the principalship. All of these school leaders believed that walk-throughs were vital opportunities to engage in dialogue about instructional and leadership practice as a way to support "genuine and meaningful adult development," as one mentor-principal put it. Betty Gonzalez-Soto, principal of CS 211, explained their value:

Walk-throughs provide a snapshot of the instruction and learning that takes place in a school. Natural outcomes of this practice are reflection and dialogue. A "win-win" situation emerges. The learning community grows in awareness through discussion. Ideas develop and springboard into plans that support the delivery of instruction.

During walk-throughs, these mentor-principals explained, the central idea is to "engage in dialogue about instructional practice" in what several of them referred to as "a nonjudgmental" and supportive way to improve practice. The focus is on "learning." For the mentor-principals, walk-throughs were a way to engage in dialogue and collect data about instructional success and areas for growth; they were also a way to support the assistant principals' growth and learning, as well as their leadership development. When conducting and modeling walk-throughs, the mentor-principals let me know that they followed guidelines from *Principles of Learning* (Center for Professional Development, Saint Paul Public Schools, 2006; www.thecenter.spps.org/pol.html).

The mentor-principals, as a group, explained to me that engaging in regular, ongoing walk-throughs with the assistant principals provided important opportunities "to model how to engage in dialogue," reflect on instructional goals, and establish explicit expectations for supporting "improved teaching and learning." Some also found it helpful to invite an instructional expert to join them in classroom observations.

The dialogue that ensued between mentor-principals and assistant principals included how to "identify and celebrate best practices in instructional leadership in the classroom"; how to engage in dialogue about what was observed and, specifically, the pros and cons of any instructional strategy; how to discuss and assess data related to successful and unsuccessful instructional practices; and how to offer appropriate and "nonjudgmental feedback." One of the most important ways these principals said they supported adult learning while modeling walk-throughs was by offering questions as a starting point for engaging in dialogue and reflecting on practice. Questions often focused on how leadership might support teachers in their quest to improve instructional practice.

When I asked the mentor-principals why they thought these walk-throughs supported the assistant principals' learning and development, several themes emerged. From the mentor-principals' perspectives, what made them work was that they could engage in "having real conversations" and "careful listening." They also voiced that it was very important "to be precise and *concise* because of the pressure of time" when modeling walk-throughs and when conducting them in general. When I asked them how they figured out how to support the assistant principals' growth, learning, and leadership development, they were unified in their response. As one mentor-principal put it, "The assistant principals were open and honest about their needs for learning and growing, and so I customized my support to meet *their needs*." One other central theme emerged that resonated with all of the mentor-principals; as one voiced it, "Establishing trust was key. It allowed us to make a connection. A willingness to listen was also very important to establishing a safe relationship" for engaging in meaningful dialogue toward learning.

The assistant principals told me that one of the "very important" aspects of being able to engage in honest dialogue with the mentor-principals and to ask them for help in supporting learning was "confidentiality." The majority of them agreed that they deeply appreciated the "collegial support" from the mentor-principals and said that their dialogue was helpful in terms of "learning how to get the job done well without being obsessed with perfection."

To illuminate the value of walk-throughs as a tool for learning by engaging in collegial inquiry, I present one principal's experiences. Principal John Quattrocchi, who leads The School By-The-Sea, a public middle school—PS 43—in Far Rockaway, New York, was a firm believer in the importance of employing walk-throughs as a tool for learning with the assistant principals he mentored and with teachers in his school.

Walk-throughs, from John's perspective, had shifted in their orientation. Originally, they were occasions that signaled an evaluation from Central Office staff. As John explained,

> Walk-throughs, the sound of that dreaded word, especially to newly assigned principals, usually meant that someone was entering the building from Central Office to create a "list of improvements" that needed to be made. Walk-throughs became a euphemism for "let's see what's wrong."

However, John emphasized that he quickly learned that "while, yes, a walk-through can indeed be used as a monitoring tool for superintendents/principals and for principals/teachers, instead it is best used as a learning tool." He further commented that he felt this kind of learning tool supports adult learning across the system. As he explained, "And, yes, superintendents can learn from principals, and, yes, principals can learn from teachers and, YES YES—teachers can learn from one another!!"

As John explained, Learning Walks can be used as a "tool of discovery." As he put it,

> It is imperative that we use the Learning Walk as a tool of discovery—to discover the best practices that exist in the classroom next-door or on the floor above, for it might be one of those practices that will help that kid who just isn't getting it.

For Learning Walks to be most effective, however, they must be implemented in a way that supports adults in learning from each other. Like many other principals, John believed that Learning Walks are most powerful when dialogue and inquiry are "focused."

> [Dialogues] can be focused on how a particular skill in a particular content area is taught, or perhaps they might be focused on a particular pedagogical or classroom management strategy, or perhaps they might be conducted as part of a particular child study; for example, what might work with a particular child?

John, while acknowledging the importance of monitoring progress and holding all accountable for student learning, continued by advocating strongly for employing Learning Walks as a tool that supports collegial inquiry through collegial learning. In his words,

> So while, of course, there is a need for all involved to be monitored and accountable, let's use the Learning Walk to discover what's right and what's worth replicating—colleague to colleague. Let's leave the supervisor/subordinate discussion, as pertaining to walk-throughs, for another day.

Work in Small Groups. The principals in my 2004 research and school leaders in my more recent research emphasized the ways in which dialogue in smaller group meetings, often (but not always) contexts initiated by teachers themselves, serve as an important support for adult learning. The majority explained that in study groups, research groups, support groups, book groups, and critical friends groups—as well as in grade-level and department meetings—teachers engaged in dialogue that was essential to reflective practice as they worked to improve instructional practice and/or develop or assess curricula.

During these smaller group meetings, most school leaders shared that their teachers engaged in dialogue that enabled them to reflect on their instructional practice (purposefulness). Such dialogue helped them to become more aware of what things were working well for them *and for others* in their classrooms, as well as the challenges and obstacles they and others needed help managing or overcoming (awareness or mindfulness). Most of these school leaders remarked that this kind of dialogue was—as Dr. Jim Scott of the Punahou School in Honolulu, Hawaii, put it—"invigorating for teachers and the school."

Principal Deborah O'Neil of St. Peter's Catholic School in Cambridge, Massachusetts, (a Catholic, low-resource, preK–8 school) told me that a variety of study groups existed at her school. Some of these emerged organically from the teachers, and others she asked adults to join. There was, for example, what she called a "study group" that engaged in dialogue to question various areas of the school's curricula and programs. This group included Deborah and several of her teachers, as well as teachers and principals from neighboring Catholic schools. Another "study group" at her school was composed of teachers who met often to engage in dialogue and reflection about children who were having difficulty and were getting help from the school's special education teacher. Deborah believed that these group meetings fostered important professional learning because they gave teachers the opportunity to exercise their "professional judgment and to engage in dialogue with colleagues about that judgment."

Many of the school leaders in my research confirmed that teachers often form their own study or research groups. For example, at the Trotter School in Boston, the teachers themselves generated study and research groups in which they engaged in dialogue about instructional practice. As the principal, Joe Shea, explained,

> I would literally walk into classrooms and [be] watching or evaluating and look in the back, and there'd be a camera . . . running. And I'd say [to myself], "What is this? Why is that camera there?" I wouldn't say anything until after the day, and then I'd go to the teacher and say, "Why was that camera in there?" [The teacher] would reply, "Oh, I'm . . . taping myself, because I'm bringing it to the study group and we're going to critique [my lesson]."

Joe proudly let me know that "65 percent of the teachers ended up belonging to one or the other of the teacher study groups." Through dialogue and reflecting on their practice, teachers were able to reconsider aspects of their teaching, focusing on what worked well and what didn't work. While a core group of teachers started these groups at his school, they were successful in attracting many other teachers, who grew interested in this kind of dialogue about instructional practice. (Another type of group that is often initiated by teachers is the book group, discussed below in the section "Practices Used by Teachers With Other Teachers.")

Like other school leaders, Joe reported that in grade-level meetings, which occurred for 90 minutes twice a month, teachers engaged in dialogue and reflection on practice by collaboratively developing rubrics for assessment, planning classes, as well as reflecting on their ideas about scoring and discussing student work. They were engaged in important dialogue and "problem solving," as Joe remarked. With meeting time extended from 45 minutes to 90 minutes, Joe observed that

> they can do things like look at student work, score student work together, talk about what happens. Okay, now we know we've got a group of kids that are scoring in level two, what do we need to do to get them to three? [How can we] develop a rubric that will help our kids do it? Do you want to take the state's rubric? I mean, how do you want to go from here?

Another fairly common forum for engaging in dialogue and reflection about practice that several school leaders named was support groups for teachers, especially new teachers. For example, Principal Kathleen Perry of Lake Worth Community High School in Lake Worth, Florida, told me about the dialogue and reflection that occurred in support groups for new teachers at her school. In these groups, new teachers (*new* meaning new to her school but not necessarily new to teaching) engaged in dialogue with fellow new teachers within a particular discipline, usually a department chair, another more experienced teacher from another discipline, one of the school administrators, and the technology coordinator. Teachers in these support groups engaged in dialogue about their expectations and the things that were working or not working in their classes (awareness or mindfulness) and, in so doing, developed a sense of their shared experiences. Questions about their instructional practice and their experience guided the dialogue. Kathleen explained that they worked to address all questions: "The only question that's a silly question is the one that's not asked." She emphasized, "The idea is to provide them with a support group through that first year. And especially for our beginning teachers, we think it's extremely important."

In addition to securing time in the schedule for teachers and other adults to engage in dialogue, another important strategy that many school leaders used to support teachers' engagement in dialogue was providing books to groups or to all teachers in the school. School leaders across all types of schools of all resource levels in my 2004 and more recent research focused on this practice. The majority believed that this practice supports teacher learning.

In many schools, I was told that teachers used the books as subjects of their dialogue and reflection in their study group conversations. At other schools, teachers shared this kind of resource. For example, Jack Thompson, while serving as head of Palm Beach Day School, Palm Beach, Florida, explained that at his school, they often purchased 25–30 copies of a book so that the 40 teachers had to share copies with each other. That seemed "to generate conversation about the book that it wouldn't otherwise," and Jack felt that this kind of dialogue supported adult learning in very important and often informal ways. In addition, at the beginning of the year, teachers were grouped with six to seven other teachers across disciplines to engage in dialogue and reflection about the same book that had been assigned for faculty reading over the summer. In these and other forums for dialogue and reflection, Jack encouraged teachers to consider and try new ideas in their teaching, even if they did not like the changes that resulted: "Just the consideration of an idea and the reasonable rejection thereof is personal development."

Curriculum Development. Dr. Dan White, head of Seabury Hall School, Makawao, Hawaii, explained that teachers engaged in dialogue, which enabled them to reflect on their practice (purposefulness), as they worked collaboratively to develop curricula at his school. In examining their practice and curricula through dialogue, teachers generated and shared the new knowledge they gained with each other and linked it to current and future practices (mindfulness), especially with respect to considering how to employ technology to enhance curricula and pedagogy. In general, Dan emphasized this dialogic approach to learning with and from peers because he felt "there is often this inattentiveness to what's at home. . . . You tend to have to go off-campus to get knowledge. Oh, gosh, there's a lot of it around you." Dan believed in the importance of inviting teachers to "share with each other their knowledge" and felt that this "kind of conversation about curriculum, with your peers, *within the school* [is critical], [and] it's important to acknowledge that's of value." The teachers engaged in dialogue and shared decision making to eliminate a course called Judeo-Christian Heritage and create a new course called Sacred Traditions of the West. The faculty regularly engaged in dialogue as a team to create this course, which was to be team taught.

Faculty Meetings. Another way in which many of the principals and assistant principals in my research encouraged reflective practice through dialogue was by altering the focus of faculty meetings from practicalities and procedures to shared inquiry and dialogue about larger, more important issues. Some of the principals and assistant principals reported that they tried to use faculty meetings as a time to engage in dialogue about accountability issues, assessment, school self-evaluation reports or Quality Review, alignment between school mission and instructional practices, development of a shared mission, and/or ideas for change and implementation of new programs. This opportunity for dialogue helped all in their communities to learn from diverse perspectives they shared.

In fact, close to one-third of the principals in my 2004 research and most of the school leaders in my research since then reported that they were working diligently to find other avenues (e.g., memos, e-mail, newsletters) for communicating information that traditionally had been the focus of faculty meetings so that more meeting time could be invested in discussing substantive issues. Faculty meetings in many of these schools, the leaders explained, had become important opportunities for teachers and principals to dialogue about issues such as creating mission statements, performing evaluation, improving the advisory period, and changing the physical plant, for example.

At Principal Annette Kunin's public "neighborhood" elementary school in New York City, with more than 350 ethnically and racially diverse students, the entire faculty worked together to engage in dialogue and reflection, mostly during faculty meeting time, to refine their school's "mission statement" and develop a "road map for success" for improving the implementation of "academic and enrichment programs." Annette felt that this was a "first step" before the faculty could together assess how they were implementing "academic and enrichment programs during the school day that [led] to sustained student growth in English Language Arts and Math."

As a community, the school selected three programs (Enrichment Clusters, Exemplars, and Community Service). Annette explained that during the 07–08 academic year, they engaged in dialogue to reflect on, examine, and critique current programs and their implementations. At the year's end, Annette proudly shared that, as a result of dialogue, inquiry, research, and reflection, there was "increased collaboration between teachers," a sense of "shared vision," and an increased "sense of renewal, purpose, and professionalism," among other things. The teachers saw themselves as both "learners and facilitators" in this process of inquiry and improvement, which was grounded in dialogue and reflection.

Principal Deborah O'Neil of St. Peter's School in Cambridge, Massachusetts, felt that it was important for faculty meetings to focus on issues that related to what teachers were doing in their classrooms so that other teachers had opportunities to hear about each other's practice. She believed that this type of reflective "dialogue" supported everyone's learning. As she recalled,

> When I came here, I felt that it was important in faculty meetings for us to discuss not just . . . what's the traffic pattern in the driveway and those kinds of things but to really be talking about what are we doing in our classrooms, because I have an opportunity as I go around to see all of the wonderful things that are happening [in classrooms]. But unless we have a forum for discussing it, then it's so difficult for a teacher to see another teacher's practice. It's difficult for a teacher to appreciate what's going on next door.

She explained that dialogue and reflection about instructional practice had become the cornerstone of faculty meetings.

Similarly, faculty meetings at Dr. Jim Scott's Punahou School in Honolulu, Hawaii, were forums for engaging in dialogue and reflection about important aspects of the school and its constituents. For example, Jim explained that as a school community, they engaged in dialogue and serious reflection as they examined issues such as student and faculty evaluation, ways to improve the high school advisory period, and changes to the physical plant. He felt evaluation was a necessary component of school life. He "welcomed" and encouraged dialogue around this and other important issues and felt that engaging in dialogue as a school community included a constant process of rethinking, comparing results to expectations, and reconsidering what has been taken for granted. In his words, his faculty were "always looking for ways to improve" and engaging in dialogue with each other during faculty meetings, which served as one of many forums for this practice.

Conflict Resolution. A few of the principals in my research said that they themselves use dialogue to resolve conflict and understand it better, and they "encourage" teachers to do the same. Several of them made a point of sharing that conflict sometimes emerges between factions of faculty who are "either for or against" a particular change initiative. Some school leaders commented that conflict can build awareness and lead to better solutions or proposals for change and that they work to communicate this message to other adults within the school.

For example, Jim Scott offered that his school was "interested as a community as to how people know that a change is important to do." As a leader, he felt that "disagreement can be done in an atmosphere of collegiality," and as he commented further, "That's still hard." Yet he believed that cultures can be "strong enough and good enough to resolve . . . differences and move on." This can happen by engaging in dialogue. He referenced Sara Lawrence Lightfoot's (1985) book, *The Good High School*, and confirmed his agreement with Lawrence Lightfoot's idea that "what makes a . . . school good" is how the adults in the school community disagree.

Practice 3: Reflection Through Decision Making

School leaders in my research employed collegial inquiry to engage in inquiry and shared decision making at their schools through having honest conversations about *how to* engage in decision-making processes and through making shared decisions (e.g., about schoolwide goals, dilemmas and challenges, and alignment of mission and practice). These leaders felt that engaging in the processes of shared inquiry and decision making builds individual and school capacity.

For example, Sr. Barbara Rogers, head of Convent of the Sacred Heart School in Newton, Massachusetts, discussed the importance of ensuring that the teachers in her school had a clear sense of the educational mission and that they made shared decisions based on the priorities of that mission. Everyone, she asserted, must "feel ownership" of the school's foundational principles. This, in her view, supported both individual and organizational capacity building. In addition, Sister Rogers emphasized that engaging in shared decision making and reflection supported her own growth:

> I appreciate the opportunity to talk about [the mission] because it makes me think about it and articulate it. . . . I think institutionally we [as a community] really try to do that all the time. Why am I deciding that? What's the principle [from the school's mission] on which I'm operating?

In her school, community members engaged in private writing before engaging in shared decision making. For example, teachers were regularly invited to reflect in writing about how their teaching embodied or related to the mission and to make decisions based on this relationship. Sr. Rogers explained that she intentionally invited teachers to write and talk about "what their own challenges are" in connecting practice to the mission, since she believed this supports individual and collective learning, as well as more informed shared decisions. "We all love the opportunity to talk about what's most important to us. . . . What's most important for faculty is they feel attended to so that they can attend fully to the children." Such contexts support adult learning.

Some school leaders employed collegial inquiry to engage in decisions related to assessing different programs and their effectiveness. For example, at the Punahou High

School in Hawaii, Dr. Jim Scott and his school community employed collegial inquiry to engage in shared decision making about how to assess and improve their school's professional development program; the goal was for it to include more opportunities for teachers to engage in reflection. The school as a community decided how to evaluate their program, not "just for quality control" but to build into it more opportunities for reflection and "frequent and consistent and thoughtful feedback."

Reflecting on practice to engage in shared decision making was part of the fabric of many school cultures, these leaders explained. For instance, at the Mather Elementary School in Dorchester, Massachusetts, Kim Marshall explained that while he was serving as principal, one of the larger projects at his school that involved teachers engaging in collegial inquiry to make shared decisions was the Early Literacy and Learning Initiative (ELLI) program.

Teachers, according to Kim, engaged in collegial inquiry to make decisions about rubrics they created and how to assess them. One of the qualities that Kim liked about this program was that it "left lots of professional decisions up to the teachers as they went along," and it supported teacher reflection and assessment of their practices. As the principal, Kim felt that he needed to create conditions that would "make it possible for that to happen" by providing the time and space for teachers to engage in collegial inquiry. Kim discussed how the school—as a whole—took on the problem of improving practice as a "school problem." Members of the school community (teachers and Kim) engaged in various inquiry initiatives to think and make decisions together about how to improve. He described how together they reflected on and engaged in dialogue to improve curricula and practice.

Practice 4: Reflection Through Helping and Advising Others

In my recent research, most of the school leaders reported that encouraging and, in some cases, financially supporting teachers to attend and/or deliver workshops are important opportunities for teachers to engage in collegial inquiry. Also, teachers then share their thinking and reflections with the school community, which can consider new learnings and ideas. In addition, while less common in my recent research, in-house and out-of-school sabbaticals (during which teachers conducted research and then shared learnings with their school communities) were named as important by close to one-third of the principals in my 2004 research.

In many cases, these leaders explained that teachers, either individually or as a team, conducted research by investigating programs or models of practice in other schools (e.g., advisory programs, literacy program models) and then lead an inquiry process at their own schools about how best to adapt or adopt models for their particular context. In addition to conducting research, the teacher or teacher team was regarded as expert in sharing new information and, in most of these schools, served as a "resource"—or consultant—to others once they have decided how to adjust and implement the new program or model.

For instance, at the Punahou School, Dr. Jim Scott explained that teams of teachers engaged in collegial inquiry as they visited and studied other middle schools to learn more about the conditions under which middle school students learn best. After analyzing learnings from their research, these teams of teachers served as experts within their school. Jim placed a lot of emphasis on research and engaging in inquiry and reflection since he believed that these practices are essential for building and sustaining healthy school climates. He saw a part of learning as "continuously questioning the status quo" and tried to spur that kind of questioning and inquiry by modeling and supporting faculty research and by creating conditions for engaging in reflection, sharing expertise, and serving as consultants.

In my recent research, the majority of school leaders explained that, in their schools, several teachers, department chairs, and other adults served on inquiry teams, which conduct research to understand better the student achievement data from the lower one-third of their classes. These teams engaged in collegial inquiry as they conducted research, examined data, and developed intervention strategies, which were then shared with others in the school community. Members of the inquiry team then served as internal experts and consultants to other teachers within the school.

Most of the school leaders named as important creating the conditions for teachers to share expertise, conduct research, and serve as consultants to other adults within and beyond the school. From their perspective, these practices lead to adult learning because, as principal Kathleen Perry of Lake Worth Community High School in Florida put it, it "encourages the sharing of ideas."

Practices Used by Principals With Fellow Principals

Having space and carving out the time to engage in dialogue and reflection with fellow principals this year was, for me, like taking a bubble bath.

—Principal Mary McDermott, New York City

In this section, I will share one example from my recent research of principals engaging in collegial inquiry with fellow principals. As I mentioned in reviewing the recent professional development literature, as a field, we have become more aware of the pressing need for securing spaces for principals to engage in collegial inquiry with fellow principals. New York City principal Mary McDermott's words in the opening passage capture perfectly the sentiment that many principals in my research have expressed. While engaging in collegial inquiry on a regular basis with fellow principals is critically important, it often feels like a luxury.

A particularly powerful theme in my 2004 research was principals' expressed need for ongoing communities wherein they can engage in dialogue with fellow principals and reflect on their leadership practice. When I asked each of them individually how they re-new themselves, all but one spontaneously discussed a craving to "regularly reflect with colleagues." Engaging in ongoing collegial inquiry with peers, they emphasized, would enable them to support their "*own* development" as effective leaders, while also supporting the development of others. Only three of these principals, however, were benefiting from reflective practice communities in which they engaged in collegial inquiry.

Nearly all of the principals in my recent research, whether participating in regular collegial inquiry groups with fellow principals or not, emphasized that engaging in ongoing collegial inquiry and reflection would help them more effectively exercise leadership, feel less isolated in their work, avoid burnout, and care for themselves as leaders. My research suggests the importance of prioritizing contexts wherein principals can engage in regular collegial inquiry with fellow principals. This, I have learned, enables principals to learn from each other, to grow, to feel better supported, and to exercise leadership more effectively.

Principals say that engaging in collegial inquiry with colleagues helps them learn how to manage better the multiple and often overwhelming demands of their work and engage in self-assessment and self-improvement. Below I share one powerful example of how engaging in collegial inquiry with fellow principals supported learning, leadership, and development and helped to sustain principals in their important work.

As I mentioned in Chapter 4, I have been learning with and from a group of nearly 50 experienced urban principals from across the nation who serve as facilitators of monthly conversations with less experienced principals to support the learning and development of the newer principals. During these monthly meetings, the group engages in collegial inquiry as they share their leadership challenges and dilemmas and learn from each other. These principals are members of the National School Leaders Network (NSLN), founded and lead by Dr. Elizabeth Neale. In addition to facilitating monthly three-hour "conversations," as NSLN refers to them, the experienced principals (who serve as "facilitators" of collegial inquiry among stable groups of 10 to 12 newer principals, called "networks") meet three times a year for two- or three-day retreats to engage in collegial inquiry, learn from each other, and strengthen their own expertise as facilitators by discussing the successes, challenges, and obstacles of facilitation and their work to promote the adult learning and leadership of newer principals.

One main purpose of both the monthly meetings and the facilitator retreats is to engage in collegial inquiry so principals work together to learn from individual leadership problems; to process experiences and leadership dilemmas together; and to share ideas for improving leadership, schools, and student achievement. NSLN believes that to enhance leadership, self-development is essential. This occurs through engaging in "conversation," or collegial inquiry, as I call it. The central focus of NSLN is to provide principals with such contexts wherein they can engage in collegial inquiry throughout the year to strengthen their leadership and learn from colleagues. According to the recent *NSLN Network Evaluation Report* (Intrator & Scribner, 2008), close to 95 percent of the NSLN principals explained that their participation both improved their leadership and positively influenced their work within schools to support teacher development.

At a recent retreat for the more than 50 principal-facilitators, participants engaged in collegial inquiry to share and discuss the successes, challenges, and obstacles they encountered during the past academic year as they worked to support the growth and development of the new principals in their individual networks. Following is a list of some of the more common successes they named:

- Monthly conversations helped to build "camaraderie," "courage," and "trust"—all of which are needed to share leadership experiences and to learn from each other.
- "It doesn't matter where we are [what type of school, where the school is located, what grade levels]; as a group we realized we all share common leadership dilemmas and problems."

- "This was the best professional development I've ever had as a principal; we discussed real problems, real issues, and real leadership dilemmas."
- "Our conversations went deeper over time, and this facilitated our learning."
- "Engaging in honest conversations and learning from each other had a real impact on our schools."
- The conversations helped all of us "to explore challenges" that are normally kept private (for example, "What happens when a principal says, 'I don't know'? How do teachers perceive that?")

Nearly all agreed that securing the space and time to engage in collegial inquiry with fellow principals was an important way to support not only their own growth and development but also the development of their schools.

A few of the more common challenges the facilitator-principals named included the difficulty of "reaching everyone in the group" if the size of the group exceeded ten members, varying attendance due to weather conditions and sometimes difficult scheduling "due to overlapping commitments."

Overall, though, there was unanimous agreement among the principal-facilitators and members of their networks that their dialogue and collegial inquiry supported adult learning and leadership development. Thinking together about how to "improve leadership," how to solve leadership dilemmas, and how to "better support teachers" within their schools helped them to work more effectively in their schools and to become "better leader[s]." Engaging in collegial inquiry with colleagues enabled them to "clarify our thinking, expand on it, and build on each other's experiences and ideas," as one principal-facilitator put it. The principals nodded in agreement when one principal-facilitator offered what seemed to capture the experience of learning and growing from engaging in collegial inquiry with fellow principals: "The conversations help me to dig deeper . . . to look inward and to examine my own behaviors as a leader so that I can grow as a leader." At the very end of the retreat, another principal remarked, "I realize that every one of us [principals] is fighting a battle" and through "honest conversation we can learn from each other and support each other's growth."

Practices Used by Teachers With Other Teachers

I can feel myself growing inside, developing a bigger perspective, and thinking differently about my practice because I engage in collegial inquiry with my colleagues [fellow teachers]. I wish everyone could have this kind of experience.

—High school teacher-leader

I am grateful for all that I have learned from teachers as well as other school leaders. Below I share a few of the more common ways in which they have employed collegial inquiry with their teacher colleagues to support their own and their colleagues' learning and development.

Practice 1: Initiating Book Clubs

One of the more common ways in which teachers have employed the practice of collegial inquiry to facilitate their own and their colleagues' learning is to invite fellow teachers to participate in book clubs. The clubs usually meet monthly and focus on engaging in collegial inquiry and critical collective discussion about how material from different books informs or connects to instructional practices and how it might influence future instructional decisions. In some cases, teachers use educational texts; in others, they invite colleagues to select novels about adolescent issues (fiction and nonfiction) as a catalyst for engaging in discussion about educational practice. In addition, some of the teacher-leaders use these forums to make collective decisions about whether or not to include books in their department's curriculum.

Several teacher-leaders explained that they provided journals to members of their book clubs so that individuals could track their thinking as they read independently and record insights, questions for further discussion, and ideas that emerged from the collegial inquiry that took place during book club conversations. A few teacher-leaders who started book clubs in their schools let me know that they encouraged teachers in their groups to use their journals as a space to reflect on the discrepancies they were becoming aware of in their pedagogy.

As Rosemary Stiglic, a high school English teacher-leader from Canada who initiated a book club for teachers *and* administrators in her school, explained, "The book club was a space where teachers could talk about books but also talk about teaching reading, discuss instructional strategies, and explore the idea of the role of the learner in the reading process." The book club, in her view, created a space supportive of adult learning. She emphasized,

> What resonated with me through this experience was the power of collaborative and collective talk in examining our current practices, assumptions, and beliefs around issues of teaching and learning. Discussions about race, culturally relevant literature, and social justice issues were themes that emerged through our discussions.

Book clubs are one of the more popular ways in which teachers in my research secured a space and prioritized time for engaging in collegial inquiry as a way to learn from each other, improve practice, and make both collective and individual instructional decisions. As one teacher-leader emphasized, what she and other teachers wanted and needed were "opportunities to reflect on practice and effect change." Engaging in collegial inquiry in book clubs is a powerful way to do this.

Practice 2: Initiating Groups for Sharing Best Practices

Inviting colleagues to participate in groups wherein they share best practices is another common way in which teachers in my research have employed collegial inquiry to support their own and other adults' learning and improve instructional practice. Teachers have created structures for implementing this sharing in team meetings (cross-disciplinary and intradisciplinary) and in grade-level meetings. Most of the teachers who initiated this kind of collaboration explained that by carving out space and time to share best practices—as well as challenges they encounter in their instructional leadership (e.g., differentiating their instruction)—they were able to support their own and other adults' learning.

Many teachers told me that through an intentional discussion about best practices and the challenges of practice, which includes offering feedback and ideas to the presenter, they were purposefully inviting each teacher in the group to examine his or her own assumptions about practice, to help other colleagues examine theirs, and to learn and grow from engaging in collegial inquiry that is centered on instructional improvement. Many of the teachers emphasized the importance of establishing ground rules and shared understandings about how teachers in these groups would provide feedback to each other to support honest sharing, "risk taking," and development. In some groups, they created protocols for providing feedback. In addition, in several cases, teachers let me know that sometimes teachers modeled best practices or viewed videotapes from their own classrooms and then, as a group, engaged in collegial inquiry to learn from each other.

Practice 3: Initiating Groups on Grant and Proposal Writing

One other common way in which teachers have employed collegial inquiry with colleagues in their schools is to create groups in which teachers collaborate to write either grants to support research they would like to conduct in their classrooms or schools or proposals to present their work at conferences.

Almost all of these teachers told me that they felt such teacher collaborations created incentives for deeply reflecting on one's own practice and for learning from other people's practices. In their view, both grant and proposal writing were opportunities to support adult learning. Importantly, as many of them explained, this kind of collegial inquiry enabled them to care for *both* group and individual needs, interests, and hopes for instructional improvement.

CASE STUDY: ONE PRINCIPAL'S "RARE AND UNIQUE OPPORTUNITY" TO ENGAGE IN REFLECTIVE PRACTICE OVER TIME

Over the years, the principals in my research reported that having opportunities to engage in reflective practice with fellow principals would lessen their isolation, and almost all believed these reflective conversations would improve their leadership. In essence, just as it is true that when teachers engage in reflective practice, their practice improves and they feel renewed, so too is it true for principals. To demonstrate these lessons more deeply, I provide the detailed case of Dr. Sarah Levine's experience of engaging in reflective practice over time as she served as head-of-school at Belmont Day School in Massachusetts.[2] She said this practice allowed her to hear herself think and to grow, something she characterized as a "rare and unique opportunity."

In this case, I describe how Dr. Levine experienced reflective practice and how it opened up a space in which she could attend to and alter her thinking, reflect on her practices and assumptions, and ultimately grow. In Sarah's view, reflecting on practice helped her renewal and development as leader and human being while fostering the development of other adults.

An Evolving Vision of Leadership

During her first years as principal, Sarah's thinking about leadership to support adult learning—both her own and others'—changed in several ways, becoming more complex but also clearer. These changes inevitably affected the shape and substance of her leadership practice. From 1991 to 1995, Sarah's leadership in support of teachers' learning moved from "shared and inclusive leadership" to a more "collaborative" vision and style, then to a style that she characterized as "participatory." In this last phase, Sarah sought to apply her vision to the broader school community. These changes seemed to reflect her developing abilities to critique her vision and to change her leadership practices on behalf of that vision.

Sarah's mission was to "create a community of learners," a culture of collaboration, and a "shared language" essential to that collaboration. Creating such a culture occupied much of her time and energy, but after four-and-a-half years, Sarah believed that the ideas and cultural values her community collaboratively developed were taking hold.

Shared and Inclusive Leadership: Phase 1

In fall 1991, during our first conversation, Sarah described her thinking about her leadership in support of teacher learning as operating "on two levels—the way I would like it to be, and the way it actually is." She invited others to share ideas during work in teams and by delegating responsibility. In essence, she had created a cooperative leadership model. To introduce new ideas at faculty meetings and meetings of the Educational Team (i.e., the upper- and lower-school division directors and Sarah) and the Administrative Team (i.e., the director of admissions, business manager, director of development, and Sarah), she would "throw a lot of balls up in the air and see how people respond[ed] to them."

In her first years as head of school, Sarah strove to reinvigorate the faculty, reshape the culture of divided constituencies into a culture of collaboration, and build trust. Even though she considered herself a "high-energy" person, Sarah admitted that at times she felt "overwhelmed by the enormity of things" that came in her direction.

> Therefore, I don't always respond as well as I would like. I can also lose perspective because I get tired and because too many things come at me at once. I can be impatient. I can be overly demanding so that people don't have enough space to reach their own height. My standards for people's performance are extremely high, and sometimes it's hard for people to rise to them.

While working on a long-range planning committee (composed of faculty, trustees, and administrators) in 1991, Sarah's leadership style was "emerging" as she became more interested in learning from others' opinions while she led them. She cultivated her ability to consider others' opinions before making a decision or taking action, which helped her to "change course." Involving others in decision making also helped foster their ownership of projects. Through such activities, Sarah was "giving people actual opportunities to take a real [leadership] role and thereby experience what the complexities are."

She recognized that she was improving and growing from her mistakes as well as from her successes:

> I used to say that my leadership style was thriving on chaos. . . . And people were telling me that it got too busy and too chaotic, and so I tried to be a little bit more planful. But I still find that what I experience is that an idea gets begun and we begin working on it and it has ramifications that we didn't anticipate.

Having learned that her pace was often too fast for others and that it was sometimes difficult to envision the ramifications of specific changes, Sarah tried to "slow down" and be more "planful" to match the community's needs.

Leadership as Collaboration: Phase 2

> So [collaboration] doubles for [sharing], but I also think that the notion of inclusion can be problematic because it's very time consuming to try to be inclusive. So I'm not sure how wholeheartedly I embrace that.

In the spring of 1992, Sarah described her leadership as "collaborative" rather than "inclusive." Although she continued to be inclusive in her leadership and decision making, she found that sharing leadership was enormously time consuming. Because of the multiple daily tasks she faced and the confidentiality required by some situations, it was impossible to include everyone in her leadership at all times. However, she tried to ensure that community members felt they had input into the decisions that affected their lives at the school. Balancing inclusiveness with appropriate confidentiality required that Sarah judge what was best for the school. Her hope was that "at least in these decisions [which affect the daily lives of school community members], people feel that nobody's making a decision that directly affects them without any kind of leeway for their voice." Sarah's awareness of the complexity of such decisions, and her sensitivity to others' feelings of exclusion, rendered some decisions difficult, yet she knew they were necessary.

One important example of Sarah's collaborative leadership style during this period was when she collaborated with teachers, administrators, and staff during an inservice day throughout the self-study evaluation process. This example highlights the ways in which Sarah engaged in collaborative leadership to support the community's development. Raising the "consciousness" of the community was Sarah's aim. Her efforts to involve community members in reflective practice and collegial inquiry resulted in a collaborative and evolving list of goals for the school. Many of her goals did not make it to the final list.

Sarah's interest in greater collaboration and listening to the voices of the community played itself out in many ways. One change in Sarah's leadership practice, which she attributed to her engagement in reflective practice, entailed providing community members with leadership roles. Though Sarah invited community members into leadership roles with great frequency early in the research study, this practice changed in conjunction with her reflections on the practice. Because Sarah valued teachers' roles in leadership, she continued to offer them to faculty but with less frequency. Sarah's new thinking made her listen more keenly and communicate more frequently with a teacher before providing a leadership role to assess whether that person should take on that role at that time.

Sarah discussed her thinking and practice of providing leadership roles in interviews and conversations with me many times. For example, Sarah decided that when inviting the community to produce the school's self-study, it would be better to invite individual groups to determine if they would elect a leader or operate without a leader. In this example, Sarah was acting on her newer thinking about leadership roles, which reflected a change from her previous approach.

Sarah explained that engaging in reflective practice over time with another person (who in this case turned out to be me) to discuss the leadership practices she employed to support teacher learning provided her with a context to explore her own thinking and assumptions. In some cases, after a period of engaging in reflective practice (i.e., collegial inquiry), Sarah altered her practices. In other cases, it seemed that the context of reflection with another person helped Sarah to come to a new understanding of her own thinking and practices. Engaging in reflective practice with another person provided Sarah with an opportunity to elaborate on her thinking, evaluate her own assumptions, and share her articulated thinking with another person, she reported.

Participatory Leadership: Phase 3

The other thing I need to do as a leader is begin to be increasingly open to the interests and ideas of the faculty and staff, because I came in [to the school] with a lot of ideas about how the school should move and it really has moved in those ways.

Toward the end of the 1994 academic year, as a result of formal evaluations and informal conversations with faculty and staff, Sarah felt a need to change her leadership practices again. Sarah's interest in implementing theory in her practice was still paramount in her own leadership practices in support of adult development; however, she explained, "After [several] years, it's beginning to feel like I need a booster shot of ideas, and I'm going to be very interested to watch where that comes from." In preparation for making more "space" for the "voices of the faculty and staff," Sarah paid closer attention than ever to the directions in which the faculty and staff wanted to see the school move.

She read more widely and began to look to the faculty and community more often for ideas for improvement. The demands of preparing to run a capital campaign also gave her an opportunity to "make more space for the voices of the faculty and staff" in the daily operations of the school. At that point in her tenure as principal, she believed that strong values for "open, honest communication," a culture of trust and collaboration, an innovative curriculum, a strong work ethic, and standards for excellence were fairly well established and that it was time to focus on "listening differently" to the ideas of faculty and staff. By the summer of 1994, she had reflected on her feedback and sought to "move from a [focus on a] community of learners to a community of learners and leaders." However, she found that most faculty sought leadership roles that were limited to the classroom and interactions with other teachers and children. They wanted to be "teacher-leaders, *not* leaders who are teachers."

Sarah gave faculty and staff more time to reflect. By "not responding right away," she sought to give people more space to "develop their own styles." As a result, Sarah employed collegial inquiry more often. Sarah also made efforts to share her internal thinking with others in such a way that they felt part of a process.

As principal, she had a unique schoolwide perspective, whereas teachers, in particular, were "coming out of a near, narrow set of experiences from within their classrooms." Sarah sought to inculcate a more "global perspective" while empathizing with others' focused perspectives. To practice "participatory" leadership, she tried

> to get as many people involved in that vision as you can, so that they can respond, not only out of their own perspective, which is important, and you can respond, not only out of their own perspective, which is important, but that both of you can then put those perspectives aside and sit, for a moment, with a larger perspective.

Sarah believed that participatory leadership could decrease isolation, promote collaboration and pride, and create an environment supporting the development of both adults and children. "I know participation is linked to ownership, and ownership to effectiveness." Sarah wanted others in the community to feel "proud" of their own leadership.

By 1995, Sarah saw her leadership bridging "between theory and practice." The changes in her style reflected her changing understanding of the school's needs, as well as her own growth. As her notion of inclusiveness expanded, her practice of offering leadership roles evolved, as did the quality of her interactions with teachers and other community members.

Case Summary

As Sarah's thinking evolved, she developed new strategies to "promote growth through reflection and thinking" and to engage with conflict to bring about resolution through genuinely participatory collegial inquiry. During the final year of this ethnographic research, she spoke more often about the joy of supporting adult development. It seemed that community members had acclimated to Sarah's leadership practices and that Sarah was responding differently to community members' needs and interests. The sharing of both leadership and growth was becoming a reality.

As this case example illuminates, Sarah's thinking about her leadership in support of adult learning evolved while she reflected on her practice with a partner. As described, Sarah's thinking about how to support teacher learning and growth moved from a "shared and inclusive" vision to a "collaborative" and then to a "participatory" one. In Sarah's view, our collaborative research provided a space for her to reflect on her practices, which, she remarked, both "clarified and complicated" her thinking. Engaging in reflective practice with another person over time provided a holding environment for her growth, which she experienced as "safe." The questions asked seemed useful in facilitating reflection on her assumptions about her leadership practices. Reflecting in the company of a partner, Sarah explained, enabled her to "freely probe and examine" her own thinking and assumptions and to test new ideas.

Just as it is important to provide contexts for teachers to engage in collegial inquiry, so too is it important for principals. Reflecting on thinking and practice, as explained by the principals who benefited from it, like Sarah, and those who desired it, like so many principals in my current and 2004 research, can be a vital source of enhanced leadership, renewal, learning, and development. I have learned that Sarah's experience of engaging in collegial inquiry with one partner or several resonates with many other principals in contemporary educational systems.

CONVENINGS: PERSONAL CASE-BASED DISCUSSIONS THAT SUPPORT COLLEGIAL INQUIRY

> *One of the most valuable processes that I am experiencing during the convening is critical thinking. It occurs to me that the convening process is enabling me to practice looking at assumptions in a value-free sort of way—without judgment.*
>
> —Teacher-leader, spring 2005

Convenings are structured opportunities for adults to come together with colleagues and engage with a case to reflect on and learn from their own and other people's experiences. Each group member has the opportunity to write a case based on an experience from practice.

My teaching and research with teachers, principals, assistant principals, and aspiring superintendents have shown that inviting adults to participate in regular opportunities to discuss real-life, case-based experiences about teaching, learning, or leadership dilemmas supports adult growth and leadership development. Teachers, principals, assistant principals, and aspiring superintendents who participated in the practice of convening in my courses have reported that engaging in this practice enhanced their reflective capacities. Engaging in the practice of convening, they explained, helped them to build individual leadership development; many said that in turn, they felt more equipped to return to their schools and support the learning of other adults.

One of the reasons why these personal, case-based discussions support adult learning and development is that the person who shares his or her case benefits from listening to and learning from colleagues' perspectives, questions, and observations about assumptions that may have been unknowingly guiding the case writer's behavior during the event. Other group members learn from each other as well. Engaging in collegial inquiry about unresolved issues, dilemmas, and struggles of instructional and/or leadership practice can support adult learning and the development of enhanced leadership capacities.

What follows is a set of guidelines that I developed to help school leaders write personal cases. These are then shared with members of their group one week before the group engages in collegial inquiry. The goal of the collegial inquiry is to help the convener (i.e., case writer) learn from the case and the questions he or she poses and wants help thinking through. Group size usually ranges from 6 to 12. Groups are stable, and during a 15-week period, I invite adults in each group to sign up for one convening slot and one facilitator slot. Although in my classes I invite school leaders to write personal cases about a specific issue, experience, or moment of exercising leadership in support of another adult's development, or about a situation in which someone else was working to support their development, personal cases can also focus on other types of experiences. For example, cases can center on an instructional leadership dilemma, an experience with a difficult parent, an unresolved interpersonal conflict with a team member or supervisor, a challenging and unsettling teaching or leadership moment, a tough decision, or a challenge related to classroom management. Leaders in my classes have adjusted the focus and the length of the case to suit their school context. I invite you to do the same.

Convening

A convening is a particular kind of consultation process aimed at supporting adult learning and development. It occurs in a group and is a structured opportunity (i.e., with a protocol) to join with colleagues and engage with a case based on one's own experience or on that of another member of the group. It is helpful to remember that convenings (engaging others in your process, questions, and/or concerns about your case) are different from presentations (delivering polished talks to audiences). Convening a group around your case is your opportunity to benefit from the support and attention of a group of colleagues as they offer (a) their thoughts on your case (and your developing relationship to it) and (b) their help with the set of questions, concerns, and dilemmas that you raise about it.

The Goal of Convening

The goal of convening is to listen to and hear from group members about the case writer's (i.e., convener's) experience. This type of space for listening to alternative perspectives on and interpretations of events is designed to help the convener reconsider his or her thinking about and relationship to the events in the case. One learning outcome of the convening process is that the convener may be able to understand his or her experience from others' perspectives; another is that the convener may be able to see and understand the assumptions, which were guiding his or her actions, that were previously unknown to him or her.

When you are the convener, or case writer, the goal of your convening is to listen to group members' thinking about your case. This kind of hearing out may help you move one step further in your thinking about your case. Keep in mind that reflection on a case for purposes of learning is *not* about finding a definitive solution or coming up with many alternative courses of action. Reflection on leadership practice creates opportunities to develop your thinking and progress in your understanding. It allows you to explore and test the validity of ideas, assumptions, and governing values that drive others and us. Your case is a vehicle to get at all of that, allowing you to go from those particulars to the more general.

How Convening Supports Adult Learning

Engagement in collegial inquiry—which is the foundation of the convening process— is a powerful way to support adult learning. The group and the convening process itself serve as a holding environment for adult learning and growth. You might be wondering, how does this work?

Convening group members read each convener's case and offer written comments in response to questions posed by the case writer *before* they engage in collegial inquiry. All group members bring their written comments to the meeting where the case is discussed. Convening, or case discussion (discussed below in detail), is an opportunity for group members to offer developmental supports and challenges that will help the case writer— and all participating in the convening—grow.

During a convening, for example, group members might point to evidence in the case where they saw inconsistencies in behaviors or values described by the case writer (his or her own or other people's). This can help the convener to see events, behaviors, or experiences from different and often new perspectives, which may lead to their development of new understandings of situations and of themselves. Group members often also offer ideas and questions that can help the convener to become aware of and examine assumptions and beliefs that may have been implicitly or explicitly influencing his or her thinking and actions. By posing questions, highlighting assumptions, and offering alternative perspectives on events and behaviors, the convening process helps adults to develop new ways of thinking, to examine assumptions that often unconsciously guide thoughts and actions, and to consider alternative perspectives and new ways of acting.

Guidelines for Creating a Case

In my work with school leaders, they create a convening packet and share it with group members one week before their convening. What follows are guidelines I have developed for building a case. These can be adapted to your particular context.

To facilitate your learning during convening, it's best if your packet includes (1) a memo or cover letter to your group, (2) your case, and (3) questions you would like the group to consider. The memo or letter from you to your colleagues will orient the group to your case. You explain why your case is important to you and what you would like the group to think about in relation to the case (i.e., the dilemma, interest, burning questions, troubling situation, and/or problem that the case addresses). The memo can include important background that is needed for group members to understand the context for your case. Your case should be written as a narrative.

Questions for the group to consider should be included at the end of your case. Your questions will help to orient the group to the particular area of your case in which you would like help/consultation. In my classes, I ask that convening packets not exceed ten pages. However, some school leaders who have adopted this process have adjusted the page limit to five.

Clarifying Purpose

Case writing is like sharing an important story that matters a lot to you. When writing a case (one in which you were directly involved), it is essential to write in the first person. You will want to describe what happened and what you observed (about yourself and others). It is helpful to discuss what you were thinking and feeling at the time of the event described (i.e., "I felt that . . ." or, At that time, I believed . . .").

Focusing your case on a particular, distinct (singular), critical experience or very brief series of experiences/events, rather than trying to cover a period of months or a year, works best. Cases from which we learn the most are based on experiences that feel unresolved, troubling, or unsettling.

Also, please select a case that occurred in the past so that you have some distance from it. However, choosing a case that remains important to you and that is still ripe for room for learning and growing might keep you from going *too* far into the past. Selecting a personally important case might also make the narrative a little messy (e.g., gaps, inconsistencies, etc.). This is fine; if you knew exactly how to explain it, you probably would not have fundamental questions and concerns about it. What is most important in choosing a case experience is that it is personally meaningful, significant, and/or challenging to you. In other words, it is a situation where you feel and think room exists for personal growth.

General Criteria for Case Development

I've developed a few criteria to help adults consider experiences that could serve as potential cases. They are listed in Figure 5.1. You may want to ask adults in your school or district to write shorter cases, given time constraints. A case should be a description—not an analysis or interpretation—of the situation. In the case writer's convening, colleagues will consult to him or her about the case. At the close of the convening, after listening carefully to colleagues, the convener has an opportunity to reflect on his or her experience and learning.

Figure 5.1   Guidelines for Selecting and Structuring a Case

(a) Select an experience that was significant to you and that contains one or more issues that are of continued personal and/or professional importance to you as leader-learner and feel unresolved.

(b) A case that contains meaningful questions, dilemmas, puzzles, or challenges will provide a rich context for your own and your group's learning. Obstacles, conflicts, or dilemmas often make a case interesting and challenging. Some examples of juicy dilemmas and growth opportunities include, but are not limited to, the following:

- Negotiating role or boundary issues (e.g., with supervisors, parents, colleagues)
- Undertaking the initial stages of a challenging change initiative or project
- Working with sensitive or otherwise difficult issues
- Responding to upset or disappointed members of your school, cabinet, district, or team
- Managing a complex task (e.g., evaluation) in support of another person's development
- Attending to issues of diversity in an effort to support learning and development
- Working through sets of loyalties while attending to supporting other people's learning or in an effort to support your own learning and/or development
- Making a tough decision
- Experiencing major conflicts or feeling torn about what to do next
- Experiencing an event that caused you to examine your own governing values and/or assumptions about how best to support someone's learning
- Engaging (or being engaged) in a process or practice that was oriented toward helping other people (or you) learn
- Participating in a critical meeting

Please select an experience that is restricted and manageable so that it (the case itself) can be described in five to seven double-spaced pages.

Organizing the Case

1. *Set up the context.* Provide contextual information that you think will help readers understand the important features of the situation and your role in it. For example, you may want to consider questions such as these: Who was involved? What pertinent contextual information will help the group understand this case? What was your role in the situation or problem?

2. *Describe the event or experience.* For example, if an important meeting occurred, describe what people actually said (if possible) and did. I think you will find it helpful to describe what you thought and felt at the time of the event. The following questions might help: What alternatives did you consider to help you (or others) in

this situation? What actions did you take? What were your hopes and/or objectives? What happened as a result of your actions?

3. *Ask questions at the end of the case.* A case needs to end with a small set of questions to guide the discussion of group members; for example, What were my blind spots? Because as the case writer you will be listening (rather than speaking or responding) during the convening, these questions will help your group know how to help you. Usually, fewer questions are better (two to three). Questions enable the case writer to focus the discussion on his or her particular growth interests, requests for help, and/or needs. Make sure that (a) the areas or issues with which you are most concerned are clear and explicit in your questions and that (b) the narrative provides your group with what they need (e.g., background information, context, knowledge) to discuss your questions meaningfully. Doing so is essential to ensuring that you get as much out of your convening as possible. If you are concerned about protecting the confidentiality of people described in your case and/or the organization, it is helpful to write "confidential" on the first page of your cover memo to the group.

Establishing Ground Rules

During the first meeting and before the first case is discussed, group members will find it helpful to discuss what constitutes a safe, productive, and supportive learning environment for each person; to agree upon group norms; and to come to a shared agreement regarding confidentiality. Discussing these essential characteristics of group work will help to build a trusting and safe context for sharing experiences and learning. Many groups decide that the content of their meetings will be confidential (due to ethical considerations). A consultation group is meant to be a place where you can freely discuss your case, questions, and concerns as you refine your ideas, develop possibly new relationships to them, and listen as colleagues do the same. In Chapter 3, I offered a protocol for developing shared understandings that might be helpful to you. A sample protocol for convening is shown in Figure 5.2.

Figure 5.2   A Protocol for Engaging in Convening and Consultation

Following is a protocol I ask school leaders in my classes to employ when engaging in the convening process. Given time constraints, we use a 40-minute time block for each convening. Depending on your context, you may choose to adjust the time frame for convenings.

Brief Overview of Your Case and Questions   *5 minutes*

This five-minute period is when the convener briefly reminds the group about the following: (1) focus of your case and (2) what questions you would like group consultation on (i.e., what the group can help you with). The convener also addresses any clarifying questions group members may have about facts of the case.

Group Discussion/Consultation of Your Case   30 Minutes (total)

This 30-minute period is dedicated to group members' discussing and offering feedback on the convener's case and questions. The group will discuss the case, and all group members will listen closely to colleagues' thinking about the issues highlighted. During this discussion, the convener will need to refrain from talking and, instead, focus on listening to group comments. Group members will address case questions and share their feedback and ideas.

Pausing and Checking in With the Convener   (5 of the total 30 minutes for this section)

Midway through the group discussion of the convener's case, the facilitator will ask the group to pause for three minutes so that all can reflect on (a) what has been said, (b) the type of feedback that has been offered, and (c) the questions the convener posed in his or her case. The last two minutes of this pause are reserved for the convener to let everyone know where he or she would appreciate the group's help during the next half of the convening.

Convener Reflections   5 Minutes

This time is reserved for the convener to share his or her reflections on the convening, learnings from the discussion, and any additional reflections as they relate to possible next steps, realizations, insights, or actions. The convener may wish to summarize what has been helpful and where he or she would like to go next with his or her work and/or questions.

The convening process supports not only the convener's learning but also group members' learning. School leaders have found it to be a powerful and rich opportunity for learning. Many of them have transported and adapted this process to use in their districts, schools, departments, and teams.

CHAPTER SUMMARY

Deep approaches to learning tend to include or, better yet, start with learners' experience.

—Taylor, Marienau, & Fiddler, 2000, p. 314

Engaging in collegial inquiry and reflective practice has the potential to build trusting relationships and support individual learning and organizational capacity. As Brookfield (1995) notes, "On a personal level, it nurtures loving relationships. On a social level, it makes collective effort possible. On a political level, it undergirds the creation and maintenance of democracy" (p. 267). As many have emphasized, reflective practice is most successful and powerful when it is a collaborative effort (Brookfield; Kegan & Lahey, 2009; Osterman & Kottkamp, 2004; York-Barr et al., 2006).

In this chapter, I first presented theoretical perspectives on collegial inquiry, a form of reflective practice, as an effective approach to professional learning within schools and school systems to situate the practice as a developmental initiative within the field. Next, I discussed how adults with different ways of knowing will experience collegial inquiry and the kinds of supports and challenges that are needed to support development. I also presented a developmental view of goal setting, since it is one example of collegial inquiry that is commonly employed in schools and school systems to support adult learning and, often, organizational learning.

Next, I presented themes from my research that illuminated school leaders' thinking about why they believe collegial inquiry supports adult learning. In this section, I provided examples of how principals employ the practice with other adults in their school (i.e., reflection through writing, dialogue, and decision making). I then presented one example of how principals engage in collegial inquiry with fellow principals to support their own and each other's learning and leadership development, and I shared a few examples of how teachers employ collegial inquiry with fellow teachers. In addition, I presented a case example of how one school leader used collegial inquiry as an opportunity to reflect on her practices and assumptions and, ultimately, grow. Toward the end of the chapter, to assist you in a particularly effective form of collegial inquiry, I introduced the practice of convening (personal case-based learning) and provided a protocol for structuring cases and for engaging in the convening process. Below, I also share a tool I developed that you can employ in personal goal setting and in supporting colleagues and/or teams in goal setting.

Throughout this chapter, I have discussed why school leaders think collegial inquiry is an effective way to support adult learning and development. Inviting adults to engage in collegial inquiry accomplishes the following:

- Supports adult development and facilitates broadening of perspectives and examination of assumptions
- Enhances shared team and schoolwide decision making
- Builds interpersonal relationships
- Improves instruction and enhances leadership
- Helps adults adjust to and manage change
- Helps adults to make sense of and manage adaptive challenges
- Strengthens professional learning communities
- Empowers adults
- Develops skills for reflection and dialogue
- Builds leadership capacity on the individual, school, and system levels

Importantly, engaging in collegial inquiry supports adult learning and development by creating opportunities for teachers, assistant principals, principals, superintendents, and other school leaders to share and learn from each others' diverse perspectives. The sharing of perspectives assists adults in considering alternative perspectives; questioning their own points of view; and identifying, exploring, questioning, revising, and developing a deeper understanding of the assumptions that influence their actions. Speaking developmentally, this type of perspective broadening and self-reflection supports adults in growing toward more complex ways of knowing.

As I have discussed, engaging in collegial inquiry helps adults to explore, support, and challenge their own and other adults' thinking through different forms of writing and dialogue about thinking, feelings, ideas, proposals, and assumptions. Collegial inquiry is both a structure and a process for shared inquiry and reflection, decision making, problem solving, and development of the self through exploration. It also allows for assumptions to be surfaced and challenged, beliefs and thinking to be examined, and alternative ways of knowing and behaving and acting to be developed.

In addition, engaging in collegial inquiry with colleagues over time creates a supportive, safe context in which adults can take greater risks in sharing their thinking and in testing their assumptions. As we engage in this form of risk taking, we develop greater awareness of our assumptions and have opportunities to reflect with colleagues in ways that may allow us to envision alternative ways of thinking, acting, or behaving. Securing, prioritizing, and guarding spaces in which adults can engage in reflection and discussion will support adult development. The focus of this initiative is to create a dynamic space in which we can share thinking and assumptions. Collegial inquiry creates ongoing opportunities for adults to learn from each other as we benefit from thinking together and sharing in decision-making practice, dilemmas, and proposals for change. Put simply, engaging in collegial inquiry becomes a holding environment for growth.

APPLICATION EXERCISES

The following application exercises are offered to assist you in applying the ideas discussed in this chapter to your own context.

Exercise 1: Applying Your Learning About Collegial Inquiry as a Developmental Practice

1. Knowing what you know about adults' ways of knowing and collegial inquiry as a developmental practice, what is one way you might use collegial inquiry to support your own learning and development in your work context? What is one way you might implement a form of this practice to support *other* people's learning and growth in your work context?

2. What logistical or substantive concerns, if any, do you have at this time in terms of implementing a form of this practice to support your own and/or other people's growth?

3. How might you secure needed help to implement your ideas? Help for supporting yourself? Help with your ideas about how to support your colleagues?

Table 5.4 might help you implement your ideas in your specific and unique context.

Table 5.4   Collegial Inquiry: Supports and Challenges

Way of Knowing	Supports	Challenges
Instrumental		
Socializing		
Self-Authoring		
Self-Transforming		

Exercise 2: Goal Setting

As I discussed earlier in this chapter, a developmental stance can be very helpful when considering how best to support other adults as they engage in the goal-setting process. It can also be helpful in considering your own goals and the kinds of internal and external supports and challenges we encounter, as well as those we need to achieve them. I created Table 5.5 to assist teachers, department chairs, assistant principals, principals, and superintendents to examine their current and future goals, the supports and challenges (both logistical and developmental) from which they benefit, and the supports and challenges they feel they need to achieve their goals.

I offer Table 5.5 as a tool for you to use, if you find it helpful, in considering your own goals—or "things you're up to these days," as one school leader put it. It can be used for private reflection on your goals, or it can be shared with a colleague or supervisor. This not only can be used as a tool for personal goal setting and self-reflection but can also be employed to assess and invent team, school, or district goals.

Teachers, principals, assistant principals, department chairs, and deans of faculty with whom I have worked and learned have told me that they use this table as a touchstone for themselves and others during the academic year when they check in on their own or with other adults on their progress toward goals and their needs from both a developmental and a logistical perspective. It not only encourages self-reflection, but it also enables us to help each other grow. Adopting a developmental mindfulness when engaging in collegial inquiry in relation to individual or collective goal setting can help us to understand how we are making sense of experiences, create a space where we can help each other to surface, explore and question our assumptions, and enable us to offer developmental supports and challenges that can support growth. I hope that it provides a useful tool for you individually and in supporting your colleagues' growth, learning, and leadership development.

Table 5.5 Considering My Current and Future Goals

Goal	Current External Supports (i.e, logistical and/or developmental external supports)	Current Internal Supports (i.e, logistical and/or developmental internal supports)	Current External Challenges or Obstacles (i.e, logistical and/or developmental external challenges)	Current Internal Challenges or Obstacles (i.e, logistical and/or developmental internal challenges)	Current Practices I Use to Achieve My Goals	How Are My Current Supports, Challenges, and/or Practices Working Out?	What Are My Needs or Wishes for Supports, Challenges, and/or Practices That Would Assist Me in Working Toward My Goals?
Primary Short-Term Goal							
Primary Long-Term Goal							
Secondary Short-Term Goal							
Secondary Long-Term Goal							

REFLECTIVE QUESTIONS

One key to successful leadership is continuous personal change. Personal change is a reflection of our inner growth and empowerment.

—Robert E. Quinn, 1996, p. 3

I offer the following questions to assist you in applying the strategies outlined in this chapter to your unique work context. They can be used for internal reflection first and then to open up a team, school, or system dialogue.

1. As you reflect on your learning from this chapter, what is one thing you've learned or one insight you've had that feels important to you? In stepping forward, how will you work to implement your learning?

2. What have you experienced as three of the more important benefits of engaging in collegial inquiry with others? What have you noticed about other adults' engagement in this process? How, if at all, do the ideas presented in this chapter help you? In what ways, if any, might you apply them to your work context?

3. How do you think adults in your school or school system would describe their experience of engaging in collegial inquiry? How do you experience it?

4. What kinds of successes have you observed when adults in your school, department, or team engage in collegial inquiry? What sorts of things, if any, do you see as creating obstacles or challenges in helping adults to engage in this process? What's working well in each case, from your perspective? What would you like to see improved? Why?

5. Knowing what you do about adults who make meaning in developmentally different ways, how might you use different structures discussed in this chapter in employing collegial inquiry to support adults with diverse ways of knowing?

6. What are two practical ideas for collegial inquiry about which you have learned in this chapter that you would like to implement or encourage in your school? What small steps will you take to implement these?

6

Mentoring

*Building Meaningful
and Growth–Enhancing Relationships*

*You are so young, so before all beginning, and I want to beg you . . . to be patient
towards all that is unsolved in your heart and to try to love the questions
themselves. . . . Perhaps you will then gradually, without noticing it, live along
some distant day into the answer.*

—Rainer Maria Rilke (1929/1999), German- and French-language poet

In this chapter, I discuss the pillar practice of mentoring as one that school leaders can
employ to promote personal and professional learning and organizational growth
through a more private relationship or series of relationships. It is important to note that as
adults, we need more than one source of support for development. In fact, schools as
learning centers can also be mentoring communities in which adults share in reciprocal
mentoring relationships or networks of supports.

First, I briefly introduce the origins of mentoring as a growth-enhancing practice that
supports human development, and I review the mentoring literature on adult development and
professional development. In so doing, I suggest that a developmental mindfulness in
mentoring can be powerful for individuals, schools, and school systems. Second, I discuss how
adults with different developmental orientations will experience this practice and what types
of supports and challenges they will need. I then briefly illuminate how the purposes of

mentoring programs vary for teachers, from "spreading a mission" to exchanging information to providing both new and experienced educators with emotional support. I emphasize why school leaders value mentoring and how they think it supports adult learning. Next, I present examples from my research that illuminate how principals and assistant principals experience the practice as a support to their growth. Through these examples, I show how leaders employ this practice and describe what effective mentoring means to them; why they value it; and how it opens communication, decreases isolation, builds interdependent relationships, helps adults to manage change, and supports adult growth. In addition, I present a case of a mentoring program for teachers, a guide that includes questions to help with building effective mentoring programs and relationships, an application exercise, and reflective questions.

Almost all of the school leaders—principals, assistant principals, superintendents, and teacher-leaders—in my research use mentoring to support individual growth and organizational learning through various forms of relational partnering and adult collaboration. Many value this practice because they think that mentoring enables adults to grow; is mutually beneficial for the mentor and the mentee; and helps adults broaden their perspectives on themselves, others, and their work.

ABOUT EFFECTIVE MENTORING AND ITS VALUE

> *At its best, mentoring can be a life-altering relationship that inspires mutual growth, learning, and development. Its effects can be remarkable, profound, and enduring; mentoring relationships have the capacity to transform individuals, groups, organizations, and communities.*
>
> —Ragins & Kram, 2007, p. 3

Scholars and practitioners agree that the practice of mentoring is crucial to supporting adult learning and development. In our educational world, a lot has been written about the importance and value of using mentoring as a practice with new teachers to support their learning and development. More recently, given the changing and increasingly complex demands and expectations placed on principals and superintendents, mentoring (often referred to in the professional development literature as "coaching") has become a prominent practice that is increasingly employed to support these leaders. In fact, different kinds of "coaching" are noted in the literature. For example, most recently demand has been great for content-focused coaching, as well as leadership coaching, peer coaching, and instructional coaching. While these differentiated forms of coaching are valuable and important, my goal in this chapter is to illuminate mentoring as a developmental practice that has been found to support individual growth of leaders throughout the system. In turn, it can also support the development of schools and districts. While I briefly discuss the difference between coaching and mentoring, my primary aim is to offer a developmental view of mentoring.

In the section that follows, I discuss key themes derived from the general literature on mentoring to provide context. Next, I focus on central ideas from the professional development literature related to the mentoring of teachers. I then briefly share a few of the more prevalent themes that have emerged recently related to the ways in which principals and superintendents are engaging in mentoring today. Last, I discuss mentoring in relation to the field of adult development, illuminating central themes from the developmental literature that address mentoring. In so doing, I highlight the importance of bringing a developmental perspective to the practice of mentoring to support adult growth.

Mentoring: Origins and Overview

Just when the caterpillar thought the world was over, it became a butterfly.

—Proverb

The term *mentor*, which means "enduring" in Greek, can be traced back to Homer's *Odyssey* in the character of Mentor, who was Odysseus's friend and trusted counselor. When Odysseus left his home and family to travel on his odyssey, he gave Mentor the important responsibility of acting as teacher and protector to his son, Telemachus. For centuries, the term *mentor* has been employed to designate a wise, trusted counselor and teacher. Mentoring is one of the oldest forms of supporting human development.

Over the years, the meaning of the terms *mentor* and *mentoring* have altered, especially since the relatively recent emergence of the field of personal and professional coaching. However, scholars agree that a central characteristic of the mentoring relationship that has remained constant is that "mentoring is a developmental relationship that is embedded within a career context" (Ragins & Kram, 2007, p. 5). Historically, according to Belle Ragins and Kathy Kram, "mentoring has been defined as a relationship between an older, more experienced mentor and a younger, less experienced protégé for the purpose of helping and developing the protégé's career" (p. 5; see also Kram, 1985; Levinson, 1978; and reviews by Noe, Greenberger, & Wang, 2002; Ragins, 1999; Wanberg, Welsh, & Hezlett, 2003). In other words, traditionally, a mentor's primary task has been to help a protégé, or mentee, work more successfully and make progress in his or her career. More recently, however, several scholars and practitioners have maintained that mentors do not necessarily need to be older; younger adults serving as mentors may have wisdom to offer (Daresh, 2003; McGowan, Stone, & Kegan, 2007).

Importantly, scholars, practitioners, and researchers have noted that in today's world, there is an ongoing discussion related to the distinctions, ambiguities, and differences between *coaching* and *mentoring* (Free Management Library, n.d.; www.managementhelp.org/guiding/mentrng/mentrng.htm); many use these terms interchangeably, while others make distinctions between them.

In the literature on mentoring, the role of a mentor is commonly depicted in the following ways:

Mentors are guides. . . . they take us on a journey.

—Daloz, 1999, p. 18

A mentor . . . serves as a guide or sponsor—one who looks after, advises, protects, and takes a special interest in another's development.

—Bode, 1999, p. 118

Mentoring is an excellent tool for professional learning both for the mentor and the mentee through systemic critical reflection.

—Nicholls, 2002, p. 141

Similarly, Sharan Merriam (1983) maintains that a mentor is a friend, guide, and, above all else, a teacher.

Importantly, Lois Zachary (2000) emphasizes the essential need in this particular relationship to clarify roles, expectations, and responsibilities to avoid role confusion and to establish boundaries. Zachary suggests the following as guidelines for developing mentoring relationships:

- Establish clear expectations and ground rules.
- Show mutual respect.
- Focus on building a trusting relationship.
- Develop shared understandings and agreements as to how to handle confidentiality.
- Make commitments as to when, where, and how often to meet.

Historically, mentors have provided two central functions to their protégés: "career functions" (e.g., coaching them for advancement in their careers, increasing their exposure to others in an organization, and/or protecting them from too many external demands) and "psychosocial functions" (e.g., in the relational context of trust and intimacy, helping them to grow personally and professionally) (Ragins & Kram, 2007, p. 5). More recently, however, as the field of mentoring has evolved and in light of recent research, Ragins and Kram have identified the emergence of four central insights related to what they call "mentoring functioning." Their discoveries are as follows.

First, these authors (2007) find that the origins and outcomes of the "career" and "psychosocial" functions of mentoring are different. Career functions have been found to predict a protégé's salary and career advancement more effectively. On the other hand, psychosocial functions link more intimately with a protégé's level of satisfaction with the mentoring relationship. Second, they find noteworthy differences in degree (i.e., high, medium, or low amounts of a particular "function") and range (i.e., a mentor's capacities to meet a protégé's needs) in any one relationship and across relationships. Third, they have discovered that since relationships are dynamic and needs change, mentoring functions vary in different phases of the relationship. Last, they find that others, who are not official mentors, might also informally provide these two functions (career and psychosocial).

As these authors point out, there is no one best way to mentor, and every relationship is different. A common theme in the literature is that mentoring supports adult development in the context of a personal relationship (Daloz, 1999; Merriam, 1983, Ragins & Kram, 2007; Zachary, 2000). Most recently, however, scholars acknowledge that no single mentoring relationship can meet all of a person's human needs for growth; instead, there is agreement that mentoring relationships live and are nested in larger developmental networks (Higgins, Chandler, & Kram, 2007; McGowan et al., 2007) or "constellations of relationships" (Ragins & Kram, 2007, p. 9). These "constellations" are what I refer to as *mentoring communities*, which have important consequences for the ways in which any single mentoring relationship functions. In other words, we need mentors throughout our lives, and our need for a variety of supports and challenges changes as we grow and are influenced by context. (I discuss this idea more in the section "Mentoring in the Adult Development Literature" below.)

Mentoring in the Professional Development Literature

In the two sections that follow, I discuss what the professional development literature has to say about the value of mentoring in supporting teacher learning and in supporting the learning of superintendents, principals, and assistant principals.

Support for Teacher Learning

The ad hoc, informal nature of traditional mentoring scenarios rel[ies] heavily on the initiative, instincts, and good will of the veteran teacher and the protégé. The need to support, nurture, and retain new teachers for today's challenging classrooms requires that we become more intentional with the approaches we take to induction.

—Saphier, Freedman, & Aschheim, 2001, p. 21

As John Saphier, Susan Freedman, and Barbara Aschheim point out in the above passage, teachers—and all of us—need mentors so that we can grow personally and professionally—as educators, leaders, and human beings. In this section, I discuss a few central themes that have emerged in the extensive literature related to the importance of mentoring new teachers.

Mentoring, among other practices, has been shown to be helpful to new teachers in a variety of ways, including helping to support teacher retention (Boyer, 1999; Killion, 2000; Moir & Bloom, 2003; Saphier et al., 2001). In addition, mentoring relationships between new and veteran teachers, who are trained as mentors, have been shown to accomplish the following:

- Enhance teacher performance and student learning by promoting collegial dialogue (Holloway, 2001; Jonson, 2008; Killion, 2000; Rowley, 1999).
- Provide professional development for new and veteran teachers (Daresh, 2003; Holloway, 2001, 2004; Moir & Bloom, 2003).

- Help beginning teachers manage new challenges and develop teaching practices through reflective activities and professional conversations (Danielson, 1999; Jonson, 2008; Moir & Bloom, 2003).
- Produce both career-related and psychosocial benefits for mentors and mentees (DeLong, Gabarro, & Lees, 2008; Hegstad, 1999; Holloway, 2001; Moir & Bloom, 2003; Pappano, 2001).

In fact, John Holloway (2001), in his review of induction programs, discovered that having a trained mentor who has participated in informal induction programs benefits both the mentor and mentee professionally and psychosocially. He, like others (e.g., Moir & Bloom, 2003; Yendol-Hoppey & Dana, 2007), finds that the process of engaging in reflective practice about their own instruction practices and effectiveness helped both mentors and mentees professionally and psychosocially.

Likewise, Ellen Moir and Gary Bloom (2003) identify similar benefits for both mentors and mentees in their examination of the Santa Cruz New Teacher Project in California, an induction-mentoring program aimed at improving the quality and retention of new teachers by pairing them with trained mentors who have been identified as some of the best teachers in the district. The benefits of this program include professional replenishment for veteran teachers and increased retention of the best teachers. Importantly, in addition to these benefits, these authors also discovered that this program has produced teacher-leaders who are lifelong learners and passionate about making professional development part of the school culture. Given the need to build capacity of this sort in our schools today, this outcome is especially important.

In addition, a few common themes have emerged across the professional development literature in terms of effective mentoring for new teachers:

- To be effective mentors to beginning teachers, mentor-teachers need training in how to mentor, good communication skills, and ongoing support (Danielson, 1999; Daresh, 2003; Holloway, 2001; Moir & Bloom, 2003; Rowley, 1999).
- Mentoring requires establishing trusting relationships (DeLong et al., 2008; Hall, 2008; Hegstad, 1999; Holloway, 2001; Killion, 2000; Moir & Bloom, 2003; Pappano, 2001).
- Mentoring requires a significant amount of time, energy, and commitment (DeLong et al., 2008; Daresh, 2003; Hegstad, 1999; Holloway, 2001; Killion, 2000; Moir & Bloom, 2003; Pappano, 2001).
- Mentors need to be accepting of beginning teachers as developing individuals and professionals (Jonson, 2008; Killion, 2000; Pappano, 2001; Rowley, 1999).
- Mentors need to use reflective practices to show empathy, avoid making any rush to judgment, and help classroom teachers grow (Blank & Kershaw, 2009; Moir & Bloom, 2003; Rowley, 1999; Yendol-Hoppey & Dana, 2007).
- Mentors need to understand stage and age theories of adult development (Jonson, 2008; Rowley, 1999) and new phases of teacher development (e.g., immediate needs and broader concerns) to offer supports and strategies (Daresh, 2003; Moir & Bloom, 2003).

- Mentors need to be skilled at providing instructional support by observing mentees in the classroom and then sharing their observations and their own past experiences (e.g., through team teaching activities, mentee and mentor can observe each other, collect classroom performance data, and use it to inform improvement plans); engaging in collegial dialogue aimed at enhancing teacher performance and student learning is an essential component of mentor-mentee relationships (Jonson, 2008; Moir & Bloom, 2003; Rowley, 1999).

- Mentors can share instructional strategies with mentees, identify research that supports various strategies, and highlight advantages and disadvantages of employing a variety of instructional strategies (Blank & Kershaw, 2009; Killion, 2000; Moir & Bloom, 2003; Rowley, 1999).

As Joellen Killion (2000) wisely writes, although "most teachers construct knowledge from their experiences," they "often [share] this private knowledge with no one" (p. 3). The mentoring relationship, she emphasizes, is one in which this private knowledge can be shared to decrease feelings of isolation, enhance reflection, improve practice, and nurture learning and growth in the context of meaningful collaboration.

Support for Principal, Superintendent, and Assistant Principal Learning

For several years, and especially more recently, a critical need has emerged for mentoring among principals, assistant principals aspiring to the principalship, and superintendents. Many assert that this need has arisen because of the changing and increasingly demanding expectations and daunting responsibilities leaders encounter in modern society and because of the palpable trend of school leaders leaving the profession due to the increased stress and isolation of their roles (Dukess, 2001; Hall, 2008; Kegan & Lahey, 2009; National Staff Development Council, 2008, www.coachingschoolresults.com). The professional development literature has begun to address this need.

Pete Hall (2008) discusses several important characteristics that can support successful mentoring relationships with principals, especially those new to the profession. Among these, he emphasizes the following:

- *Developing a common frame of reference:* A shared vocabulary and concept system of what a mentor is and clarifying what a mentor can and cannot do (e.g., expectations and boundaries)
- *Investing time to clarify roles and responsibilities:* Developing a vision for working together; creating timelines for work tasks, and defining roles
- *Allocating adequate time for the relationship:* Both the mentor and the mentee committing significant time to share ideas, ask questions, engage in dialogue, and grow as professionals
- *Ensuring thoughtful mentor/mentee matching*
- *Taking time to develop trust:* Engendering deeper learning and growth by establishing trust

- *Clarifying goals and objectives, as well as action plans for reaching them*
- *Emphasizing the ways in which mistakes are opportunities for powerful learning*

Hall (2008) recommends, in addition to offering caring support, the following for mentors to facilitate learning and growth through reflection:

- Invite mentees to engage with and reflect on probing questions.
- Offer honest feedback.
- Listen actively.
- Examine decisions together.
- Suggest alternative perspectives.

In sum, he advocates for intentional mentoring to help leaders grow.

In the context of the business world, Thomas DeLong, John Gabarro, and Robert Lees (2008) review what experts on mentoring have identified as qualities and characteristics of effective mentors. These characteristics resemble threads in the educational literature.

- Mentors are trusted and credible and proceed with integrity.
- Mentors offer comments, suggestions, and ideas, which mentees must hear, in a sensitive way that allows mentees to feel heard and acknowledged.
- Mentors engage with mentees in a positive manner to help them improve performance and build capacity.
- Mentors create a context in which mentees feel safe, and not vulnerable, so as to take enough risks.
- Mentors offer support to mentees so that they can achieve larger goals.
- Mentors help mentees to envision both opportunities and challenges they may not have imagined on their own.

As I discuss later in this chapter, it is important for us to remember that the ways in which we will experience a mentor's generous offer of support will vary, depending on our own way of knowing.

Earlier, I mentioned that in the educational literature, some scholars use the terms *coaching* and *mentoring* interchangeably (Allen, 2008; Nicholls, 2002), while others do not. What is the difference between coaching and mentoring? How are these practices distinguished in the fields?

First, it is important to note that scholars and practitioners point to some overlap between these practices (Hunt & Weintraub, 2007; Kram, 1988). One distinction is that mentoring is often longer term and the relationship often has an emotional dimension (Hunt & Weintraub). While mentors may also see themselves as coaches, they are not only coaches—that is, they are devoted not only to helping an individual increase his or her ability to do the work but to supporting the mentee's personal growth and development.

One program for principals, superintendents, and various other school leaders that is widely considered effective is the Coaching School Results Program, founded by several leaders of the National Staff Development Council (NSDC)—Shirley Hord, Annette Griffin, and Carolyn Bukhair—in the spring of 2000. This program's mission is "to support and foster confident, competent, courageous school leaders who lead their schools to high performance" by coaching them "for results" (NSDC, 2008a, www.coachingschoolresults.com). NSDC purposefully selected a group of educators from across the nation who would participate in intensive training. This training was aimed at providing the essential knowledge and skills they would need to serve in a supportive coaching role with principals, superintendents, and other school leaders. One of the many intentions was for these "coaches" to help school leaders develop their skills to lead and to manage effectively the increasingly complex and multifaceted demands of school leadership (e.g., challenges associated with leading in contexts with diverse student populations and increased accountability demands).

The cornerstone of the Coaching School Results Program is that coaches offer needed support and collaboration for leaders who are in the field, grounded in the day-to-day realities of operating a school or school system. As a coach in this program, one's goal "is to assist the school leader in becoming all that he or she can be while impacting and ensuring the highest levels of achievement for his or her school and students" (NSDC, 2008b). According to founding leaders from the National Staff Development Council, the Coaching School Results Program is based on the belief that

> the most successful coaching occurs when the client is fully committed to the process. This includes identifying and clarifying goals, creating multiple possibilities for action and implementing action toward goal attainment. The coach is hired to assist the principal in achieving at his or her goals for his or her school and students. (NSDC, 2008b)

Mentoring in the Adult Development Literature

Development is more than simply change. The word implies direction. Moreover, development seems to happen not in a gradual and linear way but in distinct and recognizable leaps—is a series of spiraling plateaus rather than a smooth slope. Each plateau rests upon and represents a qualitative improvement over the previous one.

—Daloz, 1999, p. 23

Scholars rightly assert that theories of adult development offer insight into the practice of mentoring (Daloz, 1999; Drago-Severson, 2004a, 2004b; McGowan et al., 2007; Merriam, 1983; Ragins & Kram, 2007). There is a need to develop a deeper understanding of how different kinds of mentoring work for adults who have different ways of knowing and how schools and school systems can enhance mentoring relationships. How might we nurture this?

As a developmental practice, mentoring helps adults to grow and helps schools and school systems to become nurturing learning communities that provide a safe relational context, or a robust "holding environment" (Kegan, 1982, p. 115). The mentoring relationship provides a safe context for broadening perspectives, taking risks, engaging in dialogue and reflective practice, examining assumptions (our own and other people's) and behaviors, and over time, possibly reframing them. Several principles of constructive-developmental theory (Kegan, 1982, 1994, 2000) inform how mentoring supports the *process* of growth. Mentoring creates a context—a relationship or series of relationships—that enables adults to examine, learn from, and broaden their own and other people's perspectives.

In this section, I discuss a few of the fundamentals of how adult developmental theory discusses and informs the practice of mentoring. Before presenting key theoretical ideas, I describe how mentoring is traditionally defined in this field and how the leaders in my research describe the ways in which this practice supports growth.

Traditionally, mentoring has been defined in the developmental literature as a reciprocal, developmental relationship between a more experienced and a less experienced adult, commonly referred to as mentor and mentee, or protégé. The explicit intention in this relationship is for the mentor to offer guidance to the mentee in terms of developing his or her career (Kram, 1983, 1985; Levinson, 1978). This relationship can be formal or informal.

By its very character, the mentoring relationship is a private, reciprocal one that is oriented toward supporting growth. The process of dialogue, articulating perspectives, and uncovering assumptions holds the potential to facilitate the growth of both individuals. In other words, mentoring is a practice that can support both the mentee and the mentor as growing individuals (Kram, 1983; McGowan et al., 2007; Ragins & Kram, 2007) and in developing greater capacities to manage the complexities of teaching, leadership, and life. Echoing this sentiment, the school leaders in my 2004 and more recent research reported that both mentor and mentee were often invited to share their thinking about classroom practice, leadership and teaching dilemmas, and/or challenges in managing reform initiatives. In this relational practice, engaging in dialogue and expressing vulnerabilities was intrinsic to the relationship, these leaders explained. This held true whether mentoring occurred between teachers (e.g., a more experienced teacher mentoring a less experienced teacher) or principals (a more experienced principal mentoring a less experienced principal or an assistant principal). Many remarked that mentoring was not just about improving as professionals; it was, as they put it, "personal."

In these relationships, mentors and mentees have the opportunity to share and reflect on their own thinking, assumptions, and beliefs and to learn about each other's perspectives, thus broadening their own perspectives. They also become more aware of the influence of their guiding assumptions on their leadership and instructional practices. Recall that examining assumptions is one fundamental step in growth. The school leaders in my research commented on the value of this outcome. The relationship itself can promote deeper understanding of one's self; thus, it serves as a context that enables adults to grow to more complex ways of knowing.

Mentoring as a Holding Environment for Growth

How does the mentoring relationship support adult growth? How can we, as mentors, differentiate our ways of "holding" mentees in the psychological sense? How are our own developmental capacities for holding influenced by our ways of knowing, as mentors? In describing how growth happens in this relationship, Daloz (1999, 2000) brings constructive-developmental theory (Kegan, 1982, 1994) into conversation with the mentoring literature and informs our understanding of how the relationship itself is a holding environment for growth. He uses this metaphor: the mentoring relationship is a bridge for growth when it is well anchored on both sides. In other words, to support a person's growth from one way of knowing to another, the mentor—as bridge—must first join and support the person in his or her current way of sense making, providing continuity as the mentee is challenged to grow from one way of knowing toward the next (Daloz, 2000; Kegan).

Recall that a good holding environment serves three functions (Kegan, 1982). First, it must "hold well"—meaning that it affirms who the person *is* and *how* the person is currently making meaning. Mentors hold well by meeting their mentees where they are.

While good holding is essential for growth, good holding alone is not enough to support development. To grow, we simultaneously need to experience some form of challenge to our current way of knowing. Thus, the second function of a good holding environment, "letting go" or offering challenge, needs to be offered *when* a person is ready. A good holding environment or mentoring relationship needs to let go, providing challenge by way of posing questions and offering alternative perspectives. Letting go catalyzes a person to move beyond an existing way of constructing reality to a more complex way of knowing. I often refer to these developmental challenges as being where we are standing at the edges of a person's thinking in order to help him or her grow (i.e., the growing edge).

The third function of a good holding environment, and mentoring relationship, is that it stays in place to provide continuity as the person establishes a new balance—or way of knowing. While this third characteristic of a strong holding environment might be challenging to manifest in shorter-term professional learning programs, it can be created in mentoring relationships and mentoring communities.

Robust and effective mentoring relationships, as developmental holding environments, need to offer a delicate balance of supports, challenges, and continuity that are aligned with a person's way of knowing to support growth. Because the process of growing involves risks and losses as well as joys, a person is likely to experience disorientation. Therefore, a mentoring relationship or multiple mentoring relationships can serve as safe havens. Eileen McGowan, Eric Stone, and Robert Kegan (2007) explain the importance of the mentoring relationship remaining in place in this way: "The consistency of a supportive holding environment provides the individual with an anchor—something to hold on to amidst other shifting life forces" (p. 406). Given the adaptive challenges school leaders encounter in today's educational world, we need to help each other build more supportive mentoring relationships and mentoring communities. An essential component of support is trust:

when trust exists and is nurtured in a relationship, we grow freer to take risks, to ask deeper questions, and to challenge each other's ideas. Below, I describe some of the forms of support and challenge that mentors can offer.

Providing Support. Developmentalists define support in terms of the process of holding well. As Daloz (1999) explains, support is "providing a place where [a person] can contact her need for fundamental trust, the basis of growth" (p. 215). Mentors can offer support by joining a person in his or her sense making, by supporting the person in the way he or she is making sense in the moment, and by listening carefully to the way a protégé is making sense of experiences. Mentors can also serve as a guide and as an advocate as a mentee steps forward in the developmental journey by creating a safe relationship (Daloz; Kegan, 1982). Listening to a person's inner life, as Daloz reminds us, is more than simply hearing what a person says. Listening, according to Daloz, means asking, "What does it *feel* like to be the person? How does she see the world, make sense of diversity and complexity? What are the forces holding and propelling her life?" (p. 209). In addition, when timing is right, disclosing aspects of oneself can spawn a deeper relationship between mentor and mentee (Daloz). Importantly, as I discuss later in this chapter, what constitutes support and a safe, growth-enhancing relationship will vary depending on a person's way of knowing.

Providing Challenge. Providing developmentally appropriate challenges, as I note above, can stimulate growth. Mentors offer challenges that support growth by posing questions that invite mentees to think carefully about and even question their current perspectives and to consider alternatives. This oftentimes causes cognitive dissonance (e.g., the difficulty or discomfort related to holding two contradictory ideas simultaneously) in a mentee; over time, however, as a person grows, the dissonance diminishes as new ways of thinking emerge (Daloz, 1999; McGowan et al., 2007). In addition, a mentor can offer developmental challenges by setting tasks for the mentee and engaging in dialogue to analyze the tasks. As Daloz explains, "The experience of being listened to closely, of being asked questions such as . . . 'What do you want for yourself?' . . . can be of great importance in helping a person begin to formulate her own plans more clearly" (p. 226). In other words, the experience of being listened to closely *is* a precious gift.

Mentors also offer developmental challenges by setting high expectations and by being present as a mentee makes sense of his or her culture and its implicit and explicit demands. Daloz (1999) reminds us that mentors offer a map just by being who they are; however, he emphasizes that sharing developmental maps with a mentee can help a person to see his or her journey more clearly. Like Kegan (1982, 1994), Daloz stresses the importance of providing continuity to mentees during the growth process and of modeling the process of the journey.

Sustaining Mindfulness. Being mindful of how a relationship will be influenced by *both* the mentor's and the mentee's way of knowing is important, as I mentioned earlier. Our way of knowing will influence our experience of the relationship, the expectations we bring to it, and the supports and challenges that we are able to give and receive from it. A developmental mindfulness can help us better understand how a protégé, or mentee, will experience a mentor's support, advice, and guidance differently, depending on his or her way of knowing. It also helps us to consider how mentors may make sense of the experience, and it can help us to support both in this vital practice.

Understanding Mentoring in Its Broadest Sense. Importantly, a mentoring relationship will evolve over time. In light of this, our forms of support, challenges, and continuity will need to change in response as well.

In summary, mentoring relationships can be safe contexts in which adults are supported and challenged as they articulate their own thinking, assumptions, and reflections in an open way and listen to and learn from other each other's perspectives. I discuss in detail below how the ways in which an adult in a mentoring relationship will give and receive support and challenge and experience risk will be qualitatively different, depending on how a person is making meaning of experience. Another important point is that while sometimes one mentoring relationship can support developmental movement, most often, we need multiple growth-enhancing relationships that work in combination to support growth.

School leaders who understand mentoring from a developmental perspective may be better able to design mentoring programs that attend to developmental diversity and support adults, both mentors and mentees, in their mentoring practices. In addition, school leaders would be wise to bring a developmental perspective to building schools and school systems as mentoring communities. Daloz (1999) eloquently captures the importance of this developmental relationship.

> Mentors are more than simply isolated individuals who enter our lives, intervene, and depart. Rather, they are creations that emerge out of particular demands our lives make on us. When they do their work well, they help us see not only the tasks before us but also the broader context that gives those tasks meaning. . . . They remind us of our destiny. (p. 205)

MENTORING AND DEVELOPMENTAL DIVERSITY

Mentoring is a relational practice that not only helps to build meaningful and growth-enhancing relationships between individuals but also engenders the development of nurturing learning communities in schools and districts. How does the relational context of mentoring support the development of adults with different ways of knowing? What supports and challenges will foster adult growth in mentoring relationships?

A mentoring relationship is a reciprocal, developmental relationship—a context that can support not just informational learning but also the process of transformational learning. While engaging in mentoring, adults have the opportunity to take risks and grow from reflecting on practice and from examining assumptions about practice, leadership, learning, and life (one's own, perhaps one's mentor's, and other people's). This can lead to perspective broadening and the testing of assumptions, and over time, possibly the revising of assumptions, which guide our thinking and behaviors. While often we may think of mentoring as a practice that supports the growth and development of the mentee, protégé, or less experienced adult with respect to some domain of life (e.g., as teacher, as principal, and superintendent), mentoring can support the growth of *both* mentee and mentor.

A developmental awareness helps us to understand that adults with different ways of knowing will experience the mentoring relationship in different ways. Put simply, it is essential to consider that both the mentor's and the mentee's ways of knowing will influence this relationship. There are a few other important points I'd like to emphasize:

1. Their ways of knowing influence how the mentor and mentee will make sense of a mentoring relationship.

2. Mentees' needs and expectations of mentors will vary depending on their way of knowing, as will the types of supports and challenges they need in order to grow.

3. As protégés grow, their needs and expectations of mentors and the relationship will change.

4. Context matters: a person will likely have different mentoring needs depending on the context of the relationship (e.g., an aspiring principal may have needs in a principal internship that differ from those in his or her spiritual life).

5. Roles can be relative: one person might serve as a mentor to another who is less experienced in one domain of life (e.g., teaching) and as mentee of that person in another domain (e.g., learning technology).

6. Human beings have different needs and will need multiple mentors to facilitate growth in different domains (personal, professional, and spiritual), and even within the same domain of their lives, because each mentoring relationship offers its own gifts.

Relating Ways of Knowing to Mentoring

Table 6.1 illuminates how adults with different ways of knowing will likely experience mentoring and the supports and challenges mentees need to help them grow from this pillar practice. Below, I discuss how mentees with different ways of knowing will tend to experience mentoring. A developmental mindfulness can help us understand how to support the development of effective mentoring relationships in formal and informal mentoring programs.

Table 6.1 Potential Ways Mentees Experience Mentoring Based on Their Way of Knowing

Way of Knowing	Supports for Growth From Mentor	Challenges From Mentor (Growing Edge)
Instrumental Knowers	• Discuss ground rules and step-by-step guidelines as to how to engage in the relationship (setting clear goals and expectations). • Offer concrete and tangible advice, strategies, examples of how to manage troubling situations, and suggestions for how to improve practice with emphasis on explicitly explaining "right" or "wrong" ways to move forward and achieve goals. • Engaging the mentee in conversation is supportive when dialogue provides specific and concrete suggestions to follow, models to imitate, skills, and information about practice. • Ensure that mentor is experienced as a resource who possesses information, answers, and skills that he or she gives to mentee. • Give clear descriptions of ways to proceed when addressing mentee's immediate concerns and needs for improving practice (e.g., learning better skills or more effective rules to follow) or achieving concrete goals.	• Learn about multiple perspectives through engaging in dialogue. • Engage in dialogue and/or situations that require abstract thinking and scaffold the mentee through the process. • Provide opportunities that require thinking differently—and more abstractly—about not only mentee's own perspective but also the mentor's and colleagues' perspectives through discussion and reflection on own instructional and/or leadership practice and other people's practices. • Engage in conversation that gently challenges this adult to understand and evaluate self and own perspective through another person's point of view (e.g., a mentor's or a colleague's).
Socializing Knowers	• Explicitly acknowledge own beliefs and points of view by confirming and accepting the mentee's self and own beliefs. • Ensure that mentee feels known, cared for, and accepted as a person (confirming or verifying the common value of the shared relationship). • Assure mentee of your acceptance, helping this knower feel safe in taking risks and sharing own perspectives.	• Provide dialogue and other opportunities that encourage looking to oneself and one's own views and taking a risk in voicing them in the relationship. • Support the mentee in constructing own values and standards rather than coconstructing them with mentors. • Encourage the mentee to examine various loyalties he or she holds. • Through conversation, present opportunities in which the mentee can grow to tolerate and accept conflicting perspectives with regard to issues or solutions without feeling that it threatens the mentoring relationship (personally and professionally).

(Continued)

Table 6.1 (Continued)

Way of Knowing	Supports for Growth From Mentor	Challenges From Mentor (Growing Edge)
		• Help this knower distinguish and separate own feelings and responsibilities as distinct and different from the mentor's feelings. • Challenge mentee to disentangle, differentiate, and distinguish own feelings and point of view from need to be accepted by the mentor.
Self-Authoring Knowers	• Provide opportunities to demonstrate and reveal own competencies and capabilities. • Provide opportunities to learn about diverse perspectives and points of view on issues and potential paths for solutions. • Invite to critique and/or design models. • Invite and secure spaces in the context of the mentoring relationship to analyze and critique own and the mentor's work and practice. • Provide information and practices that help these knowers improve and move forward with their self-determined goals. • Confirm and accept the mentee's independence, competency, and self-governing capabilities.	• Challenge mentee to let go of investment and identification with own understanding, singular ideology (system of beliefs, values and ideas that form one's philosophy), and/or strategies without feeling internally conflicted, instead becoming more open to alternative—and opposing—ideologies. • Encourage this knower to put aside own standards for practice and/or values and open up to the mentor's and/or other people's standards and/or values for practice. • Invite the mentee to acknowledge and accept the values of the mentor and/or of others that may be in direct opposition to own. • Invite this adult to accept and understand a mentor's different approaches to problem solving and/or the process of exploring an issue or problem.
Self-Transforming Knowers Early (4/5)	• Acknowledge that this knower appreciates and has deep respect for the lived experience and perspective of others, including mentors. • Be willing to be peerlike and mutual in the sharing of experience. • Provide mentee with space within the mentoring relationship to explore own creativity and to express it openly (in terms of both personal and professional growth). • Support for experimentation and exploration will be appreciated. • Acknowledge mentee's capability for independence and autonomy, while simultaneously recognizing the need for interdependence and relationship.	• Support this mentee in sorting through own intense and sometimes disorienting emotions and thoughts; because of this knower's willingness and capacity to take advice and to hear constructive criticism, such a focus on his or her internal life is often helpful. • Gently challenge this knower to embrace critical feedback; these knowers sometimes protect themselves by avoiding it. • Avoid overwhelming this mentee; this knower will tend to withdraw from situations, events, and relationships—temporarily.

Way of Knowing	Supports for Growth From Mentor	Challenges From Mentor (Growing Edge)
Self-Transforming Knowers Later (5)	• Know that mentoring this learner is a challenge unless the mentor is in the same or a later stage. • Ensure that value of interaction is apparent: though having respect and regard for the perspectives of others, these mentees tend to become impatient unless they perceive the worth of mentoring. • Possess the capacity to engage in full relational and dialectic engagement.	• Challenge mentee to appreciate the importance of learning from others, no matter what their ways of knowing. • Support this adult in becoming permeable to the feedback of others.

The Instrumental Knower as Mentee

As Table 6.1 shows, adults who are instrumental knowers will feel supported by mentors who provide specific advice, concrete skills, and information about instructional and/or leadership practice. Instrumental knowers will feel supported by establishing clear expectations and "rules" in their work with a mentor. Mentors can support instrumental knowers' growth by encouraging them to move away from searching for the "one right way" to teach, lead, or to solve problems and toward considering other pathways or perspectives on practice. Helping these mentees to broaden their perspectives will support their growth over time. Engaging in dialogue and presenting multiple perspectives on situations, practice, and problem solving can support the development of abstract thinking.

The context of a mentoring relationship can support instrumental knowers as they grow to be able to think differently about their own, their mentors', and other colleagues' perspectives on instructional practices, change initiatives, and other issues. With a balance of developmental supports and challenges, such as those I've mentioned here, these adults can grow to consider multiple perspectives. Put simply, the mentoring relationship can be a holding environment to help these mentees to think abstractly, consider multiple perspectives, and orient toward colleagues' needs and desires rather than only their own.

The Socializing Knower as Mentee

Recall that adults who have a socializing way of knowing have developed enhanced capacities for reflection (e.g., the developmental capacity to think abstractly and to subordinate own needs and desires to those of others). Having a mentor's approval and acceptance will be of ultimate importance to these mentees. Rather than *initially* viewing the mentoring relationship as an opportunity for dialogue about professional and sometimes personal observations—leading to critical feedback—a socializing knower tends to conceive of the mentoring relationship as an arena for receiving positive reinforcement and for feeling well held. Thus, this adult can feel threatened, perceiving the feedback as critical or negative, especially when the relationship is in its earlier phases. In addition, mentees who are socializing knowers will tend to look to their mentors for their beliefs about what *should* be done and adopt them as their own.

Mentors who are supporting fellow colleagues with this way of knowing can, first of all, explicitly validate their points of view as important. This will nurture a sense of trust and safety that will likely enable socializing knowers to take greater risks in expressing themselves and asking questions, thereby facilitating growth. When inviting socializing knowers to engage in dialogue and reflection, mentors can support their growth by gradually encouraging these mentees to look inside themselves—turn inward—for what they would like to do and to voice what steps they think would matter most or be most effective. In other words, mentors can simultaneously provide guidance and expertise that socializing knowers need, while gradually challenging mentees to consider their own thinking first and to begin to act with greater independence from those they consider authorities (e.g., mentors).

Supportively challenging these mentees to search inside for their own thinking about a next step or perspective on a situation will help these adults to generate their own values and standards over time and to see themselves as authorities.

The Self-Authoring Knower as Mentee

Mentees who are self-authoring knowers have developed the capacity to appeal to an internal system when contemplating how to improve practice. They are less concerned with pleasing a mentor and more concerned with learning from a mentor's feedback and perspective. In the end, though, these mentees will decide for themselves whether or not to adopt a mentor's suggestions and how to respond in various situations and/or to various dilemmas. They are capable of looking internally for what they feel should be done and of taking a stand for their beliefs. Self-authoring mentees will view the mentoring relationship as one in which they are collaborating with another person to improve their competencies and to grow. In addition, these adults will consider a mentoring relationship to be more reciprocal (e.g., they will offer constructive feedback to mentors on their performance). Unlike adults who are socializing knowers, self-authoring knowers are able to establish boundaries with their mentors and have internal authority over their work.

Self-authoring mentees will be less concerned with external recognition and acceptance from a mentor; instead, they will internally assess a mentor's feedback and decide whether or not they need it to improve their own competencies. These adults accept that conflict and difference of opinion are natural in any relationship and can lead to enhanced perspectives, better solutions, and achievement of goals. They generate their own ideals and professional obligations. Since they are most concerned with the smooth running of their own self-systems, challenging these adults to consider perspectives that oppose their own will support growth and learning.

Over time, as a person grows from the self-authoring to the self-transforming way of knowing, a mentor can supportively challenge a mentee to question his or her personal ideology and to consider how the mentee might be made up of more than one personal ideology. This can, gradually, help a self-authoring knower to come to see that one's self is more than the smooth functioning of one's ideology; there are other parts of the self that are incomplete or not fully developed. As growth occurs, a person will begin to yearn for a fuller sense of completeness and interdependence. A person seeks to develop neglected aspects of the self and new and deeper forms of intimacy and interdependence.

The Self-Transforming Knower as Mentee

Recall that self-transforming knowers are less invested in their own identity and more open to others' perspectives. They are constantly questioning and assessing the way their self-system works and see a mentor as a potential companion in this process. They want their mentors to join them as equals in dialogue about life and work tensions, paradoxes, and competing priorities and in making room for exploring contradictions (internal and systemic). Engaging in a mentoring relationship will feel most satisfying to self-transforming knowers if their mentor (or mentors—they realize that they yearn for different mentors based on different needs) views the relationship as a partnership that aims to be mutually beneficial and growth enhancing.

Self-transforming mentees will consider mentoring relationships to be contexts in which both partners can deepen their interpersonal relationship with one another. They value opportunities for dialogue that enables them to develop a richer understanding of their own and their mentors' assumptions, ideologies, commitments, and intentions and the strengths and limitations of these. These spaces for dialogue will be experienced as a support and a developmental challenge that will support their growth. Since self-transforming mentees are able to take a perspective on their own ideology, they constantly examine why and how it works as it does. It will feel supportive when mentors accompany these knowers in this process.

Once again, I will share excerpts from two adults, Drs. David McCallum and Aliki Nicolaides, who have been identified as self-transforming knowers, to share the supports and challenges they value in mentoring relationships. Several common themes emerged: a need for multiple mentors to satisfy their needs for growth, a recognition of having different needs for growth and needing a variety of mentors, commonality as to what is experienced as developmental supports and challenges, and a desire for the mentoring relationship to be mutually growth enhancing. Please note that I am not necessarily suggesting that these same themes would emerge from a larger sample of self-transforming knowers; instead, I offer this information as a way to illuminate how these two knowers experience the pillar practice of mentoring. I hope you find this helpful.

In commenting on their experience of what they value about mentoring and about their mentors, both Aliki and David expressed the need for multiple mentors. As Aliki put it:

> Mentoring in the conventional sense does not feel right to me. . . . I understand to be a mentor is relative to the direction I am stretching towards from moment to moment. For me a mentor is learning with me while at the same time offering tremendous wisdom in the form of intimate supports and spontaneous challenges.

Like Aliki, David emphasized the importance of having a network of mentors, or a "host" of mentors in different domains of his life, depending on specific needs. Familiar with developmental growth in himself, he shared:

After years of longing for a mentor, I find myself surrounded, supported, and challenged by a host of mentors in multiple spheres of my life. I suspect that as I was emerging into and navigating my way through my self-authoring years, I was unripe for the learning that my present mentors can facilitate. There are people I consider mentors in the area of my vocation, my professional and academic lives, in my spiritual life and ongoing growth . . . and what is even more amazing to me is how diverse these men and women are.

David continued by explaining that while "incredibly grateful that so many people have willingly stepped into the circles of my life to take up this role," he realized that "I do not expect any one of them to provide for more than a few of my needs."

In explaining the supports and challenges they needed from their mentors, both Aliki and David emphasized how important it was that they share a mutual "love" and "respect" with their mentors. Both also expressed a value for mentors who offered challenges to help them grow. Aliki explained what "intimate supports" and "challenges" for growth meant to her in this way:

What I mean by intimate supports is that there is a felt sense of love, of commitment, and of respect that is mutual. What I mean by spontaneous challenges is that there is an emerging sense of discovery and revelations as to what may be my learning edge in a given moment and that my mentor in that moment recognize and illuminates for me to take the challenge and meet it without any predetermined thought and or constitution from the mentor's side.

She continued by sharing an example how one of her mentors offered both supports and challenges as she completed her doctoral dissertation. In her words, her mentor offered her

ways to stretch my methodological and concrete approaches to my [work]. Many times in what feels like very connected and intimate moments she sees something that I must do to continue to grow into myself and bring forth my self, and she demands it from me in the most loving ways.

Similarly, David echoed Aliki's desire for a mentor who offered both affirming supports and developmental challenges.

What I desire from a mentor is a sufficient amount of love and respect—*that he or she is willing to tenderly kick my ass when necessary*. I consider tough love a more respectful way of dealing with me than the soft-glove approach because this communicates that a person truly respects me.

David further explained that while he appreciated and valued when his mentors offered "appropriate and timely challenges that feel genuinely aligned with the realization my highest values and purposes," he admitted that at the same time, he was "not as graceful about receiving feedback as I'd like, but so it goes."

David and Aliki also voiced appreciation for mentors creating spaces for them to make their own "connections" and to "generate" their own insights. As David put it, "I love it when my mentors acknowledge the mutual benefit of our relationship and have the flexibility [and] maturity to be both a learner [and] peer and a mentor."

These kinds of "generative conversations," as David called them, where both mentors and mentee are learning from and with each other, were satisfying and meaningful to both Aliki and David. Similarly, Aliki noted, "What I love most are the moments when we are both collectively present to the magnificence and mystery of *life* in the *now* and are able to sit in a meaningful silence." For both Aliki and David, mentoring relationships were those where both mentors and mentees were deeply connected and where they saw and recognized all parts of each other. Importantly, both explained that they felt mentoring relationships were those in which there was a commitment to "mutual growing," as Aliki put it.

Importantly, mentoring relationships serve as developmentally appropriate "holding environments" for growth for adults in the transitional spaces between one way of knowing and the next, just as with the other pillar practices.

IMPLICATIONS: HOW OUR WAY OF KNOWING INFLUENCES THE WAY WE MENTOR

I want to highlight a few additional points about how mentors' different ways of knowing will influence how we relate to our mentees and the kinds of developmental capacities we have for offering supports and challenges to facilitate growth. Importantly, our ways of knowing will influence the expectations we bring to mentoring relationships, as well as our experience of our mentees and the relationships themselves. It is also helpful to point out, I think, that the kinds of satisfaction a person receives from serving in the role of mentor will be influenced by the mentor's way of knowing. For example, a socializing knower may feel most satisfied if assured that the mentee approves of him or her. A self-authoring knower may be less concerned with a mentee's approval and more concerned with helping the mentee to develop a sense of independence.

The main point I want to highlight here is that a mentoring relationship is one between two human beings, or more in team mentoring, and that just as in other relationships in life, each person brings his or her whole self to the relationship. In this case, we all bring our way of knowing and the strengths and limits of it to our mission of supporting another person's development. Our way of knowing enables us to possess different internal resources to supporting another's growth. In light of this, and also in light of our complex human needs, it seems wise to consider how a developmental mindfulness can help us to strengthen both informal and formal mentoring. It seems wise also, given both the complexities of life in the 21st century and our frequent need for multiple mentors, that we begin to build mentoring communities or networks of mentor-mentee relationships in our schools and school systems.

WHY AND HOW SCHOOL LEADERS EMPLOY MENTORING

> *I guess the main thing that I learned or took away from this [mentoring] work is that all adults have unique [ways of knowing] and as a mentor, if you are aware of these understandings, the more you can support their learning.*
>
> —New York City principal-mentor to assistant principals

> *Every adult has a different way of knowing, [and] these . . . can be categorized, understood, and observed. Also the understanding of these can assist one in serving as a mentor.*
>
> —New York City principal-mentor to assistant principals

The above quotations from two principals who each mentor five New York City assistant principals aspiring to the principalship illuminate a theme in my research with school leaders, regardless of their positions (principals, assistant principals, aspiring superintendent, teachers): understanding adults' ways of knowing can help mentors support their mentees and can help both people to grow.

Principals, assistant principals, aspiring superintendent, and teachers in my research emphasized that mentoring helps them and other adults in their schools to build relationships, decrease feelings of isolation, manage change, open communication, become aware of each other's thinking and assumptions, learn from broadening their perspectives, and share information and expertise.

Mentoring, the majority of these school leaders explained, provides teachers (and themselves) with vital opportunities for growth. In their view, people grow and develop in and *through* these relationships. For most school leaders in my research, the underlying philosophy behind the practice of mentoring was to share leadership, strengthen interpersonal relationships within their school communities, help adults to manage change and diversity, and of course, support adult learning and growth. According to these school leaders, mentoring, similar to the practices of teaming, providing leadership roles, and engaging in collegial inquiry, enhances relationships, supports learning and growth, and thus strengthens the broader school community.

Common themes emerged as to the ways in which the practice of mentoring supported learning and growth. I discovered that these themes—listed below—were similar regardless of whether the school leaders were discussing the practice of mentoring for teachers or for themselves. For all parties involved, mentoring was a means of accomplishing the following:

- Accessing information about how to navigate the school or school system
- Sharing advice about adjusting to new positions and roles
- Facilitating learning about the school mission and culture
- Accessing information about what the role/position (e.g., principalship, teaching) required and what the expectations were
- Tapping the emotional and logistical (e.g., nuts and bolts, strategies) support that mentees needed to carry out their roles successfully
- Providing a context for conversations that explored how to balance the multiple demands of work (a key theme among principals and assistant principals)
- Discovering creative strategies for managing the complex demands of leading (a prominent theme among principals, assistant principals, and aspiring superintendents)

Mentoring is a practice that supports the learning and growth of *both* the mentee and the more experienced or veteran teachers, school leaders stressed. Whether they were sharing expertise or knowledge or questions with other teachers in a mentoring relationship, contributing to spreading the school mission through mentoring, or leading mentoring programs, nearly all of these school leaders believed that mentoring contributed to the growth and learning of all participating teachers—and often the school community as a whole. Involvement in mentoring not only nurtured learning but also helped adults to acclimate to change.

Mentoring allows both parties in the relationship to share expertise and to support each other in learning. Nearly all of these school leaders stated that the mentoring relationship provided contexts for individual and shared reflection and dialogue, which they named as essential to supporting adult learning. As Table 6.2 shows, these school leaders implemented mentoring practices in a variety of ways for several purposes. The commonality that emerged was that in almost all of the examples of this practice, the principals remarked that mentoring was a practice that supported both the mentor's and the mentee's learning in important ways.

Two additional important learnings related to leaders' thinking about the practice of mentoring emerged from my 2004 research and again from my recent research. First, nearly all of the principals and assistant principals emphasized the profound contribution their own mentors made to support their growth and development as school leaders and more generally as people. Second, nearly all of them emphasized that they wanted to learn more about mentoring and the developmental principles that inform it. My hope is that this chapter is helpful to them and others as we continue the journey of supporting adult growth and development.

In the next section, I first briefly discuss several examples of how principals employ mentoring as a practice to support teacher learning and growth in their schools. The range

Table 6.2 Mentoring: Reasons School Leaders Employed This Practice and Examples of Mentoring Programs

Reasons to Provide Mentoring	Examples
Philosophy for mentoring programs for teachers	• Sharing and including others in leadership • Embracing and helping people manage change • Fostering diversity • Sharing knowledge and expertise • Fostering reflective practice • Strengthening interpersonal relationships • Facilitating learning and growth

Mentoring for teachers	The purposes of these programs include the following:
	
	  • Spread the mission
	  • Exchange information
	  • Provide social or relational support to new teachers and/or staff
	  • Support learning (skills, content) and growth
	
	Mentors are selected according to different criteria, depending on the program's purpose, including the following:
	
	  • Knowledge and understanding of the mission
	  • Teaching experience
	  • Disciplinary focus
	  • Common background and/or other characteristics (nonacademic)
	
	Mentoring programs are structured in various ways, including as follows:
	
	  • Pair experienced teachers with new teachers or teachers who are new to the school
	  • Pair experienced/practicing teachers with intern teachers (graduate students, interns)
	  • Mentors teach other teachers to become mentors

Mentoring by principals	• Principals mentor assistant principals who aspire to the principalship • Experienced principals mentor leaders new to the principalship

of examples reflects their belief that mentoring is a vital way to support adult learning, as well as their commitment to helping adults to manage change, grow, and build community. Next I present learnings from my research with principals who served as mentors to aspiring principals (who are assistant principals).

Examples of Principals' Use of Mentoring to Support Teachers' Growth and Learning

[Mentors] meet with their mentees constantly. They troubleshoot for them. They act as advocates for them.

—Joe Marchese, Westtown School, Westtown, Pennsylvania

The principals and assistant principals involved in my research have developed several kinds of mentoring programs for teachers at their schools. In this section, I first describe the general features of these mentoring programs and then present two examples. The first is a mentoring program for beginning teachers, which is the most common type of mentoring program that these school leaders have implemented in their schools. The second is a computer-based mentoring program, which is an example of an innovative approach to mentoring that combines group mentoring (a team approach) with the more traditional format of one-to-one relationships.

Most programs for teachers are voluntary. (Exceptions include programs in the Boston and Florida public schools where all first-year teachers are assigned mentors.) Most of the school leaders involved with these programs expressed interest in improving them, and most leaders at schools without such programs expressed interest in developing them. Program purposes vary from exchanging information to providing relational support to new and experienced teachers to "mission spreading" to supporting graduate student interns. Most often, experienced teachers volunteer or are "encouraged" or "recruited" to participate as mentors. All programs, though, are focused on supporting learning. School leaders reported that they select mentors according to a variety of criteria, including understanding of the mission; teaching experience; disciplinary focus; educational background; and other, nonacademic characteristics. Selection of mentors depends on program purposes.

I next discuss the specific ways in which principals engaged in creating mentoring practice for teachers. Some programs fell to one end of a continuum—what I refer to as a *seed* or *early* phase. In these, mentor-mentee pairs usually met during the school year for *instrumental* purposes, and these programs had an important *logistical* orientation (e.g., knowledge sharing about school/faculty rules and policies and school life). Many school leaders reported that these are "informal" programs, often also oriented toward offering vital "emotional" or "social" support. Mentor-mentee pairs were "encouraged" to meet whenever necessary, and fewer structures were in place to facilitate ongoing dialogue.

On the other end of the continuum, what I call the *more developed and comprehensive* approach, many school leaders reported having well-developed, longstanding, and highly sophisticated programs in place. In these types of programs, mentor-mentee pairs met throughout the year for *instrumental, relational,* and *dialogic* purposes (i.e., conversations that include both knowledge sharing and reflection on and into practice), and established structures supported ongoing dialogue (e.g., mentor teachers met in groups to reflect on the challenges of mentoring, and mentees met in groups or teams to reflect on their teaching and experiences as new teachers). These programs appeared to be more comprehensive and oriented toward reflective practice and collegial inquiry than those in the early phase. School leaders, for the most part, explained that both types of programs had grown to be an important part of the fabric of the school.

Programs for Beginning Teachers

Nearly all of the school leaders in my research reported that they had mentoring programs for beginning teachers. Some of these programs were not only for teachers who were new to the profession but also for teachers who were new to a particular school. In most cases, though not all, new teachers were paired with a veteran teacher. In other cases, in addition to this pairing, new teachers were invited to attend seminars—delivered by more senior faculty—and support groups for new teachers in which they engaged in collegial inquiry about their instructional practices and the challenges and joys of first-year teaching, for example. In these group meetings, at several schools, teachers discussed their expectations for support and the things that were working or not working in their classes and developed a sense of their shared experiences, thus decreasing feelings of isolation and building feelings of community.

For example, Kathleen Perry, principal of Lake Worth Community High School in Lake Worth, Florida, explained that all teachers new to her school—and to Palm Beach County School District where her school is located—had the opportunity to meet with their mentors individually and to meet with a "team" of mentors periodically. Mentors, or "buddy teachers," as Kathleen called them, are generally assigned by department chairs based on common disciplinary focus. A Beginning Teacher Team was composed of the department chairperson, the technology coordinator (who floats from team to team), a more experienced teacher within the department, and a teacher outside of the department. In Kathy's view, the team approach enabled new teachers to benefit from multiple perspectives on practice and concerns.

> The [new] teachers are getting an opportunity to meet with someone who can give them support and answer questions as it relates to their specific disciplines [and] someone who can work with them in classroom and climate and lesson planning and technology use and so forth.

When the new teachers met with their teams, Kathleen explained that sometimes she and others would invite colleagues to share a particular expertise or skill with the group. At other times, the focus was on addressing questions or sharing experiences.

> We have some people that we identify as having strengths in [particular] areas, and we'll say [to them], "Would you mind presenting something on this?" or, "Would you be [at the team meeting] to answer questions about this?" or . . . sometimes it's . . . not as formal as a stand-up presentation. It is . . . these are some things that I do. Or do you have any questions? Did you run into any troubles?

Teachers at Lake Worth Community High School also had the opportunity to participate in "new teacher support groups." These groups were composed of teachers new to the school. The new teachers met with each other throughout the year, and as Kathleen explained, they met "more frequently" during the first seven weeks of school, since this is an especially important period of transition and "adjustment." The main purpose of the "new teacher support group" was to increase a "sense of belonging," decrease feelings of isolation, engage in shared "inquiry," and help with adjustment. These groups were, in Kathleen's view, an opportunity for them to come together and say, "Wow, I didn't know it was gonna be like this, or I had this happen too." So that they can recognize that they do have some shared experiences and not feel isolated. Or to hear [from colleagues] that "that was a neat thing, it was very successful."

Kathy shared that mentoring relationships were "good things" for both seasoned and new teachers at her school. She also hoped that these experiences would encourage all teachers to continue the "practice" in informal ways after their experience in the formal program was complete.

A Computer-Based Program

While head-of-school Jack Thompson was serving at Palm Beach Day School in Palm Beach, Florida, he initiated a mentoring program in which faculty who had expertise and sophisticated skills in using computers mentored other faculty. This type of mentoring program was aimed at helping teachers feel more comfortable admitting when they were confused and getting the help they needed to grow their expertise. Mentor faculty worked with those they were mentoring in both larger groups and also one-on-one. Jack felt it was important to have both large-group instruction as well as more private mentoring, since in a large group, many faculty "feel reluctant to ask questions." At the same time, he explained that in the large group, having the computer mentors work with the entire faculty was helpful because faculty developed "a sense that someone else was working with you on this, to share and so forth." One important role of the computer mentor was, from Jack's perspective, to help faculty move from one stage of proficiency with computers to the next. As he explained,

If you're at [a particular] stage, then your computer mentor will take you to the next stage. And if you're more competent than not in your classroom, but you want to refine a technique, okay, let's go there. And . . . it is the approach we're using for the next two or three years with the computer.

Jack saw a direct connection between supporting adult learning in this computer-mentoring program and supporting student learning. If faculty "feel more computer competent," Jack emphasized, then they would feel better "personally and professionally." When this occurred, he believed that it certainly affected "the classroom" and students' learning as well.

An Example of Principals' Mentoring to Support Assistant Principals' Learning

I need a mentor.

—Experienced New York City principal, March 2008

The above passage is from a principal who has been identified as exemplary. He has been serving as a principal for more than 20 years in the New York City school system and was a teacher for nearly 15 years before that. Bob (not his real name) is one of the principals I have had the honor of working with and learning from for four years now, since he serves as a mentor-principal to assistant principals who are aspiring to the principalship. Bob *is* an experienced principal. Bob *is* an experienced and generous mentor. The assistant principals he mentors adore and appreciate the generous ways in which he gives of himself. They say he shares "pearls of wisdom" and always is able to make time "to carefully listen." And yet, I find his yearning—in the passage above—for a mentor himself, to be so real, so sincere, so authentic, so heartfelt, and so important. Having a mentor is a "gift," Bob explained immediately after voicing his desire for one. He continued by talking about his own mentors and how they inspired him to do the leadership and mentoring work he does. Still, he admitted that he would love to have a mentor. This seems to be a human need we do not outgrow; instead, it is one from which we grow.

In this section, I will share some of the learnings from my research conducted with New York City principals, like Bob, who serve as mentors to assistant principals who are aspiring to the principalship. More specifically, I will share key themes that emerged from my work with both the mentor-principals and the assistant principals they mentored: What does mentoring mean to them? What constitutes a "good mentoring relationship"? What kinds of supports did the assistant principals appreciate most from the mentor-principals? What do the mentor-principals feel most proud of in terms of their mentoring of assistant principals? As you read please notice the similarities between what these principals and assistant principals value and deeply appreciate about the mentoring relationship. I hope what follows is helpful to you as you strengthen your own mentoring program, practice, and school-as-mentoring community.

As mentioned in Chapter 4, for the past four years, I have had the honor of working with and learning from a group of experienced principals who serve as mentors to assistant principals through the New York City Educational Leadership Institute (ELI). The mentor-principals participated in three-hour workshops/seminars that I delivered four times a year for three years. These workshops focused on the pillar practices, with special emphasis on mentoring. Principal-mentors also learned about ways of knowing and the importance of shaping holding environments. Our workshops created contexts for the mentor-principals to engage in collegial inquiry about their mentoring practice, challenges encountered, how to apply the pillar practices and theory to their mentoring relationships, and the joyful moments of mentoring.

Importantly, all of the mentor-principals experienced working and learning together in our group meetings as a support to their growth and learning. They also experienced engaging as mentor in a mentoring relationship as a support for (and good developmental challenge) to their growth.

Conceptions of Mentoring

During one of our initial meetings, we discussed the idea that each of the five assistant principals these principals mentored would view the mentor differently, depending on how they, the mentees, were making meaning. We also discussed how each of the mentor-principals made sense of what it meant to be "a good mentor." For one of them, let's call him Paul, it meant, "sharing the nuances of leadership" with his mentee. He continued by explaining that his mentee let him know that he really wanted to learn "the nuts and bolts of the principalship." This was a common request for support.

At the start of each year, all of the mentor-principals and the assistant principals they mentored gathered for a forum aimed at helping them to get to know each other, understand each other's expectations, and develop a shared understanding of what kinds of supports would be helpful to the mentee. Each mentor-principal, on average, served as a mentor to five assistant principals. I designed the protocol questions and facilitated the conversation. Mentor-principals sat with their mentees at round tables (usually).

After the welcoming, I invited everyone to respond to the question, "What does mentoring mean to you?" and then, "What, from your perspective, constitutes a good and productive mentoring relationship?" We took a few minutes to freewrite or freethink in response to these questions, and then each person at the table shared. This kind of dialogue helps the mentee to clarify his or her thinking, the mentor to learn more about the mentee to be of best support, and the group to learn about each other. Nearly all of the mentors have remarked that this dialogue helped them to build an understanding of how their mentees were making sense of the mentoring relationship and the kinds of supports they thought they needed from their mentors. I share more questions that are developmentally oriented at the end of this chapter.

Below are central themes that have emerged over the years in terms of the mentees' (assistant principals) perspectives on what mentoring meant to them.

- "The sharing of best practices so that we don't have to reinvent the wheel."
- "Having someone who is on your side." (advocate)
- "Developing trust" is important. (trust)
- "Having your own personal coat of armor." (protection)
- "My mentor let himself be transparent." (transparency)
- A mentor can be informal or formal.
- A mentor is interested in "helping others take the plunge."
- A mentor makes "it safe to take risks and gives you the confidence to succeed."
- A mentor "takes someone under their wing."
- A mentor "provides guidance, protection, and direction."
- A mentor is "generous and available."
- A mentor is "an educational friend; you can say anything and know that she will keep it confidential. It's important that both mentors and mentees feel this way."

Year after year, the most common needs that mentees expressed centered on the importance of being in a mentoring relationship where trust existed, confidentiality was respected, and where it was safe to share and take risks.

Characteristics of "Good Mentors"

"When you think about a positive mentoring relationship you have had, what are some of the characteristics that made it effective? What types of things were helpful or felt especially supportive? What do you think are the characteristics of good mentoring?" These are some of the questions I asked mentees to understand their perspectives on the characteristics of a good mentor. Here are some of the themes that have emerged over the years:

- There is "mutual respect."
- "Trust."
- Respect for each other's "knowledge" and "trust in each other's judgment."
- "Helpful . . . giving me the things I will need as a principal."
- "Equilibrium in the relationship; it's not hierarchical."
- "Warm and serious."
- "A personal connection is there; it's not all business."
- "The relationship is reassuring."
- "When a mentor acts as a mirror for me; helps me hold myself up to myself . . . and asks, "What do you see?"
- "Both people can be honest."
- "Being accepting when I admit my own defeats and weaknesses."
- "Lead someone to their own knowing."
- "Relationship-based."
- "Guiding you through the process, one step at a time."
- A relationship where the mentor says, "You always can call me."
- "Engaging in real conversations."

The most common characteristics that were voiced every year were respect, trust, acceptance, availability, and honesty.

Growing in Leadership

When the assistant principals were asked by their mentor-principal, "What do you think you need most from me this year in terms of supports?" common themes emerged. The following words characterize the assistant principals' responses:

- Honesty
- Being nonjudgmental
- Reciprocity
- Patience
- Sharing of knowledge and expertise
- Confidentiality
- Encouragement/empowerment

- Time management/flexible and creative
- "I need my principal to release me for participation in this program."
- Collegial support to learn how to get the job done well without being obsessed with perfection
- To feel challenged
- To be trusted
- To "see" recommended approaches and strategies in action
- "Allow me to vent."
- "Give me feedback about: Does my set of beliefs show in my actions?"
- "Help me establish priorities and goals to accomplish."
- "Help me with a vision; help me see the process from start to end."
- Balancing instruction with administration
- Communication
- Help me "network and build professional relationships."
- How to get along with multiple principals in one building
- "Direct feedback, useful suggestions."
- Critical-reflection-dialogue with empathy, support, and a focus on successful development
- Good listening
- "Instill confidence."
- "Tell me, show me, share with me, listen to me."
- "Accept, respect, be honest."
- "Ask questions, get answers, find resources persons, visit."
- Confidentiality
- Honest feedback with ideas and differentiated suggestions and scaffolds for development
- Develop closer relationships with mentor group to increase learning through this process.
- Safety within mentor/mentee relationship and with the group

The most common requests for support that were expressed every year were trust, sharing expertise and knowledge, engaging in dialogue, and confidentiality.

What Mentors Feel Most Proud Of

When the principal-mentors were asked each year, "What do you feel most proud of in terms of your mentoring? What do you think went really well?" several themes emerged. I list the most common of these below.

- Having "real conversations about meaningful things"
- Listening to each other and being in conversation
- Knowing that the assistant principals had learned what goes into principalship

- Customizing my mentoring to meet the assistant principals' individual needs
- Using ways of knowing to help them grow
- Saying "I need to learn" as principal and helping the assistant principals to understand that
- Knowing that we learned from each other

The principal-mentors also expressed appreciation for the "gift" of working collaboratively with fellow principal-mentors and named this as a source of learning and growth. As one said—and this was a common sentiment among the groups—this work "provided a space for slowing down, giving me time to reflect with my colleagues."

AN EXAMPLE OF A MENTORING PROGRAM: LESSONS FROM THE FIELD

As discussed, one common example of mentoring across the majority of the schools in my research involved developing partnerships with local universities and building mentoring relationships between experienced teachers and student interns in undergraduate and/or master's degree programs. In the case that follows, I discuss how one principal, Dr. Sarah Levine, while serving as head of Belmont Day School in Massachusetts, designed and implemented an Associate Teachers Program in her school. This case illuminates a common and promising way to implement mentoring to support adult development.

In the Associate Teachers Program, experienced teachers assumed leadership roles each semester in mentoring newly hired teachers and graduate students from a local university, who served as associate teachers in master teachers' classrooms. The mentor's role was to support and challenge the associate teacher. Sarah believed that this program offered growth opportunities to both mentors and mentees:

> It gets teachers who are veterans to think about practice, to reflect, to explain and articulate practice. All those good things. It helps [the associates] to combine the theory that they're learning in the classrooms in the context of the live school setting.

Sarah placed high value on the practice of mentoring. "Even when we do hiring," she said, "we look for people who have mentored before, supervised before, because that's a very helpful quality." Mentors and associate teachers were paired each semester, and they shared teaching responsibilities. Since they were in the same classroom throughout the term, they observed and commented on each other's teaching, offering feedback, suggestions, and support. Although mentoring was time consuming for the more experienced teachers, who conferred with the associate teachers each day, Sarah believed that the growth opportunities for both mentors and mentees outweighed the inherent challenges and constraints.

Educating teachers so that they could better support the growth and learning of associate teachers was needed, in Sarah's view, to create a safe context in which associates could share their thinking and feelings. For experienced teachers, Sarah and the upper- and lower-school division directors facilitated workshops on how to mentor and offer support. Experienced teachers were encouraged to reflect on their teaching through collegial inquiry with associate teachers; Sarah; and June (not her real name), who was the director of the program. Sarah and the division directors also organized seminars and programs for both associate teachers and the experienced teachers. In these seminars, Sarah and the division directors taught and advised the experienced and associate teachers about effectively handling pedagogical and relational concerns and interests. Twice a week, the other experienced teachers (mentors and those who were not participating in the Associate Teachers Program) also delivered seminars for associate teachers where experiences were shared and tested. For example, one teacher presented two sessions on teaching elementary school science. These teachers were paid a small stipend to give a class or more on a particular issue.

In addition, inviting experienced teachers to share their knowledge in this role provided opportunities both for the school community to view the teacher as a leader and for the teacher to develop further as a leader. Sarah felt that one experienced teacher, Buddy (not his real name), had benefited greatly from this role. Buddy's preparation of several hands-on seminars on integrating computers into the classroom had "helped him get out of his classroom. It's helped other people see how creative he is." Sarah felt that "his positive engagement as teacher of teachers" had helped his professional development.

As mentioned earlier, Daloz (1999, 2000) suggests that effective mentoring relationships attend to both person and context. The Associate Teachers Program at Sarah's school, like others in this study, seemed to do just that. Mentors were educated to support their mentees better, and throughout the year, they were also supported in their work by Sarah and June. June said that experienced teachers appeared to be learning much from the mentoring leadership role.

> The mentor teachers are coming to me, on a very regular basis, saying, "Boy, am I learning a lot. I'm learning about teaching. I'm learning about what it is to be an adult in this school. I'm really reflecting on practice. I'm really thinking about interpersonal skills. I'm really learning as much as the associates are." The associate teachers are in touch with the knowledge base that's out there, which the experienced teachers may not have encountered when they were in school, because, you know, so much has happened in the last few years.

As for the associates, they "had some very expansive experiences, and we've turned out some wonderful teachers," Sarah said. In her view, the Associate Teachers Program not only encouraged the faculty to take more responsibility and self-authorship of their work, but it enabled the school community to "become more of a professional development school because we are in the business of teaching and training teachers."

As this case and the other examples presented in this chapter show, mentoring is a developmental practice that can help adults grow to manage better the complexities of work and life. Mentoring relationships are reciprocal and create a safe "holding environment" for growth in which both individuals can become more aware of the assumptions that guide their actions. In other words, a mentor is in a position to challenge the thinking of a mentee supportively, and the mentee can help the mentor become more aware of his or her own assumptions. Both mentor and mentee can experiment with new ways of thinking and acting.

A developmental perspective can inform the ways in which we understand how adults experience mentoring. If a person displays signs of uneasiness or frustration in a mentoring relationship, we might consider this frustration in developmental terms to support him or her.

Working on discussing practice and on solving problems in a mentoring relationship can serve as a context of learning and growth, provided that each partner in the relationship is encouraged, supported, and challenged in appropriate ways. Mentoring relationships can be safe contexts for adults to express the more complicated selves they have become—or the selves they are in the process of becoming.

A PROTOCOL FOR BUILDING MENTORING RELATIONSHIPS THAT NURTURE ADULT DEVELOPMENT

How might we build mentoring relationships that serve as safe learning and growth-enhancing contexts for adults with different ways of knowing? Since we know that what constitutes support and challenge will differ according to a person's way of knowing, it can be helpful to invite adults to dialogue about what mentoring means to them, what kinds of supports they feel they need from their mentors, and the expectations both mentor and mentee bring to the relationship. In Figure 6.1, I offer some ideas and questions that can serve as a guide, or protocol, for building mentoring relationships from a developmental perspective. I created a portion of this protocol in partnership with Victoria Marsick; we employed some of these questions with university faculty who served as mentors and mentees (faculty new to the university). When working with principals, assistant principals, and teachers who assume roles as mentor, mentee, or both, I invite them to engage in dialogue around these questions. Before they engage in shared dialogue—or collegial inquiry—I invite them to freewrite or freethink in response to the questions in Figure 6.1. Our process is to respond to one question at a time in writing and then to share thinking in mentor-mentee pairs. School leaders have found these questions valuable in terms of building their relationships.

I invite you to consider sharing these questions with mentors and mentees in your school and district. Understanding our needs and expectations for each other as we engage in mentoring can enable us to build relationships that better support adults with different ways of knowing.

Figure 6.1   A Protocol for Strengthening Mentoring Relationships

---

I. Beginnings: Starting Where Your Mentees Are

One possible starting place is to begin by understanding your mentee's conception of mentoring. You may want to encourage your mentee to keep a *journal* so that he or she can track his or her thinking over time. (You may find it helpful to keep a journal yourself as well.) You might want to begin by having a *conversation* with your mentee about your own and his or her views of what makes for a good mentoring relationship. For example, you might ask some or all of the following questions:

1. What are *your* views of mentoring? What does mentoring mean to you?
2. What are your hopes and expectations for our mentoring relationship? What kinds of supports do you think would be most helpful to you?
3. What concerns, if any, do you have at this point in time?
4. What, in your view, makes for a good mentoring relationship? What do you think are the characteristics of a good mentor?

Initial Conceptions	
1. What is mentoring?	1. What is mentoring *not*?
2. My *hopes* and *expectations* for our mentoring relationship are . . .	2. The kinds of *supports* that would be most helpful to me are . . .
3. My *concerns* about the *work* we will do together and/or about our *relationship*, at this point in time, are . . .	3. In my view, a *good mentoring relationship* is one where . . .

You could take a few minutes to jot down your thinking and then share. You may find it helpful to revisit these questions midway through the year as a check-in and again at the end of the year.

For reflection and sharing:

_____

_____

How do our views of mentoring compare?

_____

_____

What have we learned about the kinds of supports needed to support growth and learning?

_____

_____

(Continued)

Figure 6.1 (Continued)

II. Mentoring: Clarifying Objectives/Goals for Working Together

Mentoring is a relationship.

As you know, investing time and energy into establishing a trusting relationship is essential. Engaging in conversation about the following questions will help you to build a safe, trusting and productive relationship and provide an opportunity for you and your mentee to clarify goals and objectives. You will want to check in on these periodically as well.

A. Clarifying Goals and Objectives

    1. What are your own goals for your mentoring relationships?

    2. What are your mentee's goals, hopes, and objectives?

    3. What kinds of boundaries do you both want to agree upon?

B. Practical Focus

    1. In what ways does your mentee think you can be most helpful to him or her?

> You may find it useful to listen in light of what you know about adult developmental theory and meaning making.

    2. Points of Connecting: In what ways do you think you can be most helpful to your mentee?

- What kinds of *supports* (developmentally speaking) seem most important to your mentee?
- What kinds of resources can you share with him or her? Sharing information and resources is important as a supplement to interpersonal interactions. It's helpful to follow up after information or resources are shared.
- In what ways could your time together be used most effectively to support learning?
- *Identifying and using multiple pathways for communicating:* What forms of communication will work well for both of you (e.g., e-mail, checking in by phone regularly, in-person meetings)? You will want to come to agreement and schedule communication in advance.
- *Setting a regular schedule for connecting that works for you and your mentee:* As you know, flexibility is also essential. So if you or your mentee needs to reschedule an appointment, you could use that as an opportunity for briefly checking in. What are our personal and learning needs?
- *Checking in on learning:* What kind of learning is happening? How are we doing in light of expressed goals? Create a space where thoughts and feelings can be expressed honestly.
- Make room for examining assumptions about what is going on (your own and your mentee's) and for exploring tensions, should they arise.

    3. Periodically check in on the relationship and on effectiveness of your communication. Ask the following:

- How do you think things are going for us?
- In what ways is what we are doing working well for us?
- What's not working as well as we had hoped it would?
- Are there other things we could be discussing or attending to that would be more helpful?

III. Issues to Consider and Benefits of Mentoring

A. *Communication, Relating, Thinking, and Problem-Solving Styles:*[1] It's important to consider how you might match your communication style to your mentee's style, especially when engaging in problem solving. Since people have different thinking and communication styles, you will want to consider these when identifying need areas, how to listen and help most effectively, and how to engage in problem solving. Following are some questions to consider:

1. Does your mentee prefer to hear only one way to proceed or several alternatives before deciding what should be done?

2. Is your mentee's preference to engage in dialogue about the problem and a vision for the possible outcomes before investing time in brainstorming ideas about problem solving?

3. Does your mentee prefer to talk through ideas and think aloud without taking a position about what should or could be done?

4. Does your mentee prefer to think about problems and solutions privately and only speak after developing a position he or she would like to run by you?

B. *The Importance of Asking Probing and Follow-up Questions:* As you know, asking questions can help you understand how your mentee (and your mentor) is making meaning of situations, problems, and issues of concern. Asking questions can also provide you with insight into your mentee's work context and sense of his or her role. Here are a few suggestions:

1. *Clarifying Questions:* Questions that enable you to check for understanding. "When you said *Y*, did you mean . . . ?"

2. *Open-ended Questions:* Questions that are not leading and cannot be answered with a *yes* or *no.*

3. Try to understand the specifics of the situation. *How, when, where, what,* and *why* questions can help with this.

4. Try to ask for examples so that you can better understand the situation.

5. It's often helpful to ask how the person is *thinking* and also how the person is *feeling* about situations, events, challenges, and problems.

6. It can be helpful to use the following types of questions:

   o How do you know what the person was feeling? This kind of question invites a person to make connections.
   o In what ways does the person's behavior seem disconnected to his or her surroundings? This kind of question asks the person to contrast pieces of given information.
   o What do you think the person can do to improve the situation? Why would that change things? These types of questions ask a person to make inferences.
   o What trends do the data on *X* show in your school? This question encourages the person to search for patterns and to view the situation holistically.
   o Ask why? This question invites the person to share how he or she is making sense of a situation and to share his or her reasoning.

(Continued)

Figure 6.1 (Continued)

C. Communicating and Being Present: You can monitor the communication that occurs between you and your mentee and improve its quality by doing the following:

- Listen actively.
- Point out and examine assumptions about what is going on (your own and your mentee's).
- Create a space where thoughts and feelings can be expressed honestly.
- Discuss personal and learning needs.
- Discuss boundaries.
- Focus on your mentee's learning needs and goals.
- Discuss accountability.
- Make room for checking in periodically. Engage in dialogue: What's working well? What could be improved? What are we learning?

CHAPTER SUMMARY

"For the first time, I felt like somebody was looking at me."

—Young teacher, speaking of her experience being mentored

Mentoring, like all of the pillar practices, can support growth. Each person in the relationship brings his or her unique gifts to it. An experienced teacher of nearly 15 years once told me, after an all-day workshop, that she had "a profound realization" that day. She continued,

> I used to feel that if I said I needed a mentor, that I was deficient in some way. Now I understand that needing a mentor does not mean that I am deficient in some way. Now I realize it just means I, like others, may need a little help and guidance.

We *all* can learn from each other when we engage in mentoring relationships, since we *all* bring gifts to them. Mentoring is a reciprocal relationship.

In this chapter, I have discussed the pillar practice of mentoring and illuminated how and why school leaders employ it to promote personal and professional learning, as well as organizational growth. Mentoring is a practice that brings attention to the ways in which a private relationship or series of relationships can work independently and synergistically to support adult growth. As I've noted, adults may need more than one relationship as a support for development. In fact, I've suggested that for schools to be rich and textured learning centers, they also need to be mentoring communities in which adults share in reciprocal mentoring relationships or networks of supports.

To summarize, first I reviewed the professional development and adult developmental literature on mentoring and suggested that bringing these two bodies of literature together to inform each other can be powerful. In other words, I hope I have illuminated how a developmental mindfulness in mentoring can help us to support more effectively adult growth in schools and throughout school systems. Second, I discussed how adults with different ways of knowing will tend to experience mentoring and the types of supports and challenges they will need in order to grow from it. I then briefly illuminated how school leaders explained that their mentoring program purposes vary from "spreading a mission" to exchanging information to providing both new and experienced educators with emotional support. I emphasized why school leaders value mentoring and how they think it supports adult learning and growth.

Since the literature on the importance of mentoring for teachers is extensive, I focused on presenting two examples of mentoring programs for teachers. Next I discussed some of the ways in which mentor-principals and the assistant principals they mentored experience the practice of mentoring as a support to their growth. I shared how these leaders described what effective mentoring meant to them, why they valued it, the supports they desired in order to grow, and a few key themes related to what the mentor-principals felt most proud of or satisfied with in terms of their mentoring relationships. In addition, I presented a case of a mentoring program for teachers and a guide that includes questions to help with building effective mentoring programs and relationships.

Throughout, I have emphasized that nearly all of the school leaders in my research used mentoring to support individual growth and organizational learning through various forms of partnering and adult collaboration. They believed that mentoring enables adults to grow; is mutually beneficial for both the mentor and the mentee; and helps adults broaden their perspectives on themselves, others, and their work.

I also highlighted a few important issues to keep in mind.

- What constitutes safety in a mentoring relationship will be different depending on our way of knowing.
- What *doubt* means will be experienced differently depending on our way of knowing.
- The expectations we have for mentors will vary depending on our way of knowing.
- Mentors will have different capacities and internal resources for offering supports depending on their way of knowing.
- What it takes and what it means to share stories, experiences, and uncertainties about practice will vary depending on ways of knowing.
- To build safe and meaningful mentoring relationships, it is important to explore hopes, expectations, and anticipated challenges.

As Daloz (1999) eloquently states, "Our lives move rhythmically back and forth through periods of building, breaking, building, breaking, and building again, as we grow older and accommodate to the changing circumstances of our lives" (p. 55). As noted, scholars have asserted that no single mentoring relationship can meet all of a person's human needs for growth; instead, mentoring relationships live and are nested in larger developmental networks or "constellations of relationships" (Ragins & Kram, 2007, p. 9), what I refer to as *mentoring communities,* which have important consequences for the ways in which any single mentoring relationship functions. In other words, as human beings, we need mentors throughout our lives, and our needs for different sources of support and challenges change as we change and are influenced by context. As mentioned, while mentoring undoubtedly supports growth in the context of an intimate, personal, reciprocal relationship, there is a need for developing a deeper understanding of how mentoring works for adults who have different ways of knowing and how schools and school systems can enhance mentoring relationships. I hope this chapter helps with the journey. Given the adaptive challenges school leaders encounter in today's educational world, we need to help each other build more supportive mentoring relationships and mentoring communities. We have much to learn from and with each other. The practice of building mentoring communities holds great promise.

APPLICATION EXERCISE

The following application exercise is offered to assist you in applying the ideas discussed in this chapter to your own context.

1. Knowing what you know about adults' ways of knowing and mentoring as a developmental practice, what is one way you might use these ideas to enhance your own mentoring practices and/or to support your own learning and growth?

2. What logistical or substantive challenges do you think you might encounter when implementing your new idea?

3. How might you secure needed help to implement your idea?

Table 6.3 might help you to implement your ideas in your specific and unique context.

Table 6.3   Mentoring: Supports and Challenges

Way of Knowing	Supports	Challenges
Instrumental		
Socializing		
Self-Authoring		
Self-Transforming		

REFLECTIVE QUESTIONS

Good friends are like stars; you don't always see them, but you know they're always there.

—Anonymous

The following questions are offered to assist you in applying the strategies outlined in this chapter to your work context. They can be used for internal reflection first and then to open up a team, school, or system dialogue.

1. What kinds of mentoring practices are in place in your work context? How do you think they work to support adult learning? What's working well, from your perspective? What would you like to see improved? Why?

2. What is one thing you've learned from this chapter that you feel is important in terms of your own mentoring relationships or mentoring in general? In stepping forward, how will you work to implement your learning?

3. How do you think adults—as mentors or mentees—with different ways of knowing experience mentoring? What kinds of supports and challenges exist in your school or school system for supporting mentoring and for supporting mentors as they mentor others?

4. What does mentoring mean to you? You may find it helpful to consider any of the following theatrical depictions of mentoring relationships: (a) *Good Will Hunting*, (b) *A Few Good Men*, (c) *Up Close and Personal*, (d) *Men in Black*, (e) *Educating Rita*, (f) *Finding Forester*, and (g) *A Doll's House*.

5. What does being a mentor mean to you? What do you see as a mentor's role and responsibilities? You may find it helpful to recall some of your own mentors or some of the ways that you have mentored others—what were the characteristics of those relationships that made them effective for supporting learning and growth?

6. What kinds of supports might be helpful for those serving as mentors in your department? At your school? In your district?

7. What have you experienced as the benefits of working in mentoring relationships? What have you noticed about other adults' engagement in mentoring relationships? How, if at all, do the ideas presented in this chapter help you? In what ways, if any, might you apply them to mentoring practices in your work context?

8. What kinds of successes have you noticed when adults in your school, department, or school system engage in mentoring relationships? What sorts obstacles or constraints, if any, do you see to helping adults engage even more effectively in mentoring, either as mentors or mentees or both?

9. How do you think adults in your school, department, or school district would describe their experience of learning and growing from engaging in mentoring? What, if anything, do you think they would experience as the risks?

(Continued)

(Continued)

10. Knowing what you know about adults who make meaning in developmentally different ways, how might you use different structures discussed in this chapter in your own mentoring to support adults with diverse ways of knowing?

11. What are two practical ideas for mentoring that you have learned about in this chapter that you would like to implement or encourage in your school? What small steps will you take to implement these?

7

Implementing the Pillar Practices

Cases From the Field

If one advances confidently in the direction of his dreams, and endeavors to live the life which he has imagined, he will meet with success unexpected in common hours.

—Henry David Thoreau, 1854/1995, "Conclusion"

In previous chapters, I discussed how principals, assistant principals, teachers, and superintendents can support adult learning in schools by employing the pillar practices for growth, using them to build schools as learning centers that are responsive to adults' developmental needs. In describing examples of the pillar practices, I have tried to illuminate the importance of the relationship between the individual and the environment, as well as the different kinds of supports and challenges that adults with different ways of knowing need to participate in these practices effectively and to grow through that participation.

In this chapter, I present several in-depth case examples written by school leaders who employed the four pillar practices in their work to support adult development. Individually and collectively, their work shows how teaming, providing leadership roles, engaging in collegial inquiry, and mentoring can help adults broaden their perspectives, build community, manage change, and grow. The authors of these cases are school leaders who have participated in my classes, my research, or my workshops, which focused on introducing the pillar practices and the developmental underpinnings of my learning-oriented model. As you will see, while these leaders employed the pillar practices, they adjusted them to meet the needs of the adults with whom they were working—that is, they adapted the pillar practices to the context of their work. In presenting developmentally oriented examples from these leaders' experiences in diverse contexts, I hope to make the pillar practices more tangible for you.

Case 1: Providing Leadership Roles and Mentoring to Principals and Assistant Principals

Case author: Janet Lynch Aravena

Current position: Coordinator, Executive Leadership Institute's Advanced Leadership Program for Assistant Principals, New York City

Primary pillar practices discussed: Providing leadership roles and mentoring

Before assuming her current position as coordinator of the Advanced Leadership Program for Assistant Principals in 2006, Janet Lynch Aravena worked for 33 years within the New York City Public School System. For 30 of those years, she served as teacher, coach, mentor, assistant principal, and principal in a K–8 school in upper Manhattan. She describes the important influence two mentors had on her career and the initiatives on mentoring and providing leadership roles that she implemented in her school.

I am the coordinator of the Advanced Leadership Program for Assistant Principals in New York City. This program is designed to offer one year of intensive professional development and mentoring to those assistant principals aspiring to the principalship. It is one of many efforts on the part of the Executive Leadership Institute of CSA (Council of Supervisors and Administrators) to prepare its constituents for effective leadership roles in the New York City Public Schools.

Prior to September 2006, I was principal of a K–8 school in Manhattan and had served as a mentor, both as a teacher and as a principal. During those years, I became convinced that providing leadership roles and mentoring were the two very strong initiatives that would work in my school setting to continually increase student achievement. My purpose in relating some of my experiences and reflections is to share with others the power of those initiatives.

Although I never labeled it as such, transformational learning is, and has always been, the cornerstone of my personal and professional life. The challenges inherent to school leadership, insights from professional readings, self-reflection, and my work with Ellie Drago-Severson have made this very clear to me.

Growing up in Sunset Park, Brooklyn, New York, the youngest in a family of four superachievers, I was constantly trying to measure up. I became, of necessity, quite reflective about life in general and school in particular, and I realized that learning and success for me was not the seemingly effortless path it was for them. The acquisition of new information and skills—informational learning—was laborious and time consuming. Consequently, I believe that I developed a certain capacity for managing the complexities of daily life and work, and I acquired an appreciation of the differences that exist in adult development and growth.

I was fortunate in my first year of teaching to work closely with a wonderful staff developer. Although not officially a mentor, she both encouraged and guided me as I tried to find my way. "My way" was what she emphasized, and the trust that developed between us helped me to navigate through that year. I am only now fully aware of how significant and important she was to my career as an educator. Her unwavering support and her refusal to give me the answers prompted me to work harder and harder and to constantly reflect on my practice. At the end of that first year, there were massive layoffs in New York City, and of course, the new teachers were the first to go. Many of my first-year colleagues found themselves pounding the pavement, but her recommendation landed me the position in the school where I would spend the next 30 years. That lovely "School on the Hill" in the northern section of Manhattan known as Washington Heights was to be the center and foundation of my professional life. It was here that I would grow and learn from very savvy and caring colleagues as we guided our students from the mastering of their ABCs through graduation to high school.

While continuing to teach, I found myself assuming different leadership roles—department chair, dean, assistant principal, and ultimately principal of the school. All along the way, the principal served as my mentor as well as my supervisor. She led by example, stressing the qualities that define a leader, not a leadership style. She emphasized that her style was hers and that her expectation was not that I be a clone. She challenged me to find my niche. Once again, as in my first year of teaching, solutions were not provided, but what was provided was the opportunity to safely develop my own solutions through reflection and guided practice.

I had "big shoes" to fill when I became principal, but because of the mentoring I had received, I had defined my own style. I was determined not only to continue but also to increase and enhance the academic standing of my already succeeding school. To make this a reality, I decided to concentrate on providing leadership roles for qualified staff and to provide a strong mentoring component for the assistant principals and the newly hired staff. I had a very definite advantage when I became principal of the school in July 1999 in that I did not have to spend time learning the strengths and needs of the majority of the staff. I had been there for some 25 years and had worked intimately with most of them. In fact, as a teacher, I had had the opportunity to participate in an excellent professional development program offered by the United Federation of Teachers and had mentored many of my teachers throughout the years. I had mentored the "new hirees," including new mathematics teachers and teachers in other disciplines, and I learned early on how important it is for all new hires to have a person with whom they can be honest and who will listen to what they perceive as their needs.

School Initiative 1: Providing Leadership Roles

To achieve my academic goals for the school, I tapped staff members with expertise in the critical areas of literacy, mathematics, technology, and data management and formed a cabinet of six teacher-leaders in various subject areas, in addition to my two assistant principals, to work through our plan for academic achievement and professional development.

(Continued)

(Continued)

I realized that as a new principal with a leadership style that was very different from that of the charismatic former principal, I needed to "create ownership" among the staff and to make very explicit my belief in guided "bottom-up" initiatives. Little by little, other staff members were tapped to assume leadership roles in such nonacademic areas as school safety, school procedures, staff and parent communication, testing, student activities, and professional development. Our Cabinet grew, and what was created, I believe, was an atmosphere of vitality and openness that fostered conversation and learning. We all learned, one from the other.

Our Learning Walks, which followed each professional development activity, helped tremendously in ensuring that all teachers' transformational learning was being supported and that each successive professional development was tailored to helping each person manage and make sense of expectations. Our teacher-leaders in the Cabinet understood the power of the Learning Walk and how vital these walks were in moving our achievement agenda forward. Consequently, we "walked" two to three times a month. Staff and students, although hesitant at first, came to enjoy and anticipate the visits from the "walkers."

Providing leadership roles brought about some very dramatic transformations in staff members. Michelle is a good example. Michelle came to our school while I was the assistant principal. I worked with her to acclimate her to the school. Michelle's original license was elementary (K–5), but she was unable to find a position because of an overage in that license area, so she took the short route of obtaining 12 math credits to get licensed in middle-school math, a shortage area. I assigned her a mentor (Cyndie) from the Mathematics department who had a great understanding of how to work successfully with students with skill deficits to help them gain proficiency. (Cyndie would later become assistant principal and then principal of the school.) Initially, Michelle lacked self-confidence and was very defensive. She did not feel as knowledgeable as many of her colleagues. We persisted with the mentoring, and over the years Michelle developed into one of our finest teachers. She became a cabinet member for student activities, and her leadership role in that area, coupled with the additional mathematics courses she was taking, gave her a sense of confidence and self-worth—so much so, that when many of the senior teachers had retired, she was called on to lead the department. She worked with the newly hired teachers and the entire department so effectively that our middle school mathematics' scores increased to 72.25 percent proficiency.

School Initiative 2: Mentoring

The mentoring process, so beneficial for me personally throughout my career and so beneficial, I felt, for those I had mentored, became, along with providing leadership roles, the cornerstone of my plan for sustaining and increasing the academic achievement of my K–8 school. As young teachers came on staff, we assigned mentors from the ranks of our recently retired colleagues as well as from the current staff. Michelle, in addition to assuming a leadership role, became a very effective mentor. Long gone were the days when teachers came and remained for their entire career in a particular school. Teachers now came to city schools, gained experience, learned the ropes, and then moved on to more lucrative positions in the suburbs. We realized we would not be able to maintain our high academic standard unless we had a strong mentoring process in place. We knew that we either had to try to retain the young teachers for as long as we could or, failing that, make them as effective as possible for the time we did have them. Mentoring was one tool we could use to accomplish this.

In addition to mentoring teachers, I embarked on a very vigorous mentoring of my two assistant principals. Two years prior to June 2006, I decided, after 30 years, that it was time for me to retire. I wanted to pass on the principalship to one of my assistant principals in an effort to continue the culture that had produced such outstanding results over the years. Although both were eminently qualified, the decision was made to groom Cyndie, a graduate of the school and the then-current assistant principal of the middle school, as the prospective next principal. This "grooming" was a combination of training and mentoring.

My training consisted of a very conscious modeling and the delegation of tasks that otherwise would have been mine. I modeled behaviors and constantly met with Cyndie, referring to the modeling and discussing reasons for my particular courses of action. I feel strongly that modeling is not enough, though. Follow-up is essential, because so often the reason why we behave and act in certain ways is not understood or goes unnoticed. To me, it is just good teaching, and the follow-up discussions are analogous to frequent summaries during a lesson. It is very time consuming but well worth the effort.

My mentoring took place primarily in the tasks I delegated to Cyndie. She was the decision maker. I did not tell her in advance the way I felt she should work things out. During the course of her planning, we met frequently, and I peppered the conversations with open-ended questions designed to raise her consciousness. There were many times when her strategies were different from the options I would have chosen, but unless I was convinced that the outcome would not be something I could live with, I chose to let her find her own way. There were times when unanticipated results occurred and we had to pick up the pieces, but they were few and far between, and the learning made it all worthwhile. During my last year as principal, I recommended Cyndie to The Advanced Leadership Program for Assistant Principals Program (ALPAP). I was mentoring in the program that year, and Cyndie was assigned to my colleague Peter. That turned out to be a good turn of events for Cyndie. The frequent exchanges between Peter and myself gave Cyndie a very focused and intense mentoring experience. As an unofficial mentor of Cyndie and official mentor to five other assistant principals, I had the opportunity to hone my mentoring skills. There was a wonderful reciprocity of learning. Everyone was learning. Everyone was growing. Everyone was reflecting on their practice—mentors and mentees.

Case 2: Mentoring Principals

Case author: Andrew Zuckerman

Current position: Zone Executive Director, Prince George's County, Maryland, Public Schools

Primary pillar practice discussed: Mentoring

Andrew Zuckerman's job is to lead a regional zone consisting of 22 schools in Prince George's County, Maryland. One of his primary responsibilities is to facilitate the professional learning of 22 principals. Before accepting this position, he worked as an administrator and leadership coach at Achievement First, a high-achieving nonprofit charter school management organization based in New York and Connecticut. He describes how he learned to use the practice of mentoring to help others learn how to build successful charter schools.

(Continued)

─── (Continued) ───

As a leadership coach for Achievement First, a nonprofit charter school management organization, I have the privilege of working with an extraordinary group of school leaders, collectively dedicated to the mission of closing the achievement gap in our public schools. My primary purpose is to facilitate the professional development of our principals in support of their efforts to build and maintain high-achieving urban schools. Previously, I had served as a teacher and administrator at the elementary and middle school levels, helping to build two successful charter schools along the way. While my experiences taught me how to build schools from the ground up, they did not explain how to coach other adults through the process. What practices could I exercise to help others succeed at their jobs as new school leaders and to help them build their own successful schools?

Using Mentoring to Support Leadership Growth

In the learning-oriented model of leadership that Drago-Severson (2004b) describes, I have found a powerful framework for supporting principals' professional development. Like teachers, principals need opportunities to learn and grow, and the pillar practices of the learning-oriented model provide the contexts in which principal learning can take place. Informed by adult developmental principles, the learning-oriented model seeks to facilitate transformational learning—learning characterized by shifts in how people make sense of their experiences (Drago-Severson). Supporting principals in this way can help them better manage the complex demands of school leadership in the 21st century (Drago-Severson) and help them build truly high-performing schools for their students and the communities in which they serve.

In this space, I'd like to share one aspect of my learning-oriented approach to support the development of school leaders: the practice of mentoring in support of principal learning and growth. Mentoring constitutes the majority of my work supporting principals as well as the context for some of the most powerful learning moments I have experienced this year as a leadership coach. Below, I describe my approach to mentoring from a developmental perspective. First, I discuss the ways in which I establish relationships with my colleagues that can function as holding environments (Drago-Severson, 2004b) for transformational learning and growth. I then explain how the relationship itself becomes the context for reflective dialogue that challenges us to rethink our understanding of leadership, offering examples of the different supports and challenges I provide. My hope is to highlight the ways in which I utilize principles of adult development to create a mentoring experience for each of my colleagues that best facilitates their learning and growth.

Using Mentoring to Establish Contexts for Reflective Practice

Mentoring depends first on establishing strong relationships with people who can support and challenge them to grow. Since the relationship itself acts as the holding environment for transformational learning (Drago-Severson, 2004b), I am very deliberate in my approach to building relationships with my colleagues, focusing initially on establishing the trust between us that will serve as the foundation for our future work together.

I accomplish this through a series of shadowing days, during which I visit each school leader and spend several days with him or her, "attached at the hip," as one principal likes to call it. I go where the principal goes, and out of this time together we engage in meaningful discussion around a variety of issues—whether it's about work, home, or anything else on our minds. As one colleague put it, "When you spend all day together, it's hard not to get know each other."

Still, I try to remain discreet and certainly don't want to appear overbearing. I don't carry a notebook, and I don't offer feedback unless directly asked for it. Even then, I try not to pass judgment. Primarily, I offer support through affirmation of what is working well. My goal simply is to build trust and create a safe space between us that will eventually be the context for deeper reflection about practice.

Importantly, I am also learning about my colleagues as leaders and as people. I am trying to "get a good read on them," as I often say. How do they respond to specific situations? What do they see as their strengths? What do they find challenging? I watch closely their interactions with teachers, parents, and students, hoping to learn more about their approach to leadership. Knowing who they are as people will inform how I approach my relationship with them as a mentor; it will help me to think about what supports and challenges each person will need to facilitate his or her learning and growth.

As intrusive as this may sound, I've found that my colleagues don't mind my presence. In fact, it's quite the opposite: they want me around as much as possible. Indeed, what they value, above all else, are opportunities to talk to someone about their work, about their experience of being school leaders. "It's a lonely position," a principal I work with once said. My role, however, affords both of us the unique privilege of spending time with each other during school hours—sometimes over the course of a whole day, other times in shorter spurts—engaged in discussions about our leadership practice. It is precisely our time together and the conversations that grow out of it that form the basis of mentoring practice.

Using Mentoring to Support Transformational Learning

If the mentoring relationship is to become a true context for transformational learning, then over time I have to challenge my colleagues to reflect in ways that may lead to new and different ways of thinking about their leadership. In our work together, my colleagues and I talk about "looking in the mirror" at our own actions and behaviors. This requires that we step outside of ourselves and evaluate our leadership in relation to the broader school and systemic context as part of the learning process. But how exactly do we do this?

In large part, the process of reflection depends on what each leader brings to the mentoring relationship itself. What is each person's "growing edge" (Drago-Severson, 2004b, p. 127)? Some people utilize me as a thought-partner, someone who can help to reflect on particular challenges or problems by asking questions that often cast me in the role of devil's advocate. A principal, for example, may be challenged by a seemingly recalcitrant teacher. It's important to ask how that teacher might be experiencing the principal's leadership. Could the principal's own actions be the source of the teacher's frustration? The mentoring

(Continued)

relationship thus becomes the space in which I challenge my colleagues' assumptions by offering competing perspectives on various issues they are facing. In this way, mentoring is similar to collegial inquiry; it is a context for reflective dialogue that pushes both of us to think differently about various problems of practice.

However, developing awareness of our assumptions is not easy work, and for some colleagues, I need to provide greater structure to help them step outside themselves and their role as leader to see other viewpoints. As one principal said, "[I need] to think beyond myself." Often I will find ways to use data as a focal point for our reflective conversations. For example, a principal I work with did in fact experience resistance at one point from some of his teachers, who found him to be overly controlling despite his espoused values of teamwork. Yet the principal could not see the disconnect for himself, so I provided the structure to challenge his thinking. For instance, I observed, documented, and ultimately shared with him his actions so that he could see the inconsistencies between his values and his assumptions and, thus, how others might have experienced his leadership. The data was eye opening; he saw that despite his sense that he was engaging in teamwork, his actions indicated an assumption of control that he was not aware existed. As additional support, I offered him a set of strategies that he could adopt in order to act on his new understanding of leadership, one that involved more team-mindedness to bring his everyday actions in line with his espoused values.

I have no doubt the experience disoriented my colleague. It was like "seeing through a blizzard," he said, which speaks to the importance of the holding environment as a supportive context for learning and growth. Since the mentoring relationship itself acts as the holding environment, I make sure it "sticks around" (Drago-Severson, 2004b, p. 34) for many more months by continuing to provide the trust and support my colleagues need as they experience change, sometimes in powerful ways.

Achieving Growth: The Promise of the Learning-Oriented Model

My goal in the practice of mentoring is to help my colleagues grow so that they can build and sustain high-achieving schools. That they are growing is evident. One principal described the mentoring experience as "truly transformational"; he feels like a "different person at school." Another colleague commented recently that mentoring has "helped bridge my thinking between where I am and where I want to be." Still others have found value in the simple opportunity to talk to someone else about their work.

The feelings of growth and reward are mutual. I have found that the reflective practice inherent to mentoring has challenged my own assumptions about leadership and about how best to support adult learning and development. Mentoring is thus a shared context for growth, and I feel fortunate to have ongoing opportunities to work with my colleagues in this way. My hope is that the leaders with whom I work will soon serve as mentors themselves, both to teachers in their schools and to principals new to our organization. I remain heartened by the promise that mentoring and the other practices of the learning-oriented model (Drago-Severson, 2004b) bring to my work in support of school leadership.

Case 3: Leading Teachers by Listening, Teaming, and Engaging in Collegial Inquiry

Case author: Lydia Bellino

Current position: Principal, Cold Spring Harbor, New York, Public Schools

Primary practices discussed: Teaming and engaging in collegial inquiry

After working for many years as a classroom teacher, reading specialist, and staff developer, Lydia Bellino became a principal for the first time. In this case, she explains how after ten years on the job, reflective practice helped her to understand better the leadership strategies she was using and how to employ the pillar practices to become a more effective leader.

Lydia holds a master's degree in Reading and is the recipient of the New York State Reading Association Reading Teacher of the Year Award. Lydia also holds a master's degree in Organization and Leadership from Teachers College, Columbia University, and is a doctoral student working on a PhD in Literacy.

In my journey as an educator, I started as a classroom teacher, then became a reading specialist, and then spent years of work in reading-writing staff development alongside leaders in the field like Lucy Calkins and others from the Reading and Writing Project at Teachers College at Columbia University in New York. This work has always kept me grounded in the world of teaching and learning. When I heard a new school in a neighboring community was opening with a focus on early literacy, I applied for the position as principal. I dreamed the dream of bringing all I had learned about staff development to my own school, and once I was hired, I began my work as instructional leader.

Our school environment was filled with staff development presenters, courses, and study groups. My care and passion for learning and my focus on our work with children as educators were the qualities I believed made me successful before I was a principal. It was difficult for me to understand and empathize with anyone who did not seem to want to learn or reflect on their own learning. I had never thought to reflect on my ability to hold out and examine my own capacity as a leader and my singular perspective (Ackerman, Donaldson, & Van Der Bogert, 1996).

As principal, I took seriously my responsibility to answer teachers' questions and fill in the spaces between us with ideas and solutions—with information. Teachers often followed my advice, and change did occur in their practice, but it was not a result of their professional growth—the "why" was absent from our conversation. I think I believed I was helping teachers grow and making space for their learning by clearing away their issues with my steady stream of information—focusing always on increasing their knowledge in some way that I thought would help in solving things for them.

And so it was my own search for continued information and knowledge that brought me to Dr. Drago-Severson's class on leadership. Her learning-oriented model of school leadership (Drago-Severson, 2004b) challenged me to ask myself about the connections between staff

(Continued)

(Continued)

development and individual teachers' growth as educators. In her book *Helping Teachers Learn*, Dr. Drago-Severson describes a holding environment as "the context in which, and out of which, the person grows" (Kegan, as cited in Drago-Severson, p. 32) and in which "both support *and* challenge are necessary for growth" (Drago-Severson, p. 32). Ellie's class supported me in the challenge of reconceptualizing staff development and in implementing teaming, providing leadership roles, engaging in collegial inquiry, and mentoring, the four pillar practices that support adult growth and development.

Below, I invite you into my experience of implementing two of the four pillar practices—teaming and engaging in collegial inquiry—in my school, and I invite you to learn about how each of these practices looked, felt, and sounded as I tried to make each a material reality.

Teaming

All of us in schools complain and assume there will never be enough time. That is true, but in challenging my assumption about this, I learned my complaining had to do with my caring about having more time for staff development. As Robert Kegan and Lisa Lahey (2001) write, "The language of commitment tells us (and possibly others) what it is we stand for" (p. 32). I stopped complaining and started to reimagine the possibilities in our school master schedule to create space for teachers to meet once a week in small teams. I was able to form small teams of teachers each day in the late afternoon, covering their classes for 30 minutes and extending 30 minutes into afterschool time. This gave each team one hour to meet, and no one seemed to mind staying later after school.

Creating teams was an opportunity to restructure our school Child Study Team of specialists (speech, special education, psychology, social work), who met weekly and functioned largely in the way of a medical model, as they engaged in discussions of evaluations and tests rather than in conversations about teaching children. Rather than meeting as a group of experts, with individual teachers bringing their concerns to the group, the specialists each became members of different teacher teams. Drago-Severson (2004b) writes that "teaming is a practice that creates an opportunity for teachers to share their diverse perspectives . . . and grow" (p. 18). The teams created a new perspective for everyone, as the focus shifted from expert advice to real and meaningful dialogue, support, and challenge to respond to bigger questions. See Table 7.1 for examples of this transformative process.

Table 7.1   A Transformative Approach to Problem Solving, Enabled by Teaming

Issues Brought to the Team by Individual Teachers	Issues/Questions That Emerged From the Team as a Result of Collaboration
A teacher's frustration with the behavioral issues of one kindergarten child	How do we address the different developmental stages of children in kindergarten?
A teacher's question of what else she can do to help three children in her class who have social and behavioral issues	What are the unmet needs of children who act out and appear to have behavior problems?

Issues Brought to the Team by Individual Teachers	Issues/Questions That Emerged From the Team as a Result of Collaboration
A teacher's frustration by the lack of progress an "average" student is making in his class and the lack of parent support he experiences	What are our assumptions about what parents think they should do to support their children in school?
A teacher's expression of concern a child might not move to the next grade level, because this struggling special education student has still not met grade-level expectations and does not seem to benefit from general education instruction when included in her class	With Ellie's revisions to my work I now frame these conversations in this way: • Why do you think we have special education children in the general education classrooms? • What do you see as the benefits that children gain besides academics from inclusion in the general education classroom? • In your view, does inclusion matter to their identity as a member of our school? If yes, how so? If no, why not?

In the way of a challenge—one that could support growth and learning—to every team, I also asked that when there were no students to discuss, we would raise issues related to the children in our school, the field of education, or to ourselves as learners (see the last example in Table 7.1).

Drago-Severson (2004b) writes that one benefit of teaming is that it "opens communication, decreases isolation, encourages collaboration, and creates interdependency" (p. 69). The early comments of the teachers I was working with in teams, such as "It was so good just to talk," and "I don't know what I would do now if this time was taken away," confirmed these positive effects. These conversations and questions represented a shift that Dr. Drago-Severson describes as "transformational learning that helps adults better manage the complexities of work and life. [This is] in contrast to *informational learning*, which focuses on increasing the amount of knowledge and skills a person possesses" (p. 17).

I witnessed the teachers experiencing the support from their colleagues as they talked and were given the full attention of the group. Everyone in the group seemed to help the teachers and all others through the shared trust and open dialogue. Most important, I think that ultimately the child was helped in a unique way—and perhaps all of the children in the classes of the teachers present were helped indirectly as a result of the shared dialogue. How simple and profound a learning for me, as the instructional leader, to lead by listening.

Engaging in Collegial Inquiry

Reflection seems like a leisurely activity that teachers can't seem to make time for between life and work. One spring I decided to make the appointment for them, and I designed a professional development course through our local teachers' center just for the purpose of reflective practice. I set two goals for the course: take time to think and talk with colleagues as we look back over the year and take time to pay attention to how this informs your plan for the following year. Dr. Drago-Severson defines this practice, collegial inquiry, as "shared dialogue in a reflective context

(Continued)

(Continued)

that involves reflecting on one's assumptions, convictions, and values as part of the learning process" and as part of the larger concept of "reflective practice" (2004b, p. 103). As each school year ends, we discuss the annual evaluation, and individual goals are set for the following year. Principals traditionally begin this work with teachers in the spring, so I thought this inquiry course could give teachers an appointed time to think, write, and talk about their year and about their hopes and dreams for the following year as real goals. And I wanted the teachers to do what Dr. Drago-Severson often recommended: "Choose what is important and what matters to *you*." The teachers met for six weeks, with our last class in early June. Annual evaluation and goals were filled with real projects and hopes, such as the goals of visiting each other's classrooms, planning a collaborative unit of study with a colleague, and assuming a new leadership role.

Case 4: Supporting Adult Development Through Schoolwide Transformation

Case author: Dorothy Cary

Current position: Dean of Middle School Faculty, Germantown Friends School, Philadelphia

Primary practices discussed: Engaging in collegial inquiry

Dorothy Cary describes the growth and development of the teacher evaluation system at her school that occurred through collegial inquiry. She has been dean of faculty for six years; as a part of her work she evaluates teachers. At Germantown Friends, a coeducational K–12 day school in an urban area of Philadelphia, teachers are evaluated in each of their first three years and then at regular intervals thereafter. Dorothy leads the evaluation team for the first-year teachers, contributes to the second- and third-year evaluations, and leads all the evaluations of the experienced teachers in her division. The school wants these evaluations to be a vehicle for professional growth and development. As part of her job, Dorothy teaches alongside her colleagues and participates in the same evaluation program; the principal of the middle school directs her evaluation.

Germantown Friends is a Quaker school and, therefore, values personal reflection and individual insight, both of which have been an important part of the evaluation process since its inception. As we have worked to strengthen the system for evaluating experienced faculty, however, we have also come to value the practice of collegial [inquiry] as a path to personal reflection and growth.

Six years before my appointment as dean of faculty of the middle school, the school committee (board) had mandated that the school implement a formal evaluation process for experienced teachers. The idea was met with controversy, as teachers were concerned about the stability of their jobs and mistrusted the intentions of the administration. Since Friends

Schools have a long tradition of faculty leadership through work on committees, the administration had an established venue to allay these fears, making it possible to build an evaluation system that could be embraced by the whole faculty. The committee developed a process that included a written reflection and observations by two chosen peers, the department head, and the division administrator. The faculty member controlled the peer process, chose the evaluators, and met with them before and after the classroom observations. The administrator's only role in that part of the evaluation was to receive a report from the faculty member about his or her learning from the experience. Many faculty members reported that this aspect was the most valuable, because it encouraged conversations about teaching.

When I joined the Faculty Evaluation Committee, it was considering how to proceed with the second round of evaluations for experienced faculty. Many teachers felt they had "just" written a self-reflective essay and could not imagine that they had anything new to say. Many felt that not much had changed for them in the five years since their last evaluation. We came to view the evaluation as a vehicle for the growth and development of individual teachers and looked for ways to support growth. Ultimately, we decided to offer faculty choice about the form their personal reflection would take. Faculty could choose to write another essay, they could measure themselves against established rubrics, they could create a portfolio illustrating an aspect of their work on which they wanted to focus, or they could go on a weekend retreat to collaborate with colleagues.

In the committee, there was some doubt about the idea of the retreat. We wondered whether faculty would want to give up their own time on a weekend and whether they would really want to engage in collegial inquiry as a means of personal reflection. When we took the ideas back to the full faculty, we were surprised at the strong positive response garnered by the idea of a retreat. Since a retreat requires a "critical mass" of participants, we originally anticipated offering only one every other year. Instead, the retreat has consistently been the most popular choice for experienced faculty, and we have held one every year.

The school sets aside two days in the fall for the faculty who wish to participate in the retreat. Like many schools, we struggle to find even one weekend in the fall free from school conflicts. The school covers the teacher's classes for one school day, and the teachers agree to spend a half-day on a weekend. We have run them on Friday into Saturday and from Sunday afternoon into a full day on Monday. Both models seem to work equally well. Full participation is always an issue. Every year, there are those who are eager to participate but who cannot free themselves for the entire time. In those cases, we have encouraged individuals to participate when they can and asked for a more fully developed written reflection than we do from those who participate for the whole time. Some join the retreat even though they have chosen to complete another form of evaluation. They value the collegial work and the learning for its own sake.

We hold the retreat off-campus so that teachers can really be fully present for learning and not distracted by reminders of their daily existence. Quiet, a pleasant atmosphere, and good food show the teachers that we understand they need space and time to reflect on their classroom, their teaching, and themselves. At work, teachers face continuous and often overwhelming demands from children, parents, and administrators, as well as the ever present

(Continued)

(Continued)

---

need to cover material. They rarely take time for themselves. If we expect teachers to reflect and grow, we must provide time and space for it to happen.

Ellie Drago-Severson has led the retreat each year since we began to hold them. She presents three different lenses through which to view adult development, finishing with a brief overview of Kegan's constructive-developmental theory that informs her model of the pillar practices for growth. Her presence and the emphasis on learning bring intellectual weight to the retreat and help the teachers focus on their own growth and development. The format of the retreat includes time for direct instruction on reflective practice and models of adult development, as well as time for personal reflection and time to meet in pairs or small groups. The retreat itself is a model of development.

Many participants value the chance to talk with colleagues whom they rarely see on a daily basis. The teachers are at different stages of development themselves, and the discussions of the readings and the ideas can spark remarkable insights. Every teacher who has participated has benefited in some way; it has been worth the time and energy spent to bring it about.

As the number of faculty participating in the retreat grew, participants wanted to share their learning and continue the experience with those who had been on the retreat in previous years. Their learning there had created a vocabulary and a way of thinking about development that they wanted to continue beyond the weekend of the retreat. This excitement had two consequences. First, the full administration chose to go on a retreat of its own. We included all administrators, not just those directly involved with supervising or evaluating teachers. We—all of the administrators—took a day together and learned with Ellie about constructive-developmental theory and the pillar practices for growth that had emerged from her research. We were interested in learning how we could use the ideas of constructive-developmental theory and the pillar practices to facilitate teacher growth. This retreat also served to build cohesiveness in the administrative team. We too now have a common vocabulary and a common experience on which to draw.

A second concrete result from the collaborative experience of the retreat was a commitment to grade-level meetings of teachers at all grade levels throughout the school. The middle school principal had brought the idea of such weekly "core" meetings with him, and the teachers found such collaboration extremely helpful and supportive. Enthusiasm for the idea spread throughout the school by means of some teachers from the middle and upper school mixing at retreats. Word then spread to the lower school, and those teachers, who had been energized by the collaborative experience of participating in retreats, asked for a regular opportunity to meet with colleagues. Now teachers at all three school levels hold core meetings, and this practice resulted from the increased communication and the increased enthusiasm for collegial learning made possible by the retreats.

It seems appropriate that schools, institutions whose purpose is the nurturing and development of children, should also find ways to nurture and develop the adults who work with those children. Our retreats for faculty evaluation have proved to be one such avenue for adult learning. The collaboration, thoughtful collegial inquiry, and resulting positive faculty relationships have brought concrete and wide-ranging benefits to the school.

Case 5: The Pillar Practices, Hawaiian Style

Case author: Dr. Daniel E. White

Current position: Headmaster, Island Pacific Academy, Kapolei, Hawaii

Primary practices discussed: All four pillar practices

Dr. Dan White describes the content and pedagogy of a class offered in the unique public/private collaboration at the University of Hawaii–Manoa called Private School Leadership in the Pacific Basin. Prior to founding Island Pacific Academy, a PreK–12 college preparatory school of 660 students in Kapolei, Hawaii, in 2004, Dan headed three other NAIS-member independent schools and partnered in a consulting firm doing business with independent schools around the topics of governance and leadership. Currently president of the Hawaii Association of Independent Schools, Dan has also served on the Accrediting Commission for Schools of the Western Association of Schools and Colleges, developing in the process an appreciation for the self-study process as a vehicle for ongoing school improvement. He is now involved with faculty at the University of Hawaii in designing a doctoral degree program that focuses on professional practice and educational leadership.

I'm an independent school junkie. Over the past 27 years, I have headed four schools (including my current one, for which I am the founding headmaster), helped to create three others, and cofounded an MEd program to educate a new generation of leadership for independent schools. I have chaired numerous accreditation visits to independent schools and have even visited campuses on vacation trips. In short, I'm in a lifelong relationship with mission-driven schools serving public purposes in a private setting. When done right, it is work that is addictive.

The HAIS/UH Collaboration for Leadership

In summer 2003, the Hawaii Association of Independent Schools (HAIS) and the Educational Foundations Department of the University of Hawaii (UH), Manoa, launched an MEd program in Private School Leadership in the Pacific Basin. This important collaboration between the independent school community and the public research university aimed to prepare a new generation of leaders for schools in Hawaii. Patterned after a UH educational foundations program and an independent school leadership program at Teachers College in New York City, the new program offered eight in-residence courses during two summer semesters and a year-long, project-based research paper to a cohort of 25, all drawn from independent schools in Hawaii. Some of the students were deans and directors; one was a new head of school. The rest were teachers, some aspiring to positional leadership, others wanting to be better teacher-leaders. Buoyed by the success of the first two-year cohort, HAIS and UH formed a second cohort in summer 2005, drawing students from out of state as well. The second cohort completed its degree requirements in August 2006. This program is still thriving.

(Continued)

---- (Continued) ----

Introducing the students to the four pillar practices described by Eleanor Drago-Severson in *Helping Teachers Learn* (2004b) has been an important element in the education of these new leaders. Independent schools educate a higher proportion of children in Hawaii than the national average, and the state is home to three of the largest independent schools in the nation: Punahou, Kamehameha, and Iolani. The need for new leaders is increasing as many of us move closer to retirement age, and providing our successors with important tools for leadership has become a goal of HAIS.

One of the courses offered is called Social and Cultural Contexts in Education, one of those marvelously titled courses that invites a multiplicity of content choices, as long as they bear some relationship to the catalog language. As the instructor for the course, I chose to address three broad topics during the three weeks of five 150-minute class meetings: gender issues in independent schools, strategies available to independent school leaders as they work to build communities of reflective practice, and what the future holds for independent schools. Instruction for the course was collaborative, involving two other HAIS schools heads and me (primary instructor and course designer).

I taught the second part of the course, on building communities of reflexive practice, and assigned the book *Helping Teachers Learn,* which is an excellent stimulus to thinking about the leadership of teachers and teacher leadership. The book also lent itself to a collaborative approach to study, a felicitous development because the medium became the message, and the message was clear and understood both times we taught this course.

I've been in education for more than 30 years, and the idea that teacher leadership is an important and unique facet of successful schools is fairly new. Yet the concept has been around, even in schools marked by autocratic leadership. There have always been the influence leaders, the informal mentors, the quiet, can-and-will-do people who have kept schools going. Happily, we now recognize the importance of teacher leadership, manifest in both formal and informal roles.

Likewise, the concept of communities of reflective practice has emerged into our active consciousness in recent years. It, too, had often been present in spots. What school did not have people who thought deeply about what they were doing and talked frequently with colleagues about best practices? What is different now is that we name such practice, consider it essential to good schools, and strive to construct whole faculties in the image of these smaller groups of reflective practitioners. Ensuring that our future leaders in HAIS and elsewhere know the value of developing effective teacher-leaders and communities of reflective practice became a natural goal as our experience with the HAIS/UH cohort evolved.

The Collaborative Leadership Process in Action

All class members read the first four chapters of *Helping Teachers Learn* on their own. I then asked students to pick one of the four chapters on the pillar practices to present to the class along with three or four others who were also interested in that chapter. The next chapter, "Bringing It All Together," was to be dealt with on the way. The task for each group of four or five students was the same: present their chapter to the class in a manner that ensured every other student understood the importance of the pillar presented. The students were free to take as long as they needed and present in whatever fashion they chose. We used two class days for preparation, although professional pride took over and the groups found additional time to perfect their presentations.

What the Students Did

As you might expect, or surely hope, given that the collaborators were teachers and other leaders in independent schools, the presentations were fun, creative, thoughtful, and instructive. One group created a school to illustrate teamwork. Another group role-played a headmaster; an athletic director; a new young teacher; and an older, jaded teacher to examine the chapter on providing teachers with leadership roles. The group presenting the mentoring chapter played a clip from the movie *Men in Black*. Role-playing, PowerPoint presentations, audience participation, even a polling of audience attitudes were among the devices used by the students. Both times the course has been offered, the fifth group, focused on "Bringing It All Together," decided to lead the cohort in an evaluation of the entire program, quite useful to those of us running the show.

Throughout the presentations, material from the first chapters of the book—"Constructive-Developmental Theory," "Principals as Climate Shapers," and "The Impact of Financial Resources on Support for Teacher Learning"—oozed out of the seams of the activities. Groups often referred to constructive-development theory or holding environments in the course of their discussions. Every group included pauses for reflection, usually written but sometimes for discussion, in their presentation time, and a common topic among students for journaling was their own "ways of knowing." In this important way, the students internalized the insights prompted by constructive-developmental theory and saw the necessity of understanding the behavior of others in light of the various ways of knowing, which could be represented in every group.

The Effectiveness of the Approach

Student feedback about the book and the activity was uniformly positive. Certainly, an important explanation for the enthusiastic student reception of the book is the quality of the book and its arguments. Equally important, however, is the fact that the collective approach to the material was an accurate re-creation of the pillars themselves. In five class meetings, the value of the pillar practices in promoting learning among the professional educators involved was validated. The medium was the message.

Students also grasped how transferable the pillar practices might be to learners at any level of education. We were all adults, using our knowledge and experience with adult education, but the genuine joy produced in each of the cohort members from their collaborative exercise prompted an extended discussion, completely serendipitous, about learning in general.

The book and the classroom process also succeeded because the people involved had bonded as a cohort. They had the time and freedom to create a common purpose, a shared enthusiasm, and, not insignificantly, an opportunity to impress the instructor. But in each year the book and instructional approach have been used, someone in the group has wondered if the same activity could form the basis of a valuable two-day faculty retreat for a school. Why not?

What's not to like about a group of adults collaborating under the guidance of the four pillar practices? We can assume that a person who chooses to teach or lead a school likes people and finds working with others on a task to be enjoyable and often more productive than working alone might be. Being given the chance to take the lead on occasion, especially within a group in which one feels comfortable, is a healthy boost to one's self-confidence and a great way to conserve group energy (if you believe what is said about geese: that geese alternate leading the flock so that no one gets too tired bucking the headwinds).

(Continued)

(Continued)

Educators who are effective with their students manage to retain their curiosity, wanting to know how things work or how can something be done better, and collaborating with others to explore or test a hunch will often produce a multiplier effect, as one person's "aha" moment stimulates an amplifying thought in another. And mentoring—the older I get, the more I hope to be able to share some of what I have learned with others coming behind me.

I know how valuable my mentors have been to me, like the one who reminded me regularly of President Kennedy's wisdom: "When it is not necessary to decide, it is necessary not to decide." Or the one to whom I once complained, "I think I'm being used." His response: "We are all often being used. The question is, what are you being used for?" These mentors gave me responsibility, let me discover my own successes and shortcomings, and always kept me focused, with my eyes on the prize. Now is my time to give back to others.

The challenge, of course, is to create a favorable context, a school climate in which the well-being of the whole is understood to be more than the sum of the well-being of its parts yet absolutely dependent on the vitality and dynamism of each member of the school team. A graduate school class meeting during the summer as compared to the conduct of a school during the entire academic year is like a greenhouse compared to an outdoor field as a place to raise flowers. Of course, the variability of the rains, winds, temperatures, insect populations, and so on does not stop growers from trying to grow a great crop each season. The faculty retreat my students envisioned just might help to create a fertile context for the institutionalizing of the pillar practices.

Putting the Pillars Into Practice

Coincident to my instructing the course, I had been planning, and then opening, a new independent school on Oahu, in an area of the island heretofore lacking any private educational institution other than church-related schools. We opened with 191 students, doubled the enrollment in year two, and enrolled 540 students in year three (2006–07). As the founding headmaster, it has been my responsibility to create everything in the school, either literally, through my own effort, or collaboratively, through the work of people I hired. In the days and weeks before the school opened in September 2004, I noted that I would have the certainty on that first day of knowing that every mistake would be mine.

What a privilege and a luxury, though, to be able to create a school climate where none had existed before, to initiate practices the best of which one could hope would become traditions or customary patterns of behavior! What a laboratory for the pillars of practice! Time will tell whether or not we have been successful in creating a climate that routinely engages in reflective practice, sustains an atmosphere of ongoing improvement, shares responsibility for leadership, and guides the development of others as they rise to take the places of the older, more experienced hands in the school. The start we have made in creating a holding environment in which adults can grow, professionally and personally, is promising. I speak of wanting our school to be a place that is "safe" for adults as well as for the students. Institutionalizing the pillar practices, if we succeed in doing so, will serve that end. And it will make this independent school junkie feel like we've done something really well.

CHAPTER SUMMARY

In this chapter, I have shared several in-depth case examples that have been written by school leaders who employ the four pillar practices in their leadership work in a variety of contexts and with different constituencies. Their work shows how teaming, providing leadership roles, collegial inquiry, and mentoring can be implemented to help adults grow. The authors have also shared their reflections about what they experience as the need to support adult growth in schools and what they have witnessed in terms of employing the pillars to help them with their noble mission.

In presenting developmentally oriented examples of the pillar practices in action from these leaders, I hope that their creative strategies and lessons learned will be helpful to you in your noble work. They inspire me. I hope they do the same for you.

APPLICATION EXERCISE

Action Planning: Implementing the Pillar Practices

I offer this action-planning guide in case it is helpful to you personally in your own leadership role or in case you want to share it with colleagues as a potential guide to implementing one or more of the pillar practices in your work context.

You might find it useful to (1) describe or sketch a design for a pillar practice—or a modification of one—that you might employ to support adult development in your particular context; (2) illuminate your preliminary ideas about how principles of constructive-developmental theory will inform your practice/plan; and (3) include questions, dilemmas, or challenges you might encounter when implementing the practice that you want to think through first in the company of colleagues.

The following questions are offered to assist you—and your colleagues—in developing your action plan:

1. Please sketch one or more pillar practices that you would like to implement in your leadership practice in support of adult development and learning. The practice or practices you discuss can be invented—a modification of one or more of the pillar practices described in this book—or drawn from examples of the pillar practices discussed in prior chapters that are suited to your work context.

2. You may want to consider how one principle—or several principles—from constructive-developmental theory informs your thinking about how the practice or practices can support adult development. Here are some examples: How does constructive-developmental theory help you to shape your ideas/practices in a way that will support adult development? How might the practice or practices serve as a context for growth for adults with different ways of knowing? What kinds of supports and challenges will adults with different ways of knowing need in order to grow from engagement in these practices? You may find it helpful to sketch specific examples.

3. What questions seem especially important for you to consider in terms of implementing this practice in your particular context?

4. What challenges/obstacles do you think you will encounter in implementing this practice or these practices? What kinds of supports will you need to implement this practice or these practices?

5. What would you like to observe in your work context six months from now as a result of having implemented this practice or these practices?

REFLECTIVE QUESTIONS

Alone we can do so little; together we can do so much.

—Helen Keller (attributed)

I've created these questions to assist you, as a leader, in considering how to apply the strategies discussed by other leaders in this chapter to your own context. They can be used for internal reflection and to open up a group discussion.

1. What is your personal vision for shaping a culture supportive of adult learning and development? What are your personal purposes or goals in helping adults grow? What do you want your school or district to look and feel like for you and the other adults in your community?

2. What stands out for you as being especially helpful in light of what these school leaders have shared?

3. How might their lessons learned and strategies for shaping cultures supportive of adult development inform your own vision and leadership in support of adult growth?

4. What kinds of challenges or obstacles do you face in terms of creating this type of culture in your school or school system?

5. Based on what you have read and learned here, what are two ideas you'd like to employ in your practice? What are two concrete steps you can take to implement these ideas? What kinds of supports and structures might you need to do so?

8

The School as Learning Center

Stepping Forward With Hope

It's in our hands.

—Experienced principal, New York City

I begin this chapter with a story that reminds me of where the heart of this work lies. While recently delivering a workshop for the Tasmanian Principals Association in Australia, I had the honor of being introduced to the 500 or so principals by a young woman who was a senior in high school. Jennie opened her introduction by saying that she had read my first book, *Helping Teachers Learn,* and continued by explaining that she found the concept of supporting adult development so "intriguing" that she had decided to read Robert Kegan's first book, *The Evolving Self.* Obviously, all of us in the room were quite impressed and inspired by her curiosity and dedication to learning. What she said in her closing, though, is the reason I share this story. Her final remarks went something like this:

> I *totally* agree that it's important to support teachers. I understand why it's important to help teachers learn and grow. I know that when teachers feel satisfied and happy in their work, it makes a big difference in terms of how I feel in the classroom. It's not just that. It affects me and my learning.

Around the world, the need to support adult growth is palpable. While it is very important that we support adult growth for its own reasons, it is also important because it will enhance conditions for student learning. To meet the complex, adaptive demands of leading and teaching in the 21st century, we must build schools to be learning centers— that is, rich and textured mentoring communities, places where both adults and children can be nurtured to grow. In this chapter, I discuss ways in which the four pillar practices of the learning-oriented school leadership model—teaming, providing adults with leadership roles, engaging in collegial inquiry, and mentoring—can be adapted and used effectively by school leaders in different settings. Here I also discuss some of the implications of this learning-oriented model. I emphasize the importance of considering each school's particular characteristics when thinking through how to implement this model to support the learning and growth of all its members. While there is no universal tonic that can be applied to every school context and system, this learning-oriented model holds promise for serving as a map that can be adapted to different school cultures. The pillar practices, which are informed by developmental theory, are really a new way of thinking about schools as learning centers, and they can be implemented within current structures. They can help us in our continual search for improvement.

In illuminating the pillar practices and providing examples that can be employed in your school and school system, as well as by sharing the experiences of leaders like yourself, this book provides a new entry point for joining the conversation about building schools as learning centers—as mentoring communities. My greatest hope is that this work will take us one step closer to realizing our collective desire to support adult learning in schools by building cultures responsive to and respectful of adults' developmental needs—and that this will bring us closer to realizing the important national goals that are at the forefront of our educational agenda.

MEETING ADAPTIVE CHALLENGES BY BUILDING DEVELOPMENTAL CAPACITY

We can't solve problems with the same kind of thinking we used when we created them.

—Albert Einstein (attributed)

In this book, I have emphasized both the complexity of leading and teaching in today's educational world and the extraordinary adaptive challenges we face as educators. Given current pressures to improve student achievement and the quality of teaching, schools, and school systems, researchers, policymakers, and reformers are searching for promising new approaches (Kegan & Lahey, 2009; Wagner, 2003, 2007; Wagner et al., 2006).

Recall that Ronald Heifetz (1994) distinguishes between two types of problems. *Technical problems* are those for which we both understand the problem and can identify solutions to it, even if we need to call upon others for help. However, many of the kinds of challenges we encounter in education today are adaptive. *Adaptive challenges,* according to

Heifetz, involve situations in which neither the problem nor the solution is completely known. This kind of challenge requires new approaches and, often, increased developmental capacities, because of the inherent complexity in it and since it needs to be solved while we are in the midst of working on and through it. Without the appropriate tools and supports needed to meet such challenges, many principals, superintendents, and teachers leave their professions for more supportive environments (Donaldson, 2008; Murphy, 2006; Teitel, 2006). The use of effective supports for human and leadership development in schools can make the difference.

As I've noted earlier, while it is essential that principals, teachers, and superintendents are supported as they meet the technical requirements of their work (e.g., managing budgets, schedules, and personnel), the new adaptive challenges (e.g., for increasing accountability, closing the achievement gap, and instituting standards-based reform) require new approaches and more complex developmental capacities. I have suggested that to meet best these kinds of adaptive challenges, ongoing support for adult growth and new ways of working, learning, and leading together are essential. Furthermore, I have argued that while some supports can be provided externally, many must come from within the school and school system through the practice of leadership and the work we do together as we support each other's growth.

Recall that I made the point earlier that traditionally in education, we have focused on the necessity of building two kinds of capacity to improve schools and enhance student achievement: *school or organizational capacity* (i.e., the school's ability—as a functioning, working whole—to increase achievement) and *instructional capacity* (i.e., teachers' ability to provide effective instruction). I have introduced the notion of a third kind of capacity that is needed to best meet the adaptive challenges we face: *developmental capacity,* which centers on the need for educators to be supported in their learning and development. Developmental capacity concerns the cognitive, affective, interpersonal, and intrapersonal capacities that enable us to manage the demands of leadership, teaching, learning, and life. Contemporary mental demands placed on educators often exceed our developmental capacities. I have suggested that the four pillar practices, informed by developmental theory, offer a promising path for supporting growth and transformation in individuals and in the ecology of the school and system.

THE PROMISE OF BUILDING SCHOOLS AS LEARNING CENTERS

If you want to travel fast, travel alone. If you want to travel far, travel together.

—African proverb

In this book, I have emphasized a new way to facilitate the support and development of principals, teachers, and superintendents so that *together* we can more effectively shape schools and school systems into what I call learning centers, which are genuine *mentoring communities*, contexts for collaborative learning where educators better support and challenge each other to grow. Our collective goal is to help educators work through adaptive challenges, while simultaneously building leadership and human capacity. Opening up this potential will strengthen teaching and leadership and, in turn, student performance. As school leaders committed to supporting student learning, achievement, organizational change, and adult learning, we must first understand that authentic change starts with *us* and recognize the promise in supporting each other's growth.

IMPLICATIONS OF THE NEW LEARNING-ORIENTED LEADERSHIP MODEL

> *I see the opening of your potential in you as you see it in me.*
>
> —From a Tibetan/Nepali greeting, "*Namaste*"

How can we create conditions in schools that create a fertile, nurturing soil for fostering adult growth and human capacity building? How might we reshape professional learning initiatives so that they attend to supporting growth in addition to providing needed skills and information? Improving the ways in which we work, grow, and learn together in school systems and shaping them to be learning centers—*mentoring communities*—is critical. As I have suggested throughout this book, developing mentoring communities can help us to meet the challenges we face adaptively. We can support each other in developing our capacities to manage and attend to adaptive challenges by helping each other grow. The ideas and pillar practices discussed in this book can help us as we move forward in this important journey. Taken together, the pillar practices are mutually reinforcing. They are complementary yet distinctive elements that compose a new model of *learning-oriented school leadership*, which assists adults in developing the capacities to manage the complexities of teaching and leadership in 21st-century schools.

Next I discuss what I see as the more important implications of—or lessons to be learned from—this work in terms of its capacity to support adult development in schools and school systems.

Lesson 1: A developmental perspective helps with understanding that adults will experience professional learning opportunities, leadership experiences, and engagement in the pillar practices in qualitatively *different* ways.

Lesson 2: A developmental vocabulary helps us to move away from labeling adults based on behaviors and move toward a deeper understanding of our differing developmental capacities and how to support growth.

Lesson 3: Implementing any one of the pillar practices can support adult development.

Lesson 4: As adults, we need *qualitatively different kinds of supports* and *challenges,* which can be embedded in the four pillar practices, in order to grow.

Lesson 5: Learning about and attending to supporting other people's *and* our own development can help us to build schools and school systems that are better equipped to meet the challenges of our world.

What follows elaborates on these five big lessons.

- *We, as adults, can continue to grow throughout our lives provided that we benefit from appropriate supports and challenges for growth.* We must learn from each other and support each other's development.
- *All adults in schools need to be supported in their personal and professional development.* Teachers, principals, assistant principals, superintendents, and—indeed—all human beings must be embraced by this support.
- *We must develop even deeper trust and implement new ways of working together.* This includes using a developmental lens to inform how we support and challenge each other to grow while engaging in the pillar practices.
- *We need to attend to adults' ways of knowing.* All of us would be wise to have a developmental mindfulness about how adults with different ways of knowing will experience the same practices and demonstrate competencies in qualitatively different ways. To support growth, we need to attend to our own and other people's thoughts and feelings.
- *Implementing a new learning-oriented model of leadership will benefit individuals, schools, and school systems.* Principals, assistant principals, teachers, and super-intendents will serve individuals, schools, and school systems by implementing the four pillar practices—teaming, providing adults with leadership roles, engaging in collegial inquiry, and mentoring—to support adult growth in their schools and school systems.
- *Differentiating challenges and supports to meet the needs of individual adults will facilitate their growth.* Since schools are likely to be populated by adults who make sense of their experience with a diversity of ways of knowing, we need to be able to offer adults developmentally appropriate supports and challenges, which can be embedded in the four practices, for them to benefit most fully from engaging in them.
- *Attending to and caring for shaping the holding environment will provide the support necessary for growth.* Consideration of the goodness of fit or developmental match among the expectations of leaders, school culture, and an adult's capacity to meet such expectations will help in shaping "holding environments" (Kegan, 1982) that support and challenge adults with different ways of knowing. Holding environments create the conditions for us, as adults, to have the courage to take the risks that are necessary to our growth.

- *To build learning centers and mentoring communities, we would be wise to examine our expectations through a developmental lens.* It is important to consider the explicit and implicit developmental demands inherent in our expectations for each other and of our school and compare them to our developmental capacities. Engaging in the pillar practices will help adults grow to meet more complex demands and expectations, provided that structures (the supports and challenges discussed in this book) are woven into these practices to support adults with a wide variety of ways of knowing.
- *Providing challenges and supports for growth means doing so for all adults.* Principals, assistant principals, teachers, and superintendents—all need their own supports and challenges to adapt to and grow in their complex work and to make it possible for others to adapt and grow.

In his works on leaders and leadership, Howard Gardner (1995, 1997) wisely shares a characteristic common to great leaders: they embody that which they profess and even more than they profess. They lead by example and not just by espoused theories. This is another important implication of this work. In addition, as mentioned earlier, it is important to recognize the ways in which our own way of knowing influences our capacities to support and challenge adults with different ways of knowing. As we grow to demonstrate more complex ways of knowing, we have greater internal resources for supporting others and ourselves.

ATTENDING TO AND VALUING ADULTS' WAYS OF KNOWING

> *We don't see things as they are, we see them as we are.*
>
> —Anaïs Nin (attributed)

Throughout this book, I have called attention to the importance of recognizing developmental diversity and the differing kinds of supports and challenges we need in order to grow. More specifically, I have highlighted the qualitatively distinct ways in which adults with different ways of knowing will experience participation in any one of the four pillar practices composing this new learning-oriented model of school leadership. Table 8.1 summarizes, from a developmental perspective, the essential types of support and challenges for growth that adults will need when engaging in the pillar practices.

In addition, in each of the preceding chapters, I have offered additional ideas about the kinds of supports and challenges that can be threaded through the pillar practices to support growth among adults with different ways of knowing.

Since our way of knowing not only influences our experience of participating in the pillar practice but is also our filter for how *all* life experiences are interpreted, managed, and understood, it is especially important to consider our way of knowing when interacting

Table 8.1 Supports and Challenges for Adults With Different Ways of Knowing That Are Embedded in the Pillar Practices

Way of Knowing	Supports	Challenge (Growing Edge)
Instrumental Knowers	• Establish clear expectations and guidelines. • Establish ground rules and step-by-step guidelines as to how to engage in discussion shared decision making. • Provide step-by-step directions for completing tasks. • Ensure that team leaders and/or facilitators can serve as experts. • Explicitly state and agree upon timetable. • Provide examples and/or models of the rules, purposes, and goals. • Provide unambiguous prompts (questions) for written exercises. • Establish rules of engaging in dialogue with colleagues. • Openly state reasoning or argument behind perspectives. • Establish concrete outcomes and goals of process.	• Challenge this knower to learn about multiple perspectives through inquiry and dialogue. • Challenge learner to develop abstract thinking and transferability of ideas and opinions, thus enhancing capacities for perspective broadening. • Invite this adult to think differently—and more abstractly—through discussion and reflection about own practice and other people's practices. • Support this knower in moving beyond what he or she sees as the "right answers" and toward open-ended discussion that could broaden perspectives and stretch thinking. • Encourage this knower to begin to hypothesize and start to test out alternative ideas and the analysis of outcomes.
Socializing Knowers	• Openly encourage the expression of perspectives and acknowledgment of various points of view. • Create a context of acceptance and a sense of belonging. • Enable sharing of perspectives in pairs before sharing them with a larger group. • Highlight that differences of opinion do not jeopardize friendships and/or relationships. • Establish ground rules for conversations and process before inquiry begins. • Explicitly provide positive affirmation of perspectives when appropriate. • Ensure that this knower feel acceptance from colleagues and supervisors; this will help this knower feel recognized and safe in taking risks and sharing own perspectives. • Pose reflective questions that address feelings about issues or changes.	• Support this knower in considering own perspective and sharing it before learning about the perspectives of others. • Challenge this adult to articulate what he or she needs to feel supported. • Help learner to understand that conflict is okay and can serve as a support to helping everyone learn and grow. • Encourage learner to voice assumptions, as well as new thinking and behaviors, and test them in a supportive and safe context. • Challenge this knower to develop *own* beliefs and values, independent of what important others think he or she should be thinking or doing. • Support this adult in becoming less dependent on the approval and judgment of others.

(Continued)

Table 8.1 (Continued)

Way of Knowing	Supports	Challenge (Growing Edge)
Self-Authoring Knowers	• Allow some freedom in designing and/or critiquing the inquiry process and/or initiatives under consideration. • Create opportunities within reflective forums or teams for this knower to demonstrate own competency. • Create spaces within the context of collaborative work to pursue self-generated goals. • Provide opportunities to engage in dialogue that enables testing of thinking and sharing perspectives before adopting a new idea. • Provide feedback that further develops existing competencies. • Provide opportunities to critique proposed ideas and to offer feedback to authorities and team members. • Invite this knower to design learning activities. • Create spaces within reflective conversations for this knower to pose own questions and respond to them. • Emphasize becoming more competent and extending own options to achieve self-determined goals.	• Challenge this adult to consider ideas and perspectives that are in opposition to own. • Encourage learner to question own beliefs, values, and ideology. • Provide opportunities for dialogue with others that will allow this knower to see commonalities in perspectives. • Have this adult work with colleagues who have perspectives on issues or situations that are in opposition to this knower's. • Encourage learner not be wedded to any one particular way of completing a task (i.e., his or her way). • Invite this adult to welcome alternative standards for problem-solving processes that are in opposition to own preferred way. • Challenge this knower to be less invested in *own* identity, ideology, standards, and point of view and become more open to and welcoming of standards, values, and points of view that are directly opposed to own.
Self-Transforming Knowers (Early 4/5)	• Adults who are early self-transforming knowers are almost ideally suited for collegial inquiry in pairs, triads, or larger groups since the practice provides a structure for inquiry that is open yet containing, with boundaries and deadlines.	• Challenge this knower to move from the process of inquiry to action. • Support learner in identifying or affiliating with authority or impersonal systems.

Way of Knowing	Supports	Challenge (Growing Edge)
	• Opportunities to voice, appreciate, and learn from a broad diversity of perspectives. • A shared value within the partnership and/or groups for valuing and prioritizing conversation, process, and inquiry. • Resources (e.g., time and space) are placed in favor of inquiry processes. • Can endure, tolerate, and appreciate the value for and of conflict, yet these knowers have a preference for the harmony of multiple perspectives working together.	• Encourage this knower to accept that some differences cannot be resolved. • Challenge this adult to avoid getting stuck by absolutizing "flat," nonhierarchal approaches and in own capacity for relativism.
Self-Transforming Knowers (Later 5)	• Provide a clear rationale for engaging in inquiry. • Ensure that stakeholders have a felt sense of commitment. • Allow freedom within the structure of inquiry to experiment with a variety of forms of inquiry. • Ensure that a shared sense of strategic vision exists. • Allocate resources to ensure that there will be follow-through on actions determined by the group, team, or system. • Allow conflict to occur: this knower takes conflict among a diversity of perspectives for granted, is capable of helping to harmonize conflicting perspectives, and appreciates having opportunities to do so.	• Challenge this knower to remain committed when the sense of purpose is unclear. • Help learner to appreciate the time it takes to reach a practical end when others may not move at the same pace. • Challenge this knower to refrain from taking over and rushing the process. • Encourage this adult to be sensitive to the feelings of those who do not have the same capacity (e.g., for conflict).

with each other in any context. As I have emphasized in this book, adopting a developmental stance can help us to understand our own and other people's behaviors and thinking, as well as the kinds of supports and challenges that will best support our growth when engaging in the pillar practices.

For example, understanding how we make meaning of our experiences can help us to understand how differences in behaviors, feelings, and thinking are often intimately connected to differences in how a person constructs his or her experience. Adopting a developmental stance provides us with a vocabulary to discuss growth and development and to understand how to support it. In other words, it enables us to offer developmentally appropriate supports and challenges for growth. It also gives us insight into understanding that there needs to be a *good developmental match* between the demands of the environment and adult's developmental capacities; we recognize that what might be experienced as supportive to one person may be overly challenging, in a developmental sense, to another person.

Attending to developmental diversity in schools, schools systems, and all parts of our lives is important. Research has taught us that within a team, committee, school, school system—or any organization for that matter—it is likely that there will be developmental diversity—meaning that adults will have a wide range of ways of knowing that they bring to their work (Drago-Severson, Kegan, Helsing, Broderick, Popp, & Portnow, 2001b; Kegan, 1994, 2000; Kegan, Broderick, Drago-Severson, Helsing, Popp, & Portnow, 2001b). In light of this, there is an essential need to understand how to support growth among adults who have different needs and developmental orientation. This book offers practices that will help teachers, principals, assistant principals, superintendents, and other school leaders to accommodate the different learning needs, preferences, and developmental diversity among adults within schools and school systems.

While there certainly are other valid reasons for differences among adults' preferences for engagement in particular practices (e.g., age, timing, educational background, career phase, personal circumstances), it is wise and important to consider the role of development and adults' ways of knowing. Put simply, learning-oriented school leadership can help adults in schools better support each other in growing.

To develop schools as learner-centered learning centers for both children and adults, we all need to recognize and attend to developmental diversity, in addition to the many other forms of diversity we care about in schools and in our lives. While I am suggesting that a developmental perspective will aid all of us in responding better to each other's needs and strengths, I am also emphasizing the need to continue simultaneously attending to and caring about other personal and contextual characteristics to support adult learning and growth most effectively. Helping each other to exercise leadership in support of adult growth and learning ties directly to improving teaching and children's development and achievement.

This *learning-oriented model of school leadership* differs from other models commonly employed in professional development because it accomplishes the following:

- Recognizes and attends to developmental diversity.
- Centers on learning as a developmental process.

- Focuses on the person as an active meaning maker.
- Acknowledges the interplay between person and environment.
- Sees the context (whether it is a relationship, series of relationships, team, school, or school system) as a potential enhancer or inhibitor of individual growth.
- Offers pillar practices that are developmentally robust in that they can support the growth of adults with diverse ways of knowing.

This model makes an important distinction between informational learning (i.e., acquiring facts, knowledge, and skills), which is certainly important in our contemporary world, and transformational learning (i.e., increasing the cognitive, emotional, interpersonal, and intrapersonal capacities that enable us to manage the complexities of life). It also helps us to understand how we can build schools, implement leadership practices, and enhance professional learning opportunities so that they can be intentionally aimed at helping adults to grow. Adult learning and constructive-developmental theories inform this learning-oriented school leadership model; it extends Kegan's (1982, 1994, 2000) work by applying ideas derived from his theory to the practice of supporting adult growth in schools and by illuminating the kinds of support and challenges that will facilitate growth for adults with different ways of knowing. By highlighting the types of supports and challenges that can be woven into each pillar practice, the model holds promise for supporting adult growth within schools and school systems.

PUTTING THE NEW LEARNING-ORIENTED MODEL INTO PRACTICE

It takes a lot of intentional work to provide the groundwork for a positive and supportive environment. Also, I never realized that providing an environment that encouraged teacher growth was so essential. I always assumed that I was the only teacher that felt like I could grow in this profession. From a school leader's perspective, I now see that providing teachers with implicit and explicit supports and challenges not only improves the culture of the school, the achievement of the students, but also the growth of the staff. This is the type of environment I hope to provide someday.

—Julie Chiaverini, aspiring principal and teacher-leader, July 2008

Like anything worthwhile in life, supporting adult learning and building schools as learning centers require the hidden treasure of paid attention, intention, and investment, as Julie emphasizes in the opening passage. Yes, this is important work. And yes, it is hard work that will take time. And yes, we can and must do it. In this book, I have described the four pillar practices, as well as examples of how they can be employed to support adult development. In addition, I have discussed how school leaders, like yourself, have implemented the pillar practices in their schools. The four practices of this learning-oriented model can be adapted and used effectively in different settings. Below I will discuss some potential adaptations for implementation.

Of course, we need to pay close attention to an individual school's contextual features, its needs for growth, and its distinctive culture when making decisions about how to implement this model. As we know, the uniqueness of our individual context matters when considering how to refine and adapt these practices to support greater collaboration, growth, and learning.

Please recall that these four pillar practices are strong in two ways. First, they can support and challenge adults with qualitatively different ways of knowing, which provides a goodness of fit between adults' ways of knowing and the practices themselves. Second, different supports and challenges can be woven into each of the practices to accommodate adults with different ways of knowing, enabling them to grow from participating in the practices. As Figure 8.1 shows, all four practices are informed by common underlying developmental principles.

Figure 8.1   Developmental Opportunities Inherent in All Four Pillar Practices

- Articulating and sharing thinking through writing, acting, or engaging in dialogue
- Uncovering, questioning, and examining assumptions and beliefs, which guide thinking and behaviors
- Assuming more work-related responsibility
- Supporting an adult as he or she integrates (makes sense of) multiple and diverse perspectives
- Challenging and supporting one's own and another person's thinking and internal assumptions, which inform actions
- Identifying and questioning internal assumptions in a supportive context
- Encouraging risk taking
- Challenging individual, team, organizational, and/or systemic norms and values and envisioning and engaging in dialogue about alternatives
- Recognizing internal "truths" (i.e., assumptions), sharing them publicly, and testing them in safe contexts to see if they need revision
- Increasing perspective-taking abilities
- Becoming more aware of one's own or another person's motivations, actions, thinking, and justifications
- Identifying and increasing awareness of convictions (ethical, practical, personal convictions or questions)
- Becoming aware of and having opportunities to discuss personal ambiguities; contradictions; and lack of clarity in thinking, ideas, and values
- Considering and envisioning alternative ways of thinking and behaving
- Acting on new thinking—to test new ideas—in a safe context
- Learning about and considering incorporating alternative points of view
- Developing a greater sense of self-authorship and self-ownership

SOURCE: Adapted from Drago-Severson (2004b).

Among these principles, especially important are the following: articulating thinking through writing, speaking, and acting; uncovering assumptions and beliefs, which guide thinking and actions; having opportunities to engage in dialogue about dilemmas of practice, ambiguities, contradictions, and assumptions; envisioning alternative ways of thinking and behaving; considering alternative perspectives; and testing and revising assumptions in safe contexts. Over time, engagement in these pillar practices can support growth.

While school leaders will eventually want to invite adults to participate in all four practices, they may want to implement one or two at a time with different pilot groups of adults (teachers, principals, assistant principals, and/or superintendents). Importantly, adults may prefer some practices over others, especially initially. Thus, another alternative that many school leaders have found effective (as was discussed in Chapter 7) is to employ two or three of the pillar practices and provide adults with choices for participation. Such personal and contextual fine-tuning of the model honors adults' preferences, learning needs, personalities, and developmental orientations. It also gives them more ownership and can feel and *be* empowering. For example, some adults may prefer to engage in a mentoring relationship, while others may prefer to participate in a larger team. As you know, it is helpful to respect such preferences.

Please know that implementing even one practice, however, can provide a rich soil for learning and growth. Because each of the practices creates a space for adults to meet regularly; examine their thinking, assumptions, and practices; and consider alternative, new ways of thinking and practicing, implementing any one of them will support adult development.

To build systemwide mentoring communities, principals might consider working together and with superintendents to develop an overarching vision for implementing this model systemwide. Doing so would include teaching adults within the system about developmental theory and the pillar practices. I have witnessed the benefits of this approach within systems and schools where adults share a common language for discussing adult development and employ the pillar practices to support it. With time, adults will take ownership of the practices, and the practices can become a fundamental part of the school's fabric. What small steps would you like to take in terms of implementing this model?

STEPPING FORWARD

Stop. Look. And listen.

—Gloria Ladson-Billings, May 2008, Columbia University's
Teachers College, Doctoral Student Graduation Convocation Address

Recently, an experienced teacher of 25 years voiced his hopes for learning at the start of the institute I was about to deliver. He humbly shared, "I feel guilty taking time away from my teaching to be here today. I usually feel that way when I'm not caring for my students." He continued, "It is so rare that I focus on my own needs for growth and learning. It's a luxury. My hope for today is to be intellectually fed, to be nurtured, and to have a space to reflect." This is a common hope I have heard whenever I learn with and from teachers, principals, assistant principals, and superintendents. It is both a common hope and a common human yearning.

In this book, I have suggested that the most reliable and robust way of thinking about the professional growth of adults in a school and school system is through a model that is actually similar to the model that we employ when considering how best to support the growth and development of children and youth. To support youth's growth and development, we enact the three functions of the holding environment.

1. We "hold well"—meaning we recognize and confirm who the person *is* and *how* the person is currently making meaning of reality, without frustration or urgent need to make the person change or grow before being ready.

2. We let go a little bit, and only when a person is ready, by providing challenge; that is, by questioning or offering alternative ideas or perspectives for consideration.

3. A good holding environment stays in place to provide continuity to the person in the process of growth.

Throughout this book, I have called attention to the need to do the same to support adult development. I have asserted that the four pillar practices are holding environments that can support adults with a diversity of ways of knowing. I have also made clear that we need to find new ways to support genuine growth so that we can better meet and manage the adaptive challenges we face today. Last, I have emphasized that we need to do this work together.

All educational leaders (i.e., superintendents who are called to support principals' growth and development, principals who are responsible for supporting teachers' learning, and teacher-leaders who need to support fellow teachers and students) will benefit by engaging in practices that support adult growth and learning. How might superintendents nurture and provide principals with opportunities to grow? How might these influence principals' capacities to support teachers' growth and learning within their buildings? How might teachers better support each other's growth? How might assistant principals support each other's growth? I urge you to consider these important questions. And I hope this book helps you to do so.

By participating in these practices, principals, teacher-leaders, assistant principals, and superintendents can model shared inquiry, an openness to learn from and have respect for diverse perspectives, and a willingness to take risks and attend more effectively to adults' diverse needs. Implementation of the model will enable all of us to share leadership, strengthen relationships, help each other manage change, and support adult learning.

ON THE GIFT OF GIVING

I have found that among its other benefits, giving liberates the soul of the giver.

—Maya Angelou, 1993, p. 13

After learning together in a workshop that focused on the pillar practices and how and why they can be employed to support adult development, I showed the image of Picasso's *Bouquet in Hands*. I asked the group of 50 or so principals and superintendents if they saw any connections between this image and the pillar practices. "Why might I select this image as something that captures what we've been discussing?" I inquired. As you can see on the front cover of this book, the Picasso image depicts hands wrapped around a small bouquet of colorful flowers. Some of the leaders offered their reflections.

"I see three hands holding the flowers. I think it represents holding knowledge."

"The hands are holding something delicate and fragile."

"They are guiding hands—similar to the ways we lead as guides."

"It is in our hands."

"It's alive."

"It (the flowers) represent the community, students, the world. It's up to us as leaders to support adult growth in schools."

"Stems grow continuously and hold together the people in the picture; they are represented by flowers; people are delicate. Supporting growth is a delicate process. It needs care and attention."

"It takes many hands to support something beautiful."

"Growing is a process."

One principal, whose thinking appears in the opening passage, made the point that tending to the growth and development "of the adults as well as the children is in our hands." Yes, it *is* in our hands.

While I learned from all that these leaders taught me and was inspired by and appreciated all of their thoughtful responses and insights, I explained that I selected the Picasso image for another, albeit related, reason: it reminds me of the gift of giving. In Picasso's image, I said, just as in relationships where we are working to support another human being's growth, it is impossible to discern who is doing the giving and who is receiving. "That's exactly how I feel about supporting adult development," I shared. "I receive from giving. Giving is receiving." Many other school leaders have told me they share this perspective: what feels satisfying to them is giving, for in giving they are receiving.

There is great power in hope. It is my hope that this book raises our consciousness, amplifies our abilities to support growth, and encourages and strengthens us to step forward courageously in leading for adult development. I also hope that this book helps us to be more compassionate by deepening our understanding of how to support adult growth. May it enable us to listen differently and to lead by listening.

And I hope that it informs our practices for supporting adult learning within schools and school systems as we work toward realizing the hope of creating school contexts where everyone, adults and children, is nurtured and well held as they grow. This potential is in our hands and hearts.

Finally, as I stated in the Preface, I hope that you will let me know what you do in your schools and districts and in your teaching as a result of reading this book. I would welcome the chance to learn from you.

Epilogue

In my earlier book, *Helping Teachers Learn: Principal Leadership for Adult Growth and Development* (2004), I also offered ideas and approaches for supporting teacher learning that had been found to be successful for school leaders selected from across school levels, contexts, cultures, and economic circumstances. It was in *Helping Teachers Learn* that I first introduced aspiring and practicing school leaders to a new model of *learning-oriented school leadership* built upon the four pillar practices of teaming, providing leadership roles, engaging in collegial inquiry, and mentoring.

In the epilogue of *Helping Teachers Learn,* I shared with readers the story of a certain fig tree that was company to me in my growth and development as a child in the Bronx, New York. This tree was also company to my sister and five brothers during their growing and developing years. My pediatrician father and nurse mother delivered to our family fig tree what seemed like abundant attention and thoughtful care across seasons and years, at least until such time that my siblings and I began our own watch over the tree, which looked to me more like a shrub or bush than a wholesome fruit tree.

That family fig tree was a cherished successor to past generations of family fig trees, each nurtured and cared for in turn by past generations of my father's family. The care and attention that our family directed into support for the growth and development of this fig tree did more than bring a few baskets of savory figs to our dinner table as summer came to its end. The fig tree and our family's attention to it over time came to symbolize for me much of what I would come to learn and value about adult growth and development and the holding environments that we create in schools and school systems to support such growth and development. The fig tree story that I shared in *Helping Teachers Learn* concluded with gentle assurance that our family fig tree, transplanted to new soil along with my parents' move to a house only 100 feet distant, was doing just fine in the same holding environment it had long enjoyed.

In the years since publication of *Helping Teachers Learn,* I have been privileged to work closely with and learn from many school leaders in courses I have taught, in workshops and lectures I have delivered, in research I have conducted to learn from and with them, and in special programs designed to support learning and development for adults working in schools. Keen interest in the four pillar practices elaborated in this book continues to grow, as do commitments from school leaders to work harder to create holding environments that might support the growth and development of teachers and all school leaders more effectively. This growing interest in and commitment to adult growth and development is inspirational to me, as I know that the children of our schools will benefit most, and most directly, from the growth and development of our teachers and all school leaders. Yet I notice a special joy rise up in me when someone with whom I am working asks about the fig tree: "What ever happened to that fig tree you wrote about in *Helping Teachers Learn*?" the question comes. Yes, the fig tree.

In 1999, my father retired from his life's work as pediatrician to generations of families in the Bronx. Dad passed from us that same year. My mother did her best to stay in the neighborhood where her children's lives and the work she did with her husband connected her intimately with many other families. Her work over decades as a nurse in Dad's medical practice and beyond gave Mom the invigorating gift of being able to help others in ways that were important and meaningful for them and for her. However, with her children grown and building their own lives into yet another generation, Mom no longer needed the larger house that we all called home as long as she was there. With Dad's passing and the chance to live a refreshed life with fewer demands, Mom acted courageously—and with family support—to transplant herself from the Bronx to another place.

My oldest brother, Joseph, a physician himself, had retired to southwest Florida from his professional practice a year or so earlier. After several sunny visits with Joe and his family, Mom was won over big-time by the nicer climate of southwest Florida and by seeing so much sky every day "that you can see forever."

Mom loves to swim. She had been a lifeguard when she was younger. With family roots and deep commitments in the Bronx over so many years, Mom cherished those few times when she was able to travel 5 or 20 miles to enjoy restorative time in the water she also loved. Mom soon learned that she could live year-round in a nicely maintained southwest Florida community, where many seeking to escape northern winters also enjoyed the lifestyle from December or January through May. She came upon a newer development that she liked in Bonita Springs, a growing city just north of Naples on Florida's Gulf Coast.

The Bonita Springs development was positioned close to church and shopping. Mom liked the people she happened to meet who already lived in the development. Available to residents were several swimming pools and a state-of-the-art exercise center. In 2002, Mom made a permanent move from her longtime home in the Bronx to a condominium unit in Bonita Springs. Within months, my husband and I moved to the same development where Mom had resettled. Mom's resettlement led to our relocation, which, in turn, led to yet another transplant for the family fig tree.

The new owner of the old Bronx house agreed to our taking the family fig tree with us. Soon after my husband, David, and I set up our condo, David offered to move the fig tree to Florida. He traveled to New York City by car, planning to complete the drive in three days. He did. Each evening along the way, David would stop to visit with family members who also grew out of the origins of our life in the Bronx. It was sunset when David arrived at the old house.

My husband invested several hours that evening—much of it by moonlight—into carefully digging up the fig tree and preparing it for travel. The roots of the tree were bigger than David expected. They extended deeper and across a wider range of ground. Rather than use a shovel to carve out a small ball-like piece of ground, my husband had to clear away soil around the roots for several feet in all directions. Some of the larger fig tree roots needed to be cut, as surrounding ground would not give them up without a tough fight. David covered the greater root system close to the tree with burlap to keep soil and roots protected during travel. Like a friend, the important bundle of growth seemed to settle easily into the passenger seat of David's car. The fig tree was company to my husband over each mile of the hundreds they traveled south. Each rest stop along the way included attention to watering the fig tree.

On arrival at our Florida home, David replanted the fig tree in a large clay pot. The pot was approximately 24 inches deep and circular in shape, with a top diameter of about 24 inches. With tree and soil and water, the filled pot must have weighed 40 to 50 pounds. Atop a base of smaller stones placed in the bottom of the pot, my husband added nutrient-rich soil of good quality and color before carefully placing the fig tree inside. After removing the burlap covering, David added soil around each of the exposed roots to fill the clay pot to within an inch or two of its depth. Rules of our condominium association state that an architectural review committee must approve any changes to the building or the grounds. Until such time that we would know the best place to plant the fig tree permanently, David and I decided to locate the large clay pot temporarily near to a side-entry door to our garage. Our family fig tree was gone within a week, nowhere to be found.

In times of loss or need or change, it is often the wider community of care that is there for us—at times unknowingly—to offer greatest help and hope and sustenance. When my husband needed help with loosening the fig tree from its Bronx soil and preparing the tree for travel, it was Mr. Mazzucca of nearby Yonkers who offered tools, materials, and instruction. A loving gardener himself, Achilles Mazzucca was a dear and longtime friend to my parents and our family. During summer months, this reserved gentleman would come unannounced to the side door of our house, often at dinnertime, to offer beautiful vegetables and succulent fruits to our family. My father was physician to the Mazzucca children from the day of their birth, children who have grown well and themselves been blessed with beautiful children. In writing these words, the rich aroma and color of the great red tomatoes brought to us by Mr. Mazzucca comes instantly to my senses. It is summer yet again. Warm. And safe.

My husband removed our family fig tree from the Bronx soil that evening, immediately returning to Mr. Mazzucca the tools borrowed to accomplish the work. As David was set to leave Yonkers to begin his drive, Mr. Mazzucca approached the car to say good-bye. He asked David to please deliver a small gift to my mother from the Mazzucca family. Mr. Mazzucca passed to David what appeared to be no more than two small branches from a tree, each approximately 18 inches in length with moistened paper towel wrapped loosely about one end. Mr. Mazzucca showed David the small clusters of tiny white roots within the moistened paper towel. They looked like strings of thread. "These are clippings from my best fig tree," Mr. Mazzucca said. "Please give them to Mrs. Drago. She'll know what to do to make them grow." It was Mr. Mazzucca and his gift of clippings that helped us to continue a tradition of meaning and memory after the fig tree that David brought to Florida had been taken from us.

David cared for the fig tree clippings during his drive. He potted them for Mom on his arrival at Bonita Springs. Mom kept the two new growths in a sunny corner of her home over months. She watered the new plants and watched over them, hoping that they would both accept the changes of climate and location, new conditions and new beginning. It soon became clear that only one of the two new plantings would survive, despite both clippings starting out as branches from the very same fig tree.

Of course, we could not expect fruit from a fig tree so new and so young for many years to come. Nonetheless, we were all delighted to see the single fig tree doing so well with the care and support Mom created for it. As time and conditions made everyday living more challenging for my mother, she decided to move into a nearby facility where assisted living was offered for some residents and independent living for others. My husband moved the single fig tree, now grown to some two feet in height, from Mom's home to a landing midway up the stairs leading to our second-floor condominium. That move took place about a year ago. David and I wondered about how well the tree would handle this change that seemed to us relatively minor and inconsequential. We were both very surprised to witness an apparent weakening of the relocated fig tree. What could possibly be wrong?

Some of the deep green leaves of our new family fig tree began to turn brown. Some leaves fell free from their branches. (Could the plant be casting them off in rebellion?) We tried monitoring quantities and frequencies of watering. David added plant food to soil of the fig tree. Nothing seemed to help. We moved the tree to a sunnier location on our landing. Then we moved it again, this time to a location with less sun. Leaves continued to appear softer and then brown in color, curl in some cases, and then fall from the tree. Could it simply be seasonal changes affecting the plant? In surfing the Web for answers and consulting with experts at a local gardening center, David came upon the possibility that our fig tree might have outgrown its environment. It might need the extra space and room that only a larger pot could offer. After all, the roots of that original tree from the Bronx were great and far-reaching. We found our answer. Yet again in its young life, the fig tree would experience change.

So that's what happened to the fig tree of my story as first told in the epilogue of *Helping Teachers Learn*. Our new fig tree, thriving in a larger pot and new surroundings, is growing and lush. New shoots of light green seem to be renewing themselves with each passing week. As I climb the stairs on arrival home, I stop briefly at the landing to smell, look at, and visit the fig tree. We exchange a few words and trade a memory or two. The story continues to this day—and into tomorrow. Yet it is especially a story of change and growth.

The story I share with you is one of attention to and support for growth and development. Our dear family friend, Mr. Mazzucca, helped us to continue the attention to growth and development, even as the fig tree itself was changed. A mother's care given over time to new plantings helped us to continue a family tradition that was so meaningful to us. My husband and I also paid close attention, as David carried and I gave care to creating holding environments for the growth and development needed by the fig tree amidst the challenges imposed on it. Mostly, though, my story may be about the community of caring people that we need to support and hold growth and development that produces a healthy life, one we can all feel good about and celebrate.

Research Appendix

THE RESEARCH INFORMING THIS BOOK: ORIGINS AND COMMITMENTS

The research on which this book is based includes and extends my prior research, which I presented in *Helping Teachers Learn: Principal Leadership for Adult Growth and Development* (2004b). In that study, 25 principals from across the United States discussed how they worked to support and encourage teachers to support their own and others' learning collaboratively *within their schools.* My study of these leaders, a few of whom are no longer practicing principals, was built on lessons from an earlier four-and-a-half-year ethnography (Drago-Severson, 1996) in which I examined how one principal, Dr. Sarah Levine, exercised leadership on behalf of teacher development in her school. This was one of the first studies that examined this type of leadership process in schools. Since Sarah had an explicit intention to support adult learning in her school, which was documented in her published writings, her experiences represented an "ideal type" (Freidson, 1975) or "critical case" (Maxwell, 1996). It was a case from which I could learn from a principal who intentionally supported adult development in her school under best-case conditions.

In this current book, I reference this earlier case study, the later sample of 25 principals, and the research I have conducted since then with principals, teachers, superintendents, assistant principals, and other school leaders in workshops, institutes, and classes about the pillar practices and their undergirding theories. I developed a theory derived inductively from stories about how these school leaders supported teacher learning and development in their schools. This grounded theory is what I refer to as a new *learning-oriented model* of school leadership in support of adult development. Below I describe the methods of my research for this book, which builds on my prior research and learnings from working with school leaders like you.

The Principal Study

The Twenty-Five-Principal Study

I purposefully selected 25 school leaders with at least five years of experience and a responsibility for supporting teacher learning (1999–2001). The sample was diverse with respect to gender, ethnicity, number of years in leadership positions, and educational backgrounds. As Table A.1 shows, I recruited principals from three different types of

(Text continued on page 298)

Table A.1 Characteristics of the Sample in Research on Principals[1]

Type of School	Grades	Number of Years Experience	Number of Students	Number of Teachers	Name of School/Location	Student Diversity	Resource Level/ Endowment or School Budget (in $100,000s)[2]
Public							
Mr. Kim Marshall[3]	K–5	13	600	28(31)[4]	Mather School Dorchester, MA: Urban	High	Low/$2.6
Mr. Joe Shea	K–5	20	607	55	Trotter School Boston, MA: Urban	High	Low/$3.0
Dr. Mary Nash	K–8[5]	25	120	15(27)	Mary Lyons Alternative School Brighton, MA: Urban	High	Medium/$1.5[6]
Dr. Len Solo	K–8[7]	26	370	22(47)	Graham & Parks Alternative School Cambridge, MA: Urban	High	Medium/$3.2
Ms. Muriel Leonard	6–8	18	690	60	McCormick Middle School Dorchester, MA: Urban	High	Low/$3.7
Ms. Kathleen Perry	9–12 +GED[8]	31	3,167	165(180)	Lake Worth Community High School Lake Worth, FL: Urban	High	Medium–High/$37
Dr. Jim Cavanaugh	9–12 +GED	22	768	60	Watertown High School Watertown, MA: Urban	Medium–High	High/$24.5
Dr. Larry Myatt	9–12 +GED[9]	19	300	35	Fenway Pilot High School Boston, MA: Urban	High	Low–Medium/$1.9

Type of School	Grades	Number of Years Experience	Number of Students	Number of Teachers	Name of School/Location	Student Diversity	Resource Level/Endowment or School Budget (in $100,000s)[2]
Catholic							
Mrs. Deborah O'Neil	K–8	10	235	13	St. Peter's School Cambridge, MA: Urban	High	Low/$8
Sr. Barbara Rogers	5–12 (all girls)	20	325	59	Newton Country Day School of the Sacred Heart Newton, MA: Suburban	Medium	High/$6
Mr. John Clarke	9–12	8	910	67	Cardinal Newman High School West Palm, FL: Urban	High	Medium/$5.1
Sr. Judith Brady	9–12 (all girls)	35	283	24	St. Barnabas High School Bronx, NY: Urban	High	Low/$1.2
Mr. Gary LeFave	9–12	29	535	36	Matignon High School Cambridge, MA: Urban	Medium	Low/$3.2
Sr. Joan Magnetti	preK–12	24	626	58	Convent of the Sacred Heart Greenwich, CT: Suburban	Low	High/$5.2
Independent							
Mr. John (Jack) Thompson	K–9	40	352	45	Palm Beach Day School Palm Beach, FL: Suburban	Low	Medium to High/$3
Dr. Sarah Levine	preK–6	30	200	26 ft/6pt	Belmont Day School Belmont, MA	Medium	Medium
	7–12	30	840	108	Suburban Polytechnic Pasadena, CA: Urban	High	High/$30

(Continued)

Table A.1 (Continued)

Type of School	Grades	Number of Years Experience	Number of Students	Number of Teachers	Name of School/Location	Student Diversity	Resource Level/ Endowment or School Budget (in $100,000s)[2]
Dr. Dan White[10]	7–12	20	391	41	Seabury Hall Maui, HI: Rural	Medium	Low–Medium $7
Ms. Barbara Chase	9–12	21	1,065	218	Philips Andover Academy Andover, MA: Rural	Medium-High	Very High/$535
Dr. Sue David[11]	9–12	<10	Approx. 300	<75	Anonymous Suburban	Medium	High/$60
Mr. Joe Marchese[12]	9–12	30	590	87	Westtown Germantown, PA: Suburban	Medium	High/$60
Dr. Jim Scott	K–12	25	3,700	281(334)	Punahou School Honolulu, HI: Urban	High	High/$68
Mr. Scott Nelson	preK–12	16	770	125	Rye Country Day School Rye, NY: Suburban	Medium	Medium–High/$13
Ms. Mary Newman	preK–12	22	950	170	Buckingham, Browne, & Nichols Cambridge, MA: Urban	High	High/$30

Type of School	Grades	Number of Years Experience	Number of Students	Number of Teachers	Name of School/Location	Student Diversity	Resource Level/ Endowment or School Budget (in $100,000s)[2]
Mr. Jerry Zank	preK–12	30	520	62	Canterbury School Fort Myers, FL: Urban	High	Low/$800K
Ms. Shirley Mae[13]	9–12	<25	N/A	N/A	Anonymous Urban	High	N/A

1. A similar version of this chart appears in Drago-Severson (2004b).

2. As mentioned, 2000–2001 financial resource levels were determined either by using school Web site information or publication materials (e.g., district financial reports), or in a few cases, the principals themselves identified their schools' resource levels in comparison to other schools of the same type in similar locations (e.g., Florida Catholic schools). This determination, for any school type, *does not* include the principals' strategies to secure additional external grant funding (e.g., federal, state, development fundraising, or gifts). I have listed the 2000–2001 endowments of the independent and Catholic independent schools. In the case of the Boston public schools, I have also listed their approximated school budgets for the "General Fund [which] refers to money that is allocated to the schools by the city budget" (*Boston Public School Fiscal Year Report*, 2001, p. 203). I have listed the 2000–2001 operating budgets for Catholic parochial schools. Reported numbers are rounded to the nearest half million. In places where no amount appears, information was not available, or the participant preferred not to share it.

3. Principals whose names are italicized have left their positions as school principals at these schools for a variety of reasons.

4. Parenthetical numbers indicate the number of teachers *and* support staff (i.e., assistants and specialists).

5. This school is designated as an alternative school for children with special needs.

6. Dr. Nash had a great deal of autonomy over her school budget, because this school is an alternative school and was one of the first of its kind in the city. She was also able to negotiate with the district to secure additional funding for a needed afterschool program for her students, which added to the available financial resources.

7. Graham-Parks school is an alternative school based on John Dewey's philosophy of education and constructivist thinking. The classrooms are multigraded, self-contained, and open. Learning is considered to be a social activity that transpires through social interaction. Len Solo, this school's past principal, served as interim principal of a public high school in Cambridge, Massachusetts, 2001–2002.

8. Lake Worth Community High School is a magnet school with ROTC programs, bilingual programs, and day and evening GED programs.

9. Fenway High School, founded in 1983, became an alternative pilot school in 1995. This status gives the school freedom from the Boston Public School System; it receives some funding from the Boston Public School System but does not have to conform to all of the guidelines for other Boston public schools.

10. Seabury Hall is a boarding school.

11. This participant preferred to remain anonymous; therefore, I have assigned a pseudonym.

12. Westtown is a Quaker boarding school.

13. This participant preferred to remain anonymous; therefore, I have assigned a pseudonym.

schools—public, private, and Catholic. The schools also differed in grade level (i.e., elementary, middle, high school, K–12), student population, geographic location (i.e., urban, suburban, rural), financial resource levels, and level of human resource support.

Research Questions: What Was I Hoping to Learn?

My main purposes in this research were to understand what a range of principals, who served in a variety of school contexts with dramatically different resources, did in support of teacher learning and to understand why they believed their practices were effective. I addressed the following research questions:

1. How do schools leaders in different school contexts describe and understand the ways in which they exercise their leadership to promote adults' transformational learning?

2. What are the actual practices they use to support teacher learning within their schools, and why do they think that the practices are effective?

3. How do these leaders support their own development and sustain themselves in their complex and demanding work?

4. What developmental principles, if any, inform the practices these leaders employ to support transformational learning?

In this book—as in my previous book—I focus intentionally on the principals' successful practices for two main reasons. First, I want to provide readers with effective ideas for their own leadership practice in support of adult development and to provide direction for future research. A second reason I emphasize these principals' successful practices, rather than shortcomings, is that 23 of the 25 principals asked me to use their real names in my writing. I do, however, point to the challenges they encountered in exercising leadership in support of adult development.

Data Collection

Interviews. I conducted semistructured, qualitative interviews (tape-recorded and transcribed verbatim) with the 25 principals, including approximately 75 hours of initial interviews and 14 hours of follow-up interviews. These interviews lasted two to three hours, in general, though some were a little longer and others shorter.

In all but one case, I also toured the school with the principal to familiarize myself with the school context and to develop rapport with the principal before sitting down for the interview. During the tour, I took notes on my observations.

To collect comparable data, I asked the principals similar questions about specific interview topics that related to my research questions. Topics included the following:

- The principals' backgrounds and educational experiences
- Practices used to facilitate teacher learning

- The reasons they believed their initiatives on behalf of teacher learning were effective
- The ways in which their practices for teacher learning worked in their schools
- The influence of different resources on their support of adult learning
- The challenges they faced in supporting teacher learning
- The strategies they used to support their own self-renewal

I also asked questions that were specific to each principal's school context. All were invited to review and comment on hard copies of their interview transcripts. I did this because I wanted to encourage them to elaborate on their prior comments, to reflect on and add to what they had discussed during the interviews, and to omit comments that they did not want published (e.g., teachers' names they had mentioned in the interviews). All but three chose to review their interview transcripts, with six making minor syntax changes. Their additional comments were incorporated into my analysis.

Documents. To contextualize better the principals' practices for supporting adult learning and development in their schools, I analyzed approximately 60 documents, including mission statements, self-study reports, memos I received from the principals after interviews, Web sites, school budgets, speeches, principals' memos to various constituencies, and demographic data. Examining these documents proved to be important because some were mechanisms by which the principals shared their thinking with the different constituencies they served (e.g., school boards, parents, faculty, and administrators). Many of the principals explained that they used the documents as vehicles for sharing their visions and communicating policies and priorities to a range of community members on whom they depended for achievement of objectives. Weekly notices (written by several of the principals) and the self-study evaluation documents created by members of the schools' communities helped me to understand each school context.

Data Analysis: How Did I Make Sense of the Data?

I employed various analytic strategies to address each research question. These included coding for important concepts and themes (Strauss & Corbin, 1998), crafting profiles (Seidman, 1998), writing in-depth narrative summaries (Maxwell, 2005), and building matrices (Miles & Huberman, 1994). I built my understanding of the data from the participants' stories, while informing my analysis with the literature cited in this book.

My analysis had two phases. In the early phase, I wrote field notes following each interview about main themes, my observations of the school context, and how literature and theory illuminated the principal's experiences. During this early phase, analysis entailed creating a set of more than 60 codes that I employed to analyze data from all interviews, cross-checking codes from each interview, writing summary analytic memos (Maxwell & Miller, 1998), and identifying consistencies and discrepancies within and across the data.

In the later phase of analysis, I grouped interviews by school type and financial resource level to examine patterns across categories (e.g., principals' views about teaming) and within and across groups (i.e., public, Catholic, and independent schools). I created detailed narratives and visual displays (Miles & Huberman, 1994) and analyzed them through a developmental lens. More specifically, I composed analytic narrative summary memos (Maxwell, 2005) in response to key analytic questions, which I posed to understand and focus learning from data after interview transcription. These questions focused on each principal's understanding of the following:

- The rewards and challenges of supporting teacher learning
- Their role in and the practices they employed to support teacher learning
- What initiatives they employed to support teacher learning
- The ways their initiatives worked in their schools
- The changes in their thinking about how best to support teacher learning
- The ways in which they supported their own renewal

I attended to validity as I interpreted data in several ways. Multiple data sources (e.g., the interviews and the varied documents) allowed for multiple perspectives on data and interpretations. I and at least one additional researcher employed each analytic technique during all analytic phases (e.g., cross-checking codes and interpretations) to strengthen the analysis and include alternative interpretations. Throughout this process, data were examined for both confirming and disconfirming instances of themes (Miles & Huberman, 1994) to test my developing understanding (Merriam, 1998).

Last, in analyzing data, I attended to different levels of data and included multiple perspectives on their interpretation by attending to patterns that emerged from the individual narratives, from group-level patterns (e.g., resource level and school types), case write-ups, and the sample as a whole (Glaser & Strauss, 1967).

Strengths and Limitations of the Study

Since I had a sample size of 25, I was not able to conduct in-depth or ongoing observations at every principal's school, which would have enabled me to see their practices at work. However, all but one of the 25 initial interviews was conducted on-site, which allowed me to become somewhat familiar with the school contexts. In my analysis, I have been mindful of differences between espoused theory (reported practice) and theory-in-use (actual practice) (Argyris & Schön, 1974) by noting gaps and possible inconsistencies in the interview material itself.

Since all of the principals offered to continue conversations with me, I did meet with many of them a second or, in some cases, third time to check interpretations, ask additional questions, and share findings. In this research, I examined principals' support of adult development chiefly through one theoretical lens. Although other theoretical perspectives could yield valuable findings about school leadership and supporting adult growth, they are beyond the scope of this study.

Study on Supporting Leadership
for Adult Development in University Classrooms

For this study, I conducted longitudinal research from 2003 to 2005 at Harvard's Graduate School of Education in collaboration with several doctoral students, Anila Asghar, Jenni Roloff Welch, and Anne Jones, who served as teaching fellows in my graduate courses that were aimed at teaching school leaders about the pillar practices. This book carves out a slice of this research (2004).

The course in which I conducted this research was titled Leadership for Transformation Learning (LTL). In it, graduate students, who were either current or aspiring school leaders or leaders in other educational settings, examined (1) conceptions of leadership for adult development, (2) essential elements of learning environments for adults, (3) the pillar practices for growth, (4) the ways in which adult developmental theory informs the pillar practices (Brookfield, 1995; Daloz, 1999; Kegan, 1982, 1994, 2000; Mezirow, 2000), and (5) ways of caring for one's own and others' development simultaneously (Ackerman & Maslin-Ostrowski, 2002; Drago-Severson, 2004b, 2007).

I intentionally designed this course not just to deliver this content but also to enable students to *experience* the pillar practices for growth. The class structure, my pedagogy, and feedback to students on their work (written and verbal) were shaped in a way that was mindful of developmental differences to offer forms of support and challenge needed for learning.

Research Questions: What Was I Hoping to Learn?

The research questions that guided the research follow:

1. How, if at all, do these students describe and understand the ways in which course structures (LTL practices and exercises) and content (pillar practices and theories of adult learning and development) support students' leadership development, and why?

2. What do they name as the most important characteristics of the class, and how, if at all, do these aspects support their risk taking in learning?

3. What teaching practices and curricula help current and aspiring leaders to develop the capacities to create robust contexts that support adult learning in schools?

4. How might learning in LTL support changes in students' conceptions of what it means to support adult development? How, if at all, might their learning and experience in LTL influence the way in which they think about how to support adult growth in their schools?

5. How might their learning from LTL help them translate the pillar practices for adult growth and their knowledge of adult learning and development theories to their future leadership practices? How, if at all, might leaders use these practices to support their own and other adults' learning in their work in the field?

Data Collection

All 22 students completed pre- and postclass surveys. In addition, 12 students (7 master's and 5 doctoral students) from the 2004 spring semester class were purposefully selected from 15 volunteers to provide in-depth interviews. Along with two doctoral students, I used observational notes from weekly class meetings, teaching-team meetings, and teaching-journal entries to select participants for interviews, based on the following criteria:

- Diverse responses to the pre- and postclass surveys (see below)
- Prior leadership positions
- Diverse previous work contexts (e.g., K–12 schools, universities, nonprofit organizations, and churches)
- Type of graduate program (e.g., Administration, Policy, and Politics; Human Development and Psychology; Teaching and Learning)
- Availability to participate in one interview at the end of the semester (after course grades were submitted)

As noted in Table A.2, the interview sample consisted of ten women and two men, since women constituted the majority in this class. Participants were offered the option of using a pseudonym or their real names. Table A.2 presents an overview of participants' characteristics.

Table A.2   LTL Characteristics of Participants in the LTL Course

Name	Status While in LTL[1]	Most Recent Profession[1]	Hopes for Future Work[2]
Anne	Education Doctoral student (EdD) in Administration, Planning, and Social Policy (APSP)	Middle school earth science teacher in public school; co–science department head; basketball coach	"Be involved in professional development that improves instruction on a large scale."
Margaret	Education Master's (EdM) student in APSP	Lead teacher at an adult literacy program; high school French and Spanish teacher	Secondary school teacher; aspires to "have a significant role in leading professional development initiatives."
Elizabeth	EdM student in Learning and Teaching (L&T)	High school social studies teacher in public school	Teacher; hopes to apply theories to her practice; continue to develop the nonprofit education organization she created.
Tawanda	EdD student in L&T	Special education teacher for emotionally disturbed adolescent boys at a residential treatment center; mentor teacher; staff developer	Aspiring special education administrator; teacher trainer and program developer.

Name	Status While in LTL[1]	Most Recent Profession[1]	Hopes for Future Work[2]
Amy	EdM student in Arts in Education	Elementary school art teacher in both public and private schools; Character Counts coordinator	Education director at an art museum; executive director of a community arts organization.
David	Divinity Doctoral (DivD) student at a divinity school	Rector of religious parish	Rector of a parish; plans to do professional development on an interfaith basis.
Gara	EdD student in School Leadership Program	Athletic director; varsity soccer coach; history teacher; assistant dean	Doctoral student in psychology; aspiring head of school or university professor.
Matt	EdM student in L&T	Private school elementary teacher; lower school coordinator	Aspires to be a lower school head and start his own school.
Deniz	EdM in Technology in Education	English teacher in high school in Turkey	High school; leadership position.
Sue	DivD student in divinity school	Reverend	Reverend.
Svetlana	EdD student in Human Development and Psychology	Campus coordinator for a religious training institute in Boston and Latvia; tutor trainer; coordinator of a parenting and family life class at a Sunday school	University professor in developing country; setting up parenting education programs as part of university outreach work.
Kristen	EdM student in APSP	Elementary teacher; cochair of language arts curriculum; head of school's advisory committee	Start K–8 schools; curriculum and professional development.

NOTES:

1. Initial questionnaire, January 2004

2. Final questionnaire, May 2004

The main sources of data for this portion of the larger study were pre- and postclass surveys, in-depth qualitative interviews with the 12 participants, and course documents.

Surveys. At the beginning and end of the course, along with the two doctoral students, I administered surveys that I designed; all respondents voluntarily participated. The survey questions focused on four topics: (1) students' initial conceptions of what adult development was and how to support it (preclass survey) and any changes in their thinking after the course (postclass survey), (2) prior experiences related to adult development in their professional settings, (3) initial expectations (preclass survey) and postcourse reflections (postclass survey) about the course activities and experiences, and (4) the ways in which they planned to use course material in their future leadership. The pre- and postclass surveys were examined after students' final grades were submitted, in accordance with the university's Institutional Review Board policy.

The preclass survey instrument consisted of 8 closed and 13 open-ended questions and was the primary source for participant selection for the interviews. The closed questions (i.e., Likert scales) centered on participants' contextual and background information about and prior experiences of professional development. The open-ended questions helped with understanding participants' current conceptions of how to support adult leadership and learning based on prior experiences.

The postclass survey consisted of 19 open-ended questions, focusing on participants' hopes for their future work as leaders who would support adult development, their conceptions of supporting adult learning after LTL, and any experiences that supported their learning and leadership development in LTL. The findings from the portion of this study that I share in this book concern the learnings from the pre- and postclass surveys and the 12 interviews.

Interviews. We conducted and analyzed more than 24 hours of semistructured, in-depth interviews with the 12 participants (tape-recorded and transcribed verbatim). To make sure that we had comparable data, we asked participants similar questions about various topics, including their initial conceptions of adult development, their experiences of professional development in their work contexts, their learning experiences in LTL, their experience of connecting pillar practices to leadership practices in support of adult development, any changes in their conceptions of supporting adult development, and their plans—if they had them—to employ practices supportive of adult development in their future leadership.

Documents. For this part of the study, we analyzed the course syllabus, e-mail from students regarding LTL, and midterm and end-of-course evaluations. These documents provided contextual data and sources of triangulation. In addition, we analyzed class observations and notes from meetings between the teaching team and the interviewees about changes in their thinking with regard to supporting adult development.

Data Analysis: How Did I Make Sense of the Data?

There were three analytic phases in the LTL study. In Phase 1, we analyzed the pre- and postclass survey data, guided by the research questions listed above. In Phase 2, we focused on the interview questions that explored participants' conceptions of how to support adult learning and any changes in those conceptions. We also considered their ideas for incorporating their learning into their future practice as leaders in support of adult development. In Phase 3, we explored the two data sets (i.e., surveys and interviews) in light of the following analytic questions:

1. What were participants' perceptions of and practices for supporting adult development before the course?

2. What were participants' perceptions of and practices for supporting adult development after the course?

3. What from the course helped them to develop a new understanding of supporting adult development?

4. How, if at all, did their ideas about supporting adult development change? How, if at all, did conceptual change influence participants' ideas about how to support adult development in their future practice?

The initial analytic memos helped us track participants' experiences and refine later analytic questions. Prevalent codes that emerged from data indicated issues of importance to the participants that emerged from this phase in relation to supportive LTL practices. These issues included connecting theory to practice, transferring their learning to future practice, and the importance of offering other adults both supports and challenges to enable development. Next, we conducted in-depth analysis of the 12 participants' data in relation to these codes by creating matrices to compare and contrast patterns of similarities and differences within and across all cases.

New York City Principals-as-Mentors Study

For three years (2005–2008), I worked with experienced principals who mentored assistant principals aspiring to the principalship through the New York City Educational Leadership Institute (ELI). The mentors participated in three-hour workshops/seminars, which I delivered four times a year for three years. Workshops focused on learning about the pillar practices, with particular emphasis on mentoring and adult developmental theory. In addition, these workshops enabled the mentor-principals to engage in reflective conversations on how to apply the pillar practices and theory to their mentoring and the challenges and successes of their experience.

Research Questions: What Was I Hoping to Learn?

Working from pre- and post–study year surveys (using open- and closed-ended questions) and field notes from meetings, I examined the following research questions:

1. How do these mentors to aspiring principals describe and understand the ways in which the pillar practices and principles of adult development help them in their roles as mentors?

2. How do they use the pillar practices to support adult growth? What challenges do they encounter in supporting the growth of aspiring principals?

3. How do they describe and understand their reflective practice with other mentors? What are the benefits and challenges of their participation?

The principals in the study all had more than ten years of experience as principals. Nine of them were mentors during all three years of this research, and four of them were mentors and research participants for the last two years of my study.

This sample was diverse with respect to gender, ethnicity, and prior educational background.

Data Collection

Surveys. I administered pre- and post–study year surveys to the entire cohort of principal-mentors. All principals voluntarily participated in the surveys, though one principal opted not to have his 2008 responses included in my writing.

Survey questions focused on the following topics:

1. Initial conceptions of adult development and mentoring (pre–study year survey) and any changes in their thinking at the end of the year (post–study year survey)

2. Prior professional development and mentoring experiences related to adult development (challenges and successes)

3. Initial expectations for our work during the year (pre–study year survey)

4. Post-seminar reflections about activities, their learning about supporting adult development, and the pillar practices, and how, if at all, they employed their learning in their mentoring and in their schools with other adults (post–study year survey)

5. The ways in which the reflective conversations in the seminar were helpful or unhelpful in terms of the principals' support of adult development and their mentoring

6. The ways in which they planned to use seminar learnings in their future work

Field Notes. During the sessions, I took notes on the participants' experiences and reflections. For example, during the final workshop each year, I invited participants to reflect aloud on the following questions:

1. What went well in terms of your relationship with your mentees?

2. What were some of the challenges in your mentoring relationships?

3. What kinds of structures or supports would have helped you in your role as a mentor (i.e., Do you have a wish list?)?

4. What do you feel most proud of in terms of your mentoring this year?

5. What was challenging about being a mentor this year?

In the final year of this research, I also asked the following questions:

1. What went *particularly* well this year in our group work together, or what did you value about working with your fellow mentors?

2. How, if at all, did our work support you, your learning, and/or your mentoring?

3. What could we have done that would have been more helpful or supportive? And why?

4. What content and processes were most helpful in terms of building your knowledge, skills, or attitudes in your leadership and/or your mentoring practice? How so?

Data Analysis: How Did I Make Sense of the Data?

My analytic strategies for this project resembled those used in the LTL study, discussed above.

Research With School Leaders in My Workshops and Institutes

I have delivered more than 100 workshops and institutes domestically and internationally over the past ten years to principals, assistant principals, teachers, superintendents, district leaders, curriculum developers, staff developers, and coaches of aspiring and current school leaders. In this book, I present findings from field notes taken during workshops (verbatim) and from postworkshop and preinstitute surveys I administered to these school leaders to bring to life the pillar practices, the ways they have been employed, and the theory that informs them.

The analytic strategies I employed in collecting and analyzing these data resembled those discussed above in the LTL study and the New York City principal study.

Glossary

Adaptive challenges are situations and problems (e.g., increasing accountability, closing the achievement gap, and instituting standards-based reform) for which neither the problem nor the solution is clearly known or identified (Heifetz, 1994). To manage and meet these kinds of problems often requires greater cognitive complexity and new approaches since they are often solved while we are *in the process* of working on them. Such a process requires ongoing support for adult growth and new ways of working, learning, and leading together as opposed to specific training for discrete skill acquisition.

Assumptions are the taken-for-granted beliefs that guide our thoughts, actions, and convictions in the learning, teaching, and leadership processes—and in life. We hold our assumptions as Big Truths and rarely question them unless provided with opportunities that help us recognize and consider them. Examining assumptions and testing them in safe contexts allows us to learn if they are, in fact, true—and if they are not, we can revise them. Doing so is essential for growth, the development of lasting change, and the successful implementation of new practices.

Collegial inquiry is a shared dialogue in a reflective context that involves purposefully reflecting on one's assumptions, convictions, and values as part of the learning, teaching, and leadership processes. See Chapter 5.

Constructive-developmental theory is the theory informing my new learning-oriented model of leadership. It is based on two fundamental ideas: (1) people *actively make sense of* their realities, and (2) people can *change or develop* their way of knowing (developmental orientation) if they are provided with developmentally appropriate supports and challenges (Kegan, 1982, 1994, 2000). See Chapter 2 for further explication of this theory. *See also* **way of knowing**.

Development is a process of increasing differentiation and internalization (Kegan, 1982, 1994, 2000). When development occurs, a person has a broader perspective on his or her self and others and is better able to manage the complexities of work and life.

Developmental capacity refers to our cognitive, affective (emotional), interpersonal, and intrapersonal abilities to manage the complexities of our lives and work. See Chapters 1 and 2. *See also* **growth** and **transformational learning**.

Developmental demands are the implicit or explicit expectations inherent to work and life that may be beyond the developmental capacities of those expected to perform them.

Developmental diversity relates to the qualitatively different ways in which we, as adults, make sense of our life experiences. In other words, we take in and experience our realities in very different ways; therefore, we need different types of supports and challenges to grow. Since research suggests that in any school, team, or group, adults will likely make sense of their experiences in developmentally different ways, we need to attend to this type of diversity. See Chapters 1 and 2.

Goodness of fit (developmental match) concerns the match between a person's way of knowing (i.e., developmental capacities) and the implicit and explicit demands of an environment (e.g., school), practice, and/or role (e.g., leadership position).

Growth is the increases in cognitive, emotional, interpersonal (person to person), and intrapersonal (self-to-self) capacities that enable a person to manage better the complexities of work (e.g., leadership, teaching, learning, adaptive challenges) and life. With the experience of growth, or transformational learning (I use these terms interchangeably), a qualitative shift occurs in how a person actively interprets, organizes, understands, and makes sense of his or her experience. See Chapters 1 and 2.

Holding environment is a context that provides both high supports and challenges to support growth, serving three functions: (1) meeting a person at his or her developmental level; (2) challenging adults, in a developmental sense (i.e., stretching by offering alternative perspectives) to grow beyond their current level; and (3) providing continuity and stability. See Chapter 2.

Human resource levels refers to how many adults worked at each school in the 2004 research study of 25 school principals. These data were learned through Web sites, school documents, and principal reports. See Research Appendix.

Informational learning focuses on increasing the amount of knowledge and/or skills a person possesses, augmenting *what* a person knows. See Chapter 1.

Instrumental way of knowing is a system of meaning making. An instrumental knower understands the world in highly concrete terms. While able to control impulses, this knower does not have the developmental capacity to have a perspective on other people's needs, desires, and interests. See Chapter 2.

Learning centers are schools and school districts where the adults and children are well supported in their learning and development. *See also* **mentoring communities.**

Learning-oriented model of school leadership is informed by developmental theory and composed of four pillar practices—establishing teams, providing adults with leadership roles, engaging in collegial inquiry, and mentoring. This learning-oriented model can support effective, differentiated approaches to adult development in schools and school systems. The pillar practices are developmentally robust, meaning any one of them can support growth in adults with different needs, preferences, and ways of knowing (developmental orientations). See Chapter 1 and Chapter 8.

Meaning making is the sense we make of our lived experience with respect to the cognitive, affective (emotional), intrapersonal, and interpersonal aspects of self.

Mentoring is a pillar practice of the learning-oriented model. It takes myriad forms, including (1) pairing experienced teachers with new teachers, (2) pairing teachers who have deep knowledge of the school mission with other teachers, (3) pairing experienced teachers with graduate student interns from local universities, (4) pairing experienced principals with aspiring and/or newer principals, and (5) team mentoring. See Chapter 6.

Mentoring communities are schools and school districts where the adults and children are well supported in their learning and development. *See also* **learning centers.**

Object is what a person can take a perspective on, manage, be responsible for, and act on because the person is not embedded in or identified with it (Kegan, 1982).

Providing leadership roles is a pillar practice of the learning-oriented model. It is an opportunity for adults to share power and decision-making authority. As adults, we grow and develop from being responsible for an idea's development or implementation, as well as from different kinds of opportunities to assume leadership. I use the term *providing leadership roles* rather than *distributive leadership* because of the intention behind these roles, which is to offer supports and challenges to the person in a leadership role so that he or she can grow from them. See Chapter 4.

Self-authoring way of knowing is a system of meaning making. Self-authoring knowers have the capacity to take responsibility for internal authority. They can hold, prioritize, and reflect on different perspectives. Individuals with this way of knowing can assess the expectations of others by their own internally generated system of values and ideology. See Chapter 2.

Self-transforming way of knowing is a system of meaning making. Self-transforming knowers have the developmental capacity to take perspective on their own authorship, identity, and ideology, forming a meta-awareness. In other words, a person's self-system is available to the self for attention and constant judgment; there is an appreciation for and frequent questioning of how one's self-system works. These knowers are able to understand and manage tremendous amounts of complexity. Individuals with this way of knowing are substantively less invested in their own identities and more open to others' perspectives. See Chapter 2.

Socializing way of knowing is a system of meaning making. Socializing knowers have an enhanced capacity for reflection and abstract thought (i.e., to think about thinking). They can make generalizations from one context to another and have the capacity to reflect on their actions and the actions of others. Individuals with this way of knowing orient to internal psychological states and cannot take a perspective on shared mutuality or societal expectations. Approval and acceptance from authorities and valued others is ultimate for them. See Chapter 2.

Subject is what a person cannot take a perspective on because he or she is embedded in it and it is so much a part of the very fabric of the self, that person cannot look at it, be responsible for it, or see it (Kegan, 1982).

Teaming is a pillar practice of the learning-oriented model of school leadership. It provides adults with opportunities to question their own and other people's philosophies and assumptions about leadership, teaching, and learning. It provides a context, a holding environment, in which adults can examine and question their assumptions and engage in collaborative decision making. See Chapter 3.

Technical challenges are problems (e.g., managing budgets, schedules, and personnel) for which we have both the problem and solutions clearly defined. Even if we cannot solve these challenges ourselves, we can seek out an expert who can help us resolve them.

Transformational learning relates to the development of increased cognitive, emotional, interpersonal, and intrapersonal capacities that enable a person to manage better the complexities of work (e.g., leadership, teaching, learning, adaptive challenges) and life. With the experience of transformational learning, or growth (I use these terms interchangeably), a qualitative shift occurs in how a person actively interprets, organizes, understands, and makes sense of his or her experience, such that he or she develops increased capacities for better managing the complexities of daily life. See Chapters 1 and 2.

Way of knowing refers to the meaning system through which all experience is filtered and understood. It is also known as a developmental level, an order of consciousness, or a stage (Kegan, 1982, 1994). It is the filter through which we interpret our experiences, and it influences our capacities for perspective taking on self and other and the relationship between the two. It dictates how learning, teaching, leadership experiences (and all life experiences) are taken in, managed, understood, and used.

Endnotes

CHAPTER 2

1. Since this analysis was conducted in 1994 and based on prior research that employed constructive-developmental theory, these statistics are likely different now. In other words, the percentage of adults making meaning with a self-authoring way of knowing or beyond is likely slightly greater (e.g., Cook-Greuter, 2004; Torbert, 2004). In addition, other studies (Beukema, 1990; Lahey, 1986; Sonnenschein, 1990) with samples skewed toward higher socioeconomic status and education (i.e., persons with graduate and undergraduate degrees) have found that far fewer adults make meaning with an instrumental way of knowing or a combination of instrumental and socializing ways of knowing and many more make meaning with a self-authoring or self-authoring and interindividual ways of knowing.

2. Kegan has not yet identified a way of knowing beyond what he (1994) calls interindividual and what I call self-transforming.

CHAPTER 4

1. For differing perspectives on why adults might "resist," the role of "dissenters," and how to support adults as they "overcome resistance," please see Kegan & Lahey (2001, 2009). For a developmental perspective on change, see Robert Evans (2001) and Woodbury & Gess-Newsome (2002).

2. One caveat with regard to having teachers conduct peer reviews: As always, it is important to consider each context and culture. In some contexts, teachers providing feedback to colleagues is not supported by teacher unions (see Hannay, Wideman, & Seller, 2006).

3. A version of this appears in different form in Drago-Severson, Roloff Welch & Asghar (2009).

4. This case is adapted from a case that I present in different form in Drago-Severson (2004b).

CHAPTER 5

1. I acknowledge Dr. Deborah Helsing for her thoughtful help in reflecting with me about the idea of teacher awareness or mindfulness.

2. This case is adapted from a case I present in Drago-Severson (1996).

CHAPTER 6

1. Some ideas discussed in this section are adapted from Zachary (2000).

References

PREFACE

Ackerman, R., & Mackenzie, S. (Eds.). (2007). *Uncovering teacher leadership: Voices from the field.* Thousand Oaks, CA: Corwin.

Childs-Bowen, D. (2007). Principals play a key role in developing learning communities. *The Learning Principal, 2*(4), 2.

Donaldson, G. A. (2008). *How leaders learn: Cultivating capacities for school improvement.* New York: Teachers College Press.

Drago-Severson, E. (2004b). *Helping teachers learn: Principal leadership for adult growth and development.* Thousand Oaks, CA: Corwin.

DuFour, R. (2007). Professional learning communities: A bandwagon, an idea worth considering, or our best hope for high levels of learning? *Middle School Journal, 39*(1), 4–8.

Elmore, R. F. (2004). *Educating educators: A promising partnership between HGSE and public school leaders.* Cambridge, MA: Harvard Graduate School of Education. Retrieved May 19, 2009, from http://www.gse.harvard.edu/news/features/elmore07012004.html

Firestone, W. A., & Riehl, C. (Eds.). (2005). *A new agenda: Directions for research on educational leadership.* New York: Teachers College Press.

Firestone, W. A., & Shipps, D. (2005). How do leaders interpret conflicting accountabilities to improve student learning? In W. A. Firestone & C. Riehl (Eds.), *A new agenda for research in educational leadership* (pp. 81–100). New York: Teachers College Press.

Fullan, M. (2003). Implementing change at the building level. In W. Owens & L. S. Kaplan (Eds.), *Best practices, best thinking and emerging issues in school leadership* (pp. 31–36). Thousand Oaks, CA: Corwin.

Guskey, T. R. (1999, April). *New perspectives on evaluating professional development.* Paper presented at the annual meeting of the American Educational Research Association, Montreal, Canada. (ERIC Document Reproduction Service No. ED430024)

Guskey, T. R. (2000). *Evaluating professional development* (2nd ed.). Thousand Oaks, CA: Corwin.

Hargreaves, A., & Fink, D. (2006). *Sustainable leadership.* San Francisco: Jossey-Bass.

Kegan, R., & Lahey, L. L. (2009). *Immunity to change: How to overcome it and unlock the potential in yourself and your organization.* Boston: Harvard Business School Press.

Levin, H. (2006). Can research improve educational leadership? *Educational Researcher, 35*(8), 38–43.

Levine, S. L. (1989). *Promoting adult development in schools: The promise of professional development.* Boston: Allyn & Bacon.

Marzano, R. J., Waters, T., & McNulty, B. (2005). *School leadership that works: From research to results.* Alexandria, VA: Association for Supervision and Curriculum Development.

Murphy, M. (2006). Take the lead. *TES: Only connect: Networked leading* (pp. 24–25). United Kingdom: National Council for School Leadership.

Roy, P., & Hord, S. (2003). *Moving NSDC's staff development standards into practice: Innovation configurations* (Vol. 1). Oxford, OH: National Staff Development Council.

Teitel, L. (2006). *Supporting school system leaders: The state of effective training programs for school superintendents.* New York: The Wallace Foundation.

Wagner, T. (2007). Leading for change: Five habits of mind that count. *Education Week, 26*(45), 29–30.

Wagner, T., Kegan, R., Lahey, L., Lemons, R. W., Garnier, J., Helsing, D., et al. (2006). *Change leadership: A practical guide to transforming our schools.* San Francisco: Jossey-Bass.

CHAPTER 1

Ackerman, R. H., & Mackenzie, S. (Eds.). (2007). *Uncovering teacher leadership: Voices from the field.* Thousand Oaks, CA: Corwin.

Arnold, R. (2005). *Empathic intelligence: Teaching, learning, relating.* Sydney, Australia: University of New South Wales.

Barth, R. S. (1990). *Improving schools from within.* San Francisco: Jossey-Bass.

Barth, R. S. (2006). Improving relationships within the schoolhouse. *Educational Leadership, 63*(6), 8–13.

Blankstein, A. M., Houston, P. D., & Cole, R. W. (2007). *Sustaining professional learning communities.* Thousand Oaks: Corwin.

Blase, J., & Blase, J. (2001). *Empowering teachers: What successful principals do.* Thousand Oaks, CA: Corwin.

Blaydes, J. (2002). Mastering the new 3Rs. *Principal Leadership* (Middle School Ed.), *3*(2), 52–56.

Boyatzis, R., & McKee, A. (2005). *Resonant leadership.* Boston, MA: Harvard Business School Press.

Byrne-Jiménez, M., & Orr, M. (2007). *Developing effective principals through collaborative inquiry.* New York: Teachers College Press.

Childs-Bowen, D. (2007). Principals play a key role in developing learning communities. *The Learning Principal, 2*(4), 2.

Cochran-Smith, M., & Lytle, S. L. (2001). Beyond certainty: Taking an inquiry stance on practice. In A. Lieberman & L. Miller (Eds.), *Teachers caught in the action: Professional development that matters* (pp. 45–58). New York: Teachers College Press.

Cochran-Smith, M., & Lytle, S. L. (2006). Troubling images of teaching in NCLB. *Harvard Educational Review, 76*(4), 668–697.

Cohen, D. K., & Ball, D. L. (1999). Developing practice, developing practitioners: Toward a practice-based theory of professional education. In L. Darling-Hammond & G. Sykes (Eds.), *Teaching as the learning profession: Handbook of policy and practice* (pp. 3–32). San Francisco: Jossey-Bass.

Coleman, R., & Perkins, H. (2004). Thriving—not merely surviving—in the principalship. *Principal, 84*(4), 32–36.

Corcoran, T. B. (2007). *Teaching matters: How state and local policymakers can improve the quality of teachers and teaching* (RB-48). Philadelphia: University of Pennsylvania, Consortium for Policy Research in Education.

Cranton, P. (1996). *Professional development as transformational learning: New perspectives for teachers of adults.* San Francisco: Jossey-Bass.

Darling-Hammond, L. (2003). Enhancing teaching. In W. Owens & L. S. Kaplan (Eds.), *Best practices, best thinking, and emerging issues in school leadership* (pp. 75–87). Thousand Oaks, CA: Corwin.

Desforges, C. (2006, June 23). Help with the impossible. *TES: Only Connect; Networked Leading,* pp. 12–13.

Donaldson, G. A. (2008). *How leaders learn: Cultivating capacities for school improvement.* New York: Teachers College Press.

Drago-Severson, E. (1994). *What does "staff development" develop? How the staff development literature conceives adult growth.* Unpublished qualifying paper, Harvard University, Cambridge, MA.

Drago-Severson, E. (1996). *Head-of-school as principal adult developer: An account of one leader's efforts to support transformational learning among the adults in her school.* Unpublished doctoral dissertation, Harvard Graduate School of Education, Cambridge, MA.

Drago-Severson, E. (2004a). *Becoming adult learners: Principles and practices for effective development.* New York: Teachers College Press.

Drago-Severson, E. (2004b). *Helping teachers learn: Principal leadership for adult growth and development.* Thousand Oaks, CA: Corwin.

Drago-Severson, E. (2007). Helping teachers learn: Principals as professional development leaders. *Teachers College Record, 109*(1), 70–125.

DuFour, R. (2007). Professional learning communities: A bandwagon, an idea worth considering, or our best hope for high levels of learning? *Middle School Journal, 39*(1), 4–8.

Elmore, R. F. (2000). *Building a new structure for school leadership.* Washington, DC: Albert Shanker Institute.

Elmore, R. F. (2004a). *Educating educators: A promising partnership between HGSE and public school leaders.* Cambridge, MA: Harvard Graduate School of Education. Retrieved May 19, 2009, from http://www.gse.harvard.edu/news/features/elmore07012004.html

Elmore, R. F. (2004b). *School reform from the inside out: Policy, practice, and performance.* Cambridge, MA: Harvard Education Press.

Firestone, W. A., & Riehl, C. (Eds.). (2005). *A new agenda: Directions for research on educational leadership.* New York: Teachers College Press.

Firestone, W. A., & Shipps, D. (2005). How do leaders interpret conflicting accountabilities to improve student learning? In W. A. Firestone & C. Riehl (Eds.), *A new agenda for research in educational leadership* (pp. 81–100). New York: Teachers College Press.

Fullan, M. (2003). Implementing change at the building level. In W. Owens & L. S. Kaplan (Eds.), *Best practices, best thinking, and emerging issues in school leadership* (pp. 31–36). Thousand Oaks, CA: Corwin.

Fullan, M. (2005). *Leadership and sustainability: Systems thinkers in action.* Thousand Oaks, CA, and Toronto, Canada: Corwin and the Ontario Principals' Council.

Fullan, M. (2007). Leadership to the fore. In R. Ackerman & S. Mackenzie (Eds.), *Uncovering teacher leadership: Essays and voices from the field* (pp. 93–106). Thousand Oaks, CA: Corwin.

Gardner, H. (2007). *Five minds for the future.* Boston: Harvard Business School Press.

Gardner, H., Csikszentmihalyi, M., & Damon, W. (2001). *Good work: When excellence and ethics meet.* New York: Basic Books.

Garmston, R. J., & Wellman, B. M. (2009). *The adaptive school: A sourcebook for developing collaborative groups.* Norwood, MA.: Christopher-Gordon.

Guskey, T. R. (1995). Integrating school improvement programs. In J. H. Block, S. T. Everson, & T. R. Guskey (Eds.), *School improvement programs* (pp. 453–472). New York: Scholastic Press.

Guskey, T. R. (1999). *Evaluating professional development.* Thousand Oaks, CA: Corwin.

Guskey, T. R. (2000). *Evaluating professional development* (2nd ed.). Thousand Oaks, CA: Corwin.

Hammerman, J. K. (1999, April). *Towards an understanding of development in transformational teacher education.* Paper presented at the Annual Meeting of the American Educational Research Association, Montreal, Canada.

Hargreaves, A. (1994). *Changing teachers, changing times: Teachers' work and culture in the postmodern age.* London and New York: Cassell and Teachers College Press.

Hargreaves, A. (2007a). The long and short of educational change. *Education Canada, 47*(3), 16.

Hargreaves, A. (2007b). Sustainable professional learning communities. In L. Stoll & K. S. Louis (Eds.), *Professional learning communities: Divergence, depth and dilemmas* (pp. 181–195). Maidenhead, England: Open University Press.

Hargreaves, A., & Fink, D. (2006). *Sustainable leadership.* San Francisco: Jossey-Bass.

Heifetz, R. (1994). *Leadership without easy answers.* Cambridge, MA: Harvard University Press.

Hoerr, T. R. (2008). What is instructional leadership? *Educational Leadership, 65*(4), 84–85.

Hoffmann, F. J., & Johnston, J. H. (2005). Professional development for principals, by principals. *Leadership, 34*(5), 16–19.

Hord, S. M. (2007). What is a PLC? *Southwest Educational Development Laboratory Letter, XIX,* 1, 3–5.

Hord, S. M., & Sommers, W. A. (2008). *Leading professional learning communities: Voices from research and practice.* Thousand Oaks, CA: Corwin, National Staff Development, and National Association of Secondary Schools.

Houston, P. D. (1998). The ABCs of administrative shortages. *Education Week, 44,* 32.

Johnson, S. M. (1990). *Teachers at work: Achieving success in our schools.* New York: Basic Books.

Johnson, S. M. (1996). *Leading to change: The challenge of the new superintendency.* San Francisco: Jossey-Bass.

Johnson, S. M., & Next Generation of Teachers Project. (2004). *Finders and keepers.* San Francisco: Jossey-Bass.

Kegan, R. (1982). *The evolving self: Problems and process in human development.* Cambridge, MA: Harvard University.

Kegan, R. (1994). *In over our heads: The mental demands of modern life.* Cambridge, MA: Harvard University.

Kegan, R. (2000). What "form" transforms? A constructive-developmental approach to transformative learning. In J. Mezirow & Associates (Eds.), *Learning as transformation* (pp. 35–70). San Francisco: Jossey-Bass.

Kegan, R., & Lahey, L. L. (2001). *How the way we talk can change the way we work.* San Francisco: Jossey-Bass.

Kegan, R., & Lahey, L. L. (2009). *Immunity to change: How to overcome it and unlock the potential in yourself and your organization.* Boston: Harvard Business School Press.

Kelley, C., & Peterson, K. D. (2002). The work of principals and their preparation: Addressing critical needs for the twenty-first century. In M. S. Tucker & J. B. Codding (Eds.), *The principal's challenge: Leading and managing schools in an era of accountability* (pp. 247–312). San Francisco: Jossey-Bass.

Killion, J. (2000, December/January). Exemplary schools model quality staff development. *Results, 3.*

Knowles, M. S. (1978). Gearing up for the eighties. *Training and Development Journal, 32*(7), 12–14.

Langer, S., & Boris-Schacter, S. (2003). Challenging the image of the American principalship: Attempting to meet outdated community expectations forces principals to make hard choices between their professional and personal lives. *Principal, 83*(1), 14–18.

LaPointe, M., & Davis, S. H. (2006). Effective schools require effective principals. *Leadership, 36*(1), 16–19.

Leithwood, K., & Jantzi, D. (1998, April). *Distributed leadership and student engagement in school.* Paper presented at the annual meeting of the American Educational Research Association, San Diego, CA.

Leithwood, K., Seashore-Louis, K., Anderson, S., & Wahlstrom, K. (2004). *Review of research: How leadership influences student learning.* Retrieved May 19, 2009, from http://www.wallacefoundation .org/KnowledgeCenter/KnowledgeTopics/CurrentAreasofFocus/EducationLeadership/ Pages/HowLeadershipInfluencesStudent Learning.aspx

Leithwood, K., Seashore-Louis, K., Anderson, S., & Wahlstrom, K. (2004). *How leadership influences student learning.* Minneapolis; Toronto, Canada: University of Minnesota, Center for Applied Research and Educational Improvement; Ontario Institute for Studies in Education.

Levin, H. (2006). Can research improve educational leadership? *Educational Researcher, 35*(8), 38–43.

Levine, A. (2005). *Educating school leaders.* Washington DC: The Education Schools Project. Available May 19, 2009, from http://www.edschools.org

Levine, S. L. (1989). *Promoting adult development in schools: The promise of professional development.* Boston: Allyn & Bacon.

Lieberman, A., & Miller, L. (Eds.). (2001). *Teachers caught in the action: Professional development that matters.* New York: Teachers College Press.

Lugg, C. A., & Shoho, A. R. (2006). Dare public school administrators build a new social order? Social justice and the possibly perilous politics of educational leadership. *Journal of Educational Administration, 44*(3), 208–223.

Marsick, V. (2002). *Action learning conversation.* (Available from Partners for Learning and Leadership, 22 Surf Avenue, Warwick, RI 02889; http://www.partnersforlearning.com)

Marzano, R. J., Waters, T., & McNulty, B. (2005). *School leadership that works: From research to results.* Alexandria, VA: Association for Supervision and Curriculum Development.

Mezirow, J. (1991). *Transformative dimensions of adult learning.* San Francisco: Jossey-Bass.

Mezirow, J. (2000). Learning to think like an adult: Core concepts of transformation theory. In J. Mezirow & Associates (Eds.), *Learning as transformation: Critical perspectives on a theory in progress* (pp. 3–33). San Francisco: Jossey-Bass.

Mizell, H. (2007). Students learn when adults learn. *The Learning System, 3*(3), 2. Moller, G., & Pankake, A. (2006). *Lead with me: A principal's guide to teacher leadership.* Larchmont, NY: Eye On Education.

Murphy, J. (2006). *Preparing school leaders: Defining a research and action agenda.* Lanham, MD: Rowman & Littlefield Education.

Nakkula, M. J., & Ravitch, S. M. (1997). *Matters of interpretation: Reciprocal transformation in therapeutic and developmental relationships with youth.* San Francisco: Jossey-Bass.

National Association of Elementary School Principals (NAESP). (2002). *NAESP fact sheet on the principal shortage.* Retrieved from http://www.naesp.org/ContentLoad.do?contentId=1097

National Association of Elementary School Principals (NAESP). (2005). *Leading early childhood learning communities: What principals should know and be able to do.* Retrieved May 19, 2009, from http://web.naesp.org/misc/ECLC_ExecSum.pdf

National Staff Development Council. (2008). *NSDC strategic plan.* Retrieved May 19, 2009, from http://www.nsdc.org/standfor/strategy.cfm

Newmann, F. M., King, B. M., & Youngs, P. (2000). Professional development that addresses school capacity: Lessons from urban elementary schools. *American Journal of Education, 108*(4), 259–299.

Oplatka, I. (2003). School change and self-renewal: Some reflections from life stories or women principals. *Journal of Educational Change, 4*(1), 25–43.

Osterman, K. F., & Kottkamp, R. B. (2004). *Reflective practice for educators: Improving schooling through professional development* (2nd ed.). Thousand Oaks, CA: Corwin.

Parks, S. D. (2005). *Leadership can be taught: A bold approach for a complex world.* Boston: Harvard Business School Press.

Peterson, K. D. (2002). The professional development of principals: Innovations and opportunities. *Educational Administration Quarterly, 38*(2), 213–232.

Peterson, K. D., & Deal, T. E. (1998). How leaders influence the culture of schools. *Educational Leadership, 56,* 28–30.

Rallis, S. F., & Goldring, E. B. (2000). *Principals of dynamic schools taking charge of change.* Thousand Oaks, CA: Corwin.

Rallis, S. F., Tedder, J., Lachman, A., & Elmore, R. (2006). Superintendents in the classroom: From collegial conversation to collaborative action. *Phi Delta Kappan, 87*(7), 537–545.

Roy, P. (2007). Districts can make a difference. *The Learning System, 3*(2), 3.

Roy, P., & Hord, S. (2003). *Moving NSDC's staff development standards into practice: Innovation configurations* (Vol. 1). Oxford, OH: National Staff Development Council.

Samuels, C. A. (2008). Managers help principals to balance time. *Education Week, 27*(23), 18–19.

Silva, D. Y., Gimbert, B., & Nolan, J. (2000). Sliding the doors: Locking and unlocking possibilities for teacher leadership. *Teachers College Record, 102*(4), 779–804.

Silverberg, R. P., & Kottkamp, R. B. (2006). Language matters. *Journal of Research in Leadership Education, 1*(1), 1–5. Available May 19, 2009, from http://www.ucea.org/storage/JRLE/pdf/vol1_issue1_2006/Kottkamp.pdf

Sparks, D. (2002). Inner conflicts, inner strengths: An interview with Robert Kegan and Lisa Lahey. *Journal of Staff Development, 23*(3), 66–71.

Sparks, D. (2004). Broader purpose calls for higher understanding: An interview with Andy Hargreaves. *Journal of Staff Development, 25*(2), 46–50.

Sparks, D., & Loucks-Horsley, S. (1990). Models of staff development. In W. R. Houston (Ed.), *Handbook of research on teacher education* (pp. 234–250). New York: Macmillan.

Spillane, J. P., & Louis, K. S. (2002). School improvement processes and practices: Professional learning for building instructional capacity. In J. Murphy (Ed.), *The educational leadership challenge: Redesigning leadership for the 21st century* (pp. 83–104). Chicago: The University of Chicago Press.

Teitel, L. (2006). *Supporting school system leaders: The state of effective training programs for school superintendents.* New York: The Wallace Foundation.

Wagner, T. (2007). Leading for change: Five habits of mind that count. *Education Week, 26*(45), 29–30.

Wagner, T., Kegan, R., Lahey, L., Lemons, R. W., Garnier, J., Helsing, D., et al. (2006). *Change leadership: A practical guide to transforming our schools.* San Francisco: Jossey-Bass.

Youngs, P., & King, M. B. (2002). Principal leadership for professional development to build school capacity. *Educational Administration Quarterly, 38*(5), 643–670.

CHAPTER 2

Ackerman, R. H., & Mackenzie, S. V. (Eds.). (2007). *Uncovering teacher leadership: Essays and voices from the field.* Thousand Oaks, CA: Corwin.

Ackerman, R. H., & Maslin-Ostrowski, P. (2002). *The wounded leader: How real leadership emerges in times of crisis.* San Francisco: Jossey-Bass.

Arnold, R. (2005). *Empathic intelligence: Teaching, learning, relating.* Sydney, Australia: University of New South Wales.

Basseches, M. (1984). *Dialectical thinking and adult development.* Norwood, NJ: Ablex.

Baxter-Magolda, M. B. (1992). *Knowing and reasoning in college: Gender-related patterns in students' intellectual development.* San Francisco: Jossey-Bass.

Baxter-Magolda, M. B. (2009). *Authoring your life: Developing an internal voice to navigate life's challenges.* Sterling, VA: Stylus.

Belenky, M., Clinchy, B., Goldberger, N., & Tarule, J. (1986). *Women's ways of knowing.* New York: Basic Books.

Beukema, S. (1990). *Women's best friendships: Their meaning and meaningfulness.* Unpublished doctoral dissertation, Harvard University Graduate School of Education, Cambridge, MA.

Boyatzis, R., & McKee, A. (2005). *Resonant leadership.* Boston: Harvard Business School.

Broderick, M. A. (1996). *A certain doubleness: Reflexive thought and mindful experience as tools for transformative learning in the stress reduction clinic.* Unpublished doctoral dissertation, Harvard University Graduate School of Education, Cambridge, MA.

Brookfield, S. D. (1987). *Developing critical thinkers: Challenging adults to explore alternative ways of thinking and acting.* San Francisco: Jossey-Bass.

Brookfield, S. D. (1995). *Becoming a critically reflective teacher.* San Francisco: Jossey-Bass.

Cook-Grueter, S. (2004). Making the case for a developmental perspective. *Industrial and Commercial Training, 36,* 275–281.

Covey, S. R. (2005). *The 8th habit: From effectiveness to greatness.* New York: Simon & Schuster.

Cranton, P. (1994). *Understanding and promoting transformative learning: A guide for educators of adults.* San Francisco: Jossey-Bass.

Cranton, P. (1996). *Professional development as transformational learning: New perspectives for teachers of adults.* San Francisco: Jossey-Bass.

Daloz, L. A. (1983). Mentors: Teachers who make a difference. *Change, 15*(6), 24–27.

Daloz, L. A. (1986). *Effective teaching and mentoring: Realizing the transformational power of adult learning experiences.* San Francisco: Jossey-Bass.

Daloz, L. A. (1999). *Mentor.* San Francisco: Jossey-Bass.

Dixon, J. W. (1986). *The relation of social perspective stages to Kegan's stages of ego development.* Unpublished doctoral dissertation, University of Toledo, OH.

Donaldson, G. A. (2006). *Cultivating leadership in schools: Connecting people, purpose, and practice* (2nd ed.). New York: Teachers College Press.

Drago-Severson, E. (2004a). *Becoming adult learners: Principles and practices for effective development.* New York: Teachers College Press.

Drago-Severson, E. (2004b). *Helping teachers learn: Principal leadership for adult growth and development.* Thousand Oaks, CA: Corwin.

Drago-Severson, E. (2007). Helping teachers learn: Principals as professional development leaders. *Teachers College Record, 109*(1), 70–125.

Drago-Severson, E., Helsing, D., Kegan, R., Portnow, K., Popp, N., & Broderick, M. (2001a). Describing the NCSALL adult development research. *Focus on Basics, 5*(B), 3–6.

Drago-Severson, E., Kegan, R., Helsing, D., Broderick, M., Popp, N., & Portnow, K. (2001b). Three developmentally different types of learners. *Focus on Basics, 5*(B), 7–9.

Gardner, H. (1983). *Frames of mind: The theory of multiple intelligences.* New York: Basic Books.

Gardner, H. (1997). *Extraordinary minds: Portraits of 4 exceptional individuals and an examination of our own extraordinariness.* New York: Basic Books.

Gardner, H. (2007). *Five minds for the future.* Boston: Harvard Business School Press.

Gardner, H., Csikszentmihalyi, M., & Damon, W. (2001). *Good work: When excellence and ethics meet.* New York: Basic Books.

Gilligan, C. (1982). *In a different voice: Psychological theory and women's development.* Cambridge, MA: Harvard University Press.

Gilligan, C., Kegan, R., & Sizer, T. (1999). Memorial minute: William Graves Perry Jr. *Harvard Gazette Archives.* Retrieved May 19, 2009, from http://www.hno.harvard.edu/gazette/1999/05.27/mm.perry.html

Goleman, D. (1997). *Emotional intelligence: Why it can matter more than IQ.* New York: Bantam.

Goleman, D. (2007). *Social intelligence: The new science of human relationships.* New York: Bantam.

Goodman, R. (1983). *A developmental and systems analysis of marital and family communication in clinic and non-clinic families.* Unpublished doctoral dissertation, Harvard University, Cambridge, MA.

Greenwald, G. M. (1991). *Environmental attitudes: A structural developmental model.* Unpublished doctoral dissertation, University of Massachusetts, Amherst.

Guskey, T. R. (2000). *Evaluating professional development* (2nd ed.). Thousand Oaks, CA: Corwin.

Hammerman, J. K. (1999, April). *Towards an understanding of development in transformational teacher education.* Paper presented at the Annual Meeting of the American Educational Research Association, Montreal, Canada.

Heifetz, R. (1994). *Leadership without easy answers.* Cambridge, MA: Harvard University Press.

Kegan, R. (1982). *The evolving self: Problems and process in human development.* Cambridge, MA: Harvard University Press.

Kegan, R. (1994). *In over our heads: The mental demands of modern life.* Cambridge, MA: Harvard University Press.

Kegan, R. (2000). What "form" transforms? A constructive-developmental approach to transformative learning. In J. Mezirow & Associates (Eds.), *Learning as transformation* (pp. 35–70). San Francisco: Jossey-Bass.

Kegan, R., Broderick, M., Drago-Severson, E., Helsing, D., Popp, N., & Portnow, K. (2001a). *Executive summary: Toward a "new pluralism" in the ABE/ESOL classroom; Teaching to multiple "cultures of mind"* (NCSALL Monograph #19a). Boston: World Education.

Kegan, R., Broderick, M., Drago-Severson, E., Helsing, D., Popp, N., & Portnow, K. (2001b). *Toward a "new pluralism" in the ABE/ESOL classroom: Teaching to multiple "cultures of mind"* (NCSALL Monograph #19). Boston: World Education.

Kegan, R., & Lahey, L. L. (1984). Adult leadership and adult development: A constructivist view. In B. Kellerman (Ed.), *Leadership* (pp. 199–230). Englewood Cliffs, NJ: Prentice-Hall.

Kegan, R., & Lahey, L. L. (2001). *How the way we talk can change the way we work.* San Francisco: Jossey-Bass.

Kegan, R., & Lahey, L. L. (2009). *Immunity to change: How to overcome it and unlock the potential in yourself and your organization.* Boston: Harvard Business School Press.

Kindlon, D., & Thompson, M. (1999). *Raising Cain: Protecting the emotional life of boys.* New York: Ballantine Books.

King, K. M., & Kitchener, K. S. (1994). *Developing reflective judgment: Understanding and promoting intellectual growth and critical thinking in adolescents and adults.* San Francisco: Jossey-Bass.

Knefelkamp, L. L., & David-Lang, T. (2000, Spring/Summer). Encountering diversity on campus and in the classroom: Advancing intellectual and ethical development. *Diversity Digest,* p. 10.

Kohlberg, L. (1969). Stage and sequence: The cognitive-developmental approach to socialization. In R. A. Goslin (Ed.), *Handbook of socialization theory and research* (pp. 347–480). New York: Rand-McNally.

Kohlberg, L. (1984). *Stage and sequence: The cognitive developmental approach to socialization; The psychology of moral development.* San Francisco: Harper & Row.

Lahey, L. (1986). *Males and females construction of conflicts in work and love.* Unpublished doctoral dissertation, Harvard Graduate School of Education, Cambridge, MA.

Lahey, L., Souvaine, E., Kegan, R., Goodman, R., & Felix, S. (1988). *A guide to the subject-object interview: Its administration and interpretation.* Unpublished manuscript.

Levine, S. L. (1989). *Promoting adult development in schools: The promise of professional development.* Boston: Allyn & Bacon.

Levinson, D. J. (1978). *The seasons of a man's life.* New York: Ballantine Books.

Levinson, D. J. (1996). *The seasons of a woman's life.* New York: Ballantine Books.

McCallum, D. C. (2008). *Exploring the implications of a hidden diversity in group relations conference learning: A developmental perspective.* Unpublished doctoral dissertation, Teachers College, Columbia University, New York.

Mezirow, J. (1991). *Transformative dimensions of adult learning.* San Francisco: Jossey-Bass.

Mezirow, J. (1994). Understanding transformation theory. *Adult Education Quarterly, 44*(4), 222–244.

Mezirow, J. (1996). Contemporary paradigms of learning. *Adult Education Quarterly, 46*(3), 158–172.

Mezirow, J. (2000). Learning to think like an adult: Core concepts of transformation theory. In J. Mezirow (Ed.), *Learning as transformation: Critical perspectives on a theory in progress* (pp. 3–33). San Francisco: Jossey-Bass.

Moller, G., & Pankake, A. (2006). *Lead with me: A principal's guide to teacher leadership.* Larchmont, NY: Eye On Education.

Murphy, M. (2006, June 23). Take the lead. *TES: Only Connect; Networked Leading,* pp. 24–25.

Newberger, E. (1999). *The men they will become: The nature and nurture of male character.* Reading, MA: Perseus Books.

Nicolaides, A. I. (2008). *Learning their way through ambiguity: Explorations of how nine developmentally mature adults make sense of ambiguity.* Unpublished doctoral dissertation, Teachers College, Columbia University, New York.

Osterman, K. F., & Kottkamp, R. B. (1993). *Reflective practice for educators: Improving schooling through professional development.* Thousand Oaks, CA: Corwin.

Osterman, K. F., & Kottkamp, R. B. (2004). *Reflective practice for educators: Improving schooling through professional development* (2nd ed.). Thousand Oaks, CA: Corwin.

Parks-Daloz, S. (2005). *Leadership can be taught: A bold approach for a complex world.* Cambridge, MA: Harvard Business School Press.

Perry, W. G., Jr. (1970). *Forms of intellectual and ethical development in the college years.* New York: Holt, Rinehart & Winston.

Piaget, J. (1952). *The origins of intelligence in children.* New York: International Universities Press.

Piaget, J. (1963). *The origins of intelligence.* New York: Norton.

Piaget, J. (1965). *The moral judgment of the child* (M. Gabain, Trans.). New York: Free Press. (Original work published 1932)

Pollack, W. (2000). *Real boys' voices.* Melbourne: Scribe.

Popp, N., & Portnow, K. (2001, August). Our developmental perspective on adulthood. In R. Kegan, M. Broderick, E. Drago-Severson, D. Helsing, N. Popp, & K. Portnow (Eds.), *Toward a "new pluralism" in the ABE/ESOL classroom: Teaching to multiple "cultures of mind"* (pp. 43–76; NCSALL Research Monograph #19). Boston: World Education.

Sergiovanni, T. J. (1995). *The principalship: A reflective practice perspective.* Needham Heights, MA: Allyn & Bacon.

Sergiovanni, T. J. (2000). Leadership as stewardship: "Who is serving?" In *The Jossey-Bass reader on educational leadership* (pp. 269–286). San Francisco: Jossey-Bass.

Shakeshaft, C., Nowell, I., & Perry, A. (2000). Gender and supervision. In *The Jossey-Bass reader on educational leadership* (pp. 547–566). San Francisco: Jossey-Bass.

Sheehy, G. (1996). *New passages: Mapping your life across time.* New York: Ballantine.

Sheehy, G. (2006). *Passages: Predictable crises of adult life.* New York: Ballantine. (Original work published 1974)

Sobol, T. J. (2002). The principal as moral leader. In M. S. Tucker & J. B. Codding (Eds.), *The principal's challenge: Leading and managing schools in an era of accountability* (pp. 77–96). San Francisco: Jossey-Bass.

Sonnenschein, P. S. (1990). *The developments of mutually satisfying relationships between adult daughters and their mothers.* Unpublished doctoral dissertation, Harvard Graduate School of Education, Cambridge, MA.

Surrey, J. L. (1991). The "self-in-relation": A theory of women's development. In J. V. Jordan, A. G. Kaplan, J. B. Miller, I. P. Stiver, & J. L. Surrey (Eds.), *Women's growth in connection: Writings from the Stone Center* (pp. 51–66). New York: Guilford Press.

Taylor, K. (2000). *Relational aspects of adult development theory.* Paper presented at the Adult Education Research Conference, Vancouver, Canada.

Taylor, K., Marienau, C., & Fiddler, M. (2000). *Developing adult learners: Strategies for teachers and trainers.* San Francisco: Jossey-Bass.

Torbert, W. (1976). *Creating a community of inquiry: Conflict, collaboration, and transformation.* New York: Wiley.

Torbert, W. (2003). *Personal and organizational transformations though action inquiry.* Great Britain: The Cromwell Press.

Torbert, W. (2004). *Action inquiry: The secret of timely and transforming leadership.* San Francisco: Berrett-Koehler.

Wagner, T., Kegan, R., Lahey, L., Lemons, R. W., Garnier, J., Helsing, D., et al. (2006). *Change leadership: A practical guide to transforming our schools.* San Francisco: Jossey-Bass.

Winnicott, D. W. (1965). *The maturation processes and the facilitating environment.* New York: International Universities Press

York-Barr, J., Sommers, W. A., Ghere, G. S., & Montie, J. (2001). *Reflective practice to improve schools.* Thousand Oaks, CA: Corwin.

York-Barr, J., Sommers, W. A., Ghere, G. S., & Montie, J. (2006). *Reflective practice to improve schools* (2nd ed.). Thousand Oaks, CA: Corwin.

CHAPTER 3

Ackerman, R. H., & Mackenzie, S. (Eds.). (2007). *Uncovering teacher leadership: Voices from the field.* Thousand Oaks, CA: Corwin.

Argyris, C., & Schön, D.A. (1974). *Theory in practice: Increasing professional effectiveness.* San Francisco: Jossey-Bass.

Argyris, C., & Schön, D.A. (1978). *Organizational learning.* Reading, MA: Addison-Wesley.

Barth, R. S. (1996). *Surviving and thriving as superintendent of schools: Leadership lessons from modern American presidents.* Lanham, MD: Rowman & Littlefield.

Barth, R. S. (2006). Improving relationships within the schoolhouse. *Educational Leadership, 63*(6), 8–13.

Boudett, K. P., City, E. A., & Murnane, R. J. (Eds.). (2005). *Data wise: A step-by-step guide to using assessment data results to improve teaching and learning.* Cambridge, MA: Harvard Education Press.

Brookfield, S. (1995). *Becoming a critically reflective teacher.* San Francisco: Jossey-Bass.

Byrne-Jiménez, M., & Orr, M. (2007). *Developing effective principals through collaborative inquiry.* New York: Teachers College Press.

Cambron-McCabe, N. (2003). Rethinking leadership preparation: Focus on faculty learning communities. *Leadership and Policy in Schools, 2*(4), 285–298.

Childress, S., Johnson, S. M., Grossman, A., & Elmore, R. F. (2007). *Managing school districts for high performance: Cases in public education leadership.* Cambridge, MA: Harvard Education Press.

Donaldson, G. A. (2008). *How leaders learn: Cultivating capacities for school improvement.* New York: Teachers College Press.

DuFour, R. (1999). Challenging role: Playing the part of principal stretches one's talent. *Journal of Staff Development, 20*(4), 1–4.

DuFour, R. (2002). The learning-centered principal. *Educational Leadership, 59*(8), 12–15.

DuFour, R. (2007). Professional learning communities: A bandwagon, an idea worth considering, or our best hope for high levels of learning? *Middle School Journal, 39*(1), 4–8.

Eaker, R., DuFour, R., & DuFour, R. (2002). *Getting started: Reculturing schools to become professional learning communities.* Bloomington, IN: Solution Tree.

Easton, L. B. (2009). Protocols: A facilitator's best friend. *Tools for Schools, 12*(3), 1–2.

Evans, R. (1996). *The human side of change: Reform, resistance, and the real-life problems of innovation.* San Francisco: Jossey-Bass.

Evans, R. (2001). *The human side of school change: Reform, resistance, and the real-life problems of innovation.* San Francisco: Jossey-Bass.

Fullan, M. (2005). *Leadership and sustainability: Systems thinkers in action.* Thousand Oaks, CA: Corwin.

Garmston, R. J. (2007). Balanced conversations promote shared ownership. *Journal of Staff Development, 28*(4), 57–58.

Garmston, R. J., & Wellman, B. (2000). *The adaptive school: Developing and facilitating collaborative groups* (4th ed.). Norwood, MA: Christopher-Gordon.

Garmston, R. J., & Wellman, B. M. (2009). *The adaptive school: A sourcebook for developing collaborative groups.* Norwood, MA: Christopher-Gordon.

Hannay, L., Wideman, R., & Seller, W. (2006). *Professional learning to reshape teaching.* Toronto, Canada: Elementary Teachers' Federation of Ontario.

Himes, M. (1995). *Doing the truth in love.* Mahwah, NJ: Paulist Press.

Johnston, J., Knight, M., & Miller, L. (2007). Finding time for teams: Student achievement grows as district support boosts collaboration. *Journal of Staff Development, 28*(2), 14–18.

Kegan, R. (1982). *The evolving self: Problems and process in human development.* Cambridge, MA: Harvard University Press.

Kegan, R. (1994). *In over our heads: The mental demands of modern life.* Cambridge, MA: Harvard University Press.

Kegan, R. (2000). What "form" transforms? A constructive-developmental approach to transformative learning. In J. Mezirow & Associates (Eds.), *Learning as transformation: Critical perspectives on a theory in progress* (pp. 35–70). San Francisco: Jossey-Bass.

Kegan, R., & Lahey, L. L. (2001). *How the way we talk can change the way we work: Seven languages for transformation.* San Francisco: Jossey-Bass.

Kegan, R., & Lahey, L. L. (2009). *Immunity to change: How to overcome it and unlock the potential in yourself and your organization.* Boston: Harvard Business School Press.

Leithwood, K., Seashore-Louis, K., Anderson, S., & Wahlstrom, K. (2004). *How leadership influences student learning.* Minneapolis; Toronto, Canada: University of Minnesota, Center for Applied Research and Educational Improvement; Ontario Institute for Studies in Education.

McAdamis, S. (2007). A view of the future: Teamwork is daily work. *Journal of Staff Development, 28*(3), 43, 45–47.

McTighe, J. (2008). Making the most of professional learning communities. *The Learning Principal, 3*(8), 1, 4–7.

Moller, G., & Pankake, A. (2006). *Lead with me: A principal's guide to teacher leadership.* Larchmont, NY: Eye On Education.

Osterman, K. F., & Kottkamp, R. B. (2004). *Reflective practice for educators: Improving schooling through professional development* (2nd ed.). Thousand Oaks, CA: Corwin/Sage.

Richardson, J. (2008). A fresh perspective: Network gives superintendents a safe space to learn and grow. *The Learning System, 3*(6), 1, 6–7.

Rimanoczy, I., Turner, E., & Pearson, T. (2000). *The learning coach handbook.* Aventura, FL: Leadership in International Management (LIM).

Schön, D. A. (1987). *Educating the reflective practitioner.* San Francisco: Jossey-Bass.

Severson, D. I. (2006). Learning how to learn from each other. The educational possibilities possibilities of a company work improvement team. Doctoral dissertation. Cambridge: Harvard University.

Sparks, D. (2002). *Designing powerful professional development for teachers and principals.* Oxford, OH: National Staff Development Council.

Wagner, T. (2007). Leading for change: Five habits of mind that count. *Education Week, 26*(45), 29–30.

Wagner, T., Kegan, R., Lahey, L., Lemons, R. W., Garnier, J., Helsing, D.,et al. (2006). *Change leadership: A practical guide to transforming our schools.* San Francisco: Jossey-Bass.

Weiss, C. H., & Cambone, J. (2000). Principals, shared decision making, and school reform. In *The Jossey-Bass reader on educational leadership* (pp. 366–389). San Francisco: Jossey-Bass.

Wiggins, G., & McTighe, J. (2007). *Schooling by design.* Alexandria, VA: Association for Supervision and Curriculum Development.

York-Barr, J., Sommers, W. A., Ghere, G. S., & Montie, J. (2006). *Reflective practice to improve schools* (2nd ed.). Thousand Oaks, CA: Corwin.

CHAPTER 4

Blase J., & Blase, J. (2000). Principals' perspectives on shared governance leadership. *Journal of School Leadership, 10*(1), 9–35.

Blase, J., & Blase, J. (2001). *Empowering teachers: What successful principals do.* Thousand Oaks, CA: Corwin.

Cochran-Smith, M., & Lytle, S. L. (2006). Troubling images of teaching in NCLB. *Harvard Educational Review, 76*(4), 668–697.

Danielson, C. (2007). The many faces of leadership. *Educational Leadership, 65*(1), 14–19.

Donaldson, G. A. (2006). *Cultivating leadership in schools: Connecting people, purpose, and practice* (2nd ed.). New York: Teachers College Press.

Donaldson, G. A. (2007). What do teachers bring to leadership? *Educational Leadership, 60*(1), 26–29.

Donaldson, G. A. (2008). *How leaders learn: Cultivating capacities for school improvement.* New York: Teachers College Press.

Dozier, T. K. (2007). Turning good teachers into great leaders. *Educational Leadership, 65*(1), 54–58.

Drago-Severson, E. (2004b). *Helping teachers learn: Principal leadership for adult growth and development.* Thousand Oaks, CA: Corwin.

Drago-Severson, E., Roloff Welch, J., & Asghar, A. (2009). *Supporting teacher leadership: Promising practices for teachers as leaders of adult development and learning.* Manuscript submitted for publication.

DuFour, R. (2007). Professional learning communities: A bandwagon, an idea worth considering, or our best hope for high levels of learning? *Middle School Journal, 39*(1), 4–8.

Elmore, R. F. (2000). *Building a new structure for school leadership.* Washington, DC: Albert Shanker Institute.

Elmore, R. F. (2004). *Educating educators: A promising partnership between HGSE and public school leaders.* Cambridge, MA: Harvard Graduate School of Education. Retrieved May 19, 2009, from http://www.gse.harvard.edu/news/features/elmore07012004.html

Evans, R. (2001). *The human side of school change: Reform, resistance, and the real-life problems of innovation.* San Francisco: Jossey-Bass.

Farrington, J. (2007). What leadership was and what it has become. Retrieved May 19, 2009, from http://ezinearticles.com/?What-Leadership-Was-And-What-It-Has-Become&id=480082

Fullan, M. (2008). School leadership's unfinished agenda: Integrating individual and organizational development. *Education Week, 27*(32), 28, 36.

Hannay, L., Wideman, R., & Seller, W. (2006). *Professional learning to reshape teaching.* Toronto, Canada: Elementary Teachers' Federation of Ontario.

Harrison, C., & Killion, J. (2007). Ten roles for teacher leaders. *Educational Leadership, 65*(1), 74–77.

Johnson, S. M., & Donaldson, M. (2007). Overcoming the obstacles to leadership. *Educational Leadership, 65*(1), 8–13.

Kegan, R. (1982). *The evolving self: Problems and process in human development.* Cambridge, MA: Harvard University Press.

Kegan, R. (1994). *In over our heads: The mental demands of modern life.* Cambridge, MA: Harvard University Press.

Kegan, R., & Lahey, L. L. (2001). *How the way we talk can change the way we work.* San Francisco: Jossey-Bass.

Kegan, R., & Lahey, L. L. (2009). *Immunity to change: How to overcome it and unlock the potential in yourself and your organization.* Boston: Harvard Business School Press.

Lambert, L. (2002). A framework for shared leadership. *Educational Leadership, 59*(8), 37–40.

Leithwood, K., & Riehl, C. (2003). *What we know about successful school leadership.* Philadelphia: Temple University Laboratory for Student Success.

Lewis, B. (2008). *Avoiding teacher burnout: Practical tips for avoiding burnout and renewing your commitment to teaching.* Retrieved May 19, 2009, from http://k6educators.about.com/cs/helpforteachers/a/avoidburnout.htm

Nieto, S. (2003). *What keeps teachers going?* New York: Teachers College Press, 2003.

Nin, A. (n.d.). *Risk.* Retrieved May 18, 2009, from http://www.poemhunter.com/poem/risk/

Olson, L. (2008). Lack of leadership seen as a global problem. *Education Week, 27*(33), 8.

Phelps, P. (2008). Helping teachers become leaders. *Clearing House, 81*(3), 119–122.

Portin, B. (2004). The roles that principals play. *Educational Leadership, 61*(7), 13–18.

Sergiovanni, T. J. (2001). *The principalship: A reflective practice perspective* (4th ed.). Boston: Allyn & Bacon.

Simons, K. A., & Friedman, R. H. (2008). Seven systemwide solutions. *Educational Leadership, 65*(7), 64–68.

Slater, L. (2008). Pathways to building leadership capacity. *Educational Management & Administration Leadership, 36*(1), 55–69.

Woodbury, S., & Gess-Newsome, J. (2002). Overcoming the paradox of change without difference: A model of change in the arena of fundamental school reform. *Educational Policy, 16*(5), 763–782.

CHAPTER 5

Ackerman, R. H., & Mackenzie, S. V. (Eds.). (2007). *Uncovering teacher leadership: Essays and voices from the field.* Thousand Oaks, CA: Corwin.

Ackerman, R. H., & Maslin-Ostrowski, P. (2002). *The wounded leader: How real leadership emerges in times of crisis.* San Francisco: Jossey-Bass.

Argyris, C., & Schön, D. A. (1974). *Theory in practice: Increasing professional effectiveness.* San Francisco: Jossey-Bass.

Argyris, C., & Schön, D. A. (1978). *Organizational learning.* Reading, MA: Addison-Wesley.

Ball, D., & Cohen, D. (1999). Developing practice, developing practitioners: Toward a practice-based theory of professional education. In L. Darling-Hammond & G. Sykes (Eds.), *Teaching as the learning profession: Handbook of policy and practice* (pp. 3–32). San Francisco: Jossey-Bass.

Blase, J., & Blase, J. (2001). *Empowering teachers: What successful principals do.* Thousand Oaks, CA: Corwin.

Bloomberg, M., Klien, J., & Liebman, J. (2007). *Principal's guide to the quality review.* Available from the New York City Department of Education at qualityreview@schools.nyc.gov

Brookfield, S. D. (1995). *Becoming a critically reflective teacher.* San Francisco: Jossey-Bass.

Byrne-Jiménez, M., & Orr, M. T. (2007). *Developing effective principals through collaborative inquiry.* New York: Teachers College Press.

Center for Professional Development, Saint Paul Public Schools. (2006). *Principles of learning.* Retrieved May 19, 2009, from www.thecenter.spps.org/pol.html

Cochran-Smith, M. (2006). The future of teacher education: Ten promising trends (and three big worries). *Educational Leadership, 63*(6), 20–25.

Curry, M. (2008). Critical friends groups: The possibilities and limitations embedded in teacher professional communities aimed at instructional improvement and school reform. *Teachers College Record, 110*(4), 733–774.

Darling-Hammond, L. (2003). Enhancing teaching. In W. Owens & L. S. Kaplan (Eds.), *Best practices, best thinking, and emerging issues in leadership* (pp. 75–87). Thousand Oaks, CA: Corwin.

Donaldson, G. A. (2006). *Cultivating leadership in schools: Connecting people, purpose and practice* (2nd ed.). New York: Teachers College Press.

Donaldson, G. A. (2008). *How leaders learn: Cultivating capacities for school improvement.* New York: Teachers College Press.

Drago-Severson, E. (1996). *Head-of-school as principal adult developer: An account of one leader's efforts to support transformational learning among the adults in her school.* Unpublished doctoral dissertation, Harvard Graduate School of Education, Cambridge, MA.

Drago-Severson, E. (2004b). *Helping teachers learn: Principal leadership for adult growth and development.* Thousand Oaks, CA: Corwin.

Drago-Severson, E. (2007). Helping teachers learn: Principals as professional development leaders. *Teachers College Record, 109*(1), 70–125.

Elmore, R. F. (2000). *Building a new structure for school leadership.* Washington, DC: Albert Shanker Institute.

Elmore, R. F. (2004). *Educating educators: A promising partnership between HGSE and public school leaders.* Cambridge, MA: Harvard Graduate School of Education. Retrieved May 19, 2009, from http://www.gse.harvard.edu/news/features/elmore07012004.html

Elmore, R. F., & Burney, D. (1999). Investing in teacher learning: Staff development and instructional improvement. In L. Darling-Hammond & G. Sykes (Eds.), *Teaching as the learning profession: Handbook of policy and practice* (pp. 263–291). San Francisco: Jossey-Bass.

Fullan, M. (2005). *Leadership and sustainability: Systems thinkers in action.* Thousand Oaks, CA: Corwin.

Garmston, R. (2007). Collaborative culture: Balanced conversations promote shared ownership. *Journal of Staff Development, 28*(4), 57–58.

Garmston, R. J., & Wellman, B. M. (2009). *The adaptive school: A sourcebook for developing collaborative groups.* Norwood, MA: Christopher-Gordon.

Hackney, C., & Henderson, J. (1999). Educating school leaders for inquiry based democratic learning communities. *Educational Horizons, 77*(3), 67–73.

Hawley, W. D., & Valli, L. (1999). The essentials of effective professional development: A new consensus. In L. Darling-Hammond & G. Sykes (Eds.), *Teaching as the learning profession: Handbook of policy and practice* (pp. 127–150). San Francisco: Jossey Bass.

Hirsch, S., & Killion, J. (2008). Making every educator a learning educator. *Education Week, 27*(33), 24–25.

Intrator, S. M., & Kunzman, R. (2006). Starting with soul: How can we nurture teachers for the long haul? Stop putting subsistence strategies ahead of deeper needs. *Educational Leadership, 63* (6), 38–42.

Intrator, S. M., & Scribner, M. (2008, August). *NSLN network evaluation report: Executive summary.* Northampton, MA: Smith College.

Johnson, S. M., Birkeland, S., Kardos, S. M., Kauffman, D., Liu, E., & Peske, H. G. (2004). *Finders and keepers: Helping new teachers survive and thrive in our schools.* San Francisco: Jossey-Bass.

Kegan, R., & Lahey, L. L. (2009). *Immunity to change: How to overcome it and unlock the potential in yourself and your organization.* Boston: Harvard Business School Press.

Killion, J. (2000, December/January). Exemplary schools model quality staff development. *Results,* p. 3.

Lawrence Lightfoot, S. (1985). *The good high school: Portraits of character and culture.* New York: Basic Books.

Leithwood, K., Aitken, R., & Jantzi, D. (2006). *Making schools smarter: leading with evidence* (3rd ed.). Thousand Oaks, CA: Corwin.

Leithwood, K., & Hallinger, P. (Eds.). (2003). *Second international handbook on educational leadership and administration.* Dordrecht, The Netherlands: Kluwer.

Marzano, R. (2007, January). Leading the right work. *Education Update,* p. 3.

McTighe, J. (2008). Making the most of professional learning communities. *The Learning Principal, 3*(8), 1, 4–7.

Mizell, H. (2006). Ability to grow teachers is a crucial skill for principals. *The Learning System, 1*(6), 2.

Moller, G., & Pankake, A. (2006). *Lead with me: A principal's guide to teacher leadership.* Larchmont, NY: Eye On Education.

Neuman, M., & Simmons, W. (2000). Leadership for student learning. *Phi Delta Kappan, 82*(1), 9–12.

Normore, A. (2007). A continuum approach for developing school leaders in an urban district. *Journal of Research on Leadership Education, 2*(3). Available May 19, 2009, from http://www.ucea.org/storage/JRLE/pdf/v012_issue3_2007/NormoreArticle.pdf

Osterman, K. F., & Kottkamp, R. B. (1993). *Reflective practice for educators: Improving schooling through professional development.* Thousand Oaks, CA: Corwin.

Osterman, K. F., & Kottkamp, R. B. (2004). *Reflective practice for educators: Improving schooling through professional development* (2nd ed.). Thousand Oaks, CA: Corwin.

Quinn, R. E. (1996). *Deep change: Discovering the leader within.* San Francisco: Jossey-Bass.

Schön, D. (1983). *The reflective practitioner: How professionals think in action.* New York: Basic Books.

Spillane, J. P. (2006). *Distributed leadership.* San Francisco: Jossey-Bass.

Taylor, K., Marienau, C., & Fiddler, M. (2000). *Developing adult learners: Strategies for teachers and trainers.* San Francisco: Jossey-Bass.

Wagner, T., Kegan, R., Lahey, L., Lemons, R. W., Garnier, J., Helsing, D., et al. (2006). *Change leadership: A practical guide to transforming our schools.* San Francisco: Jossey-Bass.

Wideman, H., Owston, R., & Sinitskaya, N. (2007). Transforming teacher practice through blended professional development: Lessons learned from three initiatives. In C. Crawford et al. (Eds.). *Proceedings of Society for Information Technology and Teacher Education International Conference 2007* (pp. 2148–2154). Chesapeake, VA: Association for the Advancement of Computing in Education.

York-Barr, J., Sommers, W. A., Ghere, G. S., & Montie, J. (2006). *Reflective practice to improve schools: An action guide for educations* (2nd ed.). Thousand Oaks, CA: Corwin.

CHAPTER 6

Allen, D. (with Ort, S. W., Constantini, A., Reist, J., & Schmidt, J.). (2008). *Coaching whole school change: Lessons in practice from a small high school.* New York: Teachers College Press.

Blank, M. A., & Kershaw, C. A. (2009). *Mentoring as collaboration: Lessons from the field for classroom, school, and district leaders.* Thousand Oaks, CA: Corwin.

Bode, R. K. (1999). Mentoring and collegiality. In R. J. Menges and Associates (Eds.), *Faculty in new jobs: A guide to settling in, becoming established, and building institutional support* (pp. 118–144). San Francisco: Jossey-Bass.

Boyer, K. (1999). *A qualitative analysis of the impact of mentorship on new special educators' decision to remain in the field of special education.* Unpublished doctorial dissertation, George Mason University, Fairfax, VA.

Daloz, L. A. (1999). *Mentor: Guiding the journey of adult learners.* San Francisco: Jossey-Bass.

Daloz, L. A. (2000). Transformative learning for the common good. In J. Mezirow (Ed.), *Learning as transformation: Critical perspectives on a theory in progress* (pp. 103–123). San Francisco: Jossey-Bass.

Danielson, C. (1999). Mentoring beginning teachers: The case for mentoring. *Teaching and Change, 6*(3), 251–257.

Daresh, J. C. (2003). *Teachers mentoring teachers: A practical approach to helping new and experienced staff.* Thousand Oaks, CA: Corwin.

DeLong, T., Gabarro, J., & Lees, R. (2008). Why mentoring matters in a hypercompetitive world. *Harvard Business Review, 86*(1), 115–121.

Drago-Severson, E. (2004a). *Becoming adult learners: Principles and practices for effective development.* New York: Teachers College Press.

Drago-Severson, E. (2004b). *Helping teachers learn: Principal leadership for adult growth and development.* Thousand Oaks, CA: Corwin.

Dukess, L. (2001). *Meeting the leadership challenge: Designing effective principal mentor programs.* New York: New Visions for Public Schools. (ERIC Document Reproduction Service No. ED464392).

Free Management Library. (n.d.). *Mentoring.* Retrieved May 19, 2009, from http://www.managementhelp.org/guiding/mentrng/mentrng.htm

Hall, P. (2008). Building bridges: Strengthening the principal induction process through intentional mentoring. *Phi Delta Kappan, 89*(6), 449–452.

Hegstad, C. (1999). Formal mentoring as a strategy for human resource development: A review of research. *Human Resource Development Quarterly, 10*(4), 383–390.

Higgins, M. C., Chandler, D. E., & Kram, K. E. (2007). Relational engagement and developmental networks. In B. Ragins & K. Kram (Eds.), *The handbook of mentoring at work: Research, theory, and practice* (pp. 349–372). Thousand Oaks, CA: Sage.

Holloway, J. H. (2001). The benefits of mentoring. *Educational Leadership,58*(8), 85–86.

Holloway, J. H. (2004). Mentoring new leaders. *Educational Leadership, 61*(7), 87–88.

Hunt, J. M., & Weintraub, J. R. (2007). *The coaching organization.* Thousand Oaks, CA: Sage.

Jonson, K. F. (2008). Being an effective mentor: How to help beginning teachers succeed (2nd ed.). Thousand Oaks, CA: Corwin.

Kegan, R. (1982). *The evolving self: Problems and process in human development.* Cambridge, MA: Harvard University Press.

Kegan, R. (1994). *In over our heads: The mental demands of modern life.* Cambridge, MA: Harvard University Press.

Kegan, R. (2000). What "form" transforms? A constructive-developmental approach to transformative learning. In J. Mezirow & Associates (Eds.), *Learning as transformation* (pp. 35–70). San Francisco: Jossey-Bass.

Kegan, R., & Lahey, L. L. (2009). *Immunity to change: How to overcome it and unlock the potential in yourself and your organization.* Boston: Harvard Business School Press.

Killion, J. (2000, December/January). Exemplary schools model quality staff development. *Results,* p. 3.

Kram, K. E. (1983). Phases of the mentor relationship. *Academy of Management Journal, 26*(4), 608–625.

Kram, K. E. (1985). *Mentoring at work: Developmental relationships in organizational life.* Glenview, IL: Scott, Forseman.

Kram, K. E. (1988). *Mentoring at work: Developmental relationships in organizational life.* Lanham, MD: University Press of America.

Levinson, D. J. (1978). *The seasons of a man's life.* New York: Ballantine Books.

McGowan, E. M., Stone, E. M., & Kegan, R. (2007). A constructive-developmental approach to mentoring relationships. In B. R. Ragins & K. E. Kram (Eds.), *The mentoring handbook of mentoring at work: Theory, research, and practice* (pp. 401–425). Thousand Oaks, CA: Sage.

Merriam, S. (1983). Mentors and protégés: A critical review of the literature. *Adult Education Quarterly, 33*(3), 161–173.

Moir, E., & Bloom, G. (2003). Fostering leadership through mentoring. *Educational Leadership, 60*(8), 58–60.

National Staff Development Council (NSDC). (2008a). *Coaching School Results, Inc.* Retrieved May 19, 2009, from http://www.coachingschoolresults.com

National Staff Development Council (NSDC). (2008b). *The process—How it works: Professional learning to support the highest levels of school achievement.* Retrieved May 19, 2009, from http://www.coachingschoolresults.com/process.htm

Nicholls, G. (2002). Mentoring: The art of teaching and learning. In P. Jarvis (Ed.), *The theory and practice of teaching.* London: Kogan.

Noe, R. A., Greenberger, D. B., & Wang, S. (2002). Mentoring: What we know and where we might go from here. In G. R. Ferris & J. J. Martocchio (Eds.), *Research in personnel and human resources management* (Vol. 21, pp. 129–173). Greenwich, CT: Elsevier Science/JAI Press.

Pappano, L. (2001, May 13). When two teachers = one job. *Boston Sunday Globe,* p. L5–6.

Ragins, B. R. (1999). Gender and mentoring relationships: A review and research agenda for the next decade. In G. N. Powell (Ed.), *Handbook of gender and work* (pp. 347–369). Thousand Oaks, CA: Sage.

Ragins, B. R., & Kram, K. E. (2007). The roots and meaning of mentoring. In B. R. Ragins & K. E. Kram (Eds.), *The mentoring handbook of mentoring at work: Theory, research, and practice* (pp. 3–15). Thousand Oaks, CA: Sage.

Rilke, R. M. (1999). Letter four: Worpswede, near Bremen, July 16, 1903. In *Letters to a young poet* (S. Mitchell, Trans.). (Original work published 1929). Retrieved May 19, 2009, from http://www.sfgoth.com/~immanis/rilke/letter4.html

Rowley, J. B. (1999). The good mentor. *Educational Leadership, 56*(8), 20–22.

Saphier, J., Freedman, S., & Aschheim, B. (2001). *Beyond mentoring: How to nurture, support, and retain new teachers.* Newton, MA: Teachers21.

Wanberg, C. R., Welsh, E. T., & Hezlett, S. A. (2003). Mentoring research: A review and dynamic process model. *Research in Personnel and Human Resources Management, 22,* 39–124.

Yendol-Hoppey, D., & Dana, N. F. (2007). *The reflective educator's guide to mentoring: Strengthening practice through knowledge, story, and metaphor.* Thousand Oaks, CA: Corwin.

Zachary, L. J. (2000). *The mentor's guide: Facilitating effective learning relationships.* San Francisco: Jossey-Bass.

CHAPTER 7

Ackerman, R. H., Donaldson, G. A., & Van Der Bogert, R. (1996). *Making sense as a school leader: Persisting questions, creative opportunities.* San Francisco: Jossey-Bass.

Drago-Severson, E. (2004b). *Helping teachers learn: Principal leadership for adult growth and development.* Thousand Oaks, CA: Corwin.

Kegan, R., & Lahey, L. L. (2001). *How the way we talk can change the way we work: Seven languages for transformation.* San Francisco: Jossey-Bass.

Thoreau, H. D. (1995). *Walden.* Retrieved May 19, 2009, from the Project Gutenberg Website at http://www.gutenberg.org/etext/205 (Original work published 1854).

CHAPTER 8

Angelou, M. (1993). The sweetness of charity. In *Wouldn't take nothing for my journey now* (pp. 13–18). New York: Bantam.

Donaldson, G. A. (2008). *How leaders learn: Cultivating capacities for school improvement.* New York: Teachers College Press.

Drago-Severson, E. (2004b). *Helping teachers learn: Principal leadership for adult growth and development.* Thousand Oaks, CA: Corwin.

Drago-Severson, E., Kegan, R., Helsing, D., Broderick, M., Popp, N., & Portnow, K. (2001b). Three developmentally different types of learners. *Focus on Basics, 5*(B), 7–9.

Gardner, H. (1995). *Leading minds: An anatomy of leadership.* New York: Basic Books.

Gardner, H. (1997). *Extraordinary minds: Portraits of 4 exceptional individuals and an examination of our own extraordinariness.* New York: Basic Books.

Heifetz, R. (1994). *Leadership without easy answers.* Cambridge, MA: Harvard University Press.

Kegan, R. (1982). *The evolving self: Problems and process in human development.* Cambridge: Harvard University.

Kegan, R. (1994). *In over our heads: The mental demands of modern life.* Cambridge: Harvard University.

Kegan, R. (2000). What "form" transforms? A constructive-developmental approach to transformative learning. In J. Mezirow & Associates (Eds.), *Learning as transformation* (pp. 35–70). San Francisco: Jossey-Bass.

Kegan, R., Broderick, M., Drago-Severson, E., Helsing, D., Popp, N., & Portnow, K. (2001b). *Toward a "new pluralism" in the ABE/ESOL classroom: Teaching to multiple "cultures of mind"* (NCSALL Monograph #19). Boston: World Education.

Kegan, R., & Lahey, L. L. (2009). *Immunity to change: How to overcome it and unlock the potential in yourself and your organization.* Boston: Harvard Business School Press.

Murphy, J. (2006). *Preparing school leaders: Defining a research and action agenda.* Lanham, MD: Rowman & Littlefield Education.

Teitel, L. (2006). Supporting school system leaders: The state of effective training programs for school superintendents. New York: The Wallace Foundation.

Wagner, T. (2003). Reinventing America's schools. *Phi Delta Kappan, 84*(9), 665–668.

Wagner, T. (2007). Leading for change: Five habits of mind that count. *Education Week, 26*(45), 29–30.

Wagner, T., Kegan, R., Lahey, L., Lemons, R. W., Garnier, J., Helsing, D., et al. (2006). *Change leadership: A practical guide to transforming our schools.* San Francisco: Jossey-Bass.

RESEARCH APPENDIX

Ackerman, R. H., & Maslin-Ostrowski, P. (2002). *The wounded leader: How real leadership emerges in times of crisis.* San Francisco: Jossey-Bass.

Argyris, C., & Schön, D. (1974). *Theory in practice: Increasing professional effectiveness.* San Francisco: Jossey-Bass.

Boston Public School Fiscal Year Report. (2001, March 3). Boston: Boston Public Schools.

Brookfield, S. (1995). *Becoming a critically reflective teacher.* San Francisco: Jossey-Bass.

Daloz, L. (1999). *Mentor: Guiding the journey of adult learners.* San Francisco: Jossey-Bass.

Drago-Severson, E. (1996). *Head-of-school as principal adult developer: An account of one leader's efforts to support transformational learning among the adults in her school.* Unpublished doctoral dissertation, Harvard Graduate School of Education, Cambridge, MA.

Drago-Severson, E. (2004b). *Helping teachers learn: Principal leadership for adult growth and development.* Thousand Oaks, CA: Corwin.

Drago-Severson, E. (2007). Helping teachers learn: Principals as professional development leaders. *Teachers College Record, 109*(1), 70–125.

Freidson, E. (1975). *Doctoring together: A study of professional social control.* Chicago: University of Chicago Press.

Glaser, B. G., & Strauss, A. L. (1967). *The discovery of grounded theory: Strategies for qualitative research.* Hawthorne, NY: Aldine de Gruyter.

Kegan, R. (1982). *The evolving self: Problems and process in human development.* Cambridge, MA: Harvard University.

Kegan, R. (1994). *In over our heads: The mental demands of modern life.* Cambridge, MA: Harvard University.

Kegan, R. (2000). What "form" transforms? A constructive-developmental approach to transformative learning. In J. Mezirow & Associates (Eds.), *Learning as transformation* (pp. 35–70). San Francisco: Jossey-Bass.

Maxwell, J. A. (1996). *Qualitative research design: An interactive approach.* Thousand Oaks, CA: Sage.

Maxwell, J. A. (2005). *Qualitative research design: An interactive approach* (2nd ed.). Thousand Oaks, CA: Sage.

Maxwell, J. A., & Miller, B. (1998). *Categorization and contextualization as components of qualitative data analysis.* Unpublished manuscript.

Merriam, S. B. (1998). *Qualitative research and case study applications in education.* San Francisco: Jossey-Bass.

Mezirow, J. (2000). Learning to think like an adult: Core concepts of transformation theory. In J. Mezirow & Associates (Eds.), *Learning as transformation: Critical perspectives on a theory in progress* (pp. 3–33). San Francisco: Jossey-Bass.

Miles, M. B., & Huberman, A. M. (1994). *An expanded sourcebook: Qualitative data analysis* (2nd ed.). Thousand Oaks, CA: Sage.

Seidman, I. (1998). *Interviewing as qualitative research.* New York: Teachers College Press.

Strauss, A., & Corbin, J. (1998). *Basics of qualitative research: Techniques and procedures for developing grounded theory.* Thousand Oaks, CA: Sage.

GLOSSARY

Heifetz, R. (1994). *Leadership without easy answers.* Cambridge, MA: Harvard University Press.

Kegan, R. (1982). *The evolving self: Problems and process in human development.* Cambridge, MA: Harvard University.

Kegan, R. (1994). *In over our heads: The mental demands of modern life.* Cambridge, MA: Harvard University.

Kegan, R. (2000). What "form" transforms? A constructive-developmental approach to transformative learning. In J. Mezirow & Associates (Eds.), *Learning as transformation* (pp. 35–70). San Francisco: Jossey-Bass.

Index

CORWIN

A SAGE Company

The Corwin logo—a raven striding across an open book—represents the union of courage and learning. Corwin is committed to improving education for all learners by publishing books and other professional development resources for those serving the field of PreK–12 education. By providing practical, hands-on materials, Corwin continues to carry out the promise of its motto: **"Helping Educators Do Their Work Better."**

NSDC's purpose: Every educator engages in effective professional learning every day so every student achieves.